Praise for the previous edition
iPhone and iPad in Action

D0886163

Everything you need to know about these devices of the future.
—Berndt Hamboeck, pmOne

Apple should make this its official iPhone and iPad development book.
—Jason Jung, Rockwell

Gets you up to speed and developing in a snap.
—Clint Tredway, Developed It

Don't launch Xcode without this book.
—Ted Neward, Neward & Associates

Exactly what iNeed for iPhone development.
—Christopher Haupt, Webvanta.com

It's wonderful to have all the material that covers development for multiple Apple mobile devices in one volume.
—Glenn Stokol, Oracle Corporation

A good first place to start instead of wading through multiple Apple documents.
—Gershon Kagan, Tegrity, Inc.

Brandon, Christopher, and Shannon have created the quintessential book for iPhone and iPad development.
—Daniel McGraw, Software Engineer

Brandon Trebitowski will take you up and over the iOS learning curve with his enjoyable writing style and excellent example code. iPhone and iPad in Action is a must-have addition to your programming library—even for 20-year Objective-C veterans like me!
—Andrew Stone, CEO of stone.com

iOS 4 in Action

EXAMPLES AND SOLUTIONS
FOR iPHONE & iPAD

JOCELYN HARRINGTON
BRANDON TREBITOWSKI
CHRISTOPHER ALLEN
SHANNON APPELCLINE

TECHNICAL EDITOR   JAMES HATHEWAY

MANNING
SHELTER ISLAND

For online information and ordering of this and other Manning books, please visit
www.manning.com. The publisher offers discounts on this book when ordered in quantity.
For more information, please contact

> Special Sales Department
> Manning Publications Co.
> 20 Baldwin Road
> PO Box 261
> Shelter Island, NY 11964
> Email: orders@manning.com

Manning Publications Co.   Development editors: Maria Townsend
20 Baldwin Road   Katharine Osborne
PO Box 261   Copyeditor: Tiffany Taylor
Shelter Island, NY 11964   Typesetter: Dottie Marsico
                                        Cover designer: Marija Tudor

ISBN 9781617290015
Printed in the United States of America
1 2 3 4 5 6 7 8 9 10 – MAL – 16 15 14 13 12 11

brief contents

contents

preface

When I started playing with the first-generation iPhone back in 2008, I was amazed by the simplicity and versatility of the smart phone. With the iPhone in hand, I could take pictures, navigate with GPS, tell time, and of course, play games—especially when I was bored while waiting in line at the DMV for my license plate. It's hard to believe it's only been a few years since it was introduced, but the iPhone has become an integral part of my life. The universe of applications in the App Store attracts not only the user but also inspires a lot of developers.

Developing on the iOS has been an amazing adventure for me. I have authored/coauthored a few applications in the App Store and I am also a full time iOS developer.

When I decided one year ago to join the team to work on a third edition of this book, the main goal was to power up the book with iOS 4 features for the application developer. Thanks to the previous work from Shannon, Christopher, and Brandon on the two earlier editions, this book already had a great foundation on iOS development for both iPhone and iPad.

During this time Apple never slowed down on releasing new devices, such as the iPhone 4, the iPad 2, a new-generation iPod Touch, a new iOS platform, and even a new Xcode 4 IDE for application development. We did our best to keep up with this race and include the latest technology on the iOS platform, all of which you will find in this revised version of the book.

I hope you enjoy reading this book and that it will help you develop the next Top 10 application!

JOCELYN HARRINGTON

acknowledgments

A technical book is a massive undertaking, due to the number of people required to make sure that it reads well, looks good, and is technically correct. Thus, we have to thank the entire Manning staff, without whom this book would not exist. They did more than just correct our errors and polish our words; they also helped make integral decisions about the organization and the content of the book—decisions that improved it dramatically.

In particular, we'd like to thank the four people at Manning who helped us at the most pivotal times: Troy Mott, our acquisitions editor, who initially agreed to take on the project and who stayed with us every step of the way; Maria Townsley, our development editor, who put in an incredible amount of work to ensure the quality of writing and offered tons of guidance and support along the way; Katharine Osborne who helped with the Xcode 4 updates; and Marjan Bace, our publisher, who offered some of the biggest challenges regarding content and organization and initiated some of the best improvements.

We'd also like to thank Tiffany Taylor, our copyeditor, and Katie Tennant, our proofreader. Beyond that, tech editors are crucial to the success of a book like this, so we want to thank Kalle Alm and Matt Wyman who did the technical proofread of the manuscript a number of times as it was being revised and updated, and James Hathaway who worked as the technical editor on this edition of the book during production, catching errors and minutiae that we weren't even aware of. Though it's clichéd to say, it's true: any errors that sneaked by despite their best efforts are ours, but many others were corrected by all of the people we mention—and many more who worked behind the scenes at Manning. They were crucial to the book, and we'd like to thank them all.

Finally, we'd like to thank the reviewers who generously agreed to read our manuscript as we worked on it; they improved the book immensely: Ted Neward, Jason Jung, Glenn Stokol, Gershon Kagan, Cos DiFazio, Clint Tredway, Christopher Haupt, Berndt Hamboeck, Rob Allen, Peter Scott, Lester Lobo, Frank Jania, Curtis Miller, Chuck Hudson, Carlton Gibson, Amos Bannister, Emeka Okereke, Pratik Patel, Kunal Mittal, Tyson Maxwell, TVS Murthy, Kevin Butler, David Hanson, Timothy Binkley-Jones, Carlo Bottiglieri, Barry Ezell, Rob Abbe, David M. Sinclair, Austin Ziegler, Jonas Bandi, Patrick Karjala, Greg Vaughn, Jeroen Benckhuijsen, and Alex Curylo.

JOCELYN would like to thank her husband Peter for giving her tons of support while she worked on this book. She would also like to thank Troy Mott for all the effort he contributed to this project and James Hatheway, the technical editor, who spent tons of time on this version. Last but not least, she is thankful for all the support from the important people in her life.

BRANDON would like to thank his wife Ashley for putting up with the long nights he spent working on the second edition of this book. Without her love and support, he would not have been able to complete a single chapter. He would also like to thank Matt Woodward, who introduced him to Troy Mott and provided him with the opportunity to work on this book.

CHRISTOPHER would like to thank Chris Messina for inviting him to be a founder of iPhoneDevCamp and to also thank his long-time MacHack and SmartFriends colleagues for their support and assistance.

SHANNON would like to thank Christopher, who got the book started in the first place, and Brandon and Jocelyn for taking on the revised editions.

about this book

iOS 4 in Action is an introductory book, intended to teach the basics of iOS development in a tutorial form. It's an update of *iPhone in Action,* which first appeared in 2008, and *iPhone and iPad in Action* which appeared in 2010. We encourage you to read this book straight through, from chapter 1 to 22. This will introduce the platform, show you how to program for the iPhone and iPad, and walk you through the entire process step by step.

The audience

We've done our best to make this book accessible to everyone who is interested in writing native programs for the iPhone and iPad. We hope it will be especially useful to people who are looking to dive into the iPhone/iPad arena, because it allows you to create native applications for all of Apple's iDevices.

If you want to learn about iOS programming, you should have some experience with programming in general. It'd be best if you've worked with C or at least one object-oriented language before, but that's not a necessity; if you haven't, you can read our introduction to Objective-C in chapter 2, and you should expect to do some research on your own to clarify things. There's no need to be familiar with Objective-C, Cocoa, or Apple programming in general. We'll give you everything you need to become familiar with Apple's unique programming style. You'll probably have a leg-up if you understand object-oriented concepts; but it's not necessary (and again, you'll find an introduction in chapter 2).

Roadmap

Chapter 1 explains the iOS SDK, introducing the new features in iOS 4 and covers how to install the iOS SDK.

Chapter 2 kicks things off by highlighting Objective-C, which is the programming language used on the iPhone SDK.

Chapter 3 looks at Xcode 4, the newly released tool in iOS SDK. This integrated development environment does more than just compile your code. It also helps you correct simple errors as you type and provides quick, integrated access to all the iPhone programming documents.

Chapter 4 shifts the focus to mastering Xcode by writing code for applications and debugging with Xcode.

Chapter 5 covers simple view controllers. The basic view controller is an important building block of the MVC paradigm, dividing control from view; and the table view controller provides an easy way to organize information while matching the standard iPhone OS look and feel.

Chapter 6 steps back to talk about user interaction. It covers events, which users generate by touching the screen with one or more fingers, and actions, which happen when users interact with a control object like a button or a slider.

Chapter 7 finishes our look at view controllers by examining two more-advanced possibilities. The tab bar view controller allows for modal selection between multiple pages of content, and the navigation view controller adds hierarchy to tables. Also the universal application design concept will be covered.

Chapter 8 opens the SDK toolkit by talking about data. This includes user input, such as actions and preferences; data storage, such as files; and tools that combine input and storage, such as the devices' address book.

Chapter 9 goes into more advanced data strategies. In this chapter, you learn how to store complex data in an SQLite database or by using Core Data.

Chapter 10 highlights two of the most unique features on the iPhone and iPad—the accelerometer and the GPS—showing how the iPhone can track movement through space.

Chapter 11 covers another of the device's strengths—media—by showing how to do basic work with pictures, movies, and sound.

Chapter 12 looks at working with audio. It discusses how to play and record audio using a device's microphone and speakers.

Chapter 13 provides an extensive look at graphics, centering on the iPhone's and iPad's vector graphic language, Quartz 2D. It also offers a brief overview of Core Animation and touches on OpenGL for the iOS.

Chapter 14 examines how you can use the iPhone and iPad to interact with the internet. This chapter moves through the entire hierarchy of internet communication, from low-level host connections to URLs, from web views to modern social languages like XML and JSON.

Chapter 15 takes you through the entire process of creating a multiplayer pong game on the iPhone or iPad. You learn everything about peer-to-peer communication using the Game Kit framework.

Chapter 16 walks through the new Event Kit framework on iOS 4. It also covers a great example of using Grand Central Dispatch with blocks.

Chapter 17 shows you how to handle push notifications in your applications. It also provides a simple example of how to create your own push notification server using PHP.

Chapter 18 takes an in-depth look at the Map Kit framework. It shows you everything you need in order to integrate fully functional Google maps in any application.

Chapter 19 walks you through one of the main methods for creating a virtual store in your applications. Using the Store Kit framework, you learn every step of the process, from creating products to processing purchases.

Chapter 20 covers how to implement and monetize iAd.

Chapters 21 and 22 dive into iOS 4's core feature: multitasking. We start with the basics of the application life cycle and provide you with a real example using background audio and background location.

The appendixes contain additional information that didn't fit with the flow of the main text. Appendix A contains a list of SDK objects and what they do. Appendix B features links for many websites of note for iOS programming. Appendix C includes the current information on how to deploy your SDK programs to actual devices. Appendix D shows techniques that you can use to convert iPhone applications into iPad applications.

Code conventions and downloads

Code examples appear throughout this book. Longer listings appear under clear listing headings, and shorter listings appear between lines of text. All code is set in a monospaced font like this to differentiate it from the regular text. Class names have also been set in code font; if you want to type the code into your computer, you'll be able to make it out clearly.

With the exception of a few cases of abstract code examples, all code snippets began life as working programs. You can download the complete set of programs from www.manning.com/iOS4inAction. You'll find two ZIP files there, one for each of the SDK programs. We encourage you to try the programs as you read; they include additional code that doesn't appear in the book and provide more context. In addition, we feel that seeing a program work can elucidate the code required to create it.

The code snippets in this book include extensive explanations. We often include short annotations beside the code; and sometimes numbered cueballs beside lines of code link the subsequent discussion to the code lines.

Software requirements

An Intel-based Macintosh running OS X 10.6 or higher is required to develop iOS applications. You also need to download the iOS SDK, but this is freely downloadable as soon as you sign up with Apple.

The book offers full coverage of the iOS 4 and Xcode 4.

Author Online

Purchase of *iOS4 in Action* includes free access to a private web forum run by Manning Publications where you can make comments about the book, ask technical questions, and receive help from the authors and from other users. To access the forum and subscribe to it, point your web browser to www.manning.com/iOS4inAction. This page provides information on how to get on the forum once you are registered, what kind of help is available, and the rules of conduct on the forum.

Manning's commitment to our readers is to provide a venue where a meaningful dialog between individual readers and between readers and the authors can take place. It is not a commitment to any specific amount of participation on the part of the authors, whose contribution to the AO forum remains voluntary (and unpaid). We suggest you try asking the authors some challenging questions lest their interest stray!

The Author Online forum and the archives of previous discussions will be accessible from the publisher's website as long as the book is in print.

About the title

By combining introductions, overviews, and how-to examples, the *In Action* books are designed to help learning and remembering. According to research in cognitive science, the things people remember are things they discover during self-motivated exploration.

Although no one at Manning is a cognitive scientist, we are convinced that for learning to become permanent it must pass through stages of exploration, play, and, interestingly, retelling of what is being learned. People understand and remember new things, which is to say they master them, only after actively exploring them. Humans learn in action. An essential part of an *In Action* guide is that it's example-driven. It encourages the reader to try things out, to play with new code, and explore new ideas.

There is another, more mundane, reason for the title of this book: our readers are busy. They use books to do a job or to solve a problem. They need books that allow them to jump in and jump out easily and learn just what they want just when they want it. They need books that aid them *in action*. The books in this series are designed for such readers.

about the cover illustration

The figure on the cover of *iOS4 in Action* is captioned "Russian Guard" and is taken from the four-volume *Collection of the Dresses of Different Nations* by Thomas Jefferys, published in London between 1757 and 1772. This collection, which includes beautifully hand-colored copperplate engravings of costumes from around the world, has influenced theatrical costume design ever since it was published.

The diversity of the drawings in the *Collection of the Dresses of Different Nations* speaks vividly of the richness of the costumes presented on the London stage over 200 years ago. The costumes, both historical and contemporaneous, offered a glimpse into the dress customs of people living in different times and in different countries, bringing them to life for London theater audiences.

Dress codes have changed in the last century and the diversity by region, so rich in the past, has faded away. It's now often hard to tell the inhabitant of one continent from another. Perhaps, trying to view it optimistically, we've traded a cultural and visual diversity for a more varied personal life. Or a more varied and interesting intellectual and technical life.

We at Manning celebrate the inventiveness, the initiative, and the fun of the computer business with book covers based on the rich diversity of regional and historical costumes brought back to life by pictures from collections such as this one.

Introducing iOS 4 with iPhone and iPad

This chapter covers

- Understanding Apple's iPhone and iPad technology
- Installing the iOS 4 SDK
- Anatomy of iOS
- Turning your idea into an iOS application

The iPhone and iPad provide an unforgettable user experience. It's one of the rare technologies that's so intuitive that even a toddler can use it without a user manual. iOS provides a whole platform for developers. It comes with a huge global market and one integrated distribution place: the App Store. The iOS SDK offers a rich set of APIs for developers to turn their best ideas into killer applications. The new enhancements in iOS 4 allow developers to create applications faster and easier.

In this chapter, we'll first introduce iOS 4 and then go over the key specifications of the iPhone, iPad, and iPod Touch. We'll cover the anatomy of iOS, including frameworks, windows, views, and methods. We'll also cover events, memory management, and lifecycle management before providing tips on creating a successful application. Let's start the story with the iOS platform.

1

1.1   *All for one and one for all: the iOS platform*

The iPod Touch, iPhone, and iPad (and likely future generations of Apple devices) all use iOS 4.3.1 (at the time of writing). The iOS moniker may be a bit confusing at first, but having one OS for all these devices makes it an easy and rewarding platform on which to develop. Learn how to develop for it once using the iOS SDK, and you can adapt your applications to whichever devices you like. For example, you can determine that the application will support only the devices with GPS or camera.

Let's review a bit of history on iOS. The iOS SDK was first introduced in 2007 and released in March of 2008. The third major release, iOS 3.0, was released in 2009. Prior to iOS 4.2, there was a short, fragmented OS history on the iPhone and iPad; the iPhone was running on iOS 4.0 and the iPad was on iOS 3.2. With the new iOS, all the iOS-powered devices can once again run the same OS. For developers, the experience for application development is a lot smoother and easier. The most prominent feature on iOS 4 is that iOS supports multitasking services, including playing audio, push notifications, receiving location change events, and fast app switching. We'll cover the details later in this book.

The social experience is emphasized on iOS 4 with Game Center and iTunes 10 with Ping. Game Center allows developers to create social game experiences with the Game Kit framework. For end users, it's amazing to start multiplayer games through automatching, tracking their achievements, and so on.

There are differences in developing applications for the iPad as opposed to the iPhone, but they're primarily related to the varying amount of real estate available to each device, as illustrated in figure 1.1. Obviously, the iPad has a much bigger screen for display or interaction. The content focus is to provide a rich information presentation. In the UI design, you may want to distinguish the iPad from the iPhone. For the most part, you can run the examples in this book on either the iPad or the iPhone with little adaptation. (iPhone applications are fully compatible on the iPad as is; universal applications support different experiences depending on the platform they're being run on.)

One more thing: iOS 4.3 allows applications to support printing through Airprint. Imagine that you can edit your photo with the iPad or iPhone and tap the Print button to get the photo printed out on your wi-fi printer! We'll cover this function in detail later in chapter 11.

1.2   *Understanding iPhone and iPad touch interaction*

The iPhone and iPad use a multitouch-capable capacitive touchscreen. Users access the device by tapping around with their finger. But *a finger isn't a mouse*. Generally, a finger is larger and less accurate than a more traditional pointing device. This disallows certain traditional types of UI that depend on precise selection. For example, the iPhone and iPad don't have scrollbars. Selecting a scrollbar with a fat finger would either be an exercise in frustration or require a huge scrollbar that would take up a lot of the iPhone's precious screen real estate. Apple solved this problem by allowing

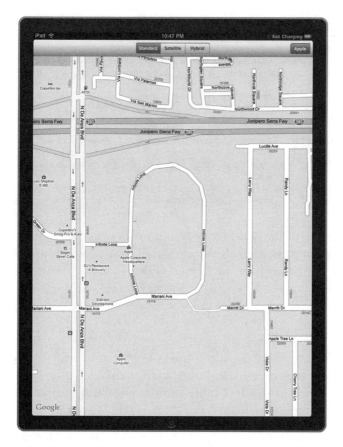

Figure 1.1 **The iPad and iPhone side by side. The primary difference between the two—the available screen real estate—is readily apparent.**

users to tap anywhere on an iPhone screen and then *flick* in a specific direction to cause scrolling.

Another interesting element of the touchscreen is shown off by the fact that a *finger isn't necessarily singular.* Recall that the iPhone and iPad touchscreens are *multi-touch.* This allows users to manipulate the device with multifinger *gestures.* Pinch-zooming is one such example. To zoom into a page, you tap two fingers on the page and then push them apart; to zoom out, you similarly push them together.

Finally, *a finger isn't persistent.* A mouse pointer is always on the display, but the same isn't true for a finger, which can tap here and there without going anywhere in between. As you'll see, this causes issues with some traditional web techniques that depend on a mouse pointer moving across the screen. It also provides limitations that may be seen throughout SDK programs. For example, there's no standard for cut and paste, a ubiquitous feature for any computer produced in the last couple of decades.

In addition to some changes to existing interfaces, the input interface introduces a number of new touches (one-fingered input) and gestures (two-fingered input), as described in table 1.1.

Table 1.1   iPhone and iPad touches and gestures allow you to accept user input in new ways.

Input	Type	Summary
Bubble	Touch	Touch and hold. Pops up an info bubble on clickable elements.
Flick	Touch	Touch and flick. Scrolls the page.
Flick, two-finger	Gesture	Touch and flick with two fingers. Scrolls the scrollable element.
Pinch	Gesture	Move fingers in relation to each other. Zooms in or out.
Tap	Touch	A single tap. Selects an item or engages an action such as a button or link.
Tap, double	Touch	A double tap. Zooms a column.

When you're designing with the SDK, many of the nuances of finger mousing are taken care of for you. Standard controls are optimized for finger use, and you have access only to the events that work on the iPhone or iPad. Chapter 6 explains how to use touches, events, and actions in iOS; as an iOS developer, you'll need to change your way of thinking about input to better support the new devices.

1.3   *Getting ready for the SDK*

The iOS software development kit (SDK) is a suite of programs available in one gargantuan (at the time of writing over 4 GB) download from Apple. It gives you the tools you need to program (Xcode—Xcode 4 is the version of the iDE used in this book), debug (Instruments), and test (Simulator) your iPhone, iPod Touch, and iPad code.

> **NOTE**   You must have an Intel-based Apple Macintosh running Mac OS X 10.6.5 or higher to use the SDK.

1.3.1   *Installing the SDK*

To obtain the SDK, download it from Apple's iOS Dev Center, which at the time of this writing is accessible at http://developer.apple.com/devcenter/ios/. You'll need to register as an iOS Developer in order to get there, but it's a fairly painless process. Note that you can also use this site to access Apple documentation and sample source code.

> **NOTE**   Xcode 4 is a free download for all members of the iOS Developer Program, which costs US$99 per year. If you're not an iOS Developer Program member, you can purchase Xcode 4 from the Mac App Store for US$4.99 or download Xcode 3 for free.

THE APPLE DOCS AND THE SDK

To see the full API documentation as well as sample code, visit http://developer .apple.com/devcenter/ios/. It contains a few introductory papers, of which we think the best are "iOS Overview" and "Learning Objective-C: A Primer," plus the complete class and protocol references for the SDK.

As we'll discuss in the next chapter, you can also access all of these docs from inside Xcode. We usually find Xcode a better interface because it allows you to click through from your source code to your local documents. Nonetheless, the website is a great source of information when you don't have Xcode handy.

Because they tend to be updated relatively frequently, we've been constantly aware of Apple's documents while writing this book, and we've done our best to ensure that what we include complements Apple's information. We'll continue to provide you with introductions to topics and to point you toward the references when there's a need for in-depth information.

After you've downloaded the SDK, you'll find that it leaves a disk image sitting on your hard drive. Double-click it to mount the disk image, and then double-click Xcode and iOS SDK in the folder that pops up to start the installation process (as shown in figure 1.2).

This will bring you through the entire install process, which will probably take 20–40 minutes. You'll also get a few licensing agreements that you need to sign off on, including the iPhone Licensing Agreement, which lists some restrictions on what you'll be able to build for the iOS-based devices.

> **Warning: installation dangers**
> The default installation of Xcode and iOS SDK will replace any existing Apple development tools you have. You'll still be able to do regular Apple development, but you'll be working with a slightly more bleeding-edge development environment.

IOS SDK LICENSING RESTRICTIONS

Although Apple is making the iOS SDK widely available for public programming, the company has placed some restrictions on what you can do with it. We expect these restrictions to change as the SDK program evolves, but what follows are some of the limitations at the time of this writing.

Among the most notable technical restrictions: you can't use the code to create plug-ins, nor can you use it to download non-SDK code. It was the latter that apparently spoiled Sun's original plans to port Java over to the iPhone. You also can use only Apple's published APIs. In addition, there are numerous privacy-related restrictions, the most important of which is that you can't log the user's location without permission. Finally, Apple has some specific application restrictions, including restrictions on apps that incorporate pornography or other objectionable content.

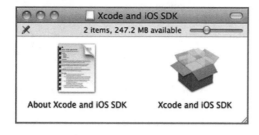

Figure 1.2 Double-clicking Xcode and iOS SDK starts your installation.

In order for your program to run on iPhones and iPads, you'll need an Apple certificate, and Apple maintains the right to refuse your cert if it doesn't like what you're doing. If you're planning to write anything that might be questionable, you should probably check whether Apple is likely to approve it first. For example, the most-used third-party software package that isn't available natively is Flash. This book is going to cover how to develop an app on iPhone or iPad with the iOS SDK. But there's another way to deliver an application to iPhone or iPad: using HTML5+JavaScript for web apps. We won't cover web application development in this book.

When the SDK finishes installing, you'll find it in the /Developer directory of your Mac system disk. Most of the programs appear in /Developer/Applications, which we suggest you make accessible using the Add to Sidebar feature in the Finder. The iOS Simulator is located separately at /Developer/Platforms/iPhoneSimulator.platform/ Developer/Applications. Because this is off on its own, you may want to add it to your Dock.

You now have everything you need to program for the iOS devices, but you won't be able to release iPhone or iPad programs on your own—that takes a special certificate from Apple. See appendix C for complete information on this process, which is critical for moving your programs from the Simulator onto a real device. The Simulator turns out to be one of several programs you've installed, each of which can be useful in SDK programming.

1.3.2   *The anatomy of the SDK*

Xcode, Instruments, and Dashcode were all available as part of the development library of Mac OS X before the iPhone came along. Many of these programs are expanded and revised for use on the iPhone, so we've opted to briefly summarize them all, in decreasing order of importance to an SDK developer:

- *Xcode 4* is the core of the SDK's integrated development environment (IDE). It's where you'll set up projects, write code in a text editor, compile code, and generally manage your applications. It supports code written in Objective-C (a superset of C that we'll cover in more depth in the next chapter) and can also parse C++ code. Interface Builder is now a part of Xcode 4, and it allows you to put together the graphical elements of your program, including windows and menus, via a quick, reliable method. You'll learn the specifics of how to use Xcode 4 in chapters 3 and 4.

- *iOS Simulator* allows you to view an iPhone or iPad screen on your desktop. It's a great help for debugging web pages. It's an even bigger help when you're working on native apps, because you don't have to get your code signed by Apple to test it out.

- *Instruments* is a program that allows you to dynamically debug, profile, and trace your program. If you were creating web apps, we would have to point you to a slew of browsers, add-ons, and remote websites to do this sort of work; but for your native apps, that's all incorporated into this one package.

- *Dashcode* is listed here only for the sake of completeness because it's part of the /Developer area. It's a graphical development environment that's used to create web-based programs incorporating HTML, CSS, and JavaScript. Dashcode is used when developing for the web; you won't use it with the iOS SDK.

JUMPING AHEAD

If you'd prefer to immediately dive into your first program, HelloWorld, head to chapter 3. You can then pop back here to see what it all means.

Figure 1.3 shows the most important developer tools. In addition to the visible tools that you've downloaded into /Developer, you've also downloaded the entire set of iOS frameworks: a huge collection of header files and source code—all written in Objective-C—that will greatly simplify your programming experience. In the next chapter, we'll look at Objective-C, the SDK's programming language. Rather than jumping straight into your first program, we instead want to touch on these foundational topics. In the next section, we'll examine some of the basics of iOS.

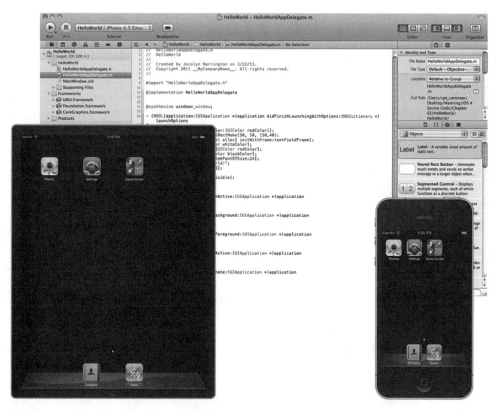

Figure 1.3 The SDK includes Xcode (top) and two instances of the iOS Simulator, running in iPad mode (bottom left) and iPhone mode (right).

1.4   *Introducing iOS*

Apple's iOS SDK provides you with a vast library of objects arranged into several frameworks. As a result, you'll spend a lot more time sending messages to objects that are ready-made for your use than creating new ones. Let's begin our look at iOS by exploring several of these objects and how they're arranged. We'll take a tour of the anatomy of iOS, at how the object hierarchy is arranged, and how iOS handles windows and views.

1.4.1   *The anatomy of iOS*

iOS's frameworks are divided into four major layers, as shown in figure 1.4.

Each of these layers contains a variety of frameworks that you can access when writing iOS SDK programs. Generally, you should prefer the higher-level layers when you're coding (those shown toward the top in the diagram).

Cocoa Touch is the framework that you'll become most familiar with. It contains the UIKit framework—which is what we spend most of our time on in this book—and the Address Book UI framework. UIKit includes window support, event support, and user-interface management, and it lets you display both text and web pages. It further acts as your interface to the accelerometers, the camera, the photo library, and device-specific information.

Figure 1.4   Apple provides you with four layers of frameworks to use when writing iOS programs.

Media is where you can get access to the major audio and video protocols built into the iPhone and iPad. Its four graphical technologies are OpenGL ES, EAGL (which connects OpenGL to your native window objects), Quartz (which is Apple's vector-based drawing engine), and Core Animation (which is also built on Quartz). Other frameworks of note include Core Audio, Open Audio Library, and Media Player.

Core Services offers the frameworks used in all applications. Many of them are data related, such as the internal Address Book framework. Core Services also contains the critical Foundation framework, which includes the core definitions of Apple's object-oriented data types, such as its arrays and sets.

Core OS includes kernel-level software. You can access threading, files, networking, other low-level I/O, and memory functions.

Most of your programming work will be done using the UIKit (UI) or Foundation (NS) framework. These libraries are collectively called Cocoa Touch; they're built on Apple's modern Cocoa framework, which is almost entirely object oriented and, in our opinion, much easier to use than older libraries. The vast majority of code in this book will be built solely using Cocoa Touch.

But you'll sometimes have to fall back on libraries that are instead based on simple C functionality. Examples include Apple's Quartz 2D and Address Book frameworks, as well as third-party libraries like SQLite. Expect object creation, memory management, and even variable creation to work differently for these non-Cocoa libraries.

When you fall back on non-Cocoa libraries, you'll sometimes have to use Apple's Core Foundation framework, which lies below Cocoa. Your first encounter with Core Foundation will be when we discuss the Address Book framework in chapter 9; we'll provide more details about how to use Core Foundation at that point.

Although Core Foundation and Cocoa are distinct classes of frameworks, many of their common variable types are *toll-free bridged*, which means they can be used interchangeably as long as you cast them. For example, `CFStringRef` and `NSString *` are toll-free bridged, as you'll see when we talk about the Address Book. The Apple class references usually point out this toll-free bridging for you.

1.4.2 *The object hierarchy of iOS*

Within these frameworks, you can access an immense wealth of classes arranged in a huge hierarchy. You'll see many of these used throughout this book, and you'll find a listing of even more in appendix A. Figure 1.5 shows many of the classes that you'll use over the next several chapters, arranged in a hierarchy. They're a fraction of what's available.

THE NS CLASSES

The NS classes come from Core Services' Foundation framework (the Cocoa equivalent of the Core Foundation framework), which contains a huge number of fundamental data types and other objects.

You should use the fundamental Cocoa classes like `NSString` and `NSArray` whenever you can, rather than C fundamentals like `char*` or a plain array. This is because they tend to play nicely with each other and with the UIKit frameworks, and therefore you're less likely to encounter bizarre errors. They also follow the memory-management rules of Objective-C (reference counting). Although it isn't shown, `NSNumber` is another class you should be aware of. Although it shouldn't be used in place of an ordinary number, it serves as a great wrapper when you need a number expressed as an object. This is useful for sending numbers via message passing. `NSNumber` is capable of holding many sorts of numerical values, from floats to integers and more.

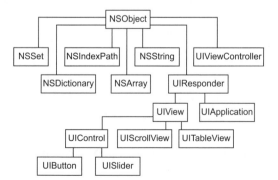

Figure 1.5 This hierarchy graph shows a small selection of the classes available in iOS.

The objects that can hold collections of values like NSArray (a numerical array) and NSDictionary (an associative array) are picky about your sticking to their NS brethren. You'll need to wrap C variables inside Cocoa classes whenever you hand off objects to these arrays. Finally, though NSString can take many sorts of objects when you're formatting a string, you should be aware that Cocoa objects may require a different formatting string than their C equivalents.

In two situations, you'll find that these NS classes can be a deficit. First, if you're using the Core Foundation framework, you'll often have to take advantage of toll-free bridging by casting variables, as you'll see starting in chapter 9, when we look at the Address Book. Second, if you're using external APIs, you may need to convert some classes into their C equivalents. Chapter 9's look at the SQLite API explores this possibility, with NSString objects often being converted to their UTF-8 equivalent.

The most important of Cocoa's Foundation objects is NSObject, which contains a lot of default behavior, including methods for object creation and memory management; you'll learn about these later in this chapter.

THE UI CLASSES

The second broad category contains the UI classes. These come from Cocoa Touch's UIKit framework, which includes all the graphical objects you'll be using as well as all the functionality for the iOS's event model, much of which appears in UIResponder. That's another topic we'll return to soon.

1.4.3   *Windows and views*

As the UI classes demonstrate, iOS is deeply rooted in the idea of a graphical user interface. Therefore, let's finish our introduction to iOS by looking at some of the main graphical abstractions embedded in the UIKit. There are three major abstractions: windows, views, and view controllers.

A *window* is something that spans the device's entire screen. An application usually has only one, and it's the overall container for everything your application does.

A *view* is the content holder in your application. You may have several of them, each covering different parts of the window or doing different things at different times. They're all derived from the UIView class. But don't think of a view as a blank container. Almost any object you use from UIKit will be a subclass of UIView that features a lot of behavior of its own. Among the major subclasses of UIView are UIControl, which gives you buttons, sliders, and other items with which users may manipulate your program, and UIScrollableView, which gives users access to more text than can appear at once.

A *view controller* does what its name suggests. It acts as the controller element of the Model-View-Controller triad and in the process manages a view, sometimes called an *application view*. As such, it takes care of events and updating for your view.

In this book, we've divided view controllers into two types. *Basic view controllers* manage a screenful of information (such as the table view controller), whereas *advanced view controllers* let a user move around among several subviews (such as the navigation bar controller and the tab bar controller).

Windows, views, and view controllers are ultimately part of a *view hierarchy*. This is a tree of objects that begins with the window at its root. A simple program may have a window with a view under it. Most programs start with a window and have a view controller under that, perhaps supported by additional view controllers, each of which controls views that may have their own subviews. We'll illustrate this concept more clearly in chapter 5 when we start looking at the basic view controllers that make this sort of hierarchy possible.

1.5 *iOS's methods*

As you've seen, iOS has a complex and deep structure of classes. In this section, we look at object creation, memory management, event response, and lifecycle management.

Two of the most important classes are NSObject and UIResponder, which contain many of the methods and properties you'll use throughout your programming. Thanks to inheritance, these important functions (and others) can be used by many different iOS objects. We cover some of these foundational methods here to provide a single reference for their usage, but we'll be sure to point them out again when you encounter them for the first time in future chapters.

1.5.1 *Object creation*

We talked earlier about how to define classes; but as we said at the time, the specifics of *how* instance objects are created from classes depend on the implementation of your framework. In iOS, the NSObject class defines how object creation works.

You'll meet a few different interfaces that are used to support object creation, but they all ultimately fall back to a two-step procedure that uses the alloc class method and the init instance method. The alloc method allocates the memory for your object and returns the object itself. The init method then sets some initial variables in that method. They usually occur through a single, nested message:

```
id newObject = [[objectClass alloc] init];
```

The alloc method from NSObject should always do the right thing for you. But when you write a new subclass, you'll almost always want to write a new init method, because that's where you define the variables that make your class what it is. Here's a default setup for an init, which would appear as part of your @implementation:

```
- (id)init
{
    if (self = [super init]) {
// Instance variables go here
    }
    return self;
}
```

This code shows all the usual requirements of an init method. First, it calls its parent to engage in its class's initialization. Then, it sets any instance variables that should be set. Last, it returns the object, usually with return self;.

The bare init is one of a few major ways you can create objects in iOS.

THE ARGUMENTATIVE ALTERNATIVE

Sometimes you'll want to send an argument with an init. You can do so with an initialization function that you name using the format initWithArgument:(argument). Other than the fact that you're sending it an argument, it works exactly like a bare init. Here's another example drawn from code you'll see in upcoming chapters:

```
[[UITextView alloc] initWithFrame:textFieldFrame];
```

Initialization methods with arguments allow you to create nonstandard objects set up in ways that you choose. They're common in UIKit.

One initialization method with an argument deserves a bit of extra mention. init-WithCoder: is a special initialization method that's called whenever you create an object with Interface Builder—and important if you want to do setup for such objects. We'll return to Interface Builder in chapter 3.

THE FACTORY METHOD ALTERNATIVE

A final sort of init supported through iOS is the factory method (class method). This is a one-step message that takes care of both the memory allocation and initialization for you. All factory methods are named with the format objecttypeWithArgument:(argument) Here's another real example:

```
[UIButton buttonWithType:UIButtonTypeRoundedRect];
```

Class (or factory) methods make messaging a little clearer. They also have the advantage of handling some memory management, which is the topic of the next major category of iOS methods.

OBJECT CREATION WRAP-UP

We've summarized the four major ways that iOS supports the creation of objects in table 1.2. As witnessed by the examples, you'll use all these methods as you move through the upcoming chapters.

Table 1.2 iOS supports several methods that you can use to create objects. Different methods are supported by different classes.

Method	Code	Summary
Simple	`[[object alloc] init];`	Plain initialization
Argument	`[[object alloc] initWithArgument:argument];`	An initialization where one or more arguments is passed to the method
Coder	`[[object alloc] initWithCoder:decoder];`	An initialization with an argument used for Interface Builder objects
Factory	`[object objecttypeWithArgument:argument];`	A one-step initialization process with an argument

1.5.2 *Memory management*

Because of power considerations, iOS doesn't support garbage collection. That means every object that's created must eventually have its memory released by hand—at least, if you don't want to introduce a memory leak into your program.

The fundamental rule of memory management in iOS is this: if you allocate memory for an object, you must release it. This is done via the `release` message (which is once again inherited from `NSObject`):

```
[object release];
```

Send that message when you've finished using an object, and you've done your proper duty as a programmer.

Note that we said you must release the memory only if you *allocated* the memory for it. You are considered to "own" the memory for an object if you created it using a method that contains *alloc, new, copy,* or *mutableCopy.* You can free memory for an object using the release message as mentioned earlier; however, an easier way in general is making use of the wonders of autorelease. (Factory methods like `UIButton`'s `buttonWithType:` return objects that are already autoreleased, so you don't need to manage their memory unless you explicitly retain it.)

THE AUTORELEASE ALTERNATIVE

If you're responsible for the creation of an object and you're going to pass it off to some other class for usage, you should autorelease the object before you send it off. This is done with the `autorelease` method:

```
[object autorelease];
```

You'll typically send the `autorelease` message just before you return the object at the end of a method. After an object has been autoreleased, it's watched over by a special `NSAutoreleasePool`. The object is kept alive for the scope of the method to which it's been passed, and then the `NSAutoreleasePool` cleans it up.

RETAINING AND COUNTING

What if you want to hold onto an object that has been passed to you and that will be autoreleased? In that case, you send it a `retain` message:

```
[object retain];
```

When you do this, you're saying you want the object to stay around, but now you've become responsible for its memory as well: you must send a `release` message at some point to balance your `retain`.

At this point, we should probably back up and explain the underlying way that iOS manages memory objects. It does so by maintaining a count of object usage. By default, it's set to 1. Each `retain` message increases that count by 1, and each `release` message reduces that count by 1. When the count drops to 0, the memory for the object is freed up.

Therefore, all memory management can be thought of as pairs of messages. If you balance every `alloc` and every `retain` with a `release`, your object will eventually be freed up when you've finished with it.

> **WARNING** Memory management can be the root cause of the bugs. Instruments is a good tool for attempting to diagnose issues with memory leaks.

Whenever you use the keyword `retain` or `alloc`, make sure to release. If the object is already released, don't try to access the released object. A good habit would be to assign `nil` to a released object and check the value isn't `nil` before accessing the object.

MEMORY MANAGEMENT WRAP-UP

Table 1.3 provides a quick summary of the methods we've looked at to manage the memory used by your objects.

Table 1.3 The memory-management methods help you keep track of the memory you're using and clean it up when you're finished.

Method	Summary
`alloc`	Part of the object-creation routine that allocates the memory for an object's usage.
`autorelease`	Request to reduce an object's memory count by 1 when it goes out of scope. This is maintained by an NSAutoreleasePool.
`release`	Reduces the object's memory count by 1.
`retain`	Increases the object's memory count by 1.

For more information on memory management, including a look at the `copy` method and how this all interacts with properties, look at Manning's *Objective-C Fundamentals* (Christopher Fairbairn, Collin Ruffenach, and Johannes Fahrenkrug, 2011). A good description of memory-management rules is also found in the "Memory Management Programming Guide" on the Mac Developer Library website.

1.5.3 *Event response*

The next-to-last category of methods that we examine for iOS is event response. Unlike object creation and memory management, we tackle this issue only briefly, because it's much better documented in chapter 6. The topic is important enough that we want to offer a quick overview of it now.

Events can appear on the iPhone or iPad in three main ways: through bare events (or actions), through delegated events, and through notification. Whereas the methods of our earlier topics all derived from `NSObject`, event response instead comes from the `UIResponder` object, whereas notification comes from the `NSNotification-Center`. You won't have to worry about accessing responder methods and properties because UIResponder is the parent of most UIKit objects, but the NSNotification-Center requires special access.

EVENTS AND ACTIONS

Most user input results in an *event* being placed into a *responder chain*. This is a linked set of objects that, for the most part, goes backward up through the view hierarchy. Any input is captured by the *first responder*, which tends to be the object the user is directly interacting with. If that object can't resolve the input, it sends it up to its *super-view* (for example, a label might send it up to its full-screen view), then to its super-view, all the way up the chain (up through the views, then up through the view controllers). If input gets all the way up the view hierarchy to the window object, it's next sent to the application itself, which tends to pass it off to an *application delegate* as a last resort.

Any of these objects can choose to handle an event, which stops its movement up the responder chain. Following the standard MVC model, you'll often build event response into UIViewController objects, which are pretty far up the responder chain.

For any UIControl objects, such as buttons, sliders, and toggles, events are often turned into *actions*. Whereas events report touches to the screen, actions instead report manipulations of the controls and are easier to read. Actions follow a slightly different hierarchy of response.

DELEGATES AND DATA SOURCES

Events can be sent to an object in a way other than via a first responder: through a *delegate*. This is an object (usually a view controller) that says it will take care of events for another object (usually a view). It's close kin to a data source, which is an object (again, usually a view controller) that promises to do the data setup and control for another object (again, usually a view).

Delegation and data sourcing are each controlled by a *protocol*, which is a set of methods the delegate or data source agrees to respond to. For example, a table's delegate might have to respond to a method that alerts it when a row in the table has been selected. Similarly, a table's data source might describe what all the rows of the table look like.

Delegates and data sources fit cleanly into the MVC model used by Objective-C, because they allow a view to hand off its work to its controller without having to worry about where each of those objects is in the responder chain.

NOTIFICATIONS

Standard event response and delegation represent two ways that objects can be alerted to standard events, such as fingers touching the screen. A third method can also be used to program many different sorts of activities, such as the device's orientation changing or a network connection closing: the notification.

Objects register to receive a certain type of notification with the NSNotification-Center and afterward may process those notifications accordingly. Again, we'll discuss this topic in chapter 6.

1.5.4   *Lifecycle management*

In this discussion, we've neglected a topic: how to recognize when objects are being created and destroyed—starting with your application. With multitasking enabled in iOS 4, you can create custom behavior before or after your application enters background mode. We'll cover more details on this topic in chapter 21.

Table 1.4 summarizes some of the important messages that will be sent as part of the lifecycle of your program. To respond to them, you fill in the contents of the appropriate methods in either an object or its delegate—which requires writing a subclass and is one of the prime reasons to do so.

Table 1.4   Several important methods let you respond to the lifecycle of your application or its individual objects.

Method	Object	Summary
`application:DidFinishLaunching WithOptions:`	`UIApplicationDelegate`	Application has loaded. You should create initial windows and otherwise start your program.
`applicationDidReceiveMemoryWarning:`	`UIApplicationDelegate`	Application received a low-memory warning. You should free up memory.
`applicationWillTerminate:`	`UIApplicationDelegate`	Application is about to end. You should free up memory and save state.
`init:`	`NSObject`	Object is being created. You should initialize it here.
`dealloc:`	`NSObject`	Object is freeing up its memory. You should release any objects that haven't been autoreleased.

Note that we've included `init:` here, because it forms a natural part of the object lifecycle. You should look at the individual Apple class references, particularly `UIApplicationDelegate`, for other methods you may want to respond to when writing programs.

With that, we've completed our look at the big-picture methods of iOS. You've not yet seen them in real use, so bookmark these pages—we'll refer to them when you begin programming in chapter 3.

1.6   *How to make an application from an idea*

At the beginning of this chapter we talked about turning great idea in to a killer application. How do you do it? Let's walk through the general steps to help make your dreams come true.

1.6.1 *The checklist*

There are several ways to build a universal application running on both the iPhone and iPad. Let's start with a handy checklist. (If you've already installed the Xcode and iOS SDK as demonstrated earlier in this chapter, you've finished half of the task.)

1 Join Apple's iOS Developer Program (US$ 99/year will give you access to submit applications to the App Store).
2 Have access to an Intel-based Mac computer with Mac OS X 10.6 or above.
3 Get a good book for beginners (this book, for example).
4 Get a test device: iPhone, iPod touch, or iPad. It will be mainly for testing during application development. If you're on a tight budget and don't already own one of these devices, you don't have to purchase one. There are test device services that provide rental equipment.
5 Get a sketchbook for the UI design, or make use of UI mocking software such as that from Balsamiq.

That's it! The last step is to learn Objective-C by reading this book and build your application with the iOS SDK. With this goal in mind, let's move on to the application concept.

1.6.2 *What's the category for your application?*

Knowing the category your application fits into will help you make a better estimate of how difficult it will be to build, which will help you plan your release date. Let's review the most common app categories.

GAMES AND ENTERTAINMENT

This category is hot and crowded. It's super competitive to create a successful application under games or entertainment. A game or entertainment application generally is heavy on media. As a developer, you should consider working with a UI designer in order to take advantage of the awesome graphic display quality of the iPhone and iPad.

Generally speaking, a game application may combine the use of the accelerometer, drawing and animations, audio, and Game Kit. Once you're familiar with the iOS SDK basics, you can jump to later chapters that will cover the iOS frameworks in detail. Chapter 15 provides complete coverage of game application development.

The difficulty level for a developer of game applications is higher compared to other categories. Fortunately, the rich UI tools on iOS provide a decent, fast prototyping environment for game developers.

RICH CONTENT APPLICATIONS

Rich content applications are commonly data oriented—for instance, a Twitter application. To allow user access data from the cloud, rich content applications provide organized data on the client side.

On the iPhone, the challenge of this rich content application is the limited screen real estate. The key to success, therefore, is in presenting the user with a good amount of well-organized data.

On the iPad, the focus is to provide rich content on one screen. The iPad screen can be compared to a book. With a detail-oriented UI design, you can add plenty of realism to your application. For example, the page-flipping animation in an iBook application allows users to flip through a digital book as if it were a traditional paper book.

This type of application needs to download data from the server and then store the data locally. Chapters 8 and 9 provide a great introduction on how to store data locally on the iPhone and iPad. Chapter 14 demos how to fetch data through Internet protocols on iOS.

NAVIGATION AND TRAVEL APPLICATIONS

This category makes more sense on the iPhone compared to the iPad. With its built-in GPS and compass, the iPhone can be used to provide the user's current location on the fly.

If you're thinking about presenting Map View on the screen, don't miss out on chapter 18, which covers the details on iOS's Map Kit framework.

With the combination of an accelerometer, GPS chip, and camera, you can build an augmented reality navigation application with iOS's hardware framework access. iOS frameworks for these hardware accesses can be found in this book.

UTILITY APPLICATIONS

The key to a successful utility application is to keep it simple. Make sure your application will focus on one major task and stick with it. The calculator application on iPhone is a good example. For a beginner, this is a relatively easy category. Moreover, it fits the needs for the creative idea or the niche market. With the knowledge acquired in the first seven chapters of this book, you'll be able to create a decent utility application.

Next, we'll cover the business model for the iOS platform.

1.6.3   *Making money with your application*

Generally speaking, there are three ways to generate profit on the iOS platform:

- *Submit a paid application.* You can price your application at the level you're happy with; the current price tier allowed on the App Store is from US$0.99 to US$999.99 (there are similar pricing tiers for each App Store market in local currencies). It should be mentioned that you have a 30% profit share with Apple.
- *Submit a free application with in-app purchase.* You can use Store Kit on iOS to generate profit through an in-app purchase. For details, please refer to chapter 19. You share 30% of all revenue through in-app purchases with Apple.
- *Submit a free application supported by advertisements.* This is a common business model for free applications. Follow the step-by-step instructions on iAd from chapter 20; you'll be able to make money with your application in no time.

You don't have to build an application for profit. Simply creating a cool application and learning a new programming technique is fun and rewarding in itself. The bottom line is if you're planning to distribute your application through the App Store, make sure you read and follow the application guidelines from the iOS Developer Center.

Finally, stay focused and don't give up! Learning a new programming language isn't easy. Try listing the key features for your application, and focus on the most important ones throughout the development process. Unless you have unlimited resources, it will be hard to put all the features you want inside one application. And even if you manage to, it may be too hard for users to figure out how to use your app. Remember: sometimes less is more.

1.7   *Summary*

In this chapter, we first explored iOS on the iPhone and iPad, and then we explained how to install the iOS SDK on your Mac. We also covered the anatomy of iOS, including objects, classes, and methods, providing the backdrop for coding in Objective-C, which follows in the next chapter. With the program environment ready, you can start the journey with iOS development.

Learning Objective-C

This chapter covers

- Introducing Objective-C
- Using messages
- Implementing classes
- Setting properties
- Learning categories and protocols

In this chapter, we'll examine all of the Objective-C elements that are applicable to iOS development. We assume that you have a good understanding of a rigorous programming language (like C), that you know the basic concepts behind object-oriented programming (OOP), and that you understand what the Model-View-Controller (MVC) architectural model is.

We're now ready to move into the world of SDK development. We'll take a quick tour to examine the programming language and frameworks you'll be using when you program with the SDK.

2.1 Introducing Objective-C

All of the SDK's programming is done in Objective-C, a full superset of C, allowing you to write any traditional C code. (There is also Objective-C++, which allows for full integration of Objective-C and C++, with some caveats.) It adds powerful object-oriented capabilities as well. These extensions come by way of the design philosophies of Smalltalk, one of the earliest object-oriented languages. Because of its origin beyond the standard boundaries of C, Objective-C's messaging code may look a little strange to you at first. But after you get the hang of it, you'll discover that it's elegant and easy to read, providing some nice improvements over traditional ANSI C code.

We'll look at Objective-C's messages, class definitions, properties, compiler directives, categories, and protocols. Although this overview gives you enough to get started with Objective-C, it can't provide all the details, particularly for more complex functionality like properties and categories. If you need more information than we've been able to provide, look at Apple's own references on the topic, particularly "Learning Objective-C: A Primer," "Object-Oriented Programming with Objective-C," and "The Objective-C 2.0 Programming Language," all of which can be found in Apple's iOS developer library.

Let's start with a look at Objective-C's big picture. It's an object-oriented language, which means it's full of classes and objects, instance variables, and methods.

As implemented by Apple and used throughout iOS's frameworks, Objective-C is built *entirely* around objects. Windows, views, buttons, sliders, and controllers all exchange information with each other, respond to events, and pass actions in order to make your program run.

A header (.h) file and a source code (.m) file together represent each object in Objective-C. Sometimes you'll access standard classes of objects that come built into the iOS frameworks, but often you'll instead subclass objects so that you can create new behaviors. When you do this, you'll add a new header file and source code file to your project that together represent the new subclass you've invented.

Although we won't dwell on it much, note that C++ code can be mixed in with Objective-C code. We leave the specifics of that for the experienced object-oriented programmer (and, as usual, there's more detail on Apple's website). You can also freely insert older C syntax; as we'll discuss shortly; this is necessary when you're working with older libraries.

With all that said, we're ready to dive into Objective-C's unique syntax. Table 2.1 summarizes the seven major elements of syntax.

Table 2.1 Objective-C code can look different from ANSI C; it depends on a handful of syntactic changes.

Syntax element	Summary
Messages	Messages send commands to objects in [bracketed] code (similar to functions in C).
Classes	Classes define object types in matched .h and .m files.
Properties	Properties allow for the easy definition of accessors and mutators (setting and getting object member variables).
Categories	Categories can be used to add to classes without subclassing.

Table 2.1 Objective-C code can look different from ANSI C; it depends on a handful of syntactic changes. *(continued)*

Syntax element	Summary
Protocols	Protocols define methods that a class promises to respond to (similar to interfaces in languages like Java).
@	@ directives are used by the compiler for a variety of purposes.
^	With iOS 4, blocks were introduced. Blocks are objects that encapsulate a unit of work—or, in less abstract terms, a segment of code—that can be executed at any time. The caret symbol (^) is used as a syntactic marker for blocks.

We offer a more technical summary at the end of this section, showing all the syntax of these elements. But first, we discuss these syntactic elements at length, in approximate order of importance.

2.2   *The message*

Objective-C's most important extension to the C programming language is the *message*. A message is sent when one object asks another to perform a specific action; it's Objective-C's equivalent to the procedural functional call. Messages are also where Objective-C's syntax varies the most from ANSI C standards—which means that when you understand them, you'll be able to read most Objective-C code.

A simple message call looks like this:

```
[receiver message];
```

Here's a real-life example that you'll meet in the next chapter:

```
[window makeKeyAndVisible];
```

That message sends the `window` object the `makeKeyAndVisible:` command, which tells it to appear and start accepting user input.

There are three ways in which this message could be slightly more complex. First, it could accept arguments; second, it could be nested; and third, it could be a call to one of a few different recipients.

2.2.1   *Messages with arguments*

Many messages include a simple command, as in the previous example. But sometimes you'll want to send one or more arguments along with a message to provide more information about what you want done. When you send a single argument, you do so by adding a colon and the argument after the message, like so:

```
[receiver message:argument];
```

Here's another real-world example:

```
[textView setText:@"These are the times ..."];
```

When you want to send multiple arguments, each additional argument is sent following a label, as shown here:

```
[receiver message:arg1 label2:arg2 label3:arg3];
```

Here's an example:

```
[myButton setTitle:@"Goodbye" forState:UIControlStateNormal];
```

This is the way in which Objective-C's messages vary the most from C's functions. You're going to come to love it. You no longer need to remember the ordering of the arguments because each gets its own title, clearly marking it. The result is much more readable.

2.2.2   Nested messages

One of the most powerful elements of Objective-C's messaging system is the fact that you can nest messages. This allows you to replace either the recipient or the argument of a message (or both) with another message. Then, the return of that nested message automatically fills in the appropriate space of the message it's nested inside.

Object creation frequently replaces the receiver in this manner:

```
[[UITextView alloc] initWithFrame:textFieldFrame];
```

The object created by sending the `alloc` message to the `UITextView` class object is then initialized. (We'll get to class objects in a moment.)

When you're passing a color as an argument, you almost always do so by nesting a call to the `UIColor` class object:

```
[textView setTextColor:[UIColor colorWithWhite:newColor alpha:1.0]];
```

Message nesting is a core Objective-C coding style, and you'll see it frequently. It also shows why Objective-C's bracketed messaging style is cool. With good use of code indentation, it can make complex concepts readable.

2.2.3   Message recipients

As you've seen over the last couple of examples, Objective-C uses two different types of objects. *Class objects* innately exist, and each represents one of the classes in your framework. They can be sent certain types of requests, such as a request to create a new object, by sending a message to the class name:

```
[class message];
```

Here's an example:

```
UIButton *myButton =
    [UIButton buttonWithType:UIButtonTypeRoundedRect];
```

Instance objects are what you're more likely to think of when you hear the term *object*. You create them yourself, and the majority of your programming time is spent manipulating them. Except for those examples of creating new objects, all of our real-life examples so far have involved instance objects.

In addition to calling an object by name, you can also refer to an object by one of two special keywords: `self` and `super`. The first always refers to the object itself, whereas the second always refers to the class's parent.

You'll often see `self` used internal to a class's source code file:

```
[self setText:@"That try men's souls. "];
```

You'll often see `super` used as part of an overridden method, where the child calls the parent's method before it executes its own behavior:

```
[super initWithFrame:frame]
```

All your message calls should follow one of these four patterns when naming its receiver: they can call something by its class name (for a class method), by its instance name (for an instance method), by the `self` keyword, or by the `super` keyword.

Now that you know how to send messages between objects, you'd probably like to know how to create those classes from which your objects are instantiated in the first place. That's the topic of the next section.

2.3   *Class definition*

As we've noted, each class tends to be represented by a matched pair of files: a header file and a source code file. To define a class, each of these files must contain a special compiler directive, which is always marked in Objective-C with an @ symbol.

First, you define the interface for the class, which is a simple declaration of its public variables and methods. You do this in the header (.h) file. Next, you define the implementation for the class, which is the content of all its methods; this is done in a source (.m) file.

Figure 2.1 shows this bifurcation graphically; we'll look at the headers and implementation files in more depth in the next few sections.

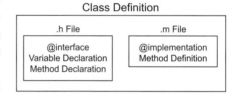

Figure 2.1   **Headers and source code files contain distinctive parts of your Objective-C classes.**

2.3.1   *The interface*

Interfaces begin with an `@interface` directive and finish with an `@end` directive. They contain instance variable declarations in curly brackets and then method declarations. The following listing shows an example of their usage. It's the first of several examples that we offer in this section that depict a fake class, `AppleTree`.

Listing 2.1   Defining the class of `Appletree`

```
/* AppleTree.h */
@interface AppleTree : UrTree
{
    NSString *appleType;
}
```

```
- (id)growFruit:(NSString *)appleColor;
@end
```

You begin the interface command with the @interface directive and end it with the @end directive. Note that the @interface directive includes not only the class name but also the name of its superclass, following a colon. It could also include a list of protocols, a topic we'll return to later in this section.

The variable declaration is entirely normal. NSString is a type that you'll meet when we look at iOS later in this chapter. Note that you don't have to declare all your variables in your @interface—those instance variables that you want to be accessible outside a particular method. You'll declare variables that are used within only individual methods inside those methods, as you'd expect.

The method declaration contains a typed description of a method with one argument, matching the syntax you've seen for messages. It also contains one other new element: it starts with a hyphen (-). That means this is an instance method, which is a method that can only be used by an instance object. Its opposite number, which is marked with a plus sign (+), is the class method, which is used by a class object. Class methods can't make use of instance variables or call install methods, because they're accessible only from an instantiated object.

The id type used as the return of growFruit: is another Objective-C innovation. Objective-C allows for dynamic typing, where type is decided at runtime. To support this, it includes the weak type of id, which can be a pointer to any object.

Before we finish our discussion of method declarations, we'd like to mention that, as with variables, you only have to declare those methods that can be called externally. Methods that remain internal to a class can remain hidden if you desire.

2.3.2 *The implementation*

After you've declared a class with an @interface, you can then define it with the @implementation directive. The following listing provides a brief example of what the implementation might look like for the AppleTree class, including a single example method.

Listing 2.2   Implementation file for the `AppleTree` class

```
/* AppleTree.m */
#import "AppleTree.h"
#import "Apple.h"
@implementation AppleTree
- (id)growFruit:(NSString *)appleColor

{

    Apple *fruit = [Apple appleWithColor:appleColor];        Definition
                                                             of method
    return fruit;

}
@end
```

The code starts with the #import directive. This is Objective-C's variant for the #include macro. It includes the file unless it's already been included, and it's the preferred alternative when using Objective-C. In this case, you include AppleTree.h, which should contain the interface described in the code snippet in listing 2.1. Without including it, you'd need to redefine all the instance variables and include the superclass in the @implementation statement. The #import helps you avoid redundant code. You also include the Apple.h file so that you can create an Apple.

As with the interface, the implementation code begins with a directive and ends with @end. In between, you describe what the method does, which includes sending a message to the Apple class object.

2.3.3   *Object instantiation*

You now have two parts of a puzzle: how to create new classes of objects and how to send messages among instantiated objects. What you're missing is how to instantiate an object from a class.

Generally, object instantiation follows the same pattern. First, you allocate memory for the object, and then you initiate any variables and perform any other setup. The precise manner in which this is done can vary from class to class. A framework usually decides how object creation works—which for our purposes means iOS. As you'll see later in this chapter, iOS specifies two methods for object instantiation: the alloc-init method and the class (or factory) method. You'll meet each of these soon, when we talk about iOS, but first let's finish up with the core syntax of Objective-C.

2.4   Properties

What we've covered so far should be sufficient for you to understand (and write) most simple Objective-C code. One other major feature in Objective-C deserves some extended discussion because of its unique syntax: the property.

2.4.1   *The purpose of properties*

Because instance variables are encapsulated, you usually have to write tons of getter and setter methods when doing OOP. This can get tedious, and you must also be careful about consistency so you don't have dozens of different syntaxes for your accessors and mutators.

Objective-C offers a solution to these problems: you can declare an instance variable as a property. When you do so, you standardize the variable's accessor and mutator methods by automatically declaring a getter and a setter. The setter is called setVariable and the getter is called variable.

For example, returning to the apples that we've been talking about in our major examples, if you define the NSString *appleType; variable as a property, the following declarations automatically occur:

```
-(void)setAppleType:(NSString *)newValue;
-(NSString *)appleType;
```

You'll never see these declarations, but they're there.

2.4.2 Setting a property

You declare an instance variable as a property by using the @property directive as part of your @interface statement. The following listing demonstrates how to do so, in the full context of the example so far.

Listing 2.3 AppleTree.h

```
@interface AppleTree : UrTree
{
    NSString *appleType;

}
@property(retain) NSString *appleType;
- (id)growFruit:(NSString *)appleColor;
@end
```

The header file shows that any property must start with the declaration of an instance variable. The @property directive then repeats that declaration. If you wish, you can stop here. You've now implicitly declared your accessor and mutator methods, and you can go and write those methods on your own if you see fit. Let's look at another example.

Listing 2.4 AppleTree.m

```
#import "AppleTree.h"
#import "Apple.h"
@implementation AppleTree
@synthesize appleType;
- (id)growFruit:(NSString *)appleColor
{
    Apple *fruit = [Apple appleWithColor:appleColor];
    return fruit;
}
@end
```

Objective-C will also write these methods for you if you ask it to. This is done with the @synthesize declaration in the @implementation statement. This creates accessor methods that read and set the variable by the simple methods you'd expect. The setter method is by default of type assign, but you can choose a different method using property attributes, which we'll talk about down the road.

2.4.3 Using the accessors

If you're not doing anything fancy, you can immediately use your class's default getter and setter methods, as shown in the following three examples:

```
NSString *chosenType = [AppleTree appleType];
[AppleTree setAppleType:@"Washington Red"];
[AppleTree setAppleType:myAppleType];
```

In addition to providing you with automatically created accessors and mutators, properties also give you access to a bit of syntactic sugar, which can make using them that much easier.

2.4.4   *The dot syntax*

Objective-C offers a dot syntax that makes it easy to use an object's accessor and mutator methods (whether you synthesized them or created them yourself). The following are the dot-syntax equivalents to the messages you sent earlier:

```
NSString *chosenType = AppleTree.appleType;
AppleTree.appleType = @"Washington Red";
AppleTree.appleType = myAppleType;
```

The dot syntax can also be nested, just as you can nest messages. In the following example, the `treeType` property returns a `tree` object that has an `AppleType` property:

```
Apple.treeType.AppleType
```

With that in hand, you should now be able to write simpler and more intuitive code.

2.4.5   *Property complexities*

There are several complexities of properties that we've opted not to delve into here. First, property declarations can include attributes. They let you change getter and setter names, change setter assignment methods, modify memory management (retain, autorelease, and so on), set nonatomic accessors (which are accessors that can be interrupted by the CPU scheduler while in use), and determine whether the property is read-only or read-write. These can all be set as part of the `@property` line.

Second, another directive called `@dynamic` lets you add accessor and mutator methods at runtime.

Third, it's possible to override default values that you've synthesized through normal method creation as part of your `@implementation`.

A variety of information about properties is available in Apple's Objective-C reference; if you need to delve into any of these complexities, you should refer to that.

2.5   *The @ directive*

We're almost finished with our overview of Objective-C, but we want to alert you to one other frequently used bit of syntax. As you've seen, the `@` symbol denotes a compile directive. It's a core part of class definition, and it's required for properties. You'll also see it in a few other places in Objective-C code.

Sometimes an `@` is used to create variables of certain types, most frequently a variable of type `NSString *`. You saw this in a few of the messaging examples. You include the `@` symbol, followed by the string value you want to set:

```
NSString *mySample = @"What does this have to do with apples?";
```

In chapter 6, you'll also encounter the `@selector` directive, which is used to create a variable of type `SEL`. This is a method selector, which is what you use when you want to pass the name of a method as an argument, as will occur when we get to events and actions. A standard usage looks like this:

```
SEL mySelector = @selector(growFruit:);
```

There are many other directives you can use in Objective-C. Our purpose here is to highlight those you're most likely to see in this book and most likely to use in introductory SDK programming.

> **TIP** Forgetting to mark a string with an @ is the most common error in iOS programming, so keep an eye out for this one! (Without the @, you'll have a C-style `char*` string, which is almost certainly not what you want.)

2.6 Categories and protocols

It's important to touch on two final elements of Objective-C: the category and the protocol. We broadly define what they do, but we won't delve too deeply into their details. To learn more, refer to *Objective-C Fundamentals* by Manning Publications.

2.6.1 The category

Categories are used if you want to add behavior to a class without subclassing. As usual, you do so by creating a new pair of files containing `@interface` and `@implementation` code. This time, you no longer need to worry about the superclass name but must include a category name in parentheses, as follows:

```
@interface AppleTree (MyAppleChanges)
@implementation AppleTree (MyAppleChanges)
```

As a result, the categorized methods and variables that you describe for the classes are added to the core class definition in your program.

We don't use categories in this book.

2.6.2 The protocol

A protocol is effectively an interface that's not tied to a class. It declares a set of methods, listing their arguments and their returns. Classes can then state that they're using the protocol in their own `@interface` statements. For example, if you had a `Growing` protocol that was used by plants and animals alike, you could define its usage as follows:

```
@interface AppleTree : UrTree <Growing>
```

The `AppleTree` class would be promising that it would respond to all the methods defined in the `Growing` protocol.

You won't be creating any new protocols in this book. But you'll use existing ones, because within Apple's iOS, they're tied integrally to the MVC model. Views hand off protocol descriptions of how they should be used to view controllers via `datasource` and `delegate` properties—both topics that we'll introduce when we talk about iOS.

With that, the shine has gone off our apples, so we'll return to real-life examples when we move on. But first, having provided an overview of a whole new programming language in an impossibly short number of pages, we'll summarize what you've learned.

2.7   *Wrapping up Objective-C*

Table 2.2 summarizes the syntax specifics of the Objective-C elements that we've been discussing. This table can serve as a quick reference whenever you want to revisit how Objective-C code works differently from traditional C.

Table 2.2   Objective-C uses many typical object-oriented coding elements, but its syntax is somewhat unique.

Object-oriented element	Syntax
Object messaging	`[recipient message];`

Class creation	`/* .h file */`
	`@interface class: super`
	`    declarations`
	`@end`
	`/* .m file */`
	`@implementation class`
	`    definitions`
	`@end`

Method declaration	`- (return type)instancemethod:arguments` `+ (return type)classmethod:arguments`
Property declaration	`@property (Property Behavior Modifiers) variable;`
Property synthesis	`@synthesize property;`
Property accessor	`[object property];`
Property mutator	`[object setProperty:value];`
Property dot syntax	`object.property`
Category declaration	`@interface class: super (category)` `@implementation class: super (category)`
Protocol declaration	`@interface class: super <protocol>`

And with that, we've completed our look at the syntax and structure of the Objective-C programming language. But that's only half of the foundation you need in order to use the SDK. You also need to be familiar with the specific methods and programming styles provided by iOS's extensive set of frameworks.

2.8   *Summary*

Objective-C is your programming language for creating iOS applications. It's an object-oriented version of C that has some unique syntax thanks to its elegant Smalltalk inspiration. After you get used to it, you'll find it simple and easy to read.

Now that we've completed our Objective-C primer, let's dive into putting Objective-C to use in Xcode 4 in chapter 3.

Using Xcode 4

This chapter covers

- What's new in Xcode 4
- Creating your HelloWorld application
- Using the Interface Builder editor under Xcode 4
- Creating the AppleStock application

Now that you have Xcode and the iOS SDK installed, and you've learned a bit about the puzzle pieces needed to build an application, you're ready to write your first HelloWorld application. The main purpose of this chapter is to show you the new features in Xcode 4 and how Xcode works. Using a traditional HelloWorld application, we'll look at the parts of a standard application, and you'll learn how to build and run your first iOS application. Then we'll look at how Interface Builder works under Xcode 4. And last, you'll create the AppleStock application, which shows how to create new objects, manipulate them graphically, and use the inspector window.

3.1 Introducing Xcode 4

At the time of this writing, Xcode 4 is a brand-new release to iOS developers. With a new user interface, Xcode 4 also includes a lot more changes under the hood. Let's first look at the new features in Xcode 4.

When Xcode 4 was first introduced at Apple's WWDC 2010, developers were excited and looked forward to the new features in Xcode 4. Compared to Xcode 3, Xcode 4 is more powerful, more tightly integrated, easier to use, and great for organizing your projects.

Note that you can have both Xcode 4 and Xcode 3 installed on your Mac at the same time, and the existing project will be fully compatible in Xcode 4.

Let's look at the advantages in Xcode 4:

- *Single-window interface*—You can create a workspace and add multiple projects under the same workspace and edit them in the same window. In Xcode 4, Interface Builder is fully integrated as part of the Xcode application, making it much easier to connect objects between the source code and the graphic design interface.
- *Source control*—Although this isn't an exciting topic, Xcode 4 makes it a lot easier to control and compare the new changes with version control and Git. New projects are even given the option to automatically have a Git repository created. Version Editor provides the side-by-side view for any two versions of a file.
- *LLVM 2.0 compiler includes full support for C, Objective-C, and C++*—The benefit is in the speed of compiling and linking, as well as improvements to syntax highlighting and code completion driven by the new LLVM parser.
- *Powerful debug support*—The Fix-it feature presents the potential solution for the issue inside the program.
- *Scheme concept*—Instead of creating each platform as a build target, you can use Xcode Schemes to collectively define targets to build, the configuration to be used, and the associated tests to execute.

There are more features in Xcode 4. You can find out the details from the iOS Dev Center. Now let's launch the Xcode 4 application on your Mac.

3.2 *Using Xcode 4 to create the HelloWorld application*

In this section, you'll work through creating your first iOS application with step-by-step instructions under Xcode 4. The goal is to get you started programming with Xcode and teach you how to write code and run the application on the iOS Simulator.

3.2.1 *Creating a new project*

Through the default installation path, you can launch Xcode 4 from the Developer directory (typically located at Macintosh HD > Developer > Applications > Xcode). An even easier way to launch Xcode is to use Spotlight: press Command-spacebar, type xcode, and then press Enter. The first time you launch the Xcode 4 program, you'll see the Welcome to Xcode window, as shown in figure 3.1.

Figure 3.1 **The Welcome to Xcode window appears when Xcode launches.**

Select Create a New Xcode Project (or choose File > New > New Project), and you're immediately prompted to choose a template for your new project, as shown in figure 3.2.

The template you choose will fill your project with default frameworks, default files, default objects, and even default code. As you'll see, it'll be a great help in jump-starting your own coding.

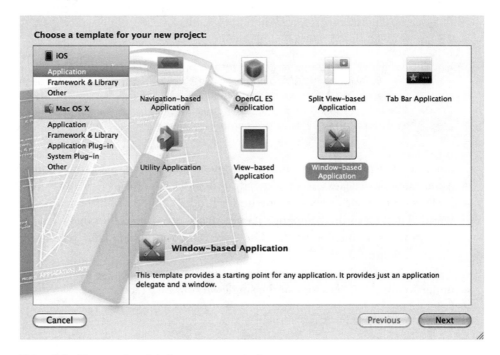

Figure 3.2 **Choose a template for your new project.**

Templates for new projects

When you're creating a new project in Xcode, you always have the option to select from among several templates, as shown in figure 3.2, each of which gives you a different basis for your code. Besides a Window-Based Application, you can create a project as a View-Based Application, a Tab Bar Application, a Navigation-Based Application, a Utility Application, a Split View-Based Application, or an OpenGL ES Application.

Most of these templates will involve view controllers, which you won't encounter for a couple of chapters. We provide you with an overview for now so you can see the possibilities that Xcode offers:

- A Window-Based Application is entirely minimalist. It provides a starting point for your application with the application delegate and window.
- A View-Based Application has a bit more functionality. It includes a basic view controller that allows you to add custom content. You'll use it in chapter 5 (and most of the time thereafter).
- A Tab Bar Application creates a tab bar along the bottom of the screen that allows you to switch between multiple views. The template does this by creating a tab bar controller and then defining what each of its views looks like. You'll use it in chapter 7.
- A Navigation-Based Application sets you up with a navigation controller, a navigation bar along the top, and a table view in the middle of the page so you can easily build hierarchical applications. You'll also use it in chapter 7.
- A Utility Application defines a flip-side controller that has two sides, the front side containing an info button that allows you to call up the backside. This is the last view controller we'll explore in chapter 7.
- An OpenGL ES Application is another minimalistic application. The difference from the Window-Based Application is that it includes GL frameworks, sends the glView messages to get it started, and otherwise sets certain GL properties. We won't get to GL until chapter 13, and even then we'll only touch on it lightly.
- A Split View-Based Application is a split view controller–based application that works only on the iPad. You'll use this template in chapter 7.

For your first program, go with the simplest template you can find: Window-Based Application. Select Next. You can specify options for your project, as shown in figure 3.3.

First, enter your project's name under Product Name. In this example, use Hello-World. Then fill in the company's name. Make sure to select iPhone from the Device Family option. (Note that neither Use Core Data nor Include Unit Tests is selected, as shown in figure 3.3.)

Click Next, and choose where to save this new project. You're ready to start coding under Xcode. Now, let's look at the single-window interface.

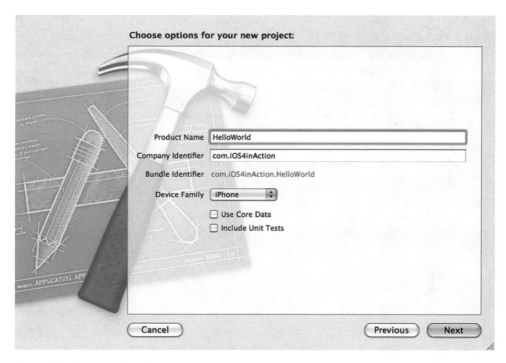

Figure 3.3 Choose options for your new project.

3.2.2 Getting familiar with the workspace window

As you can see in figure 3.4, Xcode 4's single workspace window contains a lot of information. The toolbar is on the top of the Xcode workspace window, and it offers a few commonly used commands for quick access. Below the toolbar, the window is divided into three main areas or sections: Navigator area on the left pane, Editor area in the center, and Utility area on the right pane. (Note that by using the default setting, the Utility area is hidden. You can show the utility view by selecting View > Utilities > Show Utilities, or clicking the Utility View button on the top-right-corner toolbar.)

The Navigator area contains a list of all the files that are being used in your project, organized by type. Whenever you need to add new frameworks, images, databases, or other files to your project, you can do so under the Navigator.

Select any .h file in the project in the Navigator area, and the contents appear in the Editor area in the center. When you select the HelloWorld application under the Navigator area (the top-level node of the tree, which also lists the iOS Build Target), the Editor area is the place to change the product information, such as the application icon, launching image, build setting, and so on.

The Utility area shows the selected file information. It's split into two sections: on the top is the identity info, and on the bottom is the library.

Now that you have an overview of the Xcode single-window interface, let's zoom in to the Navigator area and learn the details of the files under your HelloWorld project.

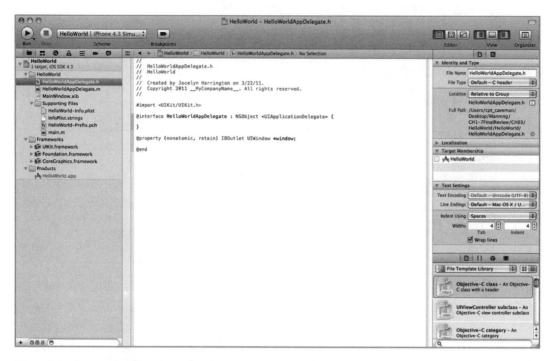

Figure 3.4   Xcode 4 in a single-window interface, which has the Navigator area on the left pane, the Editor area in the center pane, and the Utility area on the right pane

3.3   Closer look at files under the Navigation area

The HelloWorld application has three subfolders: HelloWorld, Frameworks, and Products. Let's spend some time reviewing what's under the hood.

3.3.1   HelloWorld folder

The HelloWorld folder is where you spend most of your time writing code and designing the application's interface. Click the triangle beside the HelloWorld folder to expand the contents so that you can review what it contains. You'll find one subfolder called Supporting Files and three files: HelloWorldAppDelegate.h, HelloWorldApp-Delegate.m, and MainWindow.xlb.

SUPPORTING FILES SUBFOLDER

The Supporting Files subfolder contains files that support the application. In the HelloWorld project, you can find HelloWorld-Info.plist, InfoPlist.strings, HelloWorld-Prefix.pch, and main.m. HelloWorld-Info.plist is a property list that contains information about the application, as shown in figure 3.5. It contains a number of instructions for your program compilation, the most important of which is the reference to the main nib file used in your program. InfoPlist.strings is a localization string file for your application's InfoPlist.

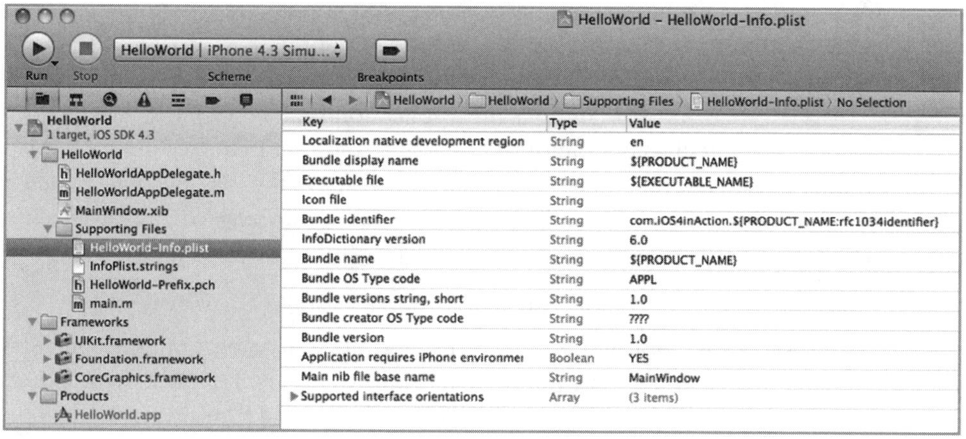

Figure 3.5   Select the project's Info.plist file to show details in the Editor area.

The HelloWorld-Prefix.pch file contains special prefix headers, which are imported into every one of your source code files.

Main.m comes with standard code generated by the project template, as you can see in the following listing.

Listing 3.1   Main.m file

```
#import <UIKit/UIKit.h>

int main(int argc, char *argv[])
{
    NSAutoreleasePool * pool = [[NSAutoreleasePool alloc] init];
    int retVal = UIApplicationMain(argc, argv, nil, nil);
        [pool release];
        return retVal;
}
```

The creation of this main routine is automatic, and you generally shouldn't have to fool with it *at all.* But it's worth understanding what's going on. You start with an #import directive, which you'll recall is Objective-C's substitute for #include. More specifically, you include the UIKit framework, the most important framework in Cocoa Touch. Notice that it's also in the helloworldxc_Prefix.pch file, but at least at the time of this writing, it's part of the default main.m file.

Notice that NSAutoreleasePool is created here. Recall that we mentioned this in our discussion of memory management in chapter 2. Note that the autorelease pool is released after you've run your application's main routine, following the standard rule that if you allocate the memory for an object, you must also release it.

The UIApplicationMain line creates your application and kicks off the event cycle. The function's arguments look like this:

```
int UIApplicationMain ( int argc, char *argv[], NSString *principalClassName,
NSString *delegateClassName);
```

As with the rest of the main.m file, you should never have to change this. But we nevertheless briefly touch on what the latter two arguments mean—although they'll usually be set to their defaults, thanks to the nil arguments.

`principalClassName` defines the application's main class, which is `UIApplication` by default. This class does a lot of the action and event controlling for your program, topics that we'll return to in chapter 6. The `UIApplication` object is created as part of this startup routine, but you'll note that no link to the object is provided. If you need to access it (and you will), you can use a `UIApplication` class method to do so:

```
[UIApplication sharedApplication];
```

This returns the application object. It's typically sent as part of a nested message to a `UIApplication` method, as you'll see in future chapters. For now, the application does two things to note: it calls up your default .xib file, and it interfaces with your application delegate.

The `delegateClassName` defines the application object's delegate, an idea introduced in chapter 2. As noted there, this is the object that responds to some of the application's messages, as defined by the `UIApplicationDelegate` protocol. Among other things, the application delegate must respond to lifecycle messages: most important, the `applicationDidFinishLaunching:` message, which runs your program's content, as we'll talk more about momentarily.

APPDELEGATE

As you've already seen, the application delegate is responsible for answering many of the application's messages. You can refer to the previous chapter for a list of some of the more important ones or to Apple's `UIApplicationDelegate` protocol reference for a complete listing.

More specifically, an application delegate should do the following:

- At launch time, it must create an application's windows and display them to the user.
- It must initialize your data.
- It must respond to "quit" requests.
- It must handle low-memory warnings.

Of these topics, the first one is the most important to you. Your application delegate files, HelloWorldAppDelegate.h and HelloWorldAppDelegate.m, start your program.

Now that you've moved past main.m, you'll be using classes, which is the sort of coding that makes up the vast majority of Objective-C code. Select HelloWorldAppDelegate.h in the Navigator area to view the source in the Editor area. You can also enable the assistant for the Editor area (choose View > Editor > Assistant). You'll see that the side-by-side editor view contains the header file in the left section and the source file in the right section, as shown in figure 3.6.

Listing 3.2 shows the HelloWorldAppDelegate header file.

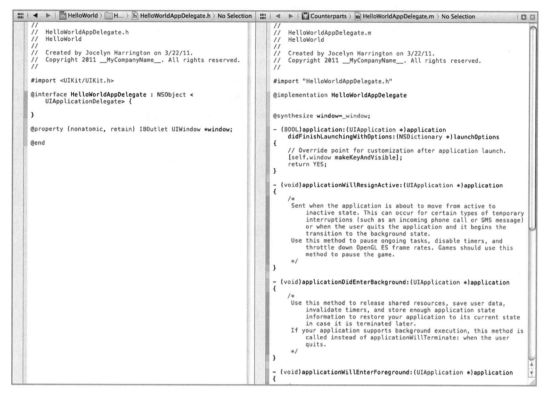

Figure 3.6 **HelloWorldAppDelegate header file and source file under editor assistant view**

Listing 3.2 HelloWorldAppDelegate's header file

```
#import <UIKit/UIKit.h>
@interface HelloWorldAppDelegate: NSObject <UIApplicationDelegate> {
}
@property (nonatomic, retain) IBOutlet UIWindow *window;
@end
```

Again, there's nothing to change here, but we want to examine the contents, both to reiterate some of the lessons you learned in the previous chapter and to give you a good foundation for work you'll do in the future.

First, an @interface line subclasses your delegate from NSObject (which is appropriate, because the app delegate is a nondisplaying class) and includes a promise to follow the UIApplicationDelegate protocol. Then @property declares window as a property. Note that this statement includes some of the property attributes, nonatomic and retain. You use the nonatomic attribute to specify that the synthesized getter method return the value directly. The retain attribute means that when a new value is assigned through the synthesized setter method, the old value will be released and the new value will be retained.

This line also includes an IBOutlet statement, which is used to mark the object as usable from Interface Builder. We'll examine this concept in more depth in the next section; for now, you only need to know that you have a window object already prepared for your application. Although you won't modify the header file in this example, you will in the future, and you'll generally be repeating the patterns you see here: creating more instance variables, including IBOutlets, and defining more properties. You may also declare methods in this header file, something that this first header file doesn't contain.

The following listing shows the application delegate's source code file, Hello-WorldAppDelegate.m.

Listing 3.3   HelloWorldAppDelegate source code

```
#import "HelloWorldAppDelegate.h"
@implementation HelloWorldAppDelegate
@synthesize window=_window;
-(BOOL)application:(UIApplication*)application
didFinishLaunchingWithOptions:(NSDictionary *)launchOptions {
    [self.window makeKeyAndVisible];
    return YES;
}
- (void)applicationWillResignActive:(UIApplication *)application{
}
- (void)applicationDidEnterBackground:(UIApplication *)application{
}
- (void)applicationWillEnterForeground:(UIApplication *)application{
}
- (void)applicationDidBecomeActive:(UIApplication *)application{
}
- (void)applicationWillTerminate:(UIApplication *)application{
}
- (void)dealloc{
    [_window release];
    [super dealloc];
}
@end
```

The source begins with an inclusion of the class's header file and an @implementation statement. The window property is also synthesized, which means the setter and getter methods will be automatically added when the program is compiled. Here window =_window means the property window is represented by the instance variable _window.

It's the content of the application:didFinishLaunchingWithOptions: method that's of most interest. As you'll recall, that's one of the iOS lifecycle messages we touched on in chapter 2. Whenever an iOS application gets entirely loaded into memory, it sends an application:didFinishLaunchingWithOptions: message to your application delegate, running that method. Note that there's already some code to display in that Interface Builder–created window.

Inside the dealloc method, the instance variable _window, which represents the property window, is released for the memory management. (Recall we mentioned that the `window` property declared in listing 3.2 will be retained through a setter accessor; if there's no `release` command here, you'll end up with a memory leak.)

MAINWINDOW.XIB

MainWindow.xib is an Interface Builder file, more broadly called a *nib file*. MainWindow creates a window, which is the root for your application to draw any other view. This is your connection to the interface design that may be used to easily create graphic interfaces for your project. We'll discuss it in depth in the next section.

3.3.2 Frameworks folder and Product folder

The Frameworks folder contains all the libraries that will be linked into your project. By default, `UIKit.framework`, `Foundation.framework`, and `CoreGraphics.framework` are automatically added by the template. The Foundation framework gives you access to NS objects, UIKit gives you access to UI objects, and CoreGraphics gives you access to various graphics functions. Later in this book, we'll cover the details on how to add a new framework to the project. For now, you can leave this folder the way it is.

The Products folder contains the products when the project compiles or builds. For the HelloWorld project, HelloWorld.app is the only product sitting under this folder. Right now, HelloWorld.app is shown in red, which means this file doesn't exist yet. You'll compile the HelloWorld project shortly, which will generate the commpiled application HelloWorld.app.

3.3.3 Building and running an application in Xcode

To compile in Xcode, navigate to Product and choose Product > Build from the drop-down menu. Your program compiles, and with a successful build, it can be launched on the iOS Simulator or an iOS device. Then choose Product > Run, and the iOS Simulator starts it up. Or, you can click the Run button in the top-left corner of the Xcode window. If you try this using the HelloWorld project you just created, you'll see the whole build and run process, resulting in an empty white screen displaying on your iOS Simulator, as shown in figure 3.7.

iOS applications run only on your iOS Simulator (or on the iPhone or iPad device); they can't be run on your Macintosh directly. Notice that by default the iPhone Simulator is started up. To switch to the iPad Simulator, navigate to the top-left Scheme menu on the Xcode window, choose iPad Simulator, and click the Run button. You'll see the iOS Simulator displaying the iPad interface.

Figure 3.7 Build and run the application on the iOS Simulator.

How to create a universal application

If you try to run the current HelloWorld application on the iPad Simulator, it will end up displaying the small iPhone window in the center of the iPad Simulator. That's because when you create this project, the project options for Device Family are set to iPhone (refer to figure 3.3).

You could create a real iPad target for this project when creating the new project for the Device Family option. Do this by selecting iPad or Universal (supports both iPhone and iPad). Because you've already created the project, there's another way to update the current project to change the device family to Universal. For details, please refer to appendix D. We won't cover the details in this chapter because the essentials have been covered. Please take this opportunity to practice on your own and gain more knowledge of Xcode by yourself.

If you later want to restart a program that you've already compiled, you can do so in one of three ways. You can click the program's icon, which should now appear in your iOS Simulator. Or, you can choose Product > Run from the Xcode menu. Finally, you can click the Run button in the Xcode window, which builds only if required and then executes your application.

That's it! With a rudimentary understanding of Xcode now in hand, you're ready to write code for your first iOS program.

3.3.4 *Writing code for HelloWorld*

We've been promising for a while that you'll be amazed by how simple it is to write things using the iOS SDK. Granted, the HelloWorld program may not be as easy as a single `printf` statement, but nonetheless it's pretty simple, considering that you're dealing with a complex, windowed UI environment.

As promised, you'll write everything inside the `application:DidFinishing-Launching` method, as shown in the next listing. The bolded code is the extra code you need to display "Hello, World!" on a window.

Listing 3.4 Presenting HelloWorld on the screen

```
-(BOOL)application:(UIApplication*)application
didFinishLaunchingWithOptions:(NSDictionary *)launchOptions {
[_window setBackgroundColor:[UIColor redColor]];
CGRect textFieldFrame = CGRectMake(50, 50, 150, 40);
UILabel *label = [[UILabel alloc] initWithFrame:textFieldFrame];
label.textColor = [UIColor whiteColor];
label.backgroundColor = [UIColor redColor];
label.shadowColor = [UIColor blackColor];
label.font = [UIFont systemFontOfSize:24];
label.text = @"Hello, World!";
[_window addSubview:label];
[label release];
[self.window makeKeyAndVisible];
return YES;
}
```

Because this is your first look at real live Objective-C code, we'll examine everything in some depth. You start by sending a message to the window object, telling it to set the background color to red. Recall back in the AppDelegate's header file, Interface Builder created the window. The IBOutlet that was defined in the header allows you to do manipulations of this sort.

Note that this line also makes use of a nested message, which we promised you'd see with some frequency. Here, you make a call to the UIColor class object and ask it to send the red color to the receiver, which then passes that on to the window. In this book, we hit a lot of UIKit classes without explaining them in depth. That's because the simpler objects all have standard interfaces; the only complexity is in which particular messages they accept. If you ever feel you need more information about a class, look at appendix A, which contains short descriptions of many objects, or see the complete class references available online at http://developer.apple.com (or in Xcode, select the class name for which you wish to find the defination, navigate to View > Utilities, and choose Quick Help. You should be able to see the documentation related to the class shown on the Utility area under the Quick Help section).

You next define where the text label is placed. You start that process by using CGRectMake to define a rectangle. Much as with Canvas, the iOS drawing uses a grid with the origin (0,0) set at the upper left. Your rectangle's starting point is 50 to the right and 50 down (50,50) from the origin. The rest of this line of code sets the rectangle to be 150 pixels wide and 40 pixels tall, which is enough room for your text.

You'll use this rectangle as a frame, which is one of the methods you can use to define a view's location. Where your view goes is one of the most important parts of your view's definition. Many classes use an initWithFrame: method, inherited from UIView, which defines location as part of the object's setup.

The frame is a rectangle that you've defined with a method like CGRectMake. Another common way to create a rectangular frame is to set it to take up your full screen with the following code snippet:

```
[[UIScreen mainScreen] bounds];
```

Sometimes you'll opt not to use the initWithFrame: method to create an object. UIButton is an example of a UIKit class that instead suggests you use a class factory method that lets you define a button shape.

In a situation like that, you must set your view's location by hand. Fortunately, this is easy to do, because UIView also offers a number of properties that you can set to determine where your view goes, even after it's been initialized. UIView's frame property can be passed as a rectangle, like the initWithFrame: method. Alternatively, you can use its center property to designate where the middle of the object goes and the bounds property to designate its size internal to its own coordinate system. All three of these properties are further explained in the UIView class reference. Note that CGRectMake is a function, not a method. It takes arguments using the old, unlabeled style of C, rather than Objective-C's more intuitive manner of using labeled arguments. When you get outside of Cocoa Touch, you'll find that many frameworks use this older paradigm. For now, all you need to know is what it does and that you needn't worry about releasing its memory. If you require more information, read the section "Using Core Foundation" in chapter 9.

The `label` is a simple class that allows you to print text on the screen. Figure 3.2 shows what the `label` (and the rest of the program) looks like.

As you'd expect, your `label` work begins with the creation of a `label` object. Note that you follow the standard methodology of nested object creation that we introduced in the previous chapter. First, you use a class method to allocate the object, and then you use an instance method to initialize it. Afterward, you send a number of messages to your object, this time using the dot syntax. We offer this as a variation from the way you set the window's background color. If you prefer, you can use the dot shorthand of `_window.backgroundColor` there, too. The two ways to access properties are equivalent.

The most important of the messages sets the label's text. You also set a font size and font color. You can even give the text an attractive black shadow, to demonstrate how easy it is to do cool stuff using iOS's objects. Every object that you use from a framework is full of properties, methods, and notifications that you can take advantage of. The best place to look up all these is the class references in Quick Help.

The final steps in your program are all pretty simple and standard. First, you connect the `label` and the window by using the window's `addSubview` method. This is a standard (and important!) method for adding views or view controllers to your window. You'll see it again and again.

Do you remember the standard rule that you must release anything you allocated? Here, that's the `label`. And that's a simple HelloWorld program, completely programmed and working, with some neat graphical nuances. Now click the Run button on Xcode's toolbar, and enjoy your first application running in the iOS Simulator (see figure 3.8)!

Although it was sufficient for this purpose, HelloWorld didn't make much use of the class creation that's possible in an object-oriented language. Sure, you depended on some existing classes—including `UIColor`, `UILabel`, and `UIWindow`—but all of your new code went into a single function, and you didn't create any classes of your own. We'll address how to create your own class in chapter 4, when you start working with new classes.

Creating a project for the iPad is almost identical to creating one for the iPhone. The main difference is that the window is much larger. We won't cover the iPad files in detail as we did for the iPhone template in the beginning of this section, because they're almost

Figure 3.8   Running HelloWorld on the iOS Simulator

the same. As mentioned earlier, the primary difference is the size of the main window. We'll discuss the iPad interface and universal application further in chapter 7.

So far, you created your first iOS application with Xcode and pure Objective-C code. Now that you're familiar with the basics of Xcode, let's move on to the next most important tool for iOS application development under Xcode: Interface Builder.

3.4   *Using Interface Builder in Xcode 4*

At the beginning of this chapter, we mentioned the new Xcode 4 interface and highlighted the single-window interface. Interface Builder is a graphical environment tool built into Xcode 4. Whenever you write an Xcode project, it includes a MainWindow.xib file that contains Interface Builder definitions for where graphical objects are placed. Every Xcode template comes with different objects prebuilt this way. Some of them have multiple, linked .xib files, with one file representing each separate screen of information.

In the project navigator, find the nib file MainWindow.xib. Click MainWindow.xib to open the document in the Interface Builder Editor pane. In the Xcode menu bar, choose View > Navigators > Hide Navigator to narrow the focus of the workspace. If the dock on the left doesn't look like the one in figure 3.9, click the button in the lower-left corner to switch the dock to outline view. In the Xcode menu, choose View > Utilities to show the Utility area on the right pane.

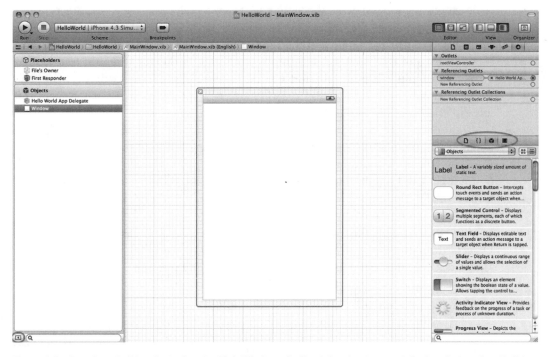

Figure 3.9   Interface Builder displaying the MainWindow.xib file. A few fundamental displays in Interface Builder are the nib document window (left), the main Editor pane in the middle, together with the Library pane (right bottom), and the Inspector pane (right top).

Let's look at what's inside Interface Builder and then quickly look at how to mock up Interface Builder objects.

3.4.1 *The anatomy of Interface Builder*

You usually access Interface Builder by selecting a .xib file in your project under Navigator area. The default .xib file is generally called MainWindow.xib. Clicking it brings up the MainWindow on the Canvas inside the Interface Builder window, showing how default objects have been designed visually, as shown in figure 3.9.

NIB VERSUS .XIB

You'll see both terms *.xib files* and *nib files* in this and later chapters. They're pretty much the same thing: a nib file is a compiled .xib file. (.xib files express the same data as nib files but in a text-based XML format.) They appear as .xib files in Xcode, but some methods call them nib files, as you'll see later in this chapter. Apple documents refer to a nib document window in Interface Builder; we've done the same here.

INTERFACE BUILDER

As you can see in figure 3.9, when you select a nib file or .xib file, the Interface Builder window will become the focus of the editor view automatically; all the files stay in the same window with your source code. Interface Builder contains a couple of important windows: the nib document dock on the left and the main Editor pane (Canvas) in the middle.

Turn on the utility view on the right panel view by selecting View > Utilities > Show Utilities or by clicking the utility view button on the top-right window. Utility view has two parts: the Inspector pane and the Library pane. The top part contains the Inspector window; and the third tab starting from the left is the Identity tab, followed by Object Attributes tab, Size tab, and Connections tab, as shown in figure 3.10. The Inspector window gives you access to a wide variety of information about an object and lets you change it.

The bottom part contains the Objects library available for Interface Builder. It's the third tab from the left on the bottom toolbar, as shown in figure 3.11. The Library window is where you can find all the UI elements that you may want to add to your program. You can start exploring the library by selecting the submenu under the Objects drop-down menu. You'll see four main classes of UI elements:

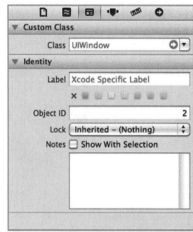

Figure 3.10   Inspector pane with Identity tab selected

- Controllers give you different ways to manage your views.
- Data Views give you different ways to display data.
- Inputs & Values give you a variety of simple input mechanisms.

- Windows, Views & Bars give you the core window and view objects, plus a variety of other elements.

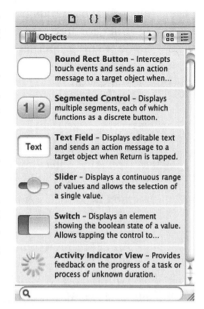

Figure 3.11   Library pane

Interface Builder is one of the most important editors within Xcode 4, so you may want to spend more time digging out the features under each tab and objects. It will definitely make your future design much smoother.

So, what's inside the nib file? Taking a closer look under the MainWindow.nib file (see figure 3.12), you find two categories: Objects and Placeholders. Interface objects are the objects that are created when the nib file is loaded. Placeholders refer to files that live outside the nib file but are connected to the contents of the nib file.

Under Placeholders in the nib file, you can see File's Owner and First Responder. The File's Owner placeholder is the main bridge between your application and the contents of the nib file. The File's Owner object is the owner of this nib file. The First Responder placeholder object represents the first object in the responder chain, which is determined dynamically at runtime by the UIKit frameworks. Don't worry if you find the concept difficult for now because we'll cover events and actions in detail in chapter 6.

A default MainWindow.xib file includes one window object. The window object is the one real object you can see on the Canvas here; you can play with it in the Editor pane on the Canvas. As you'd expect, this is the window object that was created by default in the templates you've used so far.

The Canvas in the center shows what the .xib file currently looks like. Because you used the Window-Based Application template in Xcode, there's nothing here yet. If you'd used one of the other templates, you'd see tab bars or other prebuilt elements. In any case, this is where you arrange your user interface elements as you create them.

Before you start using Interface Builder to create an application, though, we want to introduce two additional core concepts: IBOutlets and IBActions.

Figure 3.12   Contents of the MainWindow.nib file shown on the dock

IBOUTLET AND IBACTION

In order for Interface Builder–created objects to be useful, Xcode must be able to access their properties and respond to actions sent to them. This is done with `IBOutlet` and `IBAction`.

You saw an `IBOutlet` in listing 3.2, as part of the app delegate header file for your first project:

```
@property (nonatomic, retain) IBOutlet UIWindow *window;
```

An `IBOutlet` provides a link to an Interface Builder–created object. It's what you use to access that object's properties and methods. You won't see an `IBAction` until we get to chapter 6, where we'll deal with events and actions, but it's similar. You declare a method in your class, including `IBAction` as its return:

```
- (IBAction)pushButton:(id)sender;
```

An `IBAction` is a message that's executed when a specific action is applied to an Interface Builder–created object, such as when a slider moves or a button is clicked.

With the overview of Interface Builder out of the way, you're ready to create a simple application that will show a web view atop a background image.

3.4.2   *Building the AppleStock application*

Now let's build the AppleStock application. In this section, we'll look at how to create new objects, manipulate them graphically, and use the Inspector window. You can follow the step-by-step instructions to get familiar with the new tool. To give you a preview of the result, figure 3.13 shows what the AppleStock application will look like when it's finished.

CREATING A WINDOW-BASED APPLICATION

Go to Xcode 4, select File > New > New Project, and select Window-Based Application. When the prompt for the project name appears, enter `AppleStock` and your company or your own name as the project identifier. In the example, this book's name is used as the identifier, so the final project will be uniquely identified in the app store as com.iOS4inAction.AppleStock. Under Device Family, choose iPhone. The rest of the options are similar to when you created the HelloWorld application, as shown in figure 3.3.

Once the project is created under the workspace, under the project navigator on the left panel, go to the Resources folder and click the MainWindow.xib file to bring up the Interface Builder window under the Editor focus, as shown in figure 3.14.

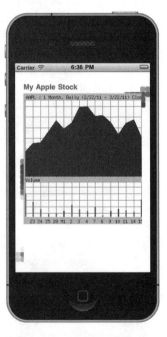

Figure 3.13   The AppleStock application in the iOS Simulator, running with a web view atop a background image

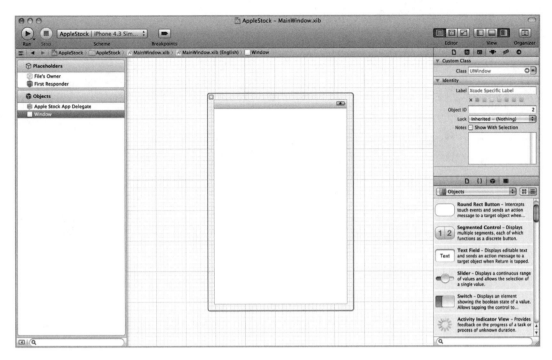

Figure 3.14   MainWindow.xib under Interface Builder

Make sure your utilities view is shown. You're now ready to create new objects on the blank Canvas in the center.

CREATING NEW OBJECTS IN INTERFACE BUILDER

Imagine a program that uses an image as a background, sets up a web view on top of that, and has a label running above everything. We'll show you how easy it is to create those entirely usable objects in Interface Builder.

You'll find the Image View object under Data Views in the Objects Library on the bottom of the utility view. Drag it over to your window in the center, and it quickly resizes to suggest a full-screen layout. You should be able to arrange it to fit exactly over the screen, and then release your mouse button to let it go. One object created!

The Web View object will be near the Image View. Drag it over to the main window. If you move it toward the center of the view, dashed lines appear: they're intended to help you center your object. If you mouse over the middle of the screen, a dashed line appears in each direction, forming a sort of crosshairs. When that happens, release the mouse button—you now have a web view in the middle of the screen. Two objects created!

Finally, select Label, which is under Inputs & Values. Drag it toward the top left of your screen, and let go. You're finished! You now have three objects laid out in Interface Builder, as shown in figure 3.15.

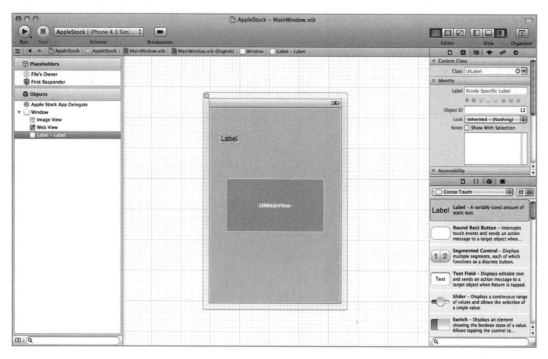

Figure 3.15   MainWindow.xib file in the center with an image view on the bottom and web view and label added in

Notice that when you mouse over and select the object in the library, a quick helper window pops up; it's helpful when you're not so familiar with all the objects at the beginning.

USING THE INSPECTOR WINDOW

Let's spend some time here to make the graphic interface look pretty. Interface Builder is an editor that focuses primarily on user interface design, so it makes sense that you can do some simple manipulation of your objects graphically. For example, if you want to change the text of your label, double-click it; then you're given the option to fill in your own text. To adjust the font color and the font size of the label, navigate to the Attributes tab under the Inspector pane on the top of the utility view, as show in figure 3.16.

Double-click the label, and type `My Apple Stock`. Don't forget to press Enter to finish the change. When you manipulated the label graphically, you changed the text to My Apple Stock for reasons that will become obvious shortly. You can see that this

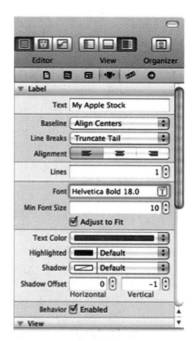

Figure 3.16   Using the inspector to update the label's text, font color, font size, and so on

change has already been made in the label's attributes. You can set a lot of other properties via this single window, with no programming required.

Do you want your text to be a nice blue? No problem: click the Text Color box. Doing so leads you to a window that offers several ways to set colors. Choose the tab that allows selection by name, and find blue on the list. You can also set shadows, alignments, font size, and a number of other text options from this panel.

In addition to the label options, the Attributes tab contains several options that relate to the view—they're the `UIView` properties that most graphical objects inherit. You can change alpha transparency, background color, and a number of other elements. For now, you can stop after having changed the color of the text and having generally seen what the Attributes tab can do.

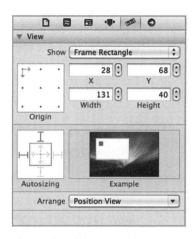

Figure 3.17 Size tab under the Inspector pane. You can change an object's position and size from the Size tab.

The Attributes tab is available to all Interface Builder objects, but it has different contents depending on the object in question. If you look at the attributes for the web view and image view objects you created, you'll see that you can set them in specific ways as well, but we'll save those for later. For now, we're concentrating on that label.

You can use the Size tab to adjust the size and position of an object. Figure 3.17 shows the options you can change here.

This tab leads off with values for size and position. Not only can you change an object's starting point, but you can also define where that starting point is, relative to the object, using the grid at the upper left. Width and height are available here too.

The Autosizing box controls how your object resizes its subviews when it resizes. For now, leave it as is; it'll be of more importance when we talk about basic view controllers in chapter 5.

Finally, the Arrange section lets you align your current object.

The Identity tab is of little use for this label, but we cover its functionality for the sake of completeness. Figure 3.18 shows what it looks like. For simple Interface Builder objects (like this example label), you use only the Interface Builder Identity section at the bottom of the Identity tab. This lets

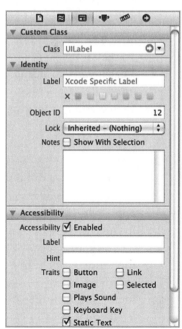

Figure 3.18 Identity tab under the Inspector window

you name your object, which makes it easier to see what you're accessing in Interface Builder. It's strictly for your own use.

The Connections tab shows an object's IBOutlets and IBActions, as shown in figure 3.19. The example label doesn't have an IBOutlet, which means it can't be accessed from Xcode yet. But this is fine; we're happy with how the label is set up in Interface Builder, and you won't need to adjust it during runtime for this example.

The Class Actions and Class Outlets sections show IBAction and IBOutlet declarations that you've made in your object's header file. For

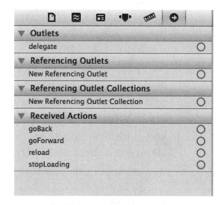

Figure 3.19 Connection tab showing a web view's IBOutlets and IBActions

example, the app delegate object has a window IBOutlet (which you've seen several times), and the web view object has a few system-defined actions, as shown in figure 3.19. These are the things to which you can build connections.

For now, leave them alone. They're not required for the label. But you have two more objects to work with in Interface Builder: the image view and the web view.

We promised you that we were going to introduce a totally new object in this section: the image view. As with web views, we'll get more into the guts of images several chapters down the line; for now, we want to show how easy it is to work with an unfamiliar object type—like the image view—in Interface Builder.

ADDING AN IMAGE

To use an image in an application, you need to add that image into your project first. That means you drag the image file into Xcode Navigator area, alongside all your other files. Generally, you should drag the images into the separate group from your source code. After dragging a file into Xcode, you'll see a confirmation prompt, as shown in figure 3.20. Make sure you select the Copy Items into Destination Group's Folder check box; this will ensure that all your resources are managed inside your project.

Once you've done that, you can go to your image view's Attributes tab in Interface Builder and select or type in the filename of your image file. In this case, it's apple.png. As soon as you enter this name, your picture should automatically pop up in Interface Builder's main window.

You then may wish to use the Attributes tab to change how the picture displays in the window (including automatically resizing it if you didn't build your image to be a specific size) or to adjust other elements. For example, we opted to change the image's alpha transparency to .5, to make it easier to see the text over the image.

If you want, you can now go ahead compile and run this program, which was built entirely in Interface Builder. You can see the results in figure 3.21.

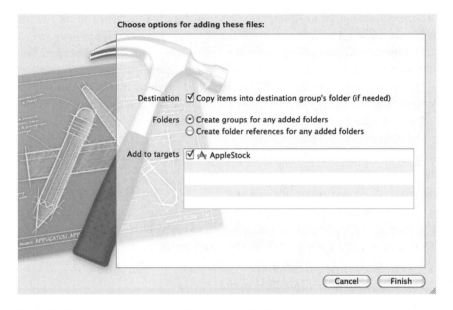

Figure 3.20 Prompt window for adding new files to the project

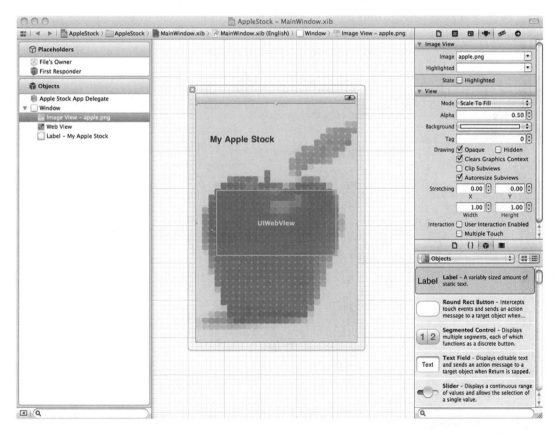

Figure 3.21 Combining graphics and text can be hard in some programming languages, but under the SDK it can be done entirely with Interface Builder. Here you see a background image with a text overlay.

The problem is that an unsightly web view box is sitting in the middle of the display. If you inspect the Attributes tab for the web view, you'll see why you didn't do anything more with it: you can't set the starting URL from inside Interface Builder.

You can do other things in Interface Builder. Specifically, you can easily resize the view. We chose to set it to 280 x 391 pixels, which various Interface Builder guidelines suggested was the right size; but you can size it by dragging the corners. We also opted to leave the Scales Page to Fit option off, which would make the web view act as if it had a viewport 980 pixels wide, like iPhone Safari. But to fill the web view window, you have to access it from the source code, which means adding a new IBOutlet to the app delegate.

CONNECTING THE DOTS IN INTERFACE BUILDER

Now it's time to code. Let's declare the web view as an `IBOutlet` in the app delegate, by connecting the outlets from app delegate to myWebView from Interface Builder.

Connecting takes a few steps with drag and drop:

1 With the MainWindow.nib file open, click the Assistant button. You see a side-by-side view under the Editor pane.

2 In the jump bar above the assistant view, select the header file in which you want to declare a new outlet. In this case, it's the AppleStockAppDelegate.h file.

3 Control-drag from a nib object to the location in the header file for the new outlet. In this case, Control-drag from the web view to the header file, and insert a new outlet (as shown in figure 3.22).

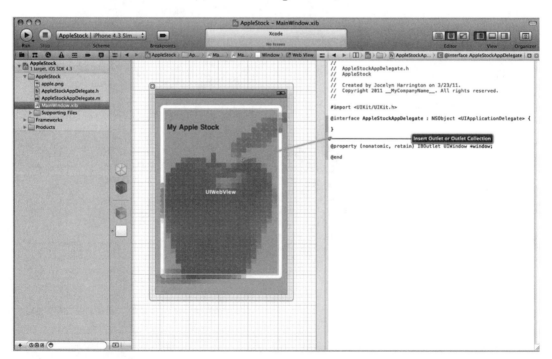

Figure 3.22   Control-drag from the web view to the app delegate header file to create a new outlet.

4 In the dialog (see figure 3.23), choose Outlet from the Connection menu, type the name of the new outlet, and click Connect. In this case, use webView as the new IBOutlet name.

Figure 3.23 Dialog box to create the Outlet connection from the nib object to the header file

That's all! Now you have the webView IBOutlet added to the header file automatically by Xcode, and it can be manipulated from within the Interface Builder editor. You can examine the app delegate's header file and source code. Notice that you have the new IBOutlet property properly declared and synthesized. Even the memory management is automatically taken care of.

ADDING CODE FOR IBOUTLET

Now it's time to add in the function to load the AppleStock's URL in the web view. Select the AppleStockAppDelegate.m file, and the implementation file will be in the Editor area (you can hide other views to focus on the source file editing). Add the code snippet from the following listing.

Listing 3.5 Create webView with automatic refresh content from Apple's stock quote

```
- (void)refreshQuote {
    NSString *url = [[NSString alloc] initWithString:@"http://quote-"
"web.aol.com/?syms=AAPL&e=NAS&action=hq&dur=1&type=mountain&hgl=1&vgl=1&vol="
"1&splits=1&div=0&w=723&h=964&gran=d"];
    [_webView loadRequest:[NSURLRequest requestWithURL:[NSURL
URLWithString:url]]];
    [url release];
}

- (BOOL)application:(UIApplication *)application
didFinishLaunchingWithOptions:(NSDictionary *)launchOptions
{
    [self refreshQuote];
    [NSTimer scheduledTimerWithTimeInterval:5 target:self
selector:@selector(refreshQuote) userInfo:nil repeats:YES];
    [self.window makeKeyAndVisible];
    return YES;
}
```

Note how you call the refreshQuote method. It's called using an NSTimer. This allows you to automatically call the refreshQuote method every so often—in this case, every 5 seconds.

Also note that you don't have to allocate the web view, nor do you have to initialize it, nor do you have to add it as a subview of your window; all those details are taken care of by Interface Builder. But after you link to the object via an outlet, you can access it like any object you created yourself.

We'll take a more complete look at how web views work in chapter 14. But we wanted to include them here to demonstrate (again) how easy it is to incorporate an unfamiliar object into your code using Interface Builder.

In addition, a web view provides a nice example of client-server integration between web design and the application—a topic that we first touched on in chapter 2 and that turns out to be pretty simple to attain using the iOS. By linking to a URL that sends dynamic content to your device, you can make a sophisticated, always-up-to-date program despite only designing the display engine on the iOS program side of things.

UPGRADING TO A UNIVERSAL APPLICATION

Follow appendix D to upgrade the current iPhone application to a universal application. Under the new MainWindow for iPad, adjust the image view's size to fit the full screen of iPad. That's it! Now click Build and Run. You'll have a nice stock chart show up in the web view and refresh every 5 seconds on the iOS Simulator.

Congrats! You just built your first application, AppleStock, in Xcode, with the major help of Interface Builder, as shown in figure 3.24.

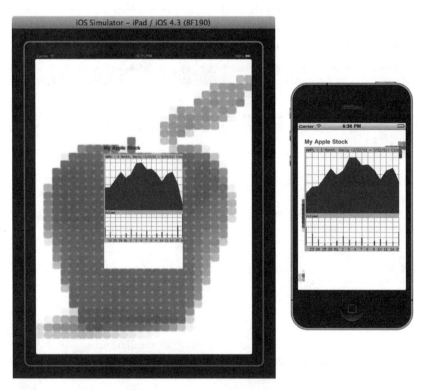

Figure 3.24   This shows what the final product looks like. An image, a label, and a dynamic web view are put together in Interface Builder with only a single line of code required. This demonstrates how simple it is to build a sophisticated interface with little work by using Interface Builder.

That brings us to the end of the AppleStock example. It presented some fundamental uses of Interface Builder that you'll encounter again and again. In particular, creating objects in Interface Builder and then adding an outlet to a header file will likely become a regular part of your iOS coding experience, so you should make sure you're entirely familiar with that process.

3.5 Summary

Xcode is ultimately the tool to build an iOS application. It's where you write the code that allows you to create, manipulate, and destroy objects. As you've seen in this chapter, it's easy to use Xcode to do some sophisticated things.

You can also create basic user interface objects visually using the Interface Builder tool under Xcode. It allows you to design objects using a graphical UI that makes their arrangement a lot easier.

In the next chapter, you'll use Xcode to create a new file and define a custom class. You'll also learn how to debug under Xcode.

Xcode and debugging

This chapter covers

- Creating a custom view in Xcode
- Learning how the debugger works

In the last chapter, you created your first HelloWorld application and an Apple-Stock application with Xcode. In this chapter, you'll build on this foundation of iOS application programming with a focus on how to create the custom view class in Xcode and how to use the Debugger to eliminate bugs during the project development lifecycle.

First, let's work on how to create a custom class together with Xcode. New programs are usually full of new classes. Here are three major reasons you may want to create new classes:

- You can create a totally new class, with different functionality from anything else. If it's a user interface class, it'll probably be a subclass of UIView. If it's not a view class, it'll probably be a subclass of NSObject.

- You can create a new class that works similarly to an old class but with some standardized differences. This new class will generally be a subclass of the old class.
- You can create a new class that has specific event responses built in. This class will also generally be a subclass of the old class.

4.1 Creating a new class in Xcode

Creating a new class with Xcode is easier than you think. In this example, you'll create a project called NewClass that will include a new class called `LabeledWebView`. It will be a subclass of `UIView`. When `LabeledWebView` is initialized, it'll display both a web page and the URL of that web page on the iPhone screen by linking together some existing classes that you used in the last chapter, such as `label` and `webview`. It will also display a toolbar at the top behind the label. In a way, it's similar to the Safari browser window on the iPhone.

Again, you'll build this project using the Window-Based Application template, and the device family is iPhone.

4.1.1 Creating a new class

When you have your new project going, the process of creating a new class (see table 4.1) is simple, with Xcode doing most of the work for you in creating the file.

In the NewClass application, choose File > New File to create a new Objective-C class (as shown in figure 4.1). Select Objective-C class, and then click Next.

Table 4.1 Three steps to create a new class in Xcode

Step	Description
1. Create your new file.	Choose File > New File. Choose the class to use as your parent from among the Cocoa Touch Classes options. Select a filename, preferably an intuitive name reflecting your object. When a subclass prompt window shows up, choose the subclass if there is one. Xcode should automatically create the header and source code files.
2. Modify your files.	If you weren't able to select your preferred class to subclass, change that now by modifying the parent class in the `@interface` line of the header file.
3. Import your object.	Add an `#import` line for your class's header in whatever file will be using it.

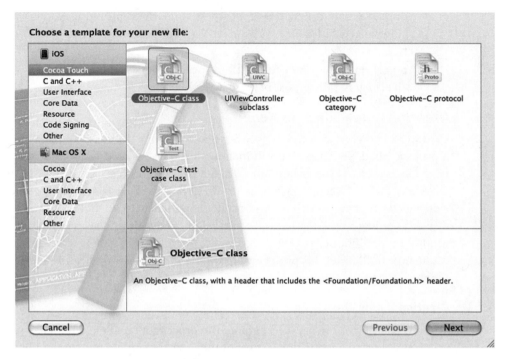

Figure 4.1   Create a new Objective-C class under iOS.

After clicking the Next button, you'll be presented with a screen to select what class the new class is inheriting from (see figure 4.2). Under the Subclass drop-down menu, choose `UIView` as the subclass option for the new class, and then click Next.

When the Save window appears, type in the name of the new class. In this example, use `LabeledWebView`.

Now import your new LabeledWebView.h file into your application delegate's .m (NewClassAppDelegate.m) file:

```
#import "LabeledWebView.h"
```

Click the Run button to make sure there are no errors in the code.

Afterward, it's a simple matter of designing your new `LabeledWebView` class with the desired functionality. As we mentioned earlier, you'll create an object that will display both a web page and the URL of that web page on the iPhone screen by linking together some existing classes.

The process has three steps, all of which we touch on in this section: you need to write your new header file, write your new source code file, and use the new class in your program.

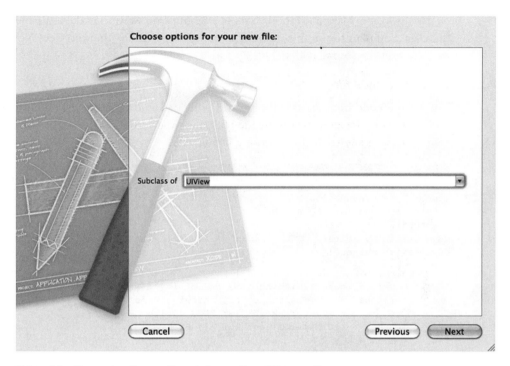

Figure 4.2 Choose `UIView` as the subclass option of the new file.

4.1.2 *The header file*

As usual, you have the start of a header file already, thanks to Xcode. The following listing shows how to expand it to create your new class.

Listing 4.1 Header file for the `LabeledWebView` class

```
#import <UIKit/UIKit.h>
@interface LabeledWebView : UIView {
    UILabel *myLabel;                                    ❶ Instance
    UIToolbar *myToolbar;                                  variables
    UIWebView *myWebView;
}
@property(nonatomic, retain) UILabel *myLabel;           ❷ Property
@property(nonatomic, retain) UIToolbar *myToolbar;         declarations
@property(nonatomic, retain) UIWebView *myWebView;
- (void)loadURL:(NSString *)url;                    ◁─── ❸ New method
@end
```

Within the header file, you make use of some common patterns that you saw back in the last chapter. First, you declare some instance variables ❶ that you want to use throughout your class. In this case, you have a label, a toolbar, and a web view. Then you define those instance variables as properties ❷.

Finally, you declare a method `loadURL:` ❸ that you want to make available outside the class. You plan to use this method to define the URL for the web view. Now you're ready to edit the source code.

4.1.3 The source code file

The source code file contains the guts of your new class. With all the new instances and properties declared in the header file, it's time to define the content inside the source code, as shown in the following listing.

Listing 4.2   Source code file for a new class

```
#import "labeledwebview.h"
@implementation labeledwebview
@synthesize myWebView;
@synthesize myToolbar;
@synthesize myLabel;

- (id)initWithFrame:(CGRect)frame {                             ❶ Create new
    if ((self = [super initWithFrame:frame])) {                    class's objects
        myToolbar = [[UIToolbar alloc] initWithFrame:
                    CGRectMake(0, 19, 320, 44)];
        myLabel = [[UILabel alloc] initWithFrame:
                    CGRectMake(10, 7, 300, 28)];
        myWebView = [[UIWebView alloc] initWithFrame:
                    CGRectMake(20,64,280,400)];
        myLabel.textColor = [UIColor whiteColor];
        myLabel.shadowColor = [UIColor blackColor];
        myLabel.adjustsFontSizeToFitWidth = YES;
        myWebView.scalesPageToFit = YES;
        [myToolbar addSubview: myLabel];
        [self addSubview:myToolbar];
        [self addSubview:myWebView];
    }
    return self;
}
- (void)setBackgroundColor:(UIColor *)color {                   ❷ Override setter
    [super setBackgroundColor:color];                             method
    [myLabel setBackgroundColor:color];
}
- (void)loadURL:(NSString *)url {                          ◁── ❸ Load URL
    [myWebView loadRequest:[NSURLRequest requestWithURL:
                        [NSURL URLWithString:url]]];
    myLabel.text = url;
}
- (void)dealloc {
    [myWebView release];
    [myToolbar release];
    [myLabel release];
    [super dealloc];
}
@end
```

Figure 4.3 shows the results of the class creation in use. Next, we'll explain the parts of the code that get you there before you put it all together in the app delegate.

Inside the source code, you first synthesize the three properties so the compiler will automatically create the setter and getter methods. You put together the pieces of your new class in the `initWithFrame:` method. As usual, you call the parent's init. Then, you create the three objects your new class will contain: a label, a toolbar, and a web view ❶. After setting some basic values for each, you make them subviews of your new `LabeledWebView` class. The code in ❷ will override the setter method for background color property. When it's called, you first pass the message to `super` and then set the label background color to match that of the parent view.

The real work occurs in the new `loadURL:` method ❸. You should be familiar with this method because you used a similar method to load the URL in the AppleStock application. (You can find more information on how `webView` loads URLs in chapter 14.) That's all you need to generate a fully functional web page, which is pretty amazing. If you play with it, you'll find that it has much of the iPhone's unique output functionality: you can pinch, tap, and zoom just like in Safari. You finish the method by setting the label to match your URL.

Figure 4.3   Brand-new class makes it easy to display a URL and call it up on the screen. You've finished the first step in building a web browser.

Your new class ends with the standard `dealloc:` method, where you clean up the objects that you allocated as part of your object creation.

In less than a page of code, you created an object that would require a lot more work if you were programming it by hand. So many tools are available to you in the iOS SDK that knocking out something like this is, as you can see, simplicity itself. You could definitely improve this example: you could link into the web view's delegate protocol to update the label whenever the web view changes. But for now, we're pleased with this example of Safari browser mockup.

4.1.4   Linking it in

Creating a new class isn't enough: you also need to use it. Add the bolded code in the following listing into the application delegate (NewClassAppDelegate.m) to use your new subclass.

Listing 4.3   Using the new class in the app delegate file

```
#import "NewClassAppDelegate.h"
#import "LabeledWebView.h"
@implementation NewClassAppDelegate
@synthesize window=_window;
- (BOOL)application:(UIApplication *)
  applicationdidFinishLaunchingWithOptions: (NSDictionary *)launchOptions
{
    LabeledWebView *myBook = [[LabeledWebView alloc]
    initWithFrame:[[UIScreen mainScreen] bounds]];
    [myBook loadURL:@"http://www.manning.com/jharrington/"];
    [myBook setBackgroundColor:[UIColor clearColor]];
    [_window addSubview:myBook];
    [myBook release];
    [self.window makeKeyAndVisible];
    return YES;
}
...
```

The code is pretty simple. First, initialize the subclass of UIView with the full screen size. Then load the URL of this book, *iOS 4 in Action*, and set the background color to transparent. The most important step is to add this new subview to the window.

That's all! Click the Run button on Xcode toolbar, and without errors during the build you should see the iOS Simulator launch with the screen shown in figure 4.3.

Now you know how to create a new Objective-C file under Xcode. In the next section, we'll cover the details of creating a new nib.

4.2   *Creating objects with Interface Builder*

In the last section, you built your first UIView subclass: the LabeledWebview class. You'll be building a lot more subclasses in your application development, and you'll often want to use Interface Builder to create a new nib file so you can connect outlets and actions to the object directly. Additionally, you don't need to crunch numbers for each subview's size because Interface Builder provides a visual design experience. How do you create a new nib file in Interface Builder? We'll cover the details in this section.

4.2.1 *Creating new nib files*

To create a new nib file under Xcode, navigate to the menu under Xcode, and choose File > New File to begin. Select User Interface under the template prompt window, as shown in figure 4.4.

You're then asked to choose a template: Application, Window, View, or Empty. You'll most often create new .xib files for view controllers, in which case you should select View. (You'll learn more about view controllers in chapter 5.) To make your new .xib file part of your existing project, save the .xib file to the main project directory.

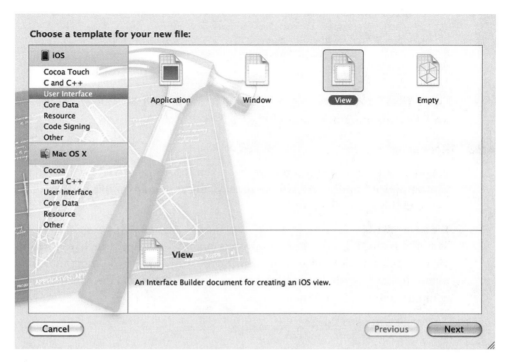

Figure 4.4   Create a new nib file under Xcode.

Table 4.2 outlines the two-step process. We say that you start the process with an "appropriate object." For a totally new object, this will probably be the blank object. But if you're making a subclass of an existing object, you should start with that object.

Table 4.2   Creating a new proxy object to link to in Interface Builder takes a couple of steps.

Step	Description
1. Create a new object.	From the Controllers section of the library, drag an appropriate object to the nib document window.
2. Change the class.	Open the Identity inspector tab, and change the class name to your new class.

After you type your new subclass name into your object's Class field (CustomWebView for example), things are automatically linked up. You'll use this technique in future chapters.

4.2.2   *Initializing Interface Builder objects*

Eventually, you'll want to do some initialization when an Interface Builder object is created. But if you try to build your setup into a standard init method, it won't work. As we've mentioned, Interface Builder objects use a special init method called `init-WithCoder:`. You must create it by hand, as follows:

```
- (id)initWithCoder:(NSCoder *)decoder {
    if (self = [super initWithCoder:decoder]) {
        // Setup code goes here
    }
    return self;
}
```

Other than its decoder argument (which you should be able to ignore), it should work like any other init method.

4.2.3 Accessing .xib files

Finally, we come to the .xib file. We've taken it for granted so far, but there are ways you can specify a different .xib file than MainWindow.xib and even ways to specify the use of multiple .xib files.

THE MAIN NIB FILE

The main .xib file is defined in <project name>-Info.plist, which you saw in the last chapter. You can look at its contents in Xcode, or you can read the XML from the command line or any text editor. It's easy to find where the main .xib file (or rather, its compiled nib twin) is defined:

```
<key>NSMainNibFile</key>
<string>MainWindow</string>
```

If you ever need to change the name of your main .xib file, do it here, using either Xcode or any text editor. Generally, we'll leave it the way it's generated by the project template.

MULTIPLE FILES

As we've mentioned, a .xib file should generally lay out the contents of a single program view. Although this has been fine for the programs so far, it becomes a limitation when you want to create more-complex programs. Fortunately, it's easy to build multiple .xib files into a single program.

New .xib files are usually loaded through view controllers, which is the topic of the next chapter. As we've discussed previously, view controllers tend to control a pageful of objects, and it makes sense that they use .xib files to help manage that. To use a new .xib file for a new page in your program, all you need to do is associate the new .xib file with the appropriate view controller.

The easiest way to do that is through Xcode's File menu. Select File > New File, and under Cocoa Touch Class select the `UIViewController` subclass. Make sure you select the With Xib for User Interface check box.

If you create a view controller, you can link in a new .xib file through its init method:

```
FlipsideViewController *viewController = [[FlipsideViewController alloc]
        initWithNibName:@"FlipsideViewController" bundle:nil];
```

If you feel a little fuzzy on the concept of view controllers, don't worry, because we're about to dive into this topic wholeheartedly in chapter 5. For now, note this connection between view controllers and the nib files.

4.2.4 *More tips under Xcode*

There's one more important window under Xcode we haven't covered yet: the Organizer window. You can launch the Organizer (see figure 4.5) by choosing Window > Organizer or by clicking the Organizer button on the Xcode toolbar.

As shown in figure 4.5, the Organizer window is used for organizing your projects and reading documentation. You can look up the Xcode 4 Developer documentation here as well.

For iOS projects, the Organizer window is also used for managing devices for development. You've learned how to run the application on the iOS Simulator, but this is the solution for launching the application on your iPhone or iPad.

Note that if you haven't created the certificate file under the iOS Provisioning Portal, you need to first head over to the iOS developer member center at http://developer.apple.com/membercenter/; then follow the step-by-step instructions

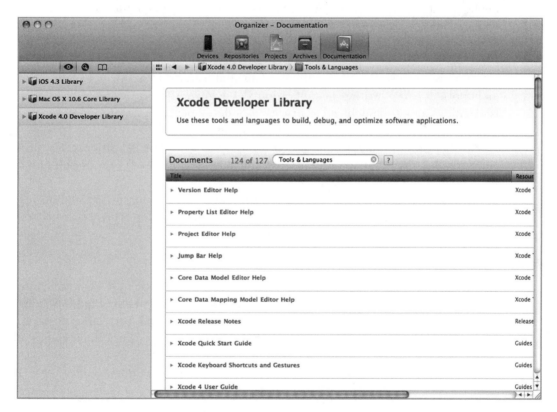

Figure 4.5   Organizer window with the Documentation tab selected

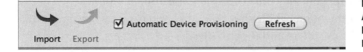

Figure 4.6 Select
Automatic Device
Provisioning under the Xcode
Devices Organizer window.

under the iOS Provisioning Portal to generate the certificate for both Developing and Distributing Provisioning profiles (needed for development/personal testing and ad hoc distribution/submitting to the App Store, respectively).

Now head back to the Xcode Organizer window, go to the Devices tab, select Provisioning Profiles, and then select the Automatic Device Provisioning option (you may need to click the Refresh button to allow the new provisioning file to be downloaded to your Mac, as shown in figure 4.6).

Xcode will use your login credentials to automatically generate the provisioning file under the iOS Provisioning Portal. Now you can plug in your device and select Use for Development to allow Xcode to automatically provision the device for development.

In the next section, we'll cover another important aspect of iOS development: debugging. You may not need all the debug functions under Xcode right now, but debugger knowledge will be handy when you inevitably encounter a bug in your application.

4.3   Debugger and Instruments

Now that we've covered some of the fundamental features in Xcode, let's talk about an important part of writing an application: debugging. Although you may have some reservations about the debugging process as a developer, it's critical to discover and remove bugs in the product development lifecycle.

Xcode provides a handy tool for debugging: Debugger. The iOS SDK package provides another important application: Instruments. These tools will provide you with a better debugging experience.

In this section, we'll cover the basics of Debugger in Xcode, such as monitoring the value of an object under the console window and setting up a breakpoint. Then we'll explore the functions under Instruments.

4.3.1   Fix-it function

While you're typing the demo application in Xcode, you'll notice the Fix-it function, as shown in figure 4.7. Under the hood, when your target is set to use the LLVM compiler, Fix-it scans your source code as you type. It's handy for correcting mistakes. When there's an error, you can see the red highlight, and if you click the icon in the gutter, you may discover the solution to your bug.

Another way to discover bugs early is by using static analysis under Xcode.

Figure 4.7   Fix-it solutions under Xcode

4.3.2   Analyze

Use static analysis to examine the semantics of your code to capture bugs early. Xcode lets you perform the analysis, examine the results, and edit your source files all from within the workspace window.

In Xcode, navigate to Product > Analyze (or click the Run button on the Xcode toolbar to activate the drop-down menu and then select Analyze). By static-analyzing code, you may discover a potential leak of an object or mismatching arguments, as shown in figure 4.8.

When you need to trace the variables inside the project, it's time to use the Debugger.

4.3.3   Debugger essentials

Under the Xcode menu, navigate to View > Show Debug Area (or click the debug view on the Xcode toolbar). When you select to show the debug area, Xcode will automati-

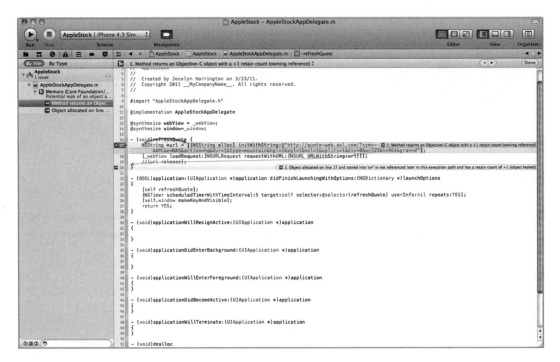

Figure 4.8   Static analysis under Xcode reports a potential leak for an object.

cally launch the Debugger toolbar on the top, the variable window at lower left, and the console window at lower right, as shown in figure 4.9.

The Xcode Debugger is a graphical interface for GDB, the underlying debugger used by Xcode. Now let's add a breakpoint to the code. You can add a breakpoint at any line in your code by single-clicking at the line number in the gutter. When that line of code is about to execute during runtime, Xcode will pause at the breakpoint so you can trace local variables, function output, and so on. Once a breakpoint is added, you'll see a blue breakpoint marker at the line number. When the Debugger is running with breakpoints on, you can trace the program's variables in the Debugger window, as shown in figure 4.10.

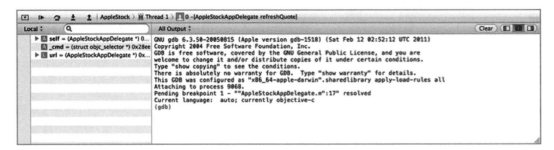

Figure 4.9   Debugger console window

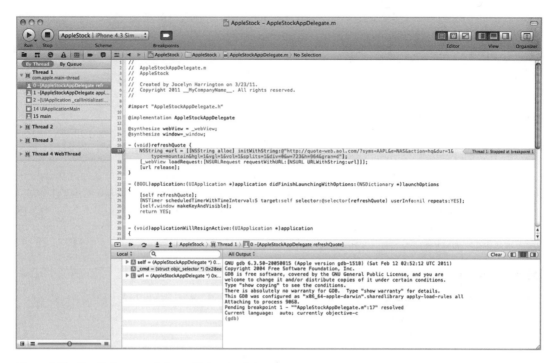

Figure 4.10 The Debugger window with breakpoints on pause

When the code is paused at the breakpoint, you can use the toolbar to step into the code line by line. If you select a thread or a stack within a thread in the debug bar, Xcode will display the corresponding source file or assembly code in the main editor. Notice that all of the variables will show up in the variable window on the bottom left.

Although you can read out the memory address for every variable, it would be nice to read out the content from the NSString on the fly. You can print out the object by typing po under the GDB console window. For example, try printing out the web view's description at the breakpoint, as shown in figure 4.11.

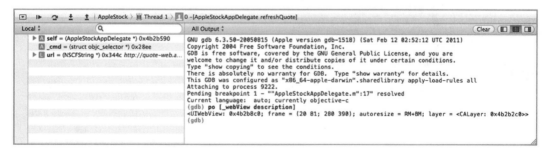

Figure 4.11 How to print out an object's details in the Debugger console window

You can also manage all the breakpoints under the Breakpoints Navigator, as shown in figure 4.12.

In the next section, we'll cover some basics under Instruments.

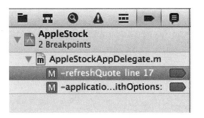

**Figure 4.12
Breakpoints Navigator window**

4.3.4   *Running Instruments from Xcode*

In the previous section, you learned how to use the Debugger under Xcode; but certain memory-allocation bugs are hard to discover with the Debugger, and that's when Instruments is useful. Under Xcode, navigate to Product > Profile (or click the Run button to bring up the drop-down menu, and then select Profile). Selecting Profile will launch Instruments with the application running on the iOS Simulator, as shown in figure 4.13.

Figure 4.13   Launching instruments from Xcode

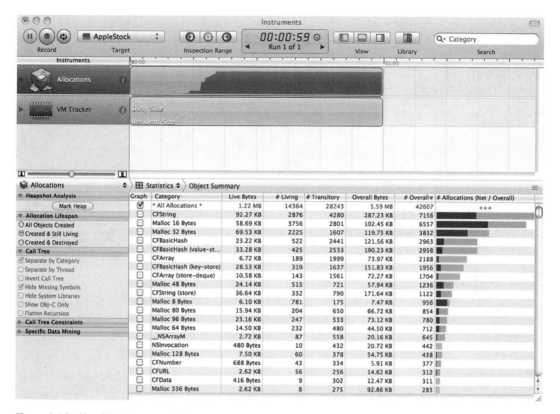

Figure 4.14   Use Allocations under Instruments to analyze the memory allocations during application runtime.

Select Allocations under the iOS Simulator. With this runtime memory-analysis tool, you can monitor and improve memory allocations (see figure 4.14).

Leaks is another trace tool under Instruments, which comes in handy for memory-related bugs. Select Leaks when Instruments launches under the template prompt window. Leaks runs with a sample of every 10 seconds by default; you can manually check for leaks by clicking the Check for Leaks Now button on the bottom-left control panel (see figure 4.15).

Once you find a leaked object, double-click that object. Instruments will show you the function name related to the memory leak.

In this section, we covered some essential debugging tools for your application development. Try to play with each tool in order to discover your preferred debugging procedure.

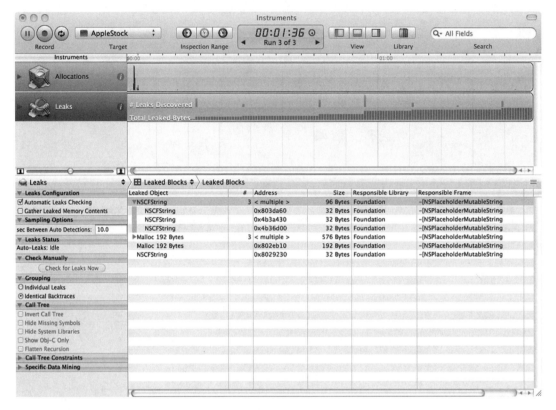

Figure 4.15   Instruments with Leaks to trace leaked blocks

4.4   Summary

In the previous chapter, we showed you how to create some simple programs using Xcode. You also have access to Interface Builder, a powerful graphic design program that allows you to lay out objects by dragging and dropping and then linking those objects back to Xcode for use there.

The example you created in this chapter, which focused on creating a new class in Xcode, provided a demo of how to mock up the iPhone Safari browser with a subclass of UIView. You may not use the Debugger for your application right away, but it will come in handy when the time comes for debugging.

Although you now have the fundamental development tools of the iOS SDK well in hand, we've neglected two of the SDK building blocks you'll use to create projects: view controllers and events. In the next three chapters, we'll cover those topics, and in the process, we'll complete our look at the iOS classes you'll use in almost any iOS program you write.

Basic view controllers

This chapter covers

- Understanding the importance of controllers
- Programming bare view controllers
- Utilizing table view controllers

So far in the last two chapters we haven't strayed far from the most fundamental building block of the SDK: the view, whether a UILabel, a UIWebView, or a UIImage-View. Ultimately, the view is only part of the story. As we mentioned when we looked at iOS, views are usually connected to view controllers, which manage events and otherwise take the controller role in the MVC model. We're now ready to begin a three-part exploration of what that all means.

In this chapter, we look at basic view controllers that manage a single page of text. With that basis, we can examine events and actions in chapter 6, correctly integrating them into the MVC model. Finally, in chapter 7, we'll return to the topic of view controllers to look at advanced classes that can be used to connect several pages of text.

Over the course of our two view controller chapters (5 and 7), we'll offer code samples that are a bit more skeletal than usual. That's because we want to provide you with the fundamental, reusable code that you'll need to use the controllers on your own. Consider chapters 5 and 7 more of a reference—although a critical one. You'll make real-world use of the controllers in the rest of this book, including when we look at events and actions in chapter 6. Right now, though, let's examine the available view controllers.

5.1   *The view controller family*

When we first talked about view controllers in chapter 2, we mentioned that they come in several flavors. These run from the bare-bones UIViewController, which is primarily useful for managing autorotation and for taking the appropriate role in the MVC model, to the more organized UITableViewController, on to a few different controllers that allow navigation across multiple pages.

All of these view controllers—and their related views—are listed in table 5.1.

Table 5.1   There are a variety of view controllers, giving you considerable control over how navigation occurs in your program.

Object	Type	Summary
UIViewController	View controller	A default controller, which controls a view. Also the basis for the flipside controller, which appears only as an Xcode template, not as a UIKit object.
UIView	View	Either your full screen or some part thereof. This is what a view controller controls, typically through some child of UIView, not this object itself.
UITableViewController	View controller	A controller that uses UITableView to organize data listings.
UITableView	View	A view that works with the UITableViewController to create a table UI. It contains UITableCells.
UITabBarController	View controller	A controller that works with a UITabBar to control multiple UIViewControllers.
UITabBar	View	A view that works with the UITabBarController to create the tab bar UI. It contains UITabBarItems.
UINavigationController	View controller	A controller used with a UINavigationBar to control multiple UIViewControllers.
UINavigationBar	View	A view that works with UINavigationController to create the navigation UI.

Table 5.1 There are a variety of view controllers, giving you considerable control over how navigation occurs in your program. *(continued)*

Object	Type	Summary
Flipside controller	View controller	A special template that supports a two-sided `UIViewController`.

`ABPeoplePickerNavigationController`
`ABNewPersonViewController`
`ABPersonViewController`
`ABUnknownPersonViewController`
`UIImagePickerController`
	View controller	Modal view controllers that allow interaction with sophisticated user interfaces for the Address Book and the photos roll.

As we've already noted, we'll be discussing these view controllers in two different chapters. Here, we'll look at the single-page view controllers: `UIViewController` and `UITableViewController`. In chapter 7, we'll examine the multipage view controllers: `UITabBarController`, `UINavigationController`, and the flipside controller. This is a clear functional split: the single-page controllers exist primarily to support the controller role of the MVC model, whereas the multipage controllers exist primarily to support navigation and may even delegate MVC work to a simpler view controller lying below them. (As for the modal controllers, we'll get to them when we cover the appropriate topics in chapters 8 and 11.)

So far, you've been programming without using view controllers, which are an important part of SDK programming. You *could* write an SDK program without them, but every SDK program *should* include them, even if you use a bare-bones view controller to manage the rotation of the screen.

5.2 The standard view controller

The plain view controller is simple to embed inside your program. But why would you want to use a view controller? That's going to be one of the topics we'll cover here. Now, we'll look at how view controllers fit into the view hierarchy, how you create them, how you expand them, and how you make active use of them. Let's get started with the most basic anatomical look at the view controller.

5.2.1 The anatomy of a view controller

A view controller is a `UIViewController` object that sits immediately above a view (of any sort). It, in turn, sits below some other object as part of the tree that ultimately goes back to an application's main window. This is shown in figure 5.1.

When we move on to advanced view controllers in chapter 7, you'll see that the use of a bare view controller can grow more complex. Bare view controllers often sit beneath advanced view controllers, to take care of the individual pages that advanced view controllers let you navigate among.

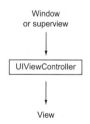

Figure 5.1 A bare view controller shows view controlling at its simplest: it sits below one object and above another.

Looking at the iOS's class hierarchy, you can see that the `UIViewController` is a direct descendent of `UIResponder`, which is a descendent of `NSObject`. It's also the parent object of all the other view controllers we'll discuss. Practically, this means that the lessons learned here also apply to all the other controllers.

But learning about how a view controller works leaves out one vital component: how do you create it?

5.2.2   *Creating a view controller*

The easiest way to incorporate a plain view controller into your project is to select a different template when you create it. The View-Based Application template should probably be your default template for programming from here on out, because it comes with a view controller built in.

As usual, the template's work is primarily done visually. When you create a new project (which we've called viewex for the purpose of this example), you can verify this by looking up the view controller's `IBOutlet` command in the program's app delegate header file:

```
ViewexViewController *viewController;
```

The app delegate's source code file further shows that the view controller's view has already been hooked up to the main window:

```
[window addSubview:viewController.view];
```

This view is a standard `UIView` that's created as part of the template. Although a view controller has only one view, that view may have a variety of subviews, spreading out into a hierarchy. We'll show you how to add a single object beneath the view in a moment, and you'll make more complete use of it in the next chapter. But before we get there, we want to step back and look at how you can create a view controller by hand if you need to.

5.2.3   *Creating another view controller*

Creating another view controller is simple. First, drag a view controller from the Library to your xib document window. Alternatively, you can `alloc` and `init` an object from the `UIViewController` class.

Second, note that the previous `IBOutlet` command shows that the controller isn't instantiated directly from the `UIViewController` class. Rather, it's instantiated from its own subclass, which has its own set of files (viewexViewController.{h|m}), named after the example project's name. This is standard operating procedure.

Because you want a view controller to do event management, you'll often need to modify some of the controller's standard event methods, so you require your own subclass. To start, the view controller class files are mostly blank, but Xcode helpfully highlights a number of standard view controller methods that you may want to modify.

After you've finished creating a bare view controller, you're mostly ready to go. But you have a slight opportunity to modify the view controller for your specific program, and that's what we'll cover next.

5.2.4 *Building up a view controller interface*

In order to correctly use a view controller, you need to build your view objects as subviews of the view controller, rather than subviews of your main window or whatever else lies above it. This is easy to do both programmatically and visually.

THE PROGRAMMATIC SOLUTION

The view controller class file gives you access to a pair of methods that can be used to set up your view controller's views. If the view controller's view is linked to a .xib file, you should use `viewDidLoad`, which will do additional work after the .xib is done loading; if you didn't first create it visually, you should instead use `loadView`.

Before you do any of this, your view controller will always start off with a standard `UIView` as its one subview. But by using these methods, you can instead create the view controller's view as you see fit, even creating a whole hierarchy of subviews if you desire.

The following code adds a simple `UILabel` to your view controller using `viewDidLoad`. In the following listing, we've chosen a humongous font that is automatically sized down so that later we can show off how rotation and resizing work:

Listing 5.1 Add a UILabel to your view controller

```
- (void)viewDidLoad {
    [super viewDidLoad];
    UILabel *myLabel = [[UILabel alloc]
        initWithFrame:[[UIScreen mainScreen] bounds]];
    myLabel.adjustsFontSizeToFitWidth = YES;
    myLabel.font = [UIFont fontWithName:@"Arial" size:60];
    myLabel.textAlignment = UITextAlignmentCenter;
    myLabel.text = @"View Controllers!";
    myLabel.backgroundColor = [UIColor grayColor];      ❶ Connects label
    [self.view addSubview:myLabel];                          as subview
    [myLabel release];
}
```

The `self.view` line is the only one of particular note ❶. It connects your label object as a subview of the view controller's `UIView`.

This example is also noteworthy because it's the first time you've definitively moved outside of your app delegate for object creation. You could have done this object creation in the app delegate, but that's often sloppy programming because this needs to be done in the view controller. Now that you have view controllers, you'll increasingly do your work in those class files. This not only better abstracts your object creation but also kicks off your support of the MVC model, because you now have controllers instantiating the views they manage. Watch for a lot more of this in the future. We'll also briefly return to the `viewDidLoad` and `loadView` methods when we talk about the bigger picture of the view controller lifecycle, shortly.

THE VISUAL SOLUTION

In the last chapter, we noted that view controllers often have their own .xib files, allowing you to have one .xib file for each page of content. That's what's going on in the program you created from the View-Based Application template. At creation, the template contains two .xib files: MainWindow.xib and viewexViewController.xib.

The MainWindow.xib file contains a view controller and a window. The all-important link to the second .xib file can be found here. If you click the view controller's Attribute tab, it helpfully shows you that the controller's content is drawn from viewexViewController(.xib). This is shown in figure 5.2.

Figure 5.2   To hook up a new .xib file to a view controller, enter its name in the view controller's attributes under NIB Name.

Now that you understand the hierarchy of .xib files that's been set up, how do you make use of them? In order to create an object as a subview of the view controller, you need to place it inside the .xib file that the view controller manages—in this case, viewexViewController.xib. To add a UILabel to your view controller, you call up the viewexViewController.xib file and then drag a label to the main display window, which should represent the existing view. Afterward, you can muck with the label's specifics in the inspector window, as usual.

Practically, there's nothing more you need to do to set up your basic view controller, but we still need to consider a few runtime fundamentals.

5.2.5   *Using your view controller*

If you've chosen to use a standard view controller, it should be because you're only managing one page of content, not a hierarchy of pages. In this situation, you don't need your view controller to do a lot, but your view controller is still important for three things, all related to event management:

- It should act as the hub for controlling its view and subviews, following the MVC model. To do this, it needs easy access to object names from its hierarchy.
- It should control the rotation of its view, which will also require resizing the view in rational ways. Similarly, it should report back on the device's orientation if queried.
- It should deal with lifecycle events related to its view.

We've split these main requirements into six topics, which we'll cover in turn.

PUTTING THE MVC MODEL TO USE

Although we've talked about the Model-View-Controller (MVC) architectural pattern, you haven't yet put it to real use. Up to this point, it's been a sort of abstract methodology for writing programs. But now that you're ready to use view controllers, you can start using MVC as a real-world ideal for programming.

As you'll recall, under MVC, the *model* is your backend data and the *view* is your frontend user interface. The *controller* sits in between, accepting user input and modifying both of the other entities. The view controller should take the role of the controller in the MVC, as the name suggests. We'll get into this more in the next chapter, but we can say confidently that event and action control *will* happen through the view controller.

We can say this confidently because you'll pretty much be forced into using MVC. A view controller is automatically set up to access and modify various elements of views that sit under it. For example, the view controller has a `title` property that is intended to be a human-readable name for the page it runs. In chapter 7, you'll learn that tab bars and navigation bars automatically pick up that information for their own use. In addition, you'll often see view controllers automatically linked up to `delegate` and `datasource` properties, so that they can respond to the appropriate protocols for their subviews.

When you start seeing view controllers telling other objects what to do, look at it through the MVC lens. You should also think about MVC as you begin to program more complex projects using view controllers.

FINDING RELATED ITEMS

If a view controller is going to act as a controller, it needs easy access to the objects that lie both above and below it in the view hierarchy. For this purpose, the view controller contains a number of properties that can be used to find other items that are connected to it. They're listed in table 5.2.

These properties will be useful primarily when we move on to advanced view controllers, because they're more likely to link multiple view controllers together. We're mentioning them here because they're related to the idea of MVC and because they're `UIViewController` properties that will be inherited by all other types of controllers.

For now, we'll leave these MVC-related properties and get into some of the more practical things you can immediately do with a view controller, starting with managing view rotation.

Table 5.2 When you begin connecting a view controller to other things, you can use its properties to quickly access references to those other objects.

Property	Summary
`modalViewController`	Reference to a temporary view controller, such as the Address Book and photo roll controllers that we'll discuss in chapter 8 and 11.
`navigationController`	Reference to a parent of the navigation controller type.
`parentViewController`	Reference to the immediate parent view controller, or nil if there is no view controller nesting.
`tabBarController`	Reference to a parent of the tab bar controller type.
`tabBarItem`	Reference to a tab bar item related to this particular view.
`view`	Reference to the controller's managed view. The view's `subviews` property may be used to dig further down in the hierarchy.

ROTATING VIEWS

Telling your views to rotate is simple. In your view controller class file, you'll find a method called shouldAutorotateToInterfaceOrientation:. In order to make your application correctly rotate, all you need to do is set that function to return the Boolean YES, as shown here:

```
- (BOOL)shouldAutorotateToInterfaceOrientation:
       (UIInterfaceOrientation)interfaceOrientation {
    return YES;
}
```

At this point, if you compile your program, you'll find that when you rotate your iPhone or iPad, the label shifts accordingly. Even better, because you set its font size to vary based on the amount of space it has, it gets larger when placed horizontally. This is a simple application of modifying your content based on the device's orientation.

You should consider one additional thing when rotating your views: whether they will resize to account for the different dimensions of the new screen.

RESIZING VIEWS

When you change your device's orientation from portrait to landscape, you change the amount of space for displaying content—for example, an iPhone goes from 320 x 480 to 480 x 320. As you just saw, when you rotated your label, it automatically resized, but this doesn't happen without some work.

A UIView (not the controller!) contains two properties that affect how resizing occurs. The autoresizesSubviews property is a Boolean that determines whether autoresizing occurs. By default, it's set to YES, which is why things worked correctly in the first view controller example. If you instead set it to NO, your view will stay the same size when a rotation occurs. In this case, your label will stay 320 pixels wide despite now being on a 480-pixel wide screen.

After you've set autoresizesSubviews, which says that resizing *will* occur, your view looks at its autoresizingMask property to decide *how* it should work. The autoresizingMask property is a bitmask that you can set with the different constants listed in table 5.3.

Table 5.3   autoresizingMask properties allow you to control how your views resize.

Constant	Summary
UIViewAutoresizingNone	No resizing
UIViewAutoresizingFlexibleHeight	Height resizing allowed
UIViewAutoresizingFlexibleWidth	Width resizing allowed
UIViewAutoresizingFlexibleLeftMargin	Width resizing allowed to left
UIViewAutoresizingFlexibleRightMargin	Width resizing allowed to right
UIViewAutoresizingFlexibleBottomMargin	Height resizing allowed to bottom
UIViewAutoresizingFlexibleTopMargin	Height resizing allowed to top

If you want to modify how your label resizes programmatically, you can do so by adding the following lines to viewDidLoad:

```
myLabel.autoresizesSubviews = YES;
myLabel.autoresizingMask = UIViewAutoresizingFlexibleHeight |
    UIViewAutoresizingFlexibleWidth;
```

Note again that these resizing properties apply to a *view*, not to the view controller. You can apply them to any view you've seen so far. There has been little need for them before you started rotating things.

Modifying the way resizing works is even easier if you do it visually. If you recall, the Resize tab of the inspector window contains an Autosizing section, as shown in figure 5.3.

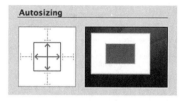

Figure 5.3 Here you can see exactly what autoresizing looks like.

You can click six different arrows that correspond to the six resizing constants other than None. Highlighting an individual arrow turns on that type of resizing. The graphic to the right of these arrows serves as a nice guide to how resizing will work.

CHECKING ORIENTATION

Now that you have an application that can rotate at will, you may occasionally want to know what orientation a user's iPhone or iPad is sitting in. You do this by querying the interfaceOrientation view controller property. It's set to one of four constants, as shown in table 5.4.

You don't have to have a view controller to look up this information. A view controller's data is kept in tune with orientation values found in the UIDevice object—a useful object that also contains other device information, such as your system version. We'll talk about it in chapter 10.

Table 5.4 The view controller's interfaceOrientation property tells you the current orientation of an iPhone or iPad.

Constant	Summary
UIInterfaceOrientationPortrait	Device is vertical, right side up.
UIInterfaceOrientationPortraitUpsideDown	Device is vertical, upside down.
UIInterfaceOrientationLandscapeLeft	Device is horizontal, tilted left.
UIInterfaceOrientationLandscapeRight	Device is horizontal, tilted right.

MONITORING THE LIFECYCLE

We've covered the major topics of loading, rotating, and resizing views within a view controller. With that under your belt, we can now look at the lifecycle events that may relate to these topics.

You saw lifecycle events in chapter 2, where we examined methods that alert you to the creation and destruction of the application, and some individual views. Given that

Table 5.5   You can use the view controller's event-handler methods to monitor and manipulate the creation and destruction of its views.

Method	Summary
loadView:	Creates the view controller's view if it isn't loaded from a .xib file.
viewDidLoad:	Alerts you that a view has finished loading. This is the place to put extra startup code if loading from a .xib file.
viewWillAppear:	Runs just before the view loads.
viewWillDisappear:	Runs just before a view disappears — because it's dismissed *or* covered.
willRotateToInterfaceOrientation:duration:	Runs when rotation begins.
didRotateToInterfaceOrientation:	Runs when rotation ends.

one of the purposes of a controller is to manage events, it shouldn't be a surprise that the UIViewController has several lifecycle methods of its own, as shown in table 5.5.

You've met loadView and viewDidLoad, which are run as part of the view controller's setup routine and which you used to add extra subviews. The viewWillAppear: message is sent afterward. The rest of the messages are sent at the appropriate times, as views disappear and rotation occurs.

Any of these methods can be overwritten to provide the specific functionality that you want when each message is sent.

OTHER VIEW METHODS AND PROPERTIES

The view controller object contains a number of additional methods that can be used to control exactly how rotation works, including controlling its animation and what header and footer bars slide in and out. These are beyond the scope of our introduction to view controllers but you can find information about them in the UIView-Controller class reference.

That's our look at the bare view controller. You now know not only how to create your first view controller but also how to use the fundamental methods and properties that you'll find in *every* view controller. But the other types of view controller also have special possibilities all their own. We'll look at these, starting with the one other view controller that's intended to control a single page of data: the table view controller.

5.3   *The table view controller*

Like the plain view controller, the table view controller manages a single page. Unlike the plain view controller, it does so in a structured manner. It automatically organizes the data in a nicely formatted table.

Our discussion of the table view controller will be similar to the discussion we just completed of the bare view controller. We'll examine its place in the view hierarchy, and then you'll learn how to create it, modify it, and use it at runtime.

Let's get started by examining the new view controller's anatomy.

5.3.1 The anatomy of a table view controller

The table view controller's setup is slightly more complex than that of the bare view controller. A `UITableViewController` controls a `UITableView`, which is an object that contains some number of `UITableViewCell` objects arranged in a single column. This is shown in figure 5.4.

By default, the controller is both the delegate and the data source of the `UITableView`. As we've previously discussed, these properties help a view hand off events and actions to its controller. The responsibilities for each of these control types are defined by a specific

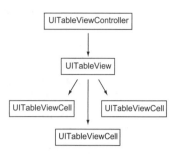

Figure 5.4 A table view controller controls a table view and its collection of cells.

protocol: `UITableViewDelegate` declares which messages the table view controller must respond to, and `UITableViewDataSource` details how it must provide the table view with content. You can look up these protocols in the same library that you've been using for class references.

Of all the view controllers, the table view controller is the trickiest to create on its own, for reasons that you'll see momentarily.

5.3.2 Creating a table view controller

The easiest way to create an application that uses a table view controller is to use the Navigation-Based template in Xcode. This provides you with a delegate and a view that contains a table view controller. It also creates some of the delegate methods required for interfacing with the table view.

Although you can quickly start an application using the Navigation-Based template, we'll discuss in detail how you can manually build a table view controller project. This will give you a better understanding of what's going on when you use the template. Table 5.6 shows the process.

Table 5.6 Creating a table view controller is simple, but it involves several steps.

Step	Description
1. Create a new project.	Open a Window-Based Application, and select iPhone from the Product drop-down menu.
2. Create a table view controller.	Create a new file containing a subclass of `UIViewController`. Then, select `UITableViewController` from the options. By default, the .xib for the view controller will be automatically created and linked. If not, you can perform step 3 manually.
3. Link your Interface Builder object.	Create an `IBOutlet` for your interface in the app delegate header file. Link an outlet from your table view controller to the `IBOutlet` in the app delegate object, using the Connections tab of the inspector window.
4. Connect your controller.	Link the controller's view to your main window.

The project-creation, object-creation, and object-linking steps pretty much follow the lessons you've already learned. You have to create the subclass for the table view controller because the class file is where you define what the table view contains; we'll cover this in more depth shortly.

Note that you use two of the more advanced visual techniques that you learned in chapter 4: first linking in a new class (by changing the Identity tab) and then creating a new connection from it to your app delegate (via the Connections tab). As a result, you end up with two connections. On the one hand, the table view controller depends on your `RootViewController` files for its own methods; on the other hand, your app delegate file links to the controller (and eventually to the methods) via its outlet. This two-part connection is common, and you should make sure you understand it before moving on.

As usual, you could elect to create this object programmatically, by using an `alloc-init` command:

```
UITableViewController *myTable = [[RootViewController alloc]
    initWithStyle:UITableViewStylePlain];
```

The following simple code finishes the table-creation process by linking in the table's view in step 4 of the process:

```
- (BOOL)application:(UIApplication *)application
    didFinishLaunchingWithOptions:(NSDictionary *)launchOptions{
    [window addSubview:myTable.view];
    [window makeKeyAndVisible];
}
```

Note that you link up your table view controller's view—not the controller itself—to your window. You've seen in the past that view controllers come with automatically created views. Here, the view is a table view.

If you want to see how that table view works, you can now click the table view to get its details. As shown in figure 5.5, it already has connections created for its `dataSource` and `delegate` properties.

Next, you need to fill the table with content.

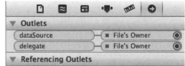

Figure 5.5   A look at the connections automatically created for a controller's table view

5.3.3   *Building up a table interface*

As the data source, the controller needs to provide the view with its content. This is why you created a subclass for your table view controller and why every one of your table view controllers should have its own subclass: each will need to fill in its data in a different way.

We've mentioned that the `UITableViewDataSource` protocol declares the methods your table view controller should pay attention to in order to correctly act as the data source. The main work of filling in a table is done by the `tableView:cellForRowAt-IndexPath:` method. When passed a row number, this method should return the `UITableViewCell` for that row of your table.

Before you can get to that method, though, you need to do some work. First, you must define the content that will fill your table. Then, you must define how large the table will be. Only then can you fill in the table using the `tableView:cellForRowAt-IndexPath:` method.

In addition to these major table view elements, we'll also cover two optional variants that can change how a table looks: accessory views and sections.

CREATING THE CONTENT

You can use numerous SDK objects to create a list of data that your table should contain. In chapter 9, we'll talk about SQLite databases; and in chapter 14, we'll discuss pulling RSS data off the Internet. For now, we stay with the SDK's simpler objects. The most obvious are `NSArray`, which produces a static indexed array; `NSMutableArray`, which creates a dynamic indexed array; and `NSDictionary`, which defines an associative array.

For this example of table view content creation, you'll create an `NSArray` containing an `NSDictionary` that itself contains color names and `UIColor` values. As you can probably guess, you'll fill this skeletal table view example with something like the color selector that you wrote back when you were learning about views in chapter 4. The code required to create your content array is shown in the following listing.

Listing 5.2 Create the content array

```
- (void)viewDidLoad {
colorList = [NSArray arrayWithObjects:
        [NSDictionary dictionaryWithObjectsAndKeys:
            @"brownColor",@"titleValue",
            [UIColor brownColor],@"colorValue",nil],
        [NSDictionary dictionaryWithObjectsAndKeys:
            @"orangeColor",@"titleValue",
            [UIColor orangeColor],@"colorValue",nil],
        [NSDictionary dictionaryWithObjectsAndKeys:
            @"purpleColor",@"titleValue",
            [UIColor purpleColor],@"colorValue",nil],
        [NSDictionary dictionaryWithObjectsAndKeys:
            @"redColor",@"titleValue",
         [UIColor redColor],@"colorValue",nil],
        nil];
    [colorList retain];
}
```

You should do this sort of setup before the view appears. Here, you do it in the `view-DidLoad` method. This method is called prior to the view appearing and is a good place to do your initialization.

The array and dictionary creations are simple. The `Apple` class references contain complete information about how to create and manipulate these objects; but, in short, you can create an `NSArray` as a listing of objects ending in a nil, and you can create an `NSDictionary` using pairs of values and keys, ending in a nil. Here, you're creating an array containing four dictionaries, each of which will fill one line of your table.

You also have to think about memory management here. Because your array was created with a class factory method, it'll be released when it goes out of scope. In order to use this array elsewhere in your class, you not only need to have defined it in your header file, but you also need to send it a retain message to keep it around. You'll release it in your dealloc method, elsewhere in the class files.

BUILDING YOUR TABLE CELLS

When you've set up a data backend for your table, you need to edit three methods in your table view controller file: two that define the table and one that fills it, as shown in the following listing. We'll explain each of these in turn.

Listing 5.3 Three methods that control how your table is created and runs

```
- (NSInteger)numberOfSectionsInTableView:(UITableView *)tableView {
    return 1;
}

- (NSInteger)tableView:(UITableView *)tableView
        numberOfRowsInSection:(NSInteger)section {
    return colorList.count;
}

- (UITableViewCell *)tableView:(UITableView *)tableView
        cellForRowAtIndexPath:(NSIndexPath *)indexPath {
static NSString *CellIdentifier = @"Cell";

    UITableViewCell *cell = [tableView
dequeueReusableCellWithIdentifier:CellIdentifier];
    if (cell == nil) {
        cell = [[[UITableViewCell alloc]
initWithStyle:UITableViewCellStyleDefault reuseIdentifier:CellIdentifier]
autorelease];
    }

    cell.textLabel.textColor= [[colorList objectAtIndex:indexPath.row]     ◁──┐
        objectForKey:@"colorValue"];
    cell.textLabel.text = [[colorList objectAtIndex:indexPath.row]           ❶
objectForKey:@"titleValue"];                                              ◁──┘

    return cell;                                             **Sets cell's text**
}                                                            **and text color**
```

All these methods should appear by default in the table view controller subclass you create, but you may need to make changes to some of them to accommodate the specifics of your table.

The first method is numberOfSectionsInTableView:. Tables can optionally include multiple sections, each of which has its own index of rows, and each of which can have a header and a footer. For this example, you're creating a table with one section, but we'll look at multiple sections before we finish this chapter.

The second method, tableView:numberOfRowsInSection:, reports the number of rows in this section. Here, you return the size of the array you created. Note that you ignore the section variable because you have only one section.

The third method, tableView:cellForRowAtIndexPath:, takes the table set up by the previous two methods and fills its cells one at a time. Although this chunk of code looks intimidating, most of it will be sitting there waiting for you the first time you work with a table. In particular, the creation of UITableViewCell will be built in. All you need to do is set the values of the cell before it's returned. Here you use your NSDictionary to set the cell's text color and text content ❶.

Also note that this is your first use of the NSIndexPath data class. It encapsulates information on rows and sections. Cells have two views that you can access. The first is the textLabel. As you saw, this contains the text displayed in the cell. The other is imageView. It's basically an icon for the cell. You can set this to an image view. See section 11.2 for more information about using UIImage.

You may want to change more than text content and color. Table 5.7 lists all the cell label features that you may want to experiment with at this point.

Table 5.7   You can modify your table cells in a variety of ways.

Property	Summary
textLabel.font	Sets the cell label's font using UIFont
textLabel.lineBreakMode	Sets how the cell label's text wraps using UILineBreakMode
textLabel.text	Sets the content of a cell label to an NSString
textLabel.textAlignment	Sets the alignment of a cell's label text using the UITextAlignment constant
textLabel.textColor	Sets the color of the cell's label text using UIColor
textLabel.selectedTextColor	Sets the color of selected text using UIColor
imageView.image	Sets the content of a cell's imageView to a UIImage
imageView.selectedImage	Sets the content of a selected cell to UIImage

Using these properties, you can make each table cell look unique, depending on the needs of your program.

ADDING ACCESSORY VIEWS

Although you didn't do so in the color-selector example, you can optionally set accessories on cells. *Accessories* are special elements that appear to the right of each list item.

Most frequently, you'll set accessories using an accessoryType constant that has four possible values, as shown in table 5.8.

Table 5.8   A cell accessory gives additional information.

Constant	Summary
UITableViewCellAccessoryNone	No accessory
UITableViewCellAccessoryDisclosureIndicator	A normal chevron: ›
UITableViewCellAccessoryDetailDisclosureButton	A chevron in a blue button: ⊙
UITableViewCellAccessoryCheckmark	A checkmark: ✔

An accessory can be set as a property of a cell:

```
cell.accessoryType = UITableViewCellAccessoryDetailDisclosureButton;
```

The normal chevron is usually used with a navigation controller, the blue chevron is typically used for configuration, and the checkmark indicates selection.

There is also an `accessoryView` property, which lets you undertake the more complex task of creating an entirely new view to the right of each list item. You create a view and then set `accessoryView` to that view:

```
cell.accessoryView = [[myView alloc] init];
```

There's an example of this in chapter 8, where you'll be working with preference tables.

ADDING SECTIONS

The example shows how to display a single section's worth of cells, but it would be trivial to rewrite the functions to offer different outputs for different sections within the table. Because of Objective-C's ease of accessing nested objects, you can prepare for this by nesting an array for each section inside a larger array:

```
masterColorList = [NSArray arrayWithObjects:colorList,otherColorList,nil];
```

Then, you return the count from this über-array for the `numberOfSections:` method:

```
return masterColorList.count;
```

You similarly return a subcount of one of the subarrays for the `tableView:numberOf-Rows:` method:

```
return [[masterColorList objectAtIndex:section] count];
```

Finally, you pull content from the appropriate subarray when filling in your cells using the same type of nested messaging.

When you're working with sections, you can also think about creating headers and footers for each section. Figure 5.6 shows what the revised application looks like so far, including two different sections, each of which has its own section header.

How do you create those section headers? As with all the methods you've seen that fill in table views, the section header messages and properties show up in the `UITableViewDataSource` protocol reference.

To create section headers, you write a `tableView:titleForHeaderInSection:` method. As you'd expect, it renders a header for each individual section.

An example of its use is shown here. You could probably do something fancier instead, such as building the section names directly into your array:

```
- (NSString *)tableView:(UITableView *)tableView
      titleForHeaderInSection:(NSInteger)section {
    if (section == 0) {
        return @"SDK Colors";
    } else if (section == 1) {
        return @"RGB Colors";
    }
    return 0;
}
```

Figure 5.6 Section headers can improve the usability of table views. Here they're shown in use on both the iPad and iPhone.

You can similarly set footers and otherwise manipulate sections according to the protocol reference.

There's still more to the table view controller. Not only do you have to work with data when you're setting it up, but you also have to do so when it's in active use, which usually occurs when the user selects individual cells.

5.3.4 Using your table view controller

We won't dwell too much on the more dynamic possibilities of the UITableView-Controller here. For the most part, you'll either use it to hold relatively static data (as you do here) or use it to interact with a navigation controller (as you'll see in chapter 7). But before we finish up with table view controllers, we'll look at one other fundamental: selection.

SELECTED CELLS

If you try the sample table view application that you've been building throughout section 5.3, you'll see that individual elements in a table view can be selected.

In table 5.7, you saw that some properties apply explicitly to selected cells. For example, the following maintains the color of your text when it's selected, rather than changing it to white, as per the default:

```
cell.textLabel.textColor =
    [[[masterColorList objectAtIndex:indexPath.section]
        objectAtIndex:indexPath.row] objectForKey:@"colorValue"];
```

To set this value, you must add this line of code to your `tableView:didSelectRowAt-IndexPath:` method. Also note that this is another example of using nested arrays to provide section- and row-specific information for a table list.

The `tableView:didSelectRowAtIndexPath:` method is the most important for dealing with selections. This method appears in the `UITableViewDelegate` protocol and tells you when a row has been selected. The message includes an index path, which, as you've already seen, contains both a row and a section number.

Here's a simple example of how you might use this method to checkmark items in your list:

```
- (void)tableView:(UITableView *)tableView
    didSelectRowAtIndexPath:(NSIndexPath *)indexPath {
    [[tableView cellForRowAtIndexPath:indexPath]
        setAccessoryType:UITableViewCellAccessoryCheckmark];
}
```

You can easily retrieve the selected cell by using the index path, and then you use that information to set the accessory value. You'll make more use of cell selection in chapter 7, when we talk about navigation controllers.

5.4   *Summary*

View controllers are the most important building blocks of the iOS SDK that you hadn't seen up to this point. As we explained in this chapter, they sit atop views of all sorts and control how those views work. Even in this chapter's simple examples, you saw some real-world examples of this control, as view controllers managed rotation, filled tables, and reacted to selections.

You can think of a view controller as being like the glue of your application. It connects your view components to the underlying models. View controllers provide interaction with the interface through `IBOutlets` and `IBActions`.

Now that we're getting into user interaction, we're ready to examine how it works in more depth, and that's the focus of the next chapter. We'll examine the underpinnings of user interaction: events and actions.

Monitoring events and actions

This chapter covers
- The SDK's event modeling
- How events and actions differ
- Creating simple event- and action-driven apps

In the previous chapter, you learned how to create the basic view controllers that fulfill the controller role of an MVC architectural model. You're now ready to start accepting user input, because you can send users to the correct object. Users can interact with your program in two ways: by using the low-level event model or by using event-driven actions. In this chapter, you'll learn the difference between the two types of interactions and how to implement them. Then we'll look at notifications, a third way that your program can learn about user actions.

Of these three models, events provide the lowest-level detail and ultimately underlie everything else (they're essential for sophisticated programs), so we'll begin with events.

6.1   *An introduction to events*

We briefly touched on the basics of event management in chapter 2. But as we said at the time, we wanted to put off a complete discussion until we could cover events in depth; we're now ready to tackle that job.

The fundamental unit of user input is the *touch*: a user puts a finger on the screen. This may be built into a multitouch or a gesture, but the touch remains the building block on which everything else is constructed. It's the basic unit that we'll examine in this chapter. In this section, we'll look at how touches and events are related. Let's start by examining the concept of a responder chain.

6.1.1   *The responder chain*

When a touch occurs in an SDK program, you have to worry about what responds to the event. That's because SDK programs are built of tens—perhaps hundreds—of different objects. Almost all of these objects are subclasses of the UIResponder class, which means they contain all the functionality required to respond to an event. What gets to respond?

The answer is embedded in the concept of the *responder chain*. This is a hierarchy of different objects that are each given the opportunity, in turn, to answer an event message.

Figure 6.1 shows an example of how an event moves up the responder chain. It starts out at the *first responder* of the *key window*, which is typically the view where the event occurred—where the user touched the screen. As we've already noted, this first responder is probably a subclass of UIResponder—which is the class reference you'll want to look to for a lot of responder functionality.

Any object in the chain may accept an event and resolve it; when that doesn't occur, the event moves farther up the list of responders. From a view, an event goes to its superview and then *its* superview, until it eventually reaches the UIWindow object, which is the superview of everything in your application. It's useful to note that from the UIWindow downward, the responder chain is the view hierarchy turned on its head; when you're building hierarchies, they do double duty.

Although figure 6.1 shows a direct connection from the first responder to the window, there can be any number of objects in this gap in a real-world program.

Often, the normal flow of the responder chain is interrupted by *delegation*. A specific object (usually a view) delegates another object (usually a view controller) to act for it. You already saw this put to use in your table view in chapter 5, but you now understand that delegation occurs as part of the normal movement up the responder chain.

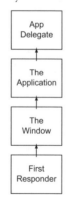

Figure 6.1   Events are initially sent to the first responder but then travel up the responder chain until they're accepted.

First responders and keyboards

Before we leave the topic of responders, we'd like to mention that the first responder is an important concept. Because this first responder is the object that can accept input, it sometimes takes a special action to show its readiness for input. This is particularly true for text objects like UITextField and UITextView, which (if editable) pop up a keyboard when they become the first responder. This has two immediate consequences.

If you want to pop up a keyboard for the text object, you can do so by turning it into the first responder:

```
[myText becomeFirstResponder];
```

Similarly, if you want to get rid of a keyboard, you must tell your text object to stop being the first responder:

```
[myText resignFirstResponder];
```

We'll discuss these ideas more when you encounter your first editable text object toward the end of this chapter.

If an event gets all the way up through the responder chain to the window and it can't deal with an event, then it moves up to the UIApplication, which most frequently punts the event to its own delegate: the *application delegate*, an object that you've been using in every program to date.

Ultimately, you, the programmer, must decide what in the responder chain will respond to events in your program. You should keep two factors in mind when you make this decision: how classes of events can be abstracted together at higher levels in your chain, and how you can build your event management using the concepts of MVC.

At the end of this section, we'll address how you can subvert this responder chain by further regulating events, but for now let's build on its standard setup.

6.1.2   *Touches and events*

Now that you know a bit about how events find their way to the appropriate object, we can dig into how they're encoded by the SDK. First, we want to offer a caveat: usually you won't need to worry about this level of detail because the standard UIKit objects generally convert low-level events into higher-level actions for you, as we discuss in the second half of this chapter. With that said, let's look at the nuts and bolts of event encoding.

The SDK abstracts events by combining a number of touches (which are represented by UITouch objects) into an event (which is represented by a UIEvent object). An event typically begins when the first finger touches the screen and ends when the last finger leaves the screen. In addition, it should generally include only those touches that happen in the same view.

In this chapter, you'll work mainly with `UITouches` (which make it easy to parse single-touch events) and not with `UIEvents` (which are more important for parsing multitouch events). Let's lead off with a more in-depth look at each.

UITOUCH REFERENCE

A `UITouch` object is created when a finger is placed on the screen, moves on the screen, or is removed from the screen. A handful of properties and instance methods can give you additional information on the touch, as detailed in table 6.1.

Table 6.1   Additional properties and methods can tell you precisely what happened during a touch event.

Method or property	Type	Summary
phase	Property	Returns a touch phase constant, which indicates whether touch began, moved, ended, or was canceled
tapCount	Property	The number of times the screen was tapped
timestamp	Property	When the touch occurred or changed
view	Property	The view where the touch began
window	Property	The window where the touch began
locationInView:	Method	The current location of the touch in the specified view
previousLocationInView:	Method	The previous location of the touch in the specified view

Together, the methods and properties shown in table 6.1 offer considerable information about a touch, including when and how it occurred.

Only the `phase` property requires additional explanation. It returns a constant that can be set to one of five values: `UITouchPhaseBegan`, `UITouchPhaseMoved`, `UITouchPhaseStationary`, `UITouchedPhaseEnded`, or `UITouchPhaseCancelled`. You'll often want to have different event responses based on exactly which phase a touch occurred in, as you'll see in the event example.

UIEVENT REFERENCE

To make it easy to see how individual touches occur as part of more complex gestures, the SDK organizes `UITouches` into `UIEvents`. Figure 6.2 shows how these two sorts of objects interrelate.

Just as with the `UITouch` object, the `UIEvent` object contains a number of properties and methods that you can use to figure out more information about your event, as described in table 6.2.

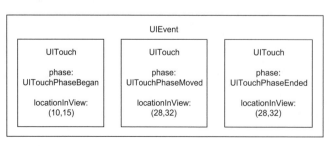

Figure 6.2   `UIEvent` objects contain a set of related `UITouch` objects.

Table 6.2   The encapsulating event object has a number of methods and properties that let you access its data.

Method or property	Type	Summary
`timestamp`	Property	The time of the event
`allTouches`	Method	All event touches associated with the receiver
`touchesForView:`	Method	All event touches associated with a view
`touchesForWindow:`	Method	All event touches associated with a window

The main use of a `UIEvent` method is to give you a list of related touches that you can break down by several means. If you want to get a list of every touch in an event, or if you want to specify just gestures on a certain part of the screen, then you can do that with `UIEvent` methods. This ends our discussion of event containers in this chapter.

Note that all of these methods compact their touches into an `NSSet`, which is an object defined in the Foundation framework. You can find a good reference for the `NSSet` at Apple's developer resources site.

THE RESPONDER METHODS

How do you access touches and/or events? You do so through a series of four different `UIResponder` methods, which are summarized in table 6.3.

Each of these methods has two arguments: an `NSSet` of touches that occurred during the phase in question and a `UIEvent` that provides a link to the entire event's worth of touches. You can choose to access either one, as you prefer; as we've said, we'll be playing with the bare touches. We're now ready to dive into an example that demonstrates how to capture touches in a real-life program.

Table 6.3   The `UIResponder` methods are the heart of capturing events.

Method	Summary
`touchesBegan:withEvent:`	Reports `UITouchPhaseBegan` event when fingers touch the screen
`touchesMoved:withEvent:`	Reports `UITouchPhaseMoved` events when fingers move across the screen
`touchesEnded:withEvent:`	Reports `UITouchPhaseEnded` events when fingers leave the screen
`touchesCancelled:withEvent:`	Reports `UITouchPhaseCancelled` events when the phone is put up to your head, or other events that might cause an external cancellation

6.2   *A touching example: the event reporter*

The sample application for events is an event reporter, which offers a variety of responses depending on how and when the device screen is touched. The sample program has two goals.

First, we want to show you a cool and simple application that you can write using events—one that should get you thinking about everything you can do.

Second, we want to show some of the low-level details of how events work in a visual form. If you take the time to code and compile this program, you'll gain a better understanding of how the various phases work as well as how tapping works.

You'll kick off this development process by creating a project named *eventreporter* that uses the View-Based Application template. That means you'll start with a view controller already in place. We'll also use this example to show how an MVC program can be structured.

6.2.1 Setting things up in Interface Builder

For this program, you'll create three new objects: two button-shaped objects that float around the screen to mark the beginning and end of touches, plus a status bar to go at the bottom of the screen and describe a few other events when they occur.

Because you want all your new objects to lie beneath the view controller in the view hierarchy, you call up the view controller's own .xib file, eventreporterView-Controller.xib. As usual, you'll add your new objects to the Main Display window that represents the view controller's view.

All this work is graphical, so we can't show the code of this programming process. But we've included a quick summary of the actions you should take (the results are shown in figure 6.3):

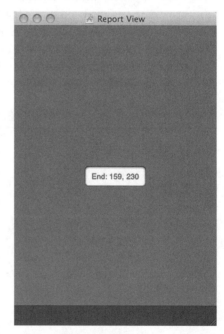

- Set the background color of the UIView to an attractive aluminum color. You do this in the Attributes Inspector, as you do most of your work in this project.
- Create a UILabel, stretch it across the bottom of the screen, and set the color to be steel. Also, clear its text so it doesn't display anything at startup.
- Create two UITextFields. This class of objects is generally used to accept input, but we opted to use the objects for pure display purposes because we like their look. (Don't worry; we'll show how to use the full functionality of a UIText-Field toward the end of this chapter.)
- Place each UITextField at the center of the screen using the handy positioning icons as guides. Set this location's coordinates to 159, 230; and set its origin to middle.

Figure 6.3 Two UITextFields (one of them hidden) and one UILabel, set against an aluminum-colored background on the iPhone, complete the object creation you need for your eventreporter project.

- For each `UITextField`, input text that lists its starting position; this will later be updated by the program as the text field moves. Deselect the user interaction–enabled option for each `UITextField` so that users can't manipulate them.

The process takes longer to explain than it takes to accomplish. You'll have a working interface in a couple of minutes.

Because you'll modify all three of these objects during the course of your program's runtime, you need to link them to variables. You should link everything to your controller, because it takes care of updates, as is appropriate under the MVC model.

The tricky thing here is that the view controller doesn't seem to appear in your eventreporterViewController.xib file—at least not by that name. Fortunately, there's a proxy for it. Because the view controller is what loads up the .xib, it appears as the file's owner in the nib document window. You can therefore connect objects to the view controller by linking them to the file's owner proxy. This is a common situation, because view controllers frequently load additional .xib files for you.

The following is your view controller's header file, eventreportViewController.h, following the addition of these `IBOutlets`. The code also contains a declaration of a method that you'll use later in this project:

```
@interface eventreporterViewController : UIViewController {
    IBOutlet UITextField *startField;
    IBOutlet UITextField *endField;
    IBOutlet UILabel *bottomLabel;
}
- (void)manageTouches:(NSSet *)touches;
@end
```

To finish this process, connect your interface objects to the `IBOutlets`, using the procedures described in chapter 4.

6.2.2 *Preparing a view for touches*

Touch events can be captured only by `UIView` objects. Unfortunately, as of this writing, there's no way to automatically delegate those touches to a view controller. Therefore, in order to manage touch events using the MVC model, you typically need to subclass a `UIView`, capture the events there, and then send messages to the view controller.

In this project, you create a new object class, `reportView`, which is a subclass of `UIView`. You then link, visually, that new class into the view controller's existing view. Open eventreporterViewController.xib, go to the Identity tab for the view object you've been using, and change its name from `UIView` to `reportView`, as you did in chapter 5 when you created a table view controller subview.

Any new methods you write into `reportView`, including methods that capture touch events, will be now reflected in your view. To clarify this setup, figure 6.4 shows the view hierarchy that you've built for your eventreporter project.

Figure 6.4 You'll connect six objects that you'll use to report events.

With a brand-new `UIView` subclass in hand, you can now write methods into it to capture touch events and forward them to its controller. This code, which appears in reportView.m, is as follows:

```
- (void) touchesBegan:(NSSet *)touches withEvent:(UIEvent *)event {
    [self.nextResponder manageTouches:touches];
}
- (void) touchesEnded:(NSSet *)touches withEvent:(UIEvent *)event {
    [self.nextResponder manageTouches:touches];
}
- (void) touchesMoved:(NSSet *)touches withEvent:(UIEvent *)event {
    [self.nextResponder manageTouches:touches];
}
```

This code is pretty simple. You're filling in standard methods so that your program will have the responses you want when those messages are sent. The overall structure of these methods reminds us of several important facts about events.

First, as promised, there are a variety of responder methods. Each of them reports *only* the events for its specific phase. So, for example, the `touchesBegan:withEvent:` method only has `UITouchPhaseBegan` touches in it. In forwarding these touches, you could keep the different phases distinct, but instead you throw everything together and sort it out on the other side.

Second, we'll comment one final time that these methods send you two pieces of information: a set of touches and an event. They're partially redundant, and which one you work with will probably depend on the work you're doing. If you're not doing complex multitouch events, then the `NSSet` of touches will probably be sufficient.

An aside on the text fields and label

If you were to code in this example, you'd discover that the program correctly responds to touch events even when the touches occur atop one of the text fields or the label at the bottom of the page. How does the program manage that when you built event response into only the `reportView`?

The answer is this: it uses the responder chain. The text fields and the label don't respond to the event methods themselves. As a result, the events are passed up the responder chain to the `reportView`, which does leap on those events, using the code you've just seen.

Third, note that you're sending the touches to the view controller by way of the `next-Responder` method. As you'll recall, the responder chain is the opposite of the view hierarchy at its lower levels, which means in this case the `nextResponder` of `report-View` is the `UIViewController`. We would have preferred to have the `UIView-Controller` naturally respond to the touches' messages, but we made use of the responder chain in the next-best way. As of this writing, the compiler warns that `next-Responder` may not know about the `manageTouches` method, but it will; you can ignore this warning.

You'll see some other ways to use the `nextResponder` method toward the end of our discussion of events.

6.2.3 Controlling your events

Intercepting touches and forwarding them up to the view controller may be the toughest part of this code. After the events get to the view controller, they run through a simple method called `manageTouches:`, as in the following listing, which shows the view controller implementation file.

> **Listing 6.1 `manageTouches`, which accepts inputs and changes views**

```
- (void)manageTouches:(NSSet *)touches {
    for (UITouch *touch in touches) {
        if (touch.phase == UITouchPhaseBegan) {               ◁┐
            CGPoint touchPos = [touch locationInView:self.view];│
            startField.center = touchPos;                       │
            startField.text = [NSString stringWithFormat:        │  ❶
                @"Begin: %3.0f,%3.0f",touchPos.x,touchPos.y];    │
        } else if (touch.phase == UITouchPhaseMoved) {      ◁┤ Determines
            bottomLabel.text = @"Touch is moving ...";        │ touch
        } else if (touch.phase == UITouchPhaseEnded)        ◁┘ phase
            {
            if (touch.tapCount > 1) {
                bottomLabel.text = [NSString stringWithFormat:
                    @"Taps: %2i",touch.tapCount];
            } else {
                bottomLabel.text = [NSString string];
            }
            CGPoint touchPos = [touch locationInView:self.view];
            endField.center = touchPos;
            endField.text = [NSString stringWithFormat:
                @"End: %3.0f,%3.0f",touchPos.x,touchPos.y];
        }
    }
}
```

Touches are sent as an `NSSet`, which can be broken apart in a number of ways, as described in the `NSSet` class reference. Here, you use a simple `for ... in` construction that lets you look at each touch in turn.

When you get a touch, the first thing you do is determine what phase it arrived in. Originally, you could have determined this information based on which method a touch arrived through, but because you combined everything you have to fall back on the `phase` property. Fortunately, it's easy to use. You match it up to one of three constants ❶, and that determines which individual actions your program undertakes.

Having different responses based on the phase in which a touch arrives is common—which is why the event methods are split up in the first place. The example demonstrates this with some distinct responses: you move your start field when touches begin, you move your end field when touches end, and you update the bottom label in both the moved and ended phases.

In the UITouchPhaseBegan response, you delve further into your touches' data by using the locationInView: method to figure out the precise coordinates where a touch occurred. You're then able to use that data to reposition your text field and to report the coordinates in the text field. You later do the same thing in the UITouch-PhaseEnded response.

Finally, you look at the tapCount in the UITouchPhaseEnded response. This is generally the best place to look at taps because the device now knows that the user's finger has come off the screen. As you can see, it's easy to both run a command based on the number of taps and to report that information.

Figure 6.5 shows the event responder in action. Imagine a finger that touches down on the space where the Begin text field is and that is currently moving across the screen.

And with that, your event reporter is complete. In addition to illustrating how a program can respond to touches, we've highlighted how the MVC model can be used in a real application.

The project contains four views: a reportView, a UILabel, and two UITextFields. It's tempting to process events in the reportView, especially because you had to create a subclass anyway, but instead you pushed the events up to the view controller and in doing so revealed *why* you want to do MVC modeling.

Because it takes on the controller role, you give the view controller access to all of its individual objects, and therefore you don't have to try to remember what object

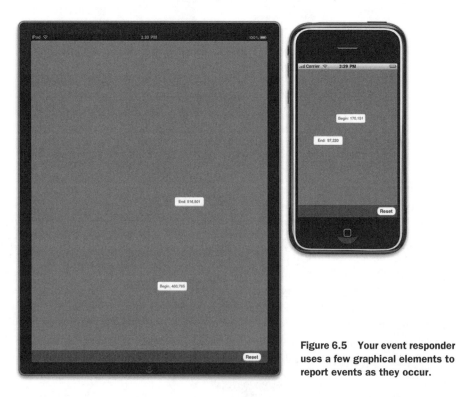

Figure 6.5 Your event responder uses a few graphical elements to report events as they occur.

knows about what other object. Tying things into the view controller, rather than scattering them randomly across your code, makes the project that much more readable and reusable, which is what most architectural and design patterns are about.

6.3   *Other event functionality*

Before we complete our discussion of events, we'd like to cover a few more topics of interest. We'll explore how to regulate the report of events in a variety of ways and then describe some deficiencies in the event model.

6.3.1   *Regulating events*

As we mentioned earlier, there are some ways that you can modify how events are reported (and whether they are at all). As you'll see, three different objects give you access to this sort of regulation: UIResponder, UIView, and UIApplication. We've listed all the notable options we'll discuss in table 6.4.

Because UIView is a subclass of UIResponder, you generally have access to the methods from both classes in most UIKit objects. You'll need to do some additional work to access the UIApplication methods.

Table 6.4   Properties in various objects allow for additional control of when events are monitored.

Method or property	Type	Summary
nextResponder	UIResponder method	Returns the next responder in the chain by default but can be modified
hitTest:withEvent:	UIView method	Returns the deepest subview containing a point by default but can be modified
exclusiveTouch	UIView property	A Boolean set to NO by default; controls whether other views in the same window are blocked from receiving events
multipleTouchEnabled	UIView property	A Boolean set to NO by default; controls whether multitouches after the first are thrown out
beginIgnoringInteractionEvents	UIApplication method	Turns off touch event handling
endIgnoringInteractionEvents	UIApplication method	Turns on touch event handling
isIgnoringInteractionEvents	UIApplication method	Tells whether the application is ignoring touch events

UIRESPONDER REGULATION

You've already seen that UIResponder is the source of the methods that let you capture events; as shown here, it's also the home of the methods that control how the responder chain works.

Most of the responder chain–related methods aren't directly used by your code; instead, they typically appear deep in frameworks. becomeFirstResponder and resignFirstResponder (which control who the first responder is) and canBecome-FirstResponder, canResignFirstResponder, and isFirstResponder (which return Booleans related to the information in question) all typically fall into this category.

The last UIResponder method, nextResponder, may be of use in your programs. As defined by UIResponder, nextResponder returns the next responder, per the normal responder chain. You used it in the example to pass your touches up.

If you want to change the normal order of the responder chain, you can do so by creating your own nextResponder function in a subclass. This new function overrides its parent method and allows your program to take a different path up your responder chain.

UIVIEW REGULATION

When you move into the UIView class methods, you can take the opposite approach by overriding hitTest:withEvent:. This method is passed a CGPoint and an event, and by default it returns the deepest subview that contains the point. By writing a new method, you can cause your responder chain to start at a different point.

The two UIView properties that we noted both work as you'd expect. exclusive-Touch declares that the view in question is the only one that can receive events (which is an alternative way you could have managed the eventreporter example, where you didn't want anything but the reportView to accept events). Meanwhile, multiple-TouchEnabled starts reporting of multitouch events, which are otherwise ignored.

UIAPPLICATION REGULATION

Finally, we come to the UIApplication methods. These lie outside the normal hierarchy of objects, and thus you can't get to them from your view objects. Instead, you need to call them directly from the UIApplication object, as shown here:

```
[[UIApplication sharedApplication] beginIgnoringInteractionEvents];
```

As you may recall from chapter 3, sharedApplication is a UIApplication class method that provides a reference to the application object. Typically, you use its return as the receiver for the beginIgnoringInteractionEvents message.

Each of the three methods listed under UIApplication works as you'd expect when you know the secret to accessing them.

6.3.2 *Other event methods and properties*

We've spent a lot of time on events, but at the same time we've only scratched the surface. Events give you low-level access to user input, but you won't use events much. Instead, you'll use the device's many control objects (and thus actions) in order to accept almost all user input.

As a result, this chapter offers you a compromise: a solid look at how events work that should suffice for those times when you do need to descend to touch management, but not all of the intricacies. The thing that we've most clearly left out is how to work with multitouch events. For that, we point you, as usual, to the Apple iOS SDK developer website. A good tutorial on multitouch events is available as part of the iOS Programming Guide; you should read if you're one of that smaller percentage of developers—such as programmers creating games and novelties—who may need access to multitouches and more complex gestures.

6.4 An introduction to actions

If you won't usually be programming directly with events, how will you access user input? The answer is by using actions. You'll typically depend on preexisting text views, buttons, and other widgets to run your programs. When using these objects, you don't have to worry about raw events. Instead, you can build programs around control events and actions that are generated by UIControls. Let's look at the UIControl object first; then, we'll examine the relationship between control events and actions and how to hook them up.

6.4.1 The UIControl object

When you were working with events, you found that the UIResponder class held many of the methods critical for event control. Similarly, you can access a lot of the methods important to SDK controls through the UIControl class.

UIControl is a child of UIView (and thus UIResponder). It's the parent of important user interface controls such as UIButton, UISwitch, UIPageControl, UISegmented-Control, UISlider, and UITextField. It's *not* used for some other control-looking objects such as UISearchBar, so you should check the Apple class references before trying to use its functionality. Also note that the higher-level UIControl class can't be used on its own; it defines the common methods used by its children.

The UIControl class contains several properties that control its basic setup, such as enabled (which determines whether it's on), highlighted (which determines its visual state), and selected (which sets Boolean state for appropriate sorts of controls, such as switches). You can also directly access a control's touch events with beginTracking-WithTouch:withEvent:, continueTrackingWithTouch:withEvent:, and endTrack-ingWithTouch:withEvent:, methods that work in a similar way to the event response functions that you played with in UIResponder. But you won't be using these methods, because they don't represent the simple advantages that you'll see when using control objects. For that, we turn to UIControl's action-target mechanism.

6.4.2 Control events and actions

The UIControl object introduces a new event-handling infrastructure that takes touch events of the sort that you might have directly handled in the previous section and (eventually) converts them into simple actions, without your having to worry about the specifics of how a user accessed a control. The complete sequence of events is outlined in figure 6.6.

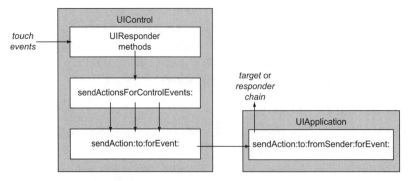

Figure 6.6 `UIControl` **objects take standard touch events and turn them into actions that are dispatched by** `UIApplication`.

When a touch event arrives at a `UIControl` object (via normal dispatching along the responder chain), the control does something unique. Inside the standard `UIResponder` methods that you used in the previous section (such as `touchesBegan:withEvent:`), a `UIControl` object turns standard touch events into special control events.

These control events broadly describe how the user has interacted with the controls rather than recording gestures. For example, they may report that a button has been pushed or a slider moved. They're divided into three categories: touch events, editing events, and a slider event. The touch events describe how a user's finger interacted with the control, the editing events describe changes to a `UITextField`, and the `UIControlEventValueChanged` event describes changes to a `UISlider`.

These control events are all enumerated in a bitmask that's defined in the `UIControl` object. An almost-complete listing of them—including some composite control events—can be found in table 6.5. We've left out only a few reserved values.

Table 6.5 `UIControl` **objects recognize a number of special events.**

Value	Summary
`UIControlEventTouchDown`	A finger touch.
`UIControlEventTouchDownRepeat`	A repeated finger touch (with `tapCount` > 1).
`UIControlEventTouchDragInside`	A finger movement ending inside the control.
`UIControlEventTouchDragOutside`	A finger movement ending just outside the control.
`UIControlEventTouchDragEnter`	A finger movement that enters the control.
`UIControlEventTouchDragExit`	A finger movement that exits the control.
`UIControlEventTouchUpInside`	A finger removed from the screen inside the control.
`UIControlEventTouchUpOutside`	A finger removed from the screen outside the control.
`UIControlEventTouchCancel`	A system event canceled a touch.
`UIControlEventValueChanged`	A slider (or other similar) object changed its value.

Table 6.5 `UIControl` objects recognize a number of special events. *(continued)*

Value	Summary
`UIControlEventEditingDidBegin`	Editing began in a `UITextField`.
`UIControlEventEditingChanged`	Editing changed in a `UITextField`.
`UIControlEventEditingDidEnd`	Editing ended in a `UITextField` due to a touch outside the object.
`UIControlEventEditingDidEndOnExit`	Editing ended in a `UITextField` due to a touch.
`UIControlEventAllTouchEvents`	Composite for all the touch-related events.
`UIControlEventAllEditingEvents`	Composite for the editing-related events.
`UIControlEventAllEvents`	Composite for all events.

After a standard event has been turned into a control event, a sequence of additional methods is called, as shown in figure 6.6. First, the `UIControl` object calls `send-ActionsForControlEvents:`. That in turn breaks down the events it's been sent and calls `sendAction:to:forEvent:` once per event. Here, the control event is turned into an action, which is a specific method that's going to be run in a specific target object. Finally, the `UIApplication` method `sendAction:to:fromSender:forEvent:` is called by the control, again once per event.

This is another situation where the application object does big-picture controlling of messaging. The application sends the action to the target object. But there's one catch: if the target that the action is being sent to has been listed as `nil`, the action is sent to the first responder instead and from there moves up the responder chain.

That process can be slightly exhausting, and fortunately you shouldn't normally need to know its details. For your purposes, you should be aware that a `UIControl` object turns a touch event first into a control event and then into an action with a specific recipient. Even better, you need to code only the last part of that conversion, from control event into targeted action.

6.4.3 Using addTarget:action:forControlEvents:

A `UIControl` object maintains an internal dispatch table that correlates control events with target-action pairs. This table says which method should be run by which object when a specified event occurs. You can add entries to this table with the `UIControl` object's `addTarget:action:forControlEvents:` method. The following example shows how it works:

```
[controlObject addTarget:recipientObject action:@selector(method)
    forControlEvents:UIControlEvents];
```

The first argument, `addTarget:`, says where the message will be sent. It's frequently set to `self`, which usually refers to a view controller that instantiated the control object.

The second argument, `action:`, is the trickiest. First, note that it uses the @ syntax that we mentioned in chapter 2. The selector should identify the name of the method that's going to be run in the target object. Second, be aware that you can send the action argument either without a colon (`method`) or with a colon (`method:`). In the latter case, the ID of the `controlObject` is sent as an argument. Be sure your receiving method is correctly defined to accept an argument if you include that colon in your selector.

The third argument, `forControlEvents:`, is a bitmasked list of possible control events, taken from table 6.5.

With all these puzzle pieces in place, you're ready to write some code that uses actions (and this method). As a simple example, you'll expand the functionality to your event reporter by adding a reset button.

6.5   *Adding a button to an application*

The simplest use of an action is probably adding a button to an application and then responding to the press of that button. As you'll see, this turns out to be a *lot* easier than digging through individual touches.

We've opted to show you how to work with a button in two ways: first by using the `addTarget:action:forControlEvents:` method that we just introduced and then visually by using an `IBAction` declaration.

Both of these examples begin with your existing eventreporter program. You'll add a simple `UIButton` to it visually. Place the button atop the label at the bottom of your page and use the `attributes` tag to label it Reset. With it in place and defined, it's ready to be linked into your program by one of two different ways.

Both examples will call a method called `resetPage:`, which restores the three changeable objects in your eventreporter to their default states. It's in eventreporter-ViewController.m, and as you can see it's entirely elementary:

```
- (void)resetPage:(id)sender {
    startField.text = @"Begin: 159,230";
    startField.center = CGPointMake(159,230);
    endField.text = @"Begin: 159,230";
    endField.center = CGPointMake(159,230);
    bottomLabel.text = [NSString string];
}
```

We can now look at the two ways you can call this method.

6.5.1   *Using addTarget:action:forControlEvents: with a button*

On the one hand, you may wish to add actions to your button programmatically. This could be the case if you created your button from within Xcode or if you created your button visually but want to change its behavior during runtime.

Your first step is bringing your button into Xcode. If you created your button visually, as we suggested earlier, you need to create an `IBOutlet` for the button, which should be old hat by now. If you didn't create your button visually, you can do so programmatically in Xcode. This probably means using the factory class method `buttonWithType:`, which lets you create either a rounded rectangle button or one of a few special buttons, like the info button. By either means, you should now have a button object available in Xcode.

Your second step is to send the `addTarget:action:forControlEvents:` message as part of your application's startup. Assuming that you're having your view controller manage the button's action, this message should be sent from the view controller's `loadView` method (if your controller was created in Xcode) or in its `viewDidLoad` method (if you created the controller in Interface Builder).

Here's what the `viewDidLoad` method of your view controller looks like when applied to a button called `myButton`:

```
- (void)viewDidLoad {
    [myButton addTarget:self action:@selector(resetPage:)
        forControlEvents:UIControlEventTouchUpInside];
    [super viewDidLoad];
}
```

This real-life example of `addTarget:action:forControlEvents:` looks much like the sample in the previous section. You're sending a message to your button that tells it to send the view controller a `resetPage:` message when the user takes their finger off the screen while touching the button.

That single line of code is all that's required; from there on out, your button will connect to your `resetPage:` method whenever it's pushed (and released).

6.5.2 Using an IBAction with a button

The other way you can link up actions to methods is to do *everything* visually. This is the preferred choice if you've created your object visually (as we've suggested) and you're not planning to change its behavior at runtime.

When you use this procedure, you don't need to make your button into an `IBOutlet`. It's effectively invisible from Xcode, which is fine, because all you care about is what happens when the button is pushed. You also don't use the somewhat complex `addTarget:action:forControlEvents:` method that we just ran through; instead, you connect things via intuitive visual means.

For the purposes of this example, start with a clean slate: with a button freshly crafted inside the interface pane and no connections yet built.

To link an interface object to an action, you must declare the method you're using as having a return of `IBAction`. This means adding the following declaration to the header file of your view controller:

```
- (IBAction)resetPage:(id)sender;
```

The implementation of the method should share the same return.
Afterward, you can go into Interface Builder and create a connection, as shown in figure 6.7.

As shown, when you're connecting a control, you're given access to the entire palette of possible control events. You select the one (or ones) that you want to connect to `IBAction`s, and then you drag over to the top-level object containing your `IBAction`. In this case, that's once again the file's owner object, which represents your view

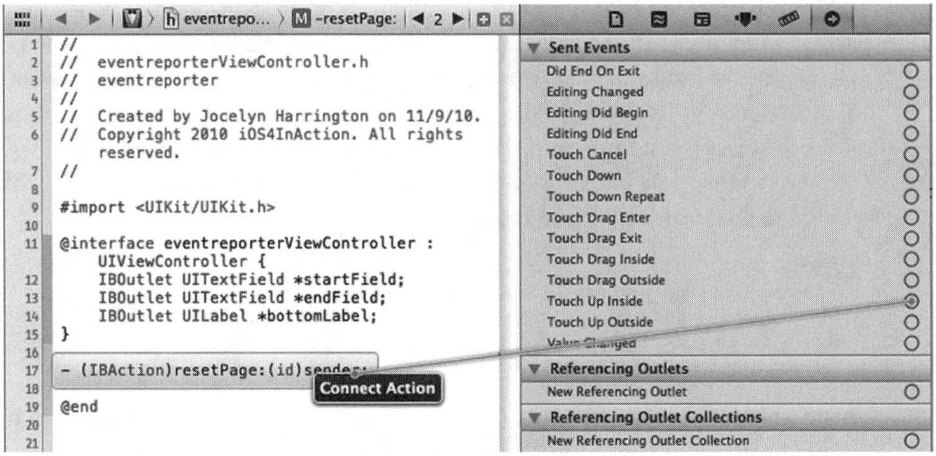

Figure 6.7 With an IBAction, there's no code, just a link.

controller. As usual, a menu pops up, this time showing possible IBActions to which
you can link your control event.

The results are almost magical. With that single graphical link, you replace the
addTarget:action:forControlEvents: call and any code of any type. The button
now links to the targeted action automagically.

What we've described so far covers the broad strokes of actions; everything else lies
in the details. If we spent less time on actions than events, it's not because actions are
less important than events, but because they're a lot simpler.

From here on, your challenge in using controls will be figuring out how individual
controls work. See appendix A for an overview of classes and the Apple Class References for specifics. But there are a few controls that we'd like to give more attention to
because they vary from the norm.

6.6   *Other action functionality*

In this section we'll look at two controls that report back different signals than the
simple button-up or button-down control events. The first is the UITextField, the
prime control for entering text, and the second is the relatively simple (but unique)
UISlider. In the process, we'll also explore the other text-based entry formats,
because they share some unique issues with UITextField.

6.6.1 *Accepting text input with UITextField*

You have four ways to display pure text in the SDK: the UILabel, the UISearchBar, the
UITextView, and the UITextField. Each has a slightly different purpose. The UILabel
and the UISearchBar are intended for short snippets of text; the UITextView is
intended for multiple lines. Each of those text objects except the UILabel is editable,
but only the UITextField is a UIControl subclass with its own control events already
defined.

If the `UITextField` sounds familiar, that's because you used it in the eventreporter example. If you go back and look at the screenshots, you'll see that the Begin and End buttons are displayed in ovals that look a lot like input boxes. As we mentioned at the time, we liked the way they looked, but they also gave us a good excuse to familiarize you with the object without getting into its details.

Usually, a `UITextField` *will* accept user input. It's intended to be used mainly for accepting short user input. The trickiest thing about using a `UITextField` is getting it to relinquish control of your device after you call up a keyboard. The following code shows the two steps needed to resolve this problem. We're assuming that you're working with a `myText` `UITextField` object visually and instantiated inside a view controller:

```
- (void)viewDidLoad {
   myText.returnKeyType = UIReturnKeyDone;
   [super viewDidLoad];
}
- (BOOL)textFieldShouldReturn:(UITextField *)textField {
  [textField resignFirstResponder];
  return YES;
}
```

Your setup of an interface object begins, pretty typically, inside its controller's `view-DidLoad` method. Here you turn the text field keyboard's Return key into a bright blue Done key, to make it clear that's how you get out. You accomplish this by using part of the `UITextInputTraits` protocol, which defines a couple of common features for objects that use keyboards.

To do anything else, you need to declare a delegate for the `UITextField` that follows the `UITextFieldDelegate` protocol. This can be done either by setting the text field's `delegate` property programmatically or by drawing a delegate link visually. (This sample code presumes you've taken the easier solution of doing so visually.) After you've done that, you can modify the `textFieldShouldReturn:` delegate method. We're assuming that the view controller has been set as the delegate, which would be typical, and which allows you to do this work in the same view controller class file.

Finally, you enter two standard lines of code into this delegate method. They tell the text field to let go of first-responder status (which, as we've previously noted, is what's necessary to make a keyboard go away) and return a YES Boolean.

With this code in place, a user can get in *and* out of a `UITextField`. To use the text field afterward, you need to monitor the text field's special control events (especially `UIControlEventEditingDidEnd`) and also look at its `text` property.

In a moment, we'll provide a sample of how that works. First, let's examine a few other text objects that aren't controls but that you might use to accept text entry.

UILABEL

The `UILabel` isn't user editable.

UISEARCHBAR

The UISearchBar looks an awful lot like a UITextField with some nuances, such as a button to clear the field and a bookmark button. Despite the similarities in style, the UISearchBar isn't a UIControl object but instead follows an entirely different methodology.

To use a UISearchBar, set its delegate to be the object of your choice, likely your view controller. Then, respond to the half-dozen messages described in UISearch-BarDelegate. The most important of these is the searchBarSearchButtonClicked: method. Be sure to include resignFirstResponder in order to clear the keyboard; then, you can take actions based on the results. There's an example of a UISearchBar in chapter 9, section 9.2.3.

UITEXTVIEW

A UITextView works like a UITextField, except that it allows users to enter many lines of text. The biggest gotcha here is that you can't use the Return key as your Done button, because users will likely want to hit Returns in their text. Instead, you must have a Done button somewhere near the top of your screen, where it can be seen when the keyboard is up. When that button is clicked, you can set the text view to resignFirst-Responder. Beyond that, you must set the UITextView's delegate property; then you can watch for delegate messages, most importantly textViewDidEndEditing:.

With the quick digression into this variety of text objects out of the way, we can now return to the other UIControl object that we wanted to discuss: UISlider.

6.6.2 *Allowing value selection with UISlider*

The slider is a simple object, but we've singled it out because it's the one other class that has its own control event, UIControlEventValueChanged. If you target this event, you'll find that it gets called whenever the slider moves, but the control event won't tell you what the new value is. To get that information, your action method must query the slider's properties.

Three properties are of particular note: value shows a slider's current value, minimumValue shows the bottom of its scale, and maximumValue shows the top of its scale. You can use value without modification if you've set your slider to return a reasonable number (as described in the class reference); or if you prefer, you can use all three properties together to determine the percentage that the slider is moved over—which is what you'll do in one final control example.

6.6.3 *A TextField/Slider mashup*

Because we want to examine two UIControl objects more closely, it makes sense to quickly mash up an example that takes advantage of both of them. You'll do this in the View-Based RGB Application, which sets the background color of a view based on the word you type into a UITextField and the selected position of a UISlider.

As usual, you create all of these objects visually. Then, go hog wild linking objects to your view controller. In all, you should create five links: an outlet each for your text field and slider, an action link for the important text field and the slider events, and a delegate link for the text field. Figure 6.8 shows what the view controller's Connections tab looks like after these have all been done.

As shown, the actions from both of the controls link into a single method, called `changeColor:`. Whenever either control is changed, this method adjusts the color of the screen accordingly. The following listing shows how.

Listing 6.2   Accessing a text field and a slider

```
- (IBAction)changeColor:(id)sender {
    int red; int green; int blue;
    if ([myText.text caseInsensitiveCompare:@"red"]
        == NSOrderedSame) {
            red = 1; green = 0; blue = 0;
    } else if ([myText.text caseInsensitiveCompare:@"blue"]
        == NSOrderedSame) {
            red = 0; green = 0; blue = 1;
    } else if ([myText.text caseInsensitiveCompare:@"green"]
        == NSOrderedSame) {
            red = 0; green = 1; blue = 0;
    } else {
            red = .5; green = .5; blue = .5;
    }
    float newShade = mySlider.value /
        (mySlider.maximumValue - mySlider.minimumValue);
    [self.view setBackgroundColor:
        [UIColor colorWithRed:red green:green blue:blue alpha:newShade]];
}
```

❶ Checks text input

❷ Calculates alpha percentage

The hardest part of working with a `UITextField` is setting it up, which you did earlier. Now that you have input coming back, all you need to do is access the `text` property and do with it as you will ❶.

Meanwhile, by working with your three slider values, you're able to easily generate a value from 0 to 1 ❷. Putting that together with the color you generated from your text field input results in a background color that you can change in two ways. Figure 6.9 takes a final look at this new program.

Would it be better to do this with a `UISegmentedControl` and a `UISlider`? Probably. But as is, it offers a quick example of how a text field works. Furthermore, it shows how you can combine action management by letting multiple controls point to a single method, a technique that will be useful in more complex programs.

As usual, more information about both of these controls is available in the Apple class references, including lots of methods and properties that we didn't talk about.

Figure 6.8   A heavily connected view controller will be a pretty normal sight as you gain experience in creating objects visually.

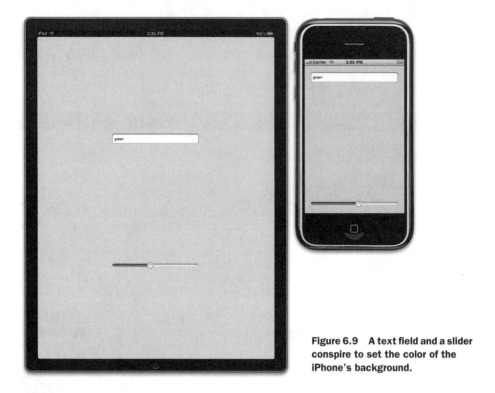

Figure 6.9   A text field and a slider conspire to set the color of the iPhone's background.

6.6.4   *Actions made easy*

Throughout the latter half of this chapter, you've seen controls that are tied to the fully fledged target-action mechanism. In the next chapter, that will change when you see the same idea in a somewhat simplified form.

Sometimes, buttons or other controls are built into other classes of objects (such as the button that can be built into the navigation bar). These controls have special methods that allow them to automatically create a target-action pair. As a result, you don't have to go through the nuisance of calling the addTarget:action:forControl-Events: method separately.

We'll point out this technique when we encounter it as part of the navigation controller.

6.6.5   *Actions in use*

There are numerous control objects that we've opted not to cover here, mainly because they use the same general principles as those we've talked about. Nonetheless, they'll remain an important factor throughout the rest of this book.

In particular, controls represent one of the main ways that users can offer input to your programs, and we'll discuss them when we talk about data in chapter 9. We'll also offer more complex programs that use a variety of controls from chapter 9 on. Through those examples, the majority of the UI controls will receive some coverage in this book.

6.7   *Introducing notifications*

As we mentioned in chapter 1, there's one other way that a program can learn about events: through notifications. When directly manipulating events or actions, as you have throughout this chapter, individual objects receive events because the events occurred in their view, because the events occurred in a subview, or because the events occurred in a view that has been delegated to them.

Notifications step outside this paradigm. Now, an object registers to receive notice when certain events occur. These are often events that lie beyond the standard view hierarchy, such as information when a network connection closes or when the device's orientation changes. Notably, these notifications are also broadcast messages: many different objects can be notified when the event occurs.

All notifications occur through the NSNotificationCenter. You must create a copy of this shared object to use it:

```
[NSNotificationCenter defaultCenter]
```

Afterward, you may use the addObserver:selector:name:object: method to request a certain notification. The Observer: is the object that receives the notification method (usually, self), the selector: is the method that is called in the observer, name: is the name of the notification (which is in the class reference), and the object: can be used if you want to restrict which objects you receive notification from (but it's usually set to nil).

For example, to receive the UIDeviceOrientationDidChangeNotification notification that we'll talk about in chapter 10, you might use the following code:

```
[[NSNotificationCenter defaultCenter] addObserver:self
  selector:@selector(deviceDidRotate:)
  name:@"UIDeviceOrientationDidChangeNotification" object:nil];
```

Overall, notification programming tends to have four steps:

1 You learn that there's a notification by reading the appropriate class reference (UIDevice in this case).
2 You may need to explicitly turn on the notification (as is indeed the case for UIDeviceOrientationDidChangeNotification).
3 You write a method that will respond to the notification (in this case, device-DidRotate:).
4 You connect the notification to the method with the NSNotificationCenter.

There is considerably more power in the notification system. Not only can you set up multiple observers, but you can also post your own notifications. If you want more information on these advanced features, you should read the class references on NSNotificationCenter, NSNotification, and NSNotificationQueue.

6.8   *Summary*

The iOS includes an extensive set of frameworks that takes care of a lot of details for you, making your programming as painless as possible. You've seen this to date in everything you've done, as sophisticated objects appear on screen with almost no work.

The same applies to the iPhone's and iPad's event system. There is a complex underlying methodology. It centers on a responder chain and granular reporting of touches and allows you to follow precise user gestures. You may occasionally have to manipulate events via these more complex means.

But the iPhone and iPad also support a higher-level iOS action system that lets programs respond to specific actions applied to controls rather than more freeform gestures. We've explained how to use both, but it's the target-action mechanism that you're more likely to rely on when programming.

With actions and events out of the way, we're ready to look at the final fundamental building block of the SDK. We've already discussed views, controls, and basic view controllers, but another category of object is critical for most SDK programming: the advanced view controller that allows for navigation over multiple screens of content.

That's the basis of the next chapter.

Advanced
view controllers

This chapter covers

- Working with navigation-based interfaces
- The flipside controller
- The split view controller
- Popover and modal view controllers
- Mixture of view controllers

When we started our look at view controllers in chapter 5, we promised that we'd return to the more advanced view controllers that manage several pages of content at once. That's the purpose of this chapter: to introduce you to the final fundamental building block of iOS that allows you to build complex multipage applications.

In this chapter, we'll take an in-depth look at three view controllers: the tab bar controller, the navigation controller, and the unique split view controller (at the time of writing, it's only available on the iPad). We'll also take a briefer look at the flipside controller that appears in one of Xcode's iOS templates and talk about some modal controllers that you'll see later in the book.

As in the previous chapter on view controllers, we'll offer skeletal examples: the main purpose is to provide you with the reusable programming frameworks that will let you use these controllers in your own programs. Let's kick off the discussion with the tab bar view controller.

7.1   The tab bar view controller

Of the multipage view controllers, the tab bar is the easiest to use because it supports simple navigation between several views. Like all the advanced view controllers, it has a complex underlying structure incorporating several objects that work in tandem.

7.1.1   The anatomy of a tab bar view controller

To function, a tab bar view controller requires a hierarchy of at least six objects:

- One `UITabBarController`
- A minimum of two `UIViewControllers`
- One `UITabBar`
- A minimum of two `UITabBarItems`

This hierarchy of objects is depicted in figure 7.1.

The tab bar controller and its associated view controllers are the heart of this setup. The tab bar controller switches off between different pages, each of which uses a view controller to manage its events. When you create them visually they are automatically hooked up, but you will you need to fill in the controllers' views when your controllers are ready to go.

The tab bar itself is created automatically when you instantiate a tab bar controller. It displays a set of radio buttons that go at the bottom of the page. Each of those buttons is a tab bar item (which is also created automatically). Each tab bar item then links to an individual view controller. Usually you shouldn't have to mess with the tab bar; you can make all the modifications you require through either the tab bar controller or the view controllers.

The connection between the tab bar controller and its tab bar is a simple delegation, as you've seen in use in previous chapters. The tab bar has a `delegate` property that's hooked up to the controller, which must respond to the `UITabBarDelegate` protocol.

The tab bar controller can also designate a `delegate`. The controller's `delegate` must follow the `UITabBarControllerDelegate` protocol. This protocol requires response to two types of high-level events: when the tab bar is rearranged and when a view controller is selected.

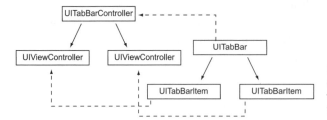

Figure 7.1   A collection of six objects (at minimum) is required to create a functioning tab bar view controller.

7.1.2 Creating a tab bar view controller

Each of the advanced view controllers has its own Xcode template that you can use to immediately instantiate the controller. Because this is your first advanced view controller, though, we'll look at how you create it by hand before we move over to simpler, template-driven object creation.

CREATING A TAB BAR VIEW CONTROLLER BY HAND

To create a tab bar view controller manually, begin with the Window-Based Application template. Use it to create a project imaginatively called *tabex*. Note that this example will work on any of the devices. After you've created the project, open the MainWindow.xib file.

Now, to create the tab bar view controller, follow these steps:

1 Drag the Tab Bar Controller object from the Library window (where you'll find it under Controllers) to the nib display window.

2 Drop the controller next to your window object. When you do that, the Tab Bar Controller Main display window appears.

3 Dismiss the old Main display; you don't need it anymore. Instead, you'll create new objects as subviews of your tab bar view controller.

The results are shown in figure 7.2.

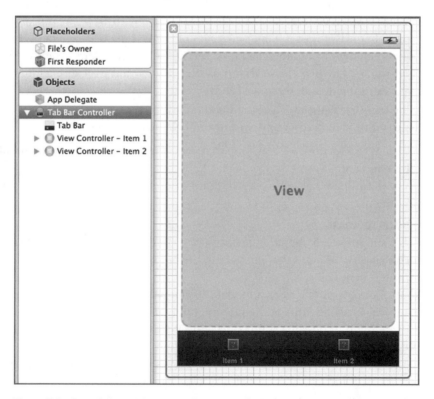

Figure 7.2 Dragging a tab bar controller to the nib display window creates the tab bar interface.

Believe it or not, that's all there is to it. All six objects of note have been created. The tab bar controller is accessible from the nib display window. The other five objects are accessible from the black bar at the bottom of the Main display window. Click a button once to get its `UIViewController` and a second time to get its `UITabBarItem`. Click in the middle of the strip (between the buttons) to access the `UITabBar`. By selecting these items, you can set their attributes, connections, size, and identity.

We took this slight diversion into the harder side of tab bar controller design to show what all the objects look like. After you've seen all the fundamental objects that are created as part of an advanced view controller, you've played the Window-Based Application template's last trick. In the future, we'll jump straight to the appropriate template for each sort of view controller—starting with the tab bar controller template.

CREATING YOUR TAB BAR THROUGH A TEMPLATE

It's even easier to create a tab bar view controller using the existing tab bar template. Select Tab Bar Application when you create a new project. This template sets you up with a tab bar controller much like the one you just created by hand, except it does three additional things:

- The template defines the tab bar controller as an `IBOutlet`, giving the app delegate access to the object `IBOutlet UITabBarController *tabBarController;`.
- The template creates the view controller for the first window as part of a special `FirstViewController` class. You'll probably want to have an individual view controller class for each tab to take care of events on a per-page basis, but that's easy to change by adding class files and adjusting the Identity tab for the view controllers. For now, leave things as they are so that we can examine how to work with the default template setup.
- The template associates a second .xib file with the second view. It does this in a way you've seen before: by defining a nib Name for the view controller.

For the rest of this section, we'll assume that you're working with this prebuilt tab bar controller template as your tabex project.

With a working tab bar controller in hand, you can begin programming multiple pages of screens.

TAB BARS AND TOOLBARS

The UIKit supports two similar interfaces, the `UITabBar` and the `UIToolBar`. They each include a strip of icons that goes along the bottom of the screen. Their main difference is in functionality.

The `UITabBar` is intended as a modal interface that changes the selections when they're tapped (usually with a permanent highlight). The purpose of the `UIToolBar` is to provide a menu of possible actions that don't change the appearance of the selection when tapped (except with a temporary highlight).

Despite their similar appearance, the two items share no inheritance other than a common ancestor in `UIView`. Consider it convergent evolution.

We'll present a fully functional example of a `UIToolBar` in chapter 11.

7.1.3 Building a tab bar interface

At this point, you have a tab bar controller that contains two tabs, each of which has relatively empty content. You also have tabs on your tab bar without pictures and without meaningful names. To build your tab bar interface, you'll want to adjust all these things.

ADDING MORE TABS

You can add tabs to the tab bar by dragging a tab bar item to the tab bar. A tab bar item and related view controller are added to the right side of your bar. Go ahead and create a third tab.

To allow for easy access to this new controller's view, you should create a new .xib file and connect the view controller to it.

CONNECTING VIEWS

When you have the right number of tabs, you can connect views to each of the tab bar's view controllers. This can be done in three ways:

- You can input views through .xib files, as noted earlier.
- If a view controller has its own class file, you can add views through the `load-View` or `viewDidLoad` method for that class.
- If a view controller doesn't have its own class file, you can load views elsewhere, such as in the app delegate's `applicationDidFinishLaunching:`.

Because the latter two view controllers don't have their own class files, you'll see how to create their views using `applicationDidFinishLaunching:`. It would probably be simpler to create their views visually, but this example will demonstrate how you can use the tab bar controller.

Although you don't have outlets for the controllers, you can link to them straight from the tab bar controller object, which you *do* have access to, thanks to that `IBOutlet` that you've already seen. This relates to a concept we discussed when talking about basic view controllers because view controllers have to do MVC management: they should give you easy access to related objects. Within the tab bar controller is a `viewControllers` property, which is an `NSArray` list of the view controllers that a tab bar controller contains.

Listing 7.1 shows how to access this information and programmatically build a couple of views for the second and third controllers within tabexAppDelegate.m. This is the skeleton of a simple program that lets you edit a text view in the first window, keep a count of what you've written in the second, and search in the third.

Listing 7.1 Tab bar controller setup

```
- (BOOL)application:(UIApplication *)application
  didFinishLaunchingWithOptions:(NSDictionary *)launchOptions

    UIViewController *secondController =
        [tabBarController.viewControllers objectAtIndex:1];
    UIViewController *thirdController =
        [tabBarController.viewControllers objectAtIndex:2];
```

❶ **Retrieves view controllers**

```
    UITextView *secondView = [[UITextView alloc]
        initWithFrame:[[UIScreen mainScreen] bounds]];
    secondView.text = @"A word count would appear here.";
    secondView.editable = NO;
    secondController.view = secondView;
    UITextView *thirdView = [[UITextView alloc]
        initWithFrame:[[UIScreen mainScreen] bounds]];
    thirdView.text = @"A search function would go here.";
    thirdView.editable = NO;
    thirdController.view = thirdView;
    [window addSubview:tabBarController.view];
    [secondView release];
    [thirdView release];
    [window makeKeyAndVisible];
    return YES;
}
```

2 Sets views

3 Displays tab bar controller

To access the view controllers, you pull elements out of an array using the appropriate NSArray calls **1**. You then associate views with each view controller, as you've done in the past **2**. Finally, you link the tab bar controller to the window, using a call that was already sitting in your file when you loaded it **3**.

You now have three modal pages (including that first controller's page, which we assume was taken care of in its class files, provided by default by the template). Each does what you want, and navigation among them is easy. But you can still do some work to make your tab bar look better.

MODIFYING THE BUTTONS

Although you have views associated with each button, the buttons say First, Second, and Third, rather than providing any useful clue as to the buttons' purpose. You can change three things on each button to improve its usability: the icon, the title, and the badge. Figure 7.3 shows the goal, which is to fill out some or all of this information for each of your tab buttons.

The *icon* is the image that appears on the tab bar item. This image can be set only when you create a tab bar item. If you were creating the tab bar programmatically, you'd use the initWithTitle:image:tag: method when creating the tab bar item. More likely, you'll go into Xcode and load a small PNG graphic that you want to use.

This process is similar to incorporating the image into your project in chapter 4. You create a transparent PNG that's approximately 30 x 30. If your image is too big, the SDK will resize it, but it's better to start at the right size. After you drag the image into your project, you can access it in the Media Library. We used a Wingdings font to create the simple images that appeared in figure 7.3.

The *title* is the word that appears on the tab bar. You can set that by going to the field in question in the Attributes Inspector and changing the text there.

If you want to later change the title during runtime, it's accessible in Xcode. The catch is that these titles aren't found in the tab bar controller. Instead, they follow the overarching idea of MVC: because a view controller is responsible for an individual view, the controller sets the title of the page. This is done with the view controller's title property, which we've mentioned before and which you'll meet again:

Figure 7.3 You can customize tab bars to make navigation clear and simple.

```
secondController.title = @"Word Count";
```

The *badge* is the little red circle that appears above the title and over the icon on the tab bar. As always, you can change this in the Attributes Inspector, but you'll usually want to do this programmatically. That's because the information in a badge is meant to be dynamic, changing as the view changes and alerting a user to new content during runtime. For example, badges tell you when you have new mail or new voicemail.

Getting to the `badge` property is a two-step process. Start with your view controller. From there, you access `tabBarItem`, which is a property of the controller that links you to its connected tab bar item, and then `badgeValue`, which is a property of the tab bar item. Fortunately, you can do all this as one nested line:

```
secondController.tabBarItem.badgeValue = @"16";
```

The 16, as it happens, is the initial character count of the main text view. If you were building a live program, you could change this count over the course of your program's runtime.

Table 7.1 summarizes the three main elements of the tab bar and how to customize them.

Table 7.1   From your view controllers, it's easy to customize the associated tab bar items.

Property	Summary	Interface Builder	Xcode
badge	Tab bar info	Yes	viewcontroller.tabBarItem.badgeValue
icon	Tab bar picture	Yes	Only at init
title	Tab bar words	Yes	viewcontroller.title

There's one more way to change both the icon and the title of a tab bar item simultaneously: by creating a tab bar item with the initWithTabBarSystemItem:tag: method. Doing so creates a tab bar using one of the constants defined under UITabBarSystemItem, each of which relates to a standard iOS function and correlates a name and a picture with that function.

You'll probably do this in the Attribute Inspector, where you select a specific identifier instead of entering a title and a picture. Because your third tab allows searches, you can initialize it as a UITabBarSystemItemSearch button, which gives it the title of Search and the picture of a magnifying glass, as shown in figure 7.3.

When you have the tab bar set up, you're ready to start using the controller.

7.1.4 *Using your tab bar controller*

The main function of a tab bar is to allow navigation between multiple pages in your application. This is an implicit function of the object, and you needn't do anything more to enable it. The rest of the tab bar controller's functionality goes beyond our basic overview of the topic, but we'll mention it briefly. The two main elements we want to consider are customization and delegation.

TAB BAR CUSTOMIZATION

One of the neat things about tab bars is that users can customize them to contain exactly the tab bar items that interest them. This can be done when the number of tab bar items exceeds the allowed space of five items. You can allow this by setting the customizableViewControllers property to include a list of view controllers that the user can change:

```
tabBarController.customizableViewControllers =
    tabBarController.viewControllers;
```

The UITabBar reference contains all the information you'll need on managing customization.

TAB BAR CONTROLLER DELEGATION

As we noted, you can set a delegate for your tab bar controller to hand off the scant amount of event management that it requires. The delegate object must follow the UITabBarControllerDelegate protocol, which is a fancy way of saying that it will respond to two specific events: one when a view controller is selected and another when the tab bar controller is customized. A protocol reference covers the specifics of this.

Two methods are associated with these protocols: `tabBarController:didEnd-CustomizingViewControllers:changed:` reports the end of tab bar customization, and `tabBarController:didSelectViewController:` reports when the user switches between controllers. The latter is probably more generally useful. For example, you might use it in the word-count example to recalculate the word-count totals whenever a user jumps to the word-count page.

Now that you have a basic example of how to navigate with a tab bar, you're ready for the next advanced controller: the navigation controller.

7.2 The navigation controller

The navigation controller is probably the most-seen user interface item on the iOS device. Whenever you have a stack of view controllers in which you can move up and down through the hierarchy, that's the navigation controller at work. It appears in the Text, Calendar, Photos, and Notes iPhone utilities, to name a few.

Working with the navigation controller is a bit harder than working with the tab bar controller, because you have to manage your hierarchy of views live as the user interacts with your program; but the SDK still keeps it simple.

As with the previous view controllers, we'll look at an overview of the class and then examine how to create, build, and use a navigation controller. Let's get started with an overview of its hierarchy.

7.2.1 The anatomy of a navigation controller

As with the tab bar controller, the navigation controller involves a hierarchy of items. The `UINavigationController` sits atop a stack of `UIViewControllers` that can be pushed or popped as a user moves up and down through it.

Each of these controllers also has an associated `UINavigationItem`, which sits in the `UINavigationBar` when it's active. Each `UINavigationItem` may also contain one or more `UIBarButtonItems`, which allow for additional action items to sit on the navigation bar.

To tie things back together, the `UINavigationBar` is also linked to the `UINavigationController` so that navigation items and view controllers stay in sync over the course of a program's runtime. Whenever a `UIViewController` loads into the `UINavigationController`, its `UINavigationItem` also loads into the `UINavigationBar`.

A minimalistic navigation controller contains just four objects: the `UINavigationController`, the `UINavigationBar`, a stack containing a single `UIViewController`, and a `UINavigationItem` (which is placed into the `UINavigationBar`). Presumably, more view controllers and associated navigation items will be added to the stack as the program runs. This is illustrated in figure 7.4.

Note how similar this diagram of navigation controller parts is to figure 7.1, the diagram of tab bar controller parts. This isn't an accident in the drawing, nor do we expect that it was an accident in Apple's design. The navigation controller works much like the tab bar controller, and you'll see familiar elements, such as the title of the view controller creating the title within the navigator.

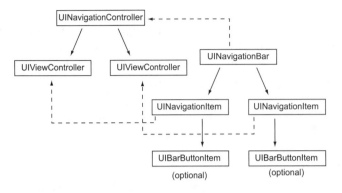

Figure 7.4   A navigation controller contains at least four objects and may be built into a complex web of interconnections.

The biggest difference is that whereas the tab bar controller presents a modal paradigm, entirely organized by the controller, the navigation controller creates a hierarchical paradigm. The navigation controller doesn't have any particular sense of the organization of the entire structure. Instead, a linked list is created, with each navigation item knowing only about the pages on either side of it.

> **A note on table views**
>
> The standard device paradigm is to do hierarchical navigation through table views, each of which contains lists of many different subpages that you can go to. As a result, despite the fact that any `UIViewController` can sit beneath a `UINavigationController`, it's usually a `UITableViewController`. This is exactly the setup you see in the navigation-based template.

7.2.2   Creating a navigation controller

To create a navigation controller, create a new project (in this example, called *navex*) using the Navigation-Based Application template. You can page through the .xib file and the Xcode listing to see what you're given. Let's start with the .xib files, whose content you can see in figure 7.5.

Mainwindow.xib contains a `UINavigationController` in the nib window with a `UINavigationBar` hidden under it. The main display window contains a `UINavigation-Item` and a `RootViewController`. The latter is a subclass of `UIViewController` created through Xcode, just as when you designed your own table controller in chapter 5. Note that this sets up the standard iPhone paradigm of navigation controllers being built atop table controllers. The table view controller's contents are instantiated through a second .xib file, RootViewController.xib, as shown in the table view controller's attributes window.

RootViewController.xib is a boring .xib file because it contains only a table view. Consider it a good example of how pairing .xib files with view controllers can keep your program well organized.

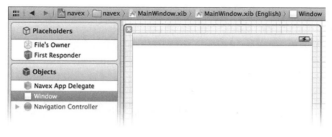

Figure 7.5 The Navigation-Based Application template contains two .xib files: one for the main view (top) and one for what appears inside the controller (bottom).

Finally, if you look at the Xcode files created by the template, you see that the navigation controller is linked to your window in the app delegate file. Among the other default files are the `RootViewController` class files you'd expect to see. Because you're working with a table view controller, you know the `RootViewController` class files will be important when you input the table view's data.

7.2.3 Completing the navigation controller

At this point, you need to do three things to complete the navigation controller: add a title, add navigation links, and (optionally) add action buttons.

ADDING A TITLE

Like the tab bar controller, the navigation controller takes its title from the title of the individual page's view controller. All you have to do is define `title` in your table view controller file:

```
self.title = @"Color List";
```

This turns out to be a critical bit of data, because it's also what the navigation controller uses as a back button when you're deeper in the hierarchy.

ADDING THE LINKS

You could theoretically use whatever method you wanted to link to additional pages via a navigational controller. The default mechanism is to use a table list, and that's the method you'll use in this example.

Design your table view controller as discussed in chapter 5, but this time give each table cell an accessory view of type UITableViewCellAccessoryDisclosureIndicator. That's the standard chevron used to indicate hierarchical navigation.

The following listing includes all the major elements required to define this navigation table in RootViewController.m.

Listing 7.2   A table for a navigator

```
- (void) viewDidLoad {
    self.title = @"Color List";
        colorList = [NSArray arrayWithObjects:
            [NSDictionary dictionaryWithObjectsAndKeys:
                @"Red",@"titleValue",
                [UIColor redColor],@"colorValue",nil],
            [NSDictionary dictionaryWithObjectsAndKeys:
                @"Green",@"titleValue",
                [UIColor greenColor],@"colorValue",nil],
            [NSDictionary dictionaryWithObjectsAndKeys:
                @"Blue",@"titleValue",
                [UIColor blueColor],@"colorValue",nil],
            nil];
        [colorList retain];
}
- (NSInteger)numberOfSectionsInTableView:(UITableView *)tableView {
    return 1;
}
- (NSInteger)tableView:(UITableView *)tableView
    numberOfRowsInSection:(NSInteger)section {

    return [colorList count];
}
- (UITableViewCell *)tableView:(UITableView *)tableView
    cellForRowAtIndexPath:(NSIndexPath *)indexPath {
    static NSString *MyIdentifier = @"MyIdentifier";
    UITableViewCell *cell = [tableView
        dequeueReusableCellWithIdentifier:MyIdentifier];
    if (cell == nil) {
    cell = [[[UITableViewCell alloc] initWithStyle:UITableViewCellStyleDefault
      reuseIdentifier:MyIdentifier] autorelease];
    } cell.textLabel.text = [[colorList objectAtIndex:indexPath.row]
    objectForKey:@"titleValue"];
    cell.textLabel.textColor = [[colorList objectAtIndex:indexPath.row]
    objectForKey:@"colorValue"];
    cell.accessoryType = UITableViewCellAccessoryDisclosureIndicator;
    return cell;
}
```

NOTE   Make sure to declare colorList in the header file.

There's nothing new here, but we've included it to clarify the rest of the discussion of the navigation controller. Figure 7.6 shows what this application looks like on both devices.

Figure 7.6 The navigation controller shown on both the iPad and iPhone

ADDING ACTIONS

If you want, you can move right on to using your navigation controller. Alternatively, you can do some extra work with buttons. In addition to the standard navigation controls, you can add buttons to the navigation bar. You do so through the `leftBar-ButtonItem` and `rightBarButtonItem` properties of the `UINavigationItem`. A left button replaces the back button, and a right button sits in the usually blank right side of the navigation bar.

As we've noted, each view controller is linked to its own navigation item. A view controller can access its navigation item through the `navigationItem` property at any time.

When you set a button, you must set it to be a `UIBarButtonItem` object, which you have to create. You can use four `init` methods, as shown in table 7.2. You'll probably instantiate the buttons in the `viewDidLoad:` method, the same place where you should initialize your array for use with the table view.

Note that all the buttons except the custom-view button come with their own target and action links. These are the simpler target-action mechanisms that we alluded to in the previous chapter. They work exactly like the more complex target-action mechanisms but are built in.

Table 7.2   You can create navigation bar button items using a variety of methods to get precisely what you want.

Method	Summary
`initWithBarButtonSystemItem:target:action:`	Creates a standard button drawn from `UIButtonSystemItem`
`initWithCustomView:`	Creates a special button
`initWithImage:style:target:action:`	Creates a button with a picture
`initWithTitle:style:target:action:`	Creates a button with a word

Here's how you can create a button as part of the page represented by your `UITableViewController`:

```
self.navigationItem.rightBarButtonItem = [[UIBarButtonItem alloc]
    initWithBarButtonSystemItem:UIBarButtonSystemItemAdd
    target:self action:@selector(changeTitle)];
```

As you can guess from the title, this button press enacts an innocuous title change, but it would be easy to redraw your table list or even to integrate that button with the navigation itself, perhaps using it as a home button.

At this point, you have a navigation controller that does precisely nothing (other than showing a gray bar with a title) and perhaps a working button. Unlike with the other controllers you've met so far, you'll need to do some runtime work to get your navigation controller operating.

7.2.4   *Using your navigation controller*

A navigation controller has one core job: to allow a user to move up and down through a hierarchy of pages.

NAVIGATING FORWARD

To allow a user to navigate to a page deeper in your hierarchy, you need to use the navigation controller's interface to push a new view controller on top of the navigation controller's stack, which then causes that new view controller's view to become the visible view in your program. This is shown in the following listing, which continues to expand on RootViewController.m.

Listing 7.3   Activating a navigation controller

```
- (void)tableView:(UITableView *)tableView
    didSelectRowAtIndexPath:(NSIndexPath *)indexPath {
    UIViewController *colorController = [[UIViewController alloc] init];
    colorController.title =
        [[tableView cellForRowAtIndexPath:indexPath].textLabel text];
    colorController.view  = [[UIView alloc] init];
    colorController.view.backgroundColor =
        [[tableView cellForRowAtIndexPath:indexPath].textLabel textColor];
    [self.navigationController
```

```
        pushViewController:colorController animated:YES];
    [colorController release];
}
```

To navigate using tables, you must modify the table view controller's `tableView:did-SelectRowAtIndexPath:` method, which you first met in chapter 5. Clearly, if you're activating your navigation controller by some other method, you'll use different means.

When a user selects an item that should lead them to the next page, you have to create the page they'll go to. You start by creating a view controller. Remember to set `title`, because it will be the title that appears in your new view controller's navigation item. Matching the title to the table cell's text is a common way to set this property.

After you've created a view controller, you need to decide how to create its default view. Here, you create a plain view. Prefer to create your view in Xcode? No problem. Use the `initWithNibName:` method when you create your view controller, visually.

Each view should have different content based on what the user selects. Here, you look at the color of the table cell's text and then set the whole view to that color. More often, you'll probably look up an `NSDictionary` element from the same array you used to fill in your table and use that information to generate a unique page. For example, it'd be easy to pull a nib name out of a dictionary.

After you've set up your new page, you send a message to the navigation controller to switch over to it. Note that you can find a reference to your navigation controller by using the view controller's `navigationController` property, another of many object links available in the view controller. The push command is simple: it adds a new page to the top of the navigation controller's stack and sends your user over to it.

NAVIGATING BACKWARD

After you've loaded a new page onto a navigation controller's stack, it appears with all the peripherals you'd expect, including a titled navigation bar with a titled back button (each based on the `title` property of the appropriate controller). This is all shown in figure 7.7.

You also don't have to worry about coding the backward navigation. Clicking the back button automatically pops the top controller off the stack without any work on your part. Moreover, if you want to play with the back button's title, the tricky part is to define the back button in the root view controller.

Go back to the `RootViewController` in the `view-DidLoad:` method, and add the following snippet to define the back button's title:

Figure 7.7 With a few simple commands, a navigation controller's setup is largely automated. Here you see the titled navigation bar with a titled back button.

```
UIBarButtonItem *backBtn = [[UIBarButtonItem alloc] initWithTitle:@"Back"
    style:UIBarButtonItemStyleDone target:nil action:nil];
self.navigationItem.backBarButtonItem = backBtn;
[backBtn release];
```

OTHER TYPES OF NAVIGATION

Navigation doesn't have to be just forward and backward. You can also do some slightly more complex things, either during setup or at runtime.

At setup, you can create a navigational hierarchy and push a user into it before they take any actions. You can see this in action in various iPhone programs. Mail always returns you to the last mailbox you were at, whereas Contacts always gives you a back button to return to the Groups page.

You can do fancy things during runtime using three navigation controller methods: `popToRootViewControllerAnimated:` (which brings you back to the top of your stack), `popToViewController:animated:` (which returns you to a specific view controller), and `popViewController-Animated:` (which pops the top controller off the stack).

They're powerful, although you have to take care when changing the standard navigation paradigm so you don't confuse your users. But, for example, you could place a `UIBarButtonItem` in your nav bar that returns you to home from deep in your hierarchy. Alternatively, you might pop the top page automatically after a user takes some action on the page that concludes its usefulness.

NAVIGATORS AND DATABASES

So far, you've built all your table view controllers—including the one embedded in this navigation controller—using arrays. This is a perfectly acceptable technique for a small, static table. But if you want a bigger or a more dynamic table, you'll probably want to use a database as your data backend. We'll present a complete example of how to do so in chapter 9, when we cover the SQLite database package.

OTHER METHODS AND PROPERTIES

There's little else to be done with the navigation controller, although you can find a few other properties in the class reference. You can set those properties to modify the look of individual `UIBarButtonItems` and to set your nav bar to be hidden.

We've now covered the two most important advanced view controllers. But before we finish our discussion of the topic, let's take a brief look at the flipside controller, which exists only as a template, not as a class in the UIKit framework. The template instead creates a subclass of `ViewController` in your program.

7.3   *Using the flipside controller*

To create a flipside controller on iPhone, choose the Utility Application template when you start a new project. Please note that this template is only available to the iPhone platform. It creates a small hierarchy of objects, as shown in figure 7.8.

The flipside controller contains three view controllers and two views. Each of the view controllers is a subclass of `UIViewController`, whereas the views are each a subclass of `UIView`.

The main view controller is called the Root-ViewController. It's loaded through MainWin-dow.xib. Much of the template's work is done, as you'd expect, through its class files. The Root-ViewController.m file loads the MainViewController (using the initWithNibName: method to load its unique nib file) and then creates a special toggleView method for when the info button at the bottom of the page is pushed. When this happens, the FlipsideView-Controller also loads. The following listing shows this standard method, which you shouldn't have to modify.

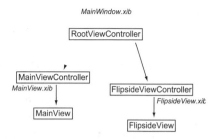

Figure 7.8 Several objects are created in a flipside controller.

Listing 7.4 The flipside toggler

```
- (IBAction)toggleView {
    if (flipsideViewController == nil) {
        [self loadFlipsideViewController];
    }
    UIView *mainView = mainViewController.view;
    UIView *flipsideView = flipsideViewController.view;
    [UIView beginAnimations:nil context:NULL];
    [UIView setAnimationDuration:1];
    [UIView setAnimationTransition:([mainView superview] ?
        UIViewAnimationTransitionFlipFromRight :
        UIViewAnimationTransitionFlipFromLeft) forView:self.view
            cache:YES];
    if ([mainView superview] != nil) {
        [flipsideViewController viewWillAppear:YES];
        [mainViewController viewWillDisappear:YES];
        [mainView removeFromSuperview];
        [infoButton removeFromSuperview];
        [self.view addSubview:flipsideView];
        [self.view insertSubview:flipsideNavigationBar
            aboveSubview:flipsideView];
        [mainViewController viewDidDisappear:YES];
        [flipsideViewController viewDidAppear:YES];
    } else {
        [mainViewController viewWillAppear:YES];
        [flipsideViewController viewWillDisappear:YES];
        [flipsideView removeFromSuperview];
        [flipsideNavigationBar removeFromSuperview];
        [self.view addSubview:mainView];
        [self.view insertSubview:infoButton
            aboveSubview:mainViewController.view];
        [flipsideViewController viewDidDisappear:YES];
        [mainViewController viewDidAppear:YES];
    }
    [UIView commitAnimations];
}
```

Because you shouldn't need to modify it, we won't cover all this code; but if you read through it, you'll find that it includes some nice nuances, including the ability to work with `UIView`'s simple animation and some different ways to call `insertSubview:`. This template provides a great example of how to connect multiple Xcode class files and multiple nib files, and reading it can serve as a great tutorial for more advanced work you'll do yourself.

For example, look at the MainWindow.xib file. Note that connections are made to two different files, as shown in figure 7.9. The app-delegate file contains a link to the root-view controller object, whereas the root-view controller file contains links to the info button object and its action. This shows the sort of organization you'll want to consider for your own projects.

Figure 7.9   Interface objects can be connected to a variety of different files.

Given that, how do you use the flipside controller? All you need to do is lay out objects in the two .xib files and/or make changes to their accompanying class files. Then, you can build controller actions, events, and other activities into the two controller files.

For example, you can make your main view red; then, you can go into the FlipsideViewController.m file and change the default background color to `green-Color` (instead of its current `flipsideColor`) to create a simple red and green flashcard, which can be used to express your interest in a conference topic. We'll also show you how to use a flipside controller to create local preferences on the back side of your program in chapter 8, section 8.2.1. If you ever need a two-sided application, the flipside controller is a great place to get started.

Now that we've explored the template view controllers that work on iPhone, we'll discuss the iPad-specific view controllers.

7.4   *The split view controller*

The split view controller is an iPad-specific view controller that allows you to separate content into different panes. Although you can implement it a few ways, by far the most common is to have a `UITableView` on the left and a `UIView` on the right. Because the split view is made of two views that you have learned about in previous chapters, we'll focus on the example instead of the individual views.

One of the major places you'll see this interface component in use is in the iPad's Mail application. The left pane of the split view controller displays all of your mail messages, whereas the right displays the content of the selected message.

7.4.1 Creating a split view controller

To create a project based on `SplitViewController`, start by selecting the Split View-Based Application template from Apple's project templates, as shown in figure 7.10. Titled the project *SplitViewx*. This will provide you with a complete basic application, including a simple data set.

You'll walk through the code and modify it to display a list of website bookmarks. When the user taps the bookmark in the left pane, it will load the website in the right one. As you modify the code, we'll explain in detail how the `SplitViewController` is constructed. Figure 7.11 shows what the application will look like.

When you first create a split view–based application, a number of files are added to your project automatically. Open MainWindow.xib, and inspect the contents. Figure 7.12 shows the various view elements you see when you click the `SplitView-Controller`.

As you can see, the `SplitViewController` is made up of two main views. The navigation bar in the left view should hint that its view is a navigation controller. The object viewer in the bottom corner confirms this. Notice that the view hierarchy is exactly the same as that for the navigation controller in section 7.2.

The right view is loaded from another nib called `DetailView`. Double-clicking the blue text labeled `DetailView` opens it and allows you to modify it as you would any other view. You'll see that later in the section when you add a web view to the example application.

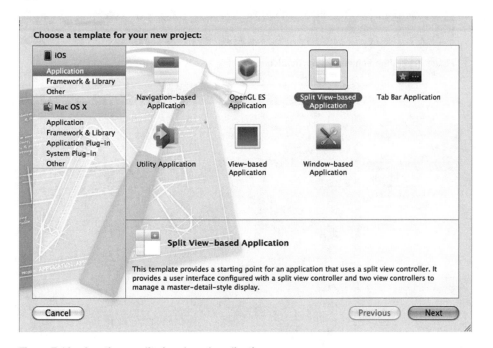

Figure 7.10 Creating a split view–based application

Figure 7.11   The bookmarks application employing a split view

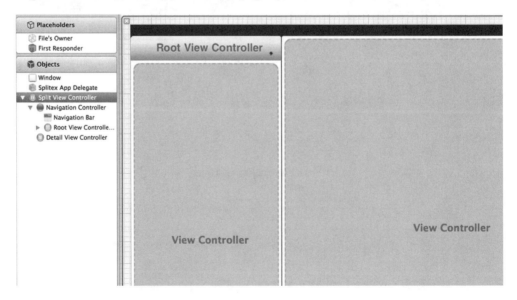

Figure 7.12   `SplitViewController` view elements

7.4.2 Building the split view controller

Now that you've seen how the views are organized, it's time to review the code necessary for them to function. As mentioned earlier, the project will contain a sample data set that you'll modify to fit the application.

The first steps are exactly the same as in section 7.2, when you created the navigation controller. You need to create an array of data, display it in the table view, and respond to actions when a row has been selected.

DECLARING THE DATA ARRAY

Open RootViewController.h, and modify the code to look like the following listing.

> **Listing 7.5 Declaring the dataset array for the SplitViewController**

```
@class DetailViewController;

@interface RootViewController : UITableViewController {
    DetailViewController *detailViewController;

    NSArray *bookmarks;                             ❶ Declares array
}                                                     of bookmarks

@property (nonatomic, retain) IBOutlet             ❷ Creates property
    DetailViewController *detailViewController;       for class
@property (nonatomic, retain) NSArray *bookmarks;

@end
```

You add ❶ and ❷ to declare the array of bookmarks to be displayed in the table. For this example, the user can't modify the bookmarks, so the array is declared as an NSArray rather than an NSMutableArray.

Now that you have your declaration, let's synthesize the property and populate the array with various bookmarks of your choice. Open RootViewController.m, and add the code in this listing.

> **Listing 7.6 Populating the dataset for the SplitViewController**

```
@synthesize bookmarks;

- (void)viewDidLoad {
    [super viewDidLoad];
    self.clearsSelectionOnViewWillAppear = NO;
    self.contentSizeForViewInPopover = CGSizeMake(320.0, 600.0);

    NSArray *_bookmarks = [[NSArray alloc]          ❶ Initializes
       initWithObjects:@"http://manning.com",          array with
      @"http://apple.com",                             URLs
      @"http://twitter.com",
      @"http://google.com",nil];

    self.bookmarks = _bookmarks;
    [_bookmarks release];
}
```

You've seen the first line earlier in the book: it synthesizes the `bookmarks` property, allowing getter and setter methods to be automatically created for it. You initialize the `bookmarks` array with strings ❶, which are the URLs to be loaded when a given cell is selected. This declaration is similar to the first method implemented in listing 7.2.

Now that your data has been initialized, you need to implement the delegate methods of the `UITableViewController` in the left pane of your `SplitView`.

TABLEVIEW DELEGATE METHODS

Because the left pane is a `UITableViewController`, you'll implement the same methods to interact with it that you did in listing 7.2. The following listing details the methods for displaying your array of bookmarks instead of the default data.

Listing 7.7   `UITableViewDelegate` methods for displaying bookmark data

```
- (NSInteger)numberOfSectionsInTableView:(UITableView *)aTableView {
    return 1;                                              Sets number of
}                                                       ❶ table sections

- (NSInteger)tableView:(UITableView *)aTableView
       numberOfRowsInSection:(NSInteger)section {
    return [bookmarks count];                              Sets number
}                                                          of rows equal
                                                           to number of
- (UITableViewCell *)tableView:(UITableView *)tableView  ❷ bookmarks
    cellForRowAtIndexPath:(NSIndexPath *)indexPath {

    static NSString *CellIdentifier = @"CellIdentifier";

    UITableViewCell *cell = [tableView
       dequeueReusableCellWithIdentifier:CellIdentifier];
    if (cell == nil) {
        cell = [[[UITableViewCell alloc]
           initWithStyle:UITableViewCellStyleDefault
           reuseIdentifier:CellIdentifier] autorelease];   Sets text ❸
        cell.accessoryType = UITableViewCellAccessoryNone;  of cell to
    }                                                       bookmark

    cell.textLabel.text = [self.bookmarks objectAtIndex:indexPath.row];
    return cell;
}
```

You first set the number of sections for the `UITableView` to 1 because your dataset doesn't have any groupings ❶. Next, you return the number of bookmarks in the array ❷. As you've seen before, this denotes the number of cells to be displayed in the `UITableView`. Finally, you set the text of the cell to the URL string of the bookmark ❸. At this point, the application has enough code to display the bookmarks; running it in the simulator looks like figure 7.13.

When you select a row in the table, the label updates with text that says something like "Row *X*", where *X* is the row number selected.

Next, we'll show you how to modify this view to do something a little more interesting. You'll add a `UIWebView` to the `DetailView` and display the page of the selected URL inside it.

Figure 7.13 A first look at your bookmark application as shown on an iPad in landscape orientation

MODIFYING THE DETAILVIEW

Start by opening DetailViewController.h and adding an IBOutlet for a UIWebView. The code is shown here.

Listing 7.8 Adding an IBOutlet for your UIWebView

```
@interface DetailViewController : UIViewController
    <UIPopoverControllerDelegate, UISplitViewControllerDelegate> {

    UIPopoverController *popoverController;
    UIToolbar *toolbar;

    id detailItem;
    UILabel *detailDescriptionLabel;

    UIWebView *webView;
}

@property (nonatomic, retain) IBOutlet UIToolbar *toolbar;

@property (nonatomic, retain) id detailItem;
@property (nonatomic, retain) IBOutlet UILabel *detailDescriptionLabel;

@property (nonatomic, retain) IBOutlet UIWebView *webView;

@end
```

At this point, the code should look pretty familiar. You declare an IBOutlet for a UIWebView. This gives you the ability to control the UIWebView from within your class. Now that the outlet has been added, be sure to synthesize it in the .m file.

Open DetailView.xib, and drag a UIWebView onto the main view. Move the label out of the way if necessary. Make sure you connect your webView outlet from the file's Owner object to the UIWebView you place on the view. (If you don't recall how to do this, refer to section 3.4.2.)

Now that all of your views have been created, it's time to implement the code that actually does something.

7.4.3 *Using your split view controller*

As you did in section 7.2.4, you'll implement the didSelectRowAtIndexPath delegate method of the UITableView to respond to the user tapping on a cell. In this example, the user taps on the cell to load the selected bookmark's website in the UIWebView.

Open RootViewController.m, and modify the code as follows:

```
- (void)tableView:(UITableView *)aTableView
  didSelectRowAtIndexPath:(NSIndexPath *)indexPath {

    detailViewController.detailItem = [bookmarks
        objectAtIndex:indexPath.row];
}
```

You don't modify the code much from the sample code given to you by the project template. Note that you set the detailItem of the detailViewController to your selected URL string. The data type of detailItem is id; this is a generic data type that can be set to any object, making the detailViewController class very dynamic.

Normally, in the didSelectRowAtIndexPath method, you'd initialize a new view controller, set its data, and push it onto the view stack. This isn't the case when you're dealing with a split view, because the detailViewController has already been initialized for you—you just want to modify its data.

The last step in displaying the web page is to tell the UIWebView to reload with the selected URL when the detailItem property is set. As mentioned earlier, when the detailItem property was synthesized, the getter and setter methods were automatically created. You can override either one of these methods to modify its functionality. This is what has been done in DetailViewController.m, because you want to update the interface when the detailItem property is modified. Although you won't modify the code in this method, you do need to modify the code in a method called from it. Open DetailViewController.m, and update the configureView method to contain the following code:

```
- (void)configureView {
    detailDescriptionLabel.text = [detailItem description];
    NSURLRequest *request = [NSURLRequest
        requestWithURL: [NSURL URLWithString:[detailItem description]]];
    [self.webView loadRequest:request];
}
```

This code should look very familiar. It's almost identical to the code you wrote in section 3.4.2 when loading the Apple stock into the web view. This code creates an NSURL-Request with the selected URL and loads it into the UIWebView.

When you run this code in the simulator, tapping on a row loads the selected URL in the web view. But one gotcha remains: the interface doesn't look right when you switch from vertical to horizontal mode. To rotate the simulator, press Cmd-left arrow or Cmd-right arrow.

7.4.4 Adjusting the interface for vertical and landscape modes

Apple is very clear that all iPad-specific apps should work correctly in both portrait and landscape modes. This is in an effort to enforce the idea that there is no wrong way to hold the device.

Currently, your web view looks fine when the device is vertical, but it's cut off when the device is rotated to be horizontal. To resolve this issue, you must implement the shouldAutorotateToInterfaceOrientation method of your DetailViewController.

You need to adjust the frame of all the view elements for a given device orientation. Doing so lets you position the view items correctly no matter how the user is holding the device. Update DetailViewController.m to include the following code.

Listing 7.9   Responding to device rotation

```
- (BOOL)shouldAutorotateToInterfaceOrientation:
   (UIInterfaceOrientation)interfaceOrientation {

    if(interfaceOrientation == UIInterfaceOrientationLandscapeLeft ||      ◄─┐  Device in
       interfaceOrientation == UIInterfaceOrientationLandscapeRight) {     ◄─┤  landscape
        self.webView.frame = CGRectMake(                                      │  mode? ❶
self.webView.frame.origin.x,                              ❷ Updates frame
        slef.webView.frame.origin.y,                         of web view
        662,                                                 for landscape
            662);                                        ◄─┘ mode
    } else {
        self.webView.frame = CGRectMake(
self.webView.frame.origin.x,                                 ❸ Updates frame
        self.webView.frame.origin.y,                            of web view
        728,                                                    for portrait
        911);                                            ◄─┘     mode
    }
    return YES;
}
```

You first determine whether the device is being held in landscape mode ❶. If so, you adjust the frame accordingly ❷. Note that the numbers used to update the frame are picked based on personal preference—you should adjust the frame to what you feel looks correct for the given orientation. Then, you update the frame of the WebView to look correct in portrait mode ❸.

So far, you've explored the view controllers that you might use as the building blocks of your own views. Tab bars, navigators, flipsides, and split views are ultimately tools that you'll use to construct other sorts of programs. But a couple types of view controllers exist to accomplish specific tasks: the modal view controller and the pop-over view controller.

7.5   *Popover and modal view controllers*

Technically, a modal view refers to a temporary view that's placed on top of all the elements of an existing view and then later dismissed. A modal view controller is a view controller that manages such a modal view. The iPhone camera is an example of a view controller that has been presented modally.

The popover view is a lightweight view intended to display data in a specific area. It's available to the iPad. In contrast to a modal view, the popover view doesn't consume the entire screen; rather, it's displayed as a context menu. In the previous example, the split view controller project template gave you a pop-over view for free when the device was in portrait mode.

7.5.1   *Creating a popover view controller*

A popover view controller is initialized with the view controller containing the view to be displayed inside it. Figure 7.14 shows what this looks like in the previous example when the device is held in portrait mode.

As you can see, it contains the data that is normally displayed in the table view on the left side of the split view. This list is displayed when the user presses the Root List button.

Let's look at the code for displaying a popover view when a button is pressed, shown in the following listing. This code is taken from Apple's example of working with popover view controllers.

Figure 7.14   A popover view

Listing 7.10   Displaying a popover view when a button is pressed

```
- (IBAction) buttonPressed:(id) sender {
    MyCustomViewController* content = [[MyCustomViewController alloc]
        init];
    UIPopoverController* aPopover = [[UIPopoverController alloc]
        initWithContentViewController:content];
    aPopover.delegate = self;
    [content release];

    self.popoverController = aPopover;
    [aPopover release];

    [self.popoverController presentPopoverFromBarButtonItem:sender
        permittedArrowDirections:UIPopoverArrowDirectionAny animated:YES];
}
```

The pattern that this code follows should be fairly familiar to you. It's similar to the code that handles a touch on a `UITableView` row. You first initialize the new view controller to display in; this controller is then used to initialize the popover. You basically tell the popover to display the view contents of the view controller it was initialized with.

Finally, you display the popover view near the button the user tapped. Fortunately, UIKit automatically handles the placing of the popover view for you. In addition, it allows you to configure the direction the arrow is pointing in, giving your popover some sort of context.

7.5.2 Creating a modal view controller

Practically, the modal views available in iOS are all "helper" programs. They let you start up a complex graphical interface that's been preprogrammed by Apple while only managing the responses. You get the advantage of lots of programming (and a standardized interface), and you don't have to do much yourself.

Whenever you want to display a modal view, you use the `UIViewController`'s `presentModalViewController:animated:` method to start it up:

```
[self presentModalViewController:myPicker animated:YES];
```

Later, you dismiss it using another `UIViewController` method:

```
[self dismissModalViewControllerAnimated::YES];
```

You can design your own modal view controllers for when you want to have users make a choice before you return them to the regular program. More commonly, you'll use picker controllers that are intended to be run as modal view controllers.

In chapter 9, you'll meet the Address Book UI people picker (as well as some related controllers that run inside a navigator), and in chapter 11 you'll meet the image picker.

7.6 Combining view controllers in universal applications

You learned how to create view controllers inside your application or start an application by using the template under iOS projects. How do you combine these view controllers inside your application for both the iPhone and iPad? In this section, we will talk about how to design universal applications for both the iPhone and iPad and how to combine the view controllers inside the project.

7.6.1 Design universal applications for the iPhone and iPad

There are multiple ways to build a universal application running on both the iPhone and iPad. But think about the user experience before you start to work on the universal application for both the iPhone and iPad. Generally speaking, the application running on the iPhone is limited to the screen size. That's why you commonly see the combination of table view controller and navigation controller on the iPhone. This pattern works great on the iPhone because the application's content is well organized under the menu selection user interface, and the information is easy to spot on the go with only one-thumb navigation on the screen.

The split view controller template is created for the iPad only, simply because there is more space available on the iPad for content display and user interactions. The user would expect much more on an iPad application, not only because the content needs to be richer compared to the iPhone, but also because the navigation on the iPad is not limited to one thumb; multitouch gestures are commonly used.

The iPhone, as we mentioned earlier, is limited to 320 x 480 size for the full-screen display. Therefore, you often see navigation controllers with a table view controller as a menu-selection user interface.

When you design an application, it's recommended that you study the difference in the users' habits between the iPhone and iPad. Next, let's talk about common cases for reusing view controllers in a universal application.

7.6.2   *Combining view controllers*

On the iPhone, you see a navigation controller as a parent view controller. A table view is the child view controller. Based on the user's selection on the table view, you can present a modal view controller or other view controller for more detailed information. A good example would be the Messages application on the iPhone.

On the iPad, you often see the split view controller template with the popover controller as a menu selection user interface. For example, the Notes application on the iPad is designed based on the split view controller template.

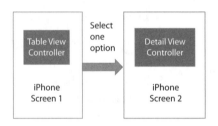

Figure 7.15   The prototype for an iPhone application with a table view controller and a detail view controller

Let's look at an example; you are about to design an application running on iPhone with a list of selections on table view. When you select one option, a detailed view controller will appear, as shown in figure 7.15.

On iPad, the split view controller will be used at the root. Under landscape mode, the menu selection is on the left in the table view and the detailed view controller is on the right side, as shown in figure 7.16.

Under portrait mode, the detailed view controller is on the screen. The menu selection becomes a button on the top screen. When you tap the button, the menu selection presents as a popover controller.

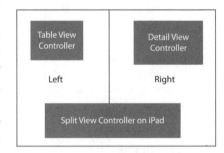

Figure 7.16   The prototype for an iPad with a split view controller contains a table view on the left and a detail view on the right.

You can separate the view controllers between the iPhone and iPad. But that's a lot of duplicate code inside this project. In this case, how do you reuse the view controllers in the iPhone on the iPad?

The common thing to do is to find the same view controllers in both projects. As shown in the prototype drawings, the table view for the menu selection and the detail view controller are in both the iPhone and iPad design.

Therefore, you can use the same detail view controller and table view controller as your split view controller's detail view controller and master view controller, respectively.

Sometimes, drawing the prototype on a sketchbook is beneficial. This process helps developers to analyze the structure of the program.

There is more than one way to design a universal application. In this section, we first looked at the user interface design differences on the iPhone and iPad; then we talked about how to combine the view controllers in the universal application. I hope you find the design pattern useful in your own practice.

7.7   *Summary*

At this point, we've finished with what we consider the basic introduction to the SDK. Because this is an introductory SDK book, our main goal has been to show you all the fundamentals before we set you loose in the wilds of iPhone and iPad programming, so you have the building blocks you need when you begin programming on your own.

Let's briefly review:

- The SDK is built on top of Objective-C and is supported by a large set of frameworks provided by iOS. (See chapters 1 and 2.)
- Programming can be done in either programmatically or visually, supporting two powerful ways to create objects. (See chapters 3 and 4.)
- Basic view controllers take the controller role of the MVC model and allow you to administer your views in a rational way. (See chapter 5.)
- Events provide low-level methods for seeing what a user is doing, whereas actions provide more sophisticated connections to buttons, sliders, text fields, and other tools. (See chapter 6.)
- Advanced view controllers provide you with a variety of ways to navigate among pages. (See chapter 7.)

Although we've completed our introduction to the iOS SDK, we're not finished yet. Our next stop is an in-depth look at the many ways to input data into an application.

Data: actions, preferences, and files

This chapter covers

- Accepting user input through controls
- Allowing user choice through preferences
- Accessing and creating files

In the preceding chapters, we offered a tutorial on the most important features of the SDK: we outlined Objective-C and iOS and explained Xcode, we examined view controllers of all types, and we looked at the standard event and action models for the iPhone and iPad. In the process, we tried to provide the strong foundation that you need to do any type of iOS programming. Armed with that knowledge, and with the extensive documentation available online (or as part of Xcode), you should be able to start programming right away.

But we also want to offer you some additional information about many of the SDK's best features. In the coming chapters, we'll touch on some of the major categories of SDK tools and show you how to use them.

We'll expand on the sample programs a bit. Having completed the introduction to the SDK, we can take advantage of your knowledge of Objective-C to incorporate at least one in-depth example in each upcoming chapter; our intent is to show how different objects can work together to create a more complex Objective-C project. We can't give you ready-to-submit App Store programs because of the breadth of what we're covering here, but expect to see some code examples that are more than a page long and that typically include some off-topic elements.

This chapter will kick off our look at the SDK toolkit with a discussion of data, which will describe many of the ways you can deal with information generally (and text specifically). We've broken this into a couple of broad categories. First, we'll look at the ways users can input data into your program, focusing on actions and preferences. Second, we'll examine ways that you can store and retrieve internal data using files.

8.1   *Accepting user actions*

The simplest way to accept new data from a user is through `UIControls`, a topic that we covered in some depth in the latter half of chapter 6 and that we're looking at again here for the sake of completeness. Table 8.1 includes some notes on the controls that you can use to accept user input.

Table 8.1   Various controls allow you to accept user input, most using simple interfaces.

Control	Summary
`UIButton`	Offers simple functionality when the user clicks a button. See section 6.5 for an example.
`UIPageControl`	A pure navigation object that allows users to move between multiple pages using a trio of dots.
`UIPickerView`	Not a `UIControl` object, but allows the user to select from a number of items in a "slot machine" selection. It includes the subclass `UIDatePicker`.
`UISearchBar`	Not a `UIControl` object, but offers similar functionality to a `UITextField`. It provides an interface that includes a single-line text input, a search button, a cancel button, and a bookmark button. See section 9.2.3 for an example.
`UISegmentedControl`	A horizontal bar containing several buttons. See section 18.1.3 for an example.
`UISlider`	A slider that allows users to input from a range of approximate values. See section 6.6.2 for an example.
`UISwitch`	An on-off button of the sort used in preferences. See section 8.2.1 for an example.
`UITextField`	A single-line text input and probably the most common control for true user input. It requires some work to make the keyboard relinquish control. See section 6.6.1 for a complete discussion and an example.

Table 8.1 Various controls allow you to accept user input, most using simple interfaces. *(continued)*

Control	Summary
UITextView	Not a `UIControl` object, but does allow the user to enter longer bits of text. As with a text field, you must have it `resignFirstResponder` status to return control to the program when the user has finished typing. As shown in the iPhone Notes utility, this is typically done with a separate Done button at the top of the interface, because the Return key is used to input returns. See section 8.3.4 for an example.
UIToolBar	Not a `UIControl` object. Instead, it's a bar meant to hold a collection of `UIBarButtonItems`, each of which can be clicked to initiate an action. The bar is easy to configure and change. See section 11.4.2 for an example.

Clearly, these controls serve a variety of uses. Many exist for pure user interface purposes, which we covered pretty extensively in chapter 6. What's of more interest here are the text-input controls (UISearchBar, UITextField, and UITextView) that you're likely to use in conjunction with files and databases. We'll look particularly at UISearchBar and UITextView, the two text inputs that we hadn't previously given much attention to, over the course of this chapter.

Not included in this table are the integrated controller pickers that allow users to input data and make choices using complex prebuilt systems. We'll discuss these pickers in later chapters.

Controls are central to any real-life program, so you'll see them throughout the upcoming chapters. Because you'll be seeing lots of examples of their use, we can now move on to the next method of user data input: preferences.

8.2   *Maintaining user preferences*

Preferences are the way an iPhone or iPad program maintains user choices, particularly from one session to another. They're a way to not only accept user input but also save it. You can use your own programmatic interface to maintain these preferences, or you can use the Settings interface provided in the iOS SDK.

If your program includes preferences that may change frequently, or if it would be disruptive for a user to leave your program to set a preference, you can create a preferences page within your program. This type of program-centric preferences page is seen in the Stocks and Maps programs, each of which has settings that can be changed on the backside of the main utility.

Alternatively, if your program has preferences that don't change that much, particularly if the defaults are usually okay, you should instead set them using the system's settings. Typically, you use this option when your configuration controls are pretty standard, because this method is limited to a specific set of possible interactions. This type of device-centric setting can be seen in the iPod, Mail, Phone, Photos, and Safari applications, all of which have their settings available under the Settings icon on the device screen.

Of the two, the latter is the Apple-preferred way of doing things, but we'll touch on both, starting with creating your own preferences page. You should feel free to use either method, based on the needs of your program; but you should most definitely *not* mix the two styles of preferences, because that's likely to be confusing for your users.

8.2.1 Creating your own preferences

You'll typically use this method of creating preferences when your application has more than basic data to store. For example, if one of your application settings is a user photo, you can't store this type of information in the built-in system settings. You need a custom interface to allow the user to pick a photo from their library.

Whenever you're writing apps, you should always do your best to match the look, feel, and methodology of Apple's existing programs. Looking through built-in programs can offer lessons about when and how to use personal preferences on your own. Here's what the personal preferences of those built-in programs can tell you:

- They're used infrequently.
- When they do appear, they're used in conjunction with a program that has only a single page of content (like Stocks) or one that has multiple identical pages of content (like Weather).
- They appear on the backside of a flipside controller.
- The preferences appear in a special list view that includes cells.

You can easily accommodate these standards when building your own programs. You'll do so over the next few examples, with the goal being to create the simple preferences table shown in figure 8.1.

DRAWING THE PREFERENCES PAGE

If you're going to create a program that has built-in preferences, you should do so using the Utility Application template. As you've previously seen, this will give you access to a flipside controller, which will allow you to create your preferences on the backside of your application.

To create the special cartouched list used by preferences, you must create a table view controller with the special `UITableViewGrouped` style. You can do this by choosing the Grouped style for your table view in the Attributes Inspector or by using the `init-WithStyle:` method in Xcode. The following code shows the latter method by creating the `UITableViewController` subclass (here called `PreferencesController`) inside the flipside controller's `viewDidLoad` method:

```
- (void)viewDidLoad {
    PreferencesController *myTableView = [[PreferencesController alloc]
        initWithStyle:UITableViewStyleGrouped];
    [self.view addSubview:myTableView.view];
}
```

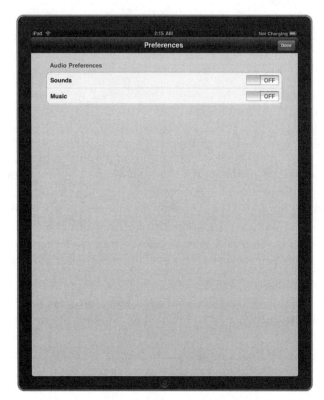

Figure 8.1   This preferences page was built from scratch on the backside of a flipside controller.

After you've done this, you can fill in your `PreferencesController`'s table view using the methods described in chapter 5. You'll probably use the cells' `accessoryView` property, because you'll want to add switches and other objects to the preference listing. The following listing shows the most important methods required to create a simple preferences page with two switches.

Listing 8.1   Following the table view methods to fill out your preferences table

```
- (id)initWithStyle:(UITableViewStyle)style {
    if (self = [super initWithStyle:style]) {
        settingsList = [NSArray arrayWithObjects:
            [NSMutableDictionary dictionaryWithObjectsAndKeys:
                @"Sounds",@"titleValue",
                @"switch",@"accessoryValue",
                [NSNumber numberWithBool:YES],
                    @"prefValue",
                @"setSounds:",@"targetValue",nil],
            [NSMutableDictionary dictionaryWithObjectsAndKeys:
                @"Music",@"titleValue",
                @"switch",@"accessoryValue",
                [NSNumber numberWithBool:YES],@"prefValue",
                @"setMusic:",@"targetValue",nil],nil];
        [settingsList retain];
        switchList = [NSMutableArray arrayWithCapacity:settingsList.count];
```

```
        for (int i = 0 ;
            i < [settingsList count] ;
            i++)    {
            if ([[[settingsList objectAtIndex:i]
                objectForKey:@"accessoryValue"] compare:@"switch"] ==
                    NSOrderedSame) {
                UISwitch *mySwitch = [[[UISwitch alloc]
                    initWithFrame:CGRectZero] autorelease];
                mySwitch.on = [[[settingsList objectAtIndex:i]
                    objectForKey:@"prefValue"] boolValue];
                [mySwitch addTarget:self
                    action:NSSelectorFromString([[settingsList
                        objectAtIndex:i] objectForKey:@"targetValue"])
                            forControlEvents:UIControlEventValueChanged];

                [switchList insertObject:mySwitch atIndex:i];
            } else {
                [switchList insertObject:@"" atIndex:i];
            }
        }
        [switchList retain];
        CGPoint tableCenter = self.view.center;
        self.view.center = CGPointMake(tableCenter.x,tableCenter.y+22);
    }
    return self;
}
- (NSInteger)numberOfSectionsInTableView:
    (UITableView *)tableView {
    return 1;
}
- (NSString *)tableView:(UITableView *)tableView
    titleForHeaderInSection:(NSInteger)section {
    return @"Audio Preferences";
}

- (NSInteger)tableView:(UITableView *)tableView
    numberOfRowsInSection:(NSInteger)section {
    return settingsList.count;
}
- (UITableViewCell *)tableView:(UITableView *)tableView
    cellForRowAtIndexPath:(NSIndexPath *)indexPath {
    static NSString *MyIdentifier = @"MyIdentifier";
    UITableViewCell *cell = [tableView
        dequeueReusableCellWithIdentifier:MyIdentifier];
    if (cell == nil) {
        cell = [[[UITableViewCell alloc]
            initWithStyle:UITableViewCellStyleDefault
            reuseIdentifier:MyIdentifier] autorelease];
    }
    cell.textLabel.text = [[settingsList objectAtIndex:indexPath.row]
        objectForKey:@"titleValue"];
    if ([switchList objectAtIndex:indexPath.row]) {
        cell.accessoryView =
            [switchList objectAtIndex:indexPath.row];
    }
    return cell;
}
```

1 Prepares switch array

2 Moves table down

3 Creates cells

4 Puts switch in accessory view

This example generally follows the table view methodology that you learned in chapter 5. You use an array to set up your table view. In addition to a title, these (mutable) dictionaries include additional info about the switch that goes into the table view, including what it should be set to and what action it should call. This example shows one nuance we mentioned before: only NSObjects can be placed in an NSDictionary, so you have to encode a Boolean value in order to use it.

The initWithStyle: method must do two other things. First, it must create a mutable array to hold all your switches for later access. You do all the creation ❶ based on settingsList (or on whatever other means you used to pull in preferences data), because if you wait until you get to the table view methods, you can't guarantee the order in which they'll be created. If you didn't fill the switch list here, you could get an out-of-bounds error—if, for example, the switch in row 1 was created before the switch in row 0. Note also that these switches are created with no particular location on the screen, because you'll place them later. Second, the method must move your table down a bit to account for the navigation bar at the top of the flipside page ❷.

The methods that define the section count, the section head, and the row count are all pretty standard. It's the method that defines the contents of the rows ❸ that's of interest, primarily because it contains code that takes advantage of the accessoryView property that we touched on in chapter 5. In this method, you read back the appropriate switch from your array and input it ❹.

There's no real functionality in this preferences page—that ultimately will depend on the needs of your program. But this skeleton should give you everything you need to get started. Afterward, you'll need to build your methods (here, setMusic: and setSounds:), which should access the switchList array, and then do the appropriate thing for your program when the switches are toggled.

Switches are the most common element of a preferences page. The other common feature that you should consider programming is the *select list*. That's usually done by creating a subpage with a table view all its own. It should be set in UITableView-Grouped style, like this table. You'll probably allow users to checkmark one or more elements in the list.

SAVING USER PREFERENCES

We're leaving one element out of this discussion: what to do with your users' preferences after they've set them. It's possible that you'll want to save user preferences only for the length of a single session, but it's our experience that it can be confusing and even annoying to users. More commonly, you should save preferences from one session to another. We offer three different ways to do so:

- *Save the preferences in a file*—Section 8.3 talks about file access. You can either save the preferences in plain text or else use a more regulated format like XML, which is covered in chapter 14.
- *Save the preferences in a database*—Sections 9.1 and 9.3 cover this.
- *Save the preferences using* NSUserDefaults—This option is discussed next.

NSUserDefaults is a storage mechanism that's specific to user preferences, so we'll cover it here.

Generally, NSUserDefaults is a persistent shared object that you can use to remember a user's preferences from one session to another. It's sort of like a preferences associative array. It has three major methods, listed in table 8.2.

Table 8.2 Notable methods for NSUserDefaults

Method	Summary
standardUserDefaults:	Class method that creates a shared defaults object.
objectForKey:	Instance method that returns an object for the key; numerous variants return specific types of objects such as strings, Booleans, and the like.
setObjectForKey:	Instance method that sets a key to the object; numerous variants set specific types of objects such as strings, Booleans, and so on.

It would be simple enough to modify the previous preferences example to use NSUserDefaults. First, you'd change the init method to create a shared defaults object and then read from it when creating the settingListing array, as shown in the following listing.

Listing 8.2 Preferences setup with NSUserDefaults

```
NSUserDefaults *myDefaults = [NSUserDefaults standardUserDefaults];
settingsList = [NSArray arrayWithObjects:
    [NSMutableDictionary dictionaryWithObjectsAndKeys:
        @"Sounds",@"titleValue",
        @"switch",@"accessoryValue",
        [NSNumber numberWithBool:[myDefaults          Extracts/sets
                                                       sound value
    boolForKey:@"soundsValue"]],@"prefValue",
        @"setSounds:",@"targetValue",nil],
    [NSMutableDictionary dictionaryWithObjectsAndKeys:
        @"Music",@"titleValue",
        @"switch",@"accessoryValue",
        [NSNumber numberWithBool:[myDefaults          Extracts/sets
            boolForKey:@"musicValue"]],@"prefValue",    music value
        @"setMusic:",@"targetValue",nil],nil];
```

The lines in which the prefValues are set are the new material here. The information is extracted from NSUSerDefaults first.

The methods called when each of these switches are moved can set and save changes to the default values. You'll want to do other things here too, but the abbreviated form of these methods is shown in the following listing.

Listing 8.3   Setting and saving `NSUserDefaults`

```
-(void)setMusic:(id)sender {
    NSUserDefaults *myDefaults = [NSUserDefaults standardUserDefaults];
    UISwitch *musicSwitch = [switchList objectAtIndex:1];
    [myDefaults setBool:musicSwitch.on forKey:@"musicValue"];
}
-(void)setSounds:(id)sender {
    NSUserDefaults *myDefaults = [NSUserDefaults standardUserDefaults];
    UISwitch *soundsSwitch = [switchList objectAtIndex:0];
    [myDefaults setBool:soundsSwitch.on forKey:@"soundsValue"];
}
```

This functionality is simple. You call up `NSUserDefaults`, set any values you want to change, and then save them. If you call up your program again, you'll find that the two switches remain in the position where you set them the last time you ran the program.

After you decide how to save your personal preferences, you'll have a skeleton for creating your own preferences page; if that's appropriate for your program, you're finished. But that's just one of two ways to let users add preference data to your program. More commonly, you'll export your settings to the main Settings program. So, how do you do that?

8.2.2 Using the system settings

When you created a personal preferences page in the previous section, you used all the iOS programming skills you've been learning to date, creating objects and manipulating them. Conversely, using the system settings is much easier: it just requires creating some files.

About bundles

Xcode allows you to tie multiple files together into a coherent whole called a *bundle*. In practice, a bundle is just a directory. Often a bundle is made opaque, so that users can't casually see its contents; in this case, it's called a *package*.

The main advantage of a bundle is that it can invisibly store multiple variants of a file, using the right one when the circumstances are appropriate. For example, an application bundle can include executable files for different chip architectures or in different formats.

When working with Xcode, you're likely to encounter three different types of bundles: framework bundles, application bundles, and settings bundles. All frameworks appear packaged as framework bundles, although that's largely invisible to you. An application bundle is what's created when you compile a program to run on your iPhone or iPad; we'll talk about how to access individual files in a bundle in the next section, when we talk about files in general. Finally, the settings bundle contains a variety of information about system settings, a topic that we'll address now.

You can find more information about how to access bundles in the `NSBundle` and `CFBundle` classes.

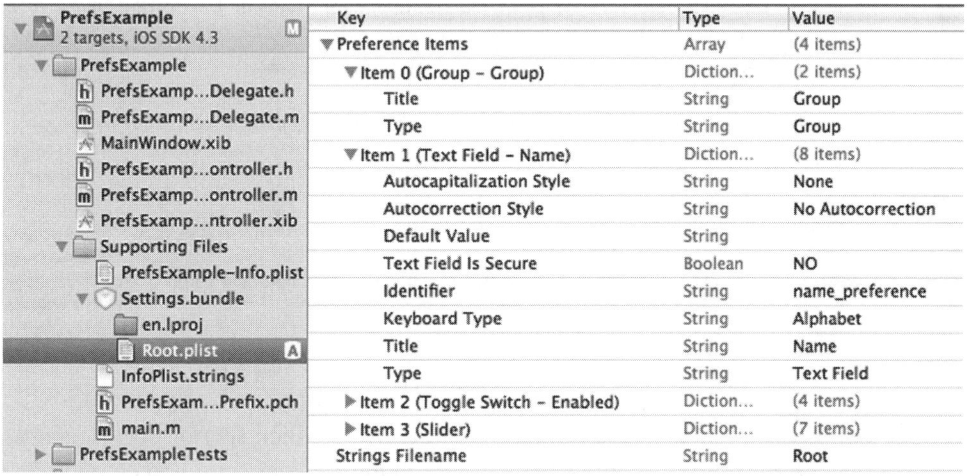

Figure 8.2 This look at system settings reveals some of Root.plist's `PreferenceSpecifiers`.

To begin using the system settings, you must create a settings bundle. You do this in Xcode by choosing the File > New File option. To date, you've only created new files using the Cocoa Touch Classes option (starting in section 3.3). Now, you should instead choose Resources in the side pane, which gives you the option to create one sort of settings file: Settings Bundle. When you do this, Settings.bundle is added to your current project.

EDITING EXISTING SETTINGS

Root.plist is an XML property list file, but as usual, you can view it in Xcode, where it appears as a list of keys and values. All of your settings appear under the `Preference-Specifiers` category, as shown in figure 8.2.

You can enter seven types of data in the Settings plist file, each of which creates a specific tool on the Settings page. Of these, four appear by default in the plist file at the time of this writing and are the easiest to modify. All seven options are shown in table 8.3.

The plist editor is simple to use and lets you easily do the vast majority of work required to create the settings for your program. You can cut and paste the existing four preferences (noted by checkmarks in table 8.3) to reorder them or create new instances of the four existing preference types. Then, you fill in their data to create preferences that look exactly like you want them.

Table 8.3 Different preference types let you create different tools on the Settings page.

Preference	Summary	Default ✓
PSChildPaneSpecifier	Points to a subpage of preferences	
PSGroupSpecifier	Contains a group header for the current table section	✓

Table 8.3   Different preference types let you create different tools on the Settings page. *(continued)*

Preference	Summary	Default ✓
PSMultiValueSpecifier	Points to a subpage containing a select list	
PSSliderSpecifier	A UISlider	✓
PSTextFieldSpecifier	A UITextField	✓
PSTitleValueSpecifier	Shows the current, unchangeable value of the preference	
PSToggleSwitchSpecifier	A UISwitch	✓

For any setting, the Type string always describes which sort of preference you're setting. Other settings define what you can change. For example, to change the text that appears in a PSGroupSpecifier, you adjust the Title string inside the PSGroup-Specifier dictionary. Changing the PSSliderSpecifier, PSTextFieldSpecifier, and PSToggleSwitchSpecifier is equally easy. The only thing to note on those is the Key string, which sets the name of the variable for the preference. You'll need that name when you want to look it up from inside your program (a topic we'll return to).

CREATING NEW SETTINGS

The remaining three preferences are a bit harder to implement because you don't have a preexisting template for them sitting in the default Root.plist file. But all you have to do is create a dictionary that contains the right values.

When you click individual rows in the plist editor, you'll see some iconic options to help you create new preferences. At any time, you can create new Preference-Specifiers (which is to say, new preferences) by clicking the plus (+) symbol to the right of the current row. You can likewise add to dictionaries or arrays by opening them and then clicking the indented row symbol to the right of the current row.

A PSTitleValueSpecifier is an unchangeable preference. It shows the preference name and a word on the Settings page. Its dictionary includes a Type (string) of PSTitleValueSpecifier, a Title (string) that defines the name of the preference, a Key (string) that defines the variable name, and a DefaultValue (string).

A PSMultiValueSpecifier is a select list that appears on a subpage. Its dictionary contains a Type (string) of PSMultiValueSpecifier, a Title (string), a Key (string), a DefaultValue (string), a Titles (array) that contains a number of String items, and a matched Values (array) that contains Number items.

Figure 8.3 shows what these two items look like, laid out in Xcode.

The last sort of setting, PSChildPaneSpecifier, does something totally different: it lets you create additional pages of preferences.

Item 5	Dictionary	(4 items)
Type	String	PSTitleValueSpecifier
Title	String	CPU Speed
Key	String	title_preference
DefaultValue	String	default
▼ Item 6	Dictionary	(6 items)
Type	String	PSMultiValueSpecifier
Title	String	Animation Type
Key	String	options_preference
DefaultValue	String ‡	0
▼ Values	Array	(3 items)
Item 1	Number	0
Item 2	Number	1
Item 3	Number	2
▼ Titles	Array	(3 items)
Item 1	String	Line Drawings
Item 2	String	Filled Polygons
Item 3	String	Full CGI

Figure 8.3   This display shows how a `PSTitleValueSpecifier` and a `PSMultiValueSpecifier` look in Xcode.

CREATING HIERARCHICAL SETTINGS

If necessary, you can have multiple pages of settings. To create a subpage, use the `PSChildPaneSpecifier` type. It should contain a `Type` (string) of `PSChildPaneSpecifier`, a `Title` (string), and a `File` (string) that contains the new plist file without an extension.

After you've done this, you need to create your new plist file. There is currently no easy "Add plist" option, so we suggest copying your existing Root.plist file, renaming it, and going from there.

We've put together an example of all seven preference types in figure 8.4. It shows the types of preference files that you can create using Apple's built-in functionality.

Now you know everything that's required to give your users a long list of preferences that they can set. But how do you use them from within Xcode?

ACCESSING SETTINGS

Settings end up encoded as variables. As you saw when looking through the plist editor, each individual preference is an `NSString`, an `NSArray`, an `NSNumber`, or a Boolean. You can access these variables using the shared `NSUserDefaults` object. We already discussed this class in the last section; it so happens that Apple's settings bundle uses it, as we suggested you might. The functionality remains the same. You can create it as follows:

```
[NSUserDefaults standardUserDefaults];
```

Figure 8.4   As seen on an iPhone, in order from top to bottom, a `Group`, a `TextField`, another `Group`, a `Switch`, a `TitleValue`, a `MultiValue`, a `ChildPane`, a third `Group`, and a `Slider`

When you've done that, you can use NSUserDefaults' objectForKey: methods, such as arrayForKey:, integerForKey:, and stringForKey:, as appropriate to access the information from the settings. For example, the following code applies a string from the settings to a label:

```
myLabel.text = [[NSUserDefaults standardUserDefaults]
    stringForKey:@"name_preference"];
```

Similarly, you can save new settings by using the various setObjectForKey: methods—although we don't think this is a particularly good idea if users are otherwise modifying these values in Settings.

There is one considerable gotcha that you must watch for: if a user hasn't yet accessed the settings for your program, then all settings without default values have a value of nil. This means you either need to create your preferences by hand or build defaults into your program, as appropriate.

Most of the time, you'll only need to retrieve the setting values, as described here; but if more is required, you should look at the class reference for NSUserDefaults.

That concludes our look at the two ways to create preferences for your programs and also at how users can input data into your program. But user input represents just one part of the data puzzle. Certainly, a lot of important data comes from users, but data can also come from various files and databases built into your program or into the device. Retrieving data from those sources is the topic of the latter half of this chapter.

8.3   *Opening files*

When we talked about bundles earlier in this chapter, you saw how the iPhone and iPad arrange their internal information for programs. That arrangement becomes vitally important when you're trying to access files that you've added to a project.

Fortunately, for the iPhone, you can look at how your program's files are arranged when you're testing applications on the Simulator. Each time you run a program, the program is compiled to a directory under ~/Library/Application Support/iPhone Simulator/Users/Applications. The specific directory has a hexadecimal name, but you can search to find the right one. Figure 8.5 shows an example of the directory for the sample program that we used to set up the system preferences example (the subdirectories are the same for any basic program). The process is similar for the iPad.

As shown, there are four directories of files for this one simple program. The majority of the content appears in the *application bundle*, which in this example is called systempreferences.app. There, you find everything you've added to your project, including text files, pictures, and databases. The other three directories you can use are Documents, Library, and tmp.

These are all intended to be used for files that are created or modified when the program is run. Documents should contain user-created information (including new or modified text files, pictures, and databases), Library should contain more programmatic items (like preferences), and tmp should contain temporary information. Each

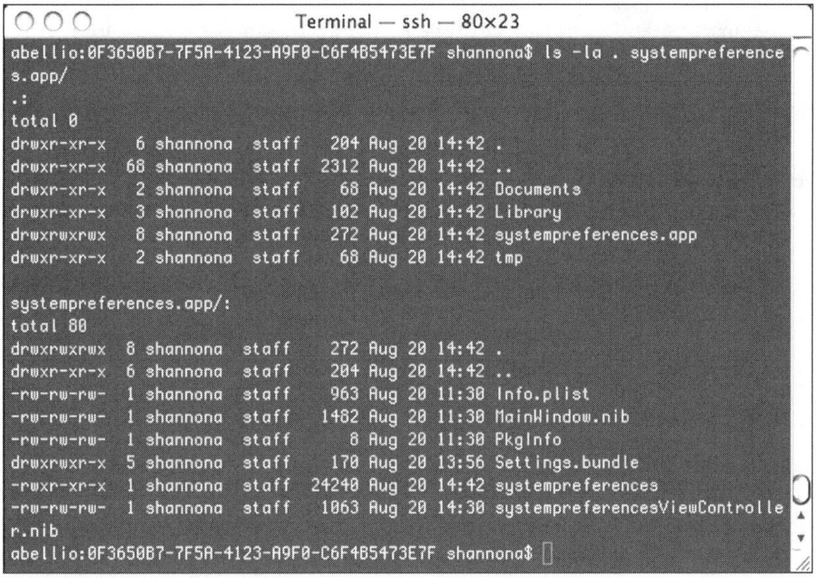

```
○ ○ ○                    Terminal — ssh — 80×23
abellio:0F3650B7-7F5A-4123-A9F0-C6F4B5473E7F shannona$ ls -la . systempreference
s.app/
.:
total 0
drwxr-xr-x    6 shannona    staff      204 Aug 20 14:42 .
drwxr-xr-x   68 shannona    staff     2312 Aug 20 14:42 ..
drwxr-xr-x    2 shannona    staff       68 Aug 20 14:42 Documents
drwxr-xr-x    3 shannona    staff      102 Aug 20 14:42 Library
drwxrwxrwx    8 shannona    staff      272 Aug 20 14:42 systempreferences.app
drwxr-xr-x    2 shannona    staff       68 Aug 20 14:42 tmp

systempreferences.app/:
total 80
drwxrwxrwx    8 shannona    staff      272 Aug 20 14:42 .
drwxr-xr-x    6 shannona    staff      204 Aug 20 14:42 ..
-rw-rw-rw-    1 shannona    staff      963 Aug 20 11:30 Info.plist
-rw-rw-rw-    1 shannona    staff     1482 Aug 20 11:30 MainWindow.nib
-rw-rw-rw-    1 shannona    staff        8 Aug 20 11:30 PkgInfo
drwxrwxr-x    5 shannona    staff      170 Aug 20 13:56 Settings.bundle
-rwxr-xr-x    1 shannona    staff    24240 Aug 20 14:42 systempreferences
-rw-rw-rw-    1 shannona    staff     1063 Aug 20 14:30 systempreferencesViewControlle
r.nib
abellio:0F3650B7-7F5A-4123-A9F0-C6F4B5473E7F shannona$ []
```

Figure 8.5   Compiled programs contain several directories full of files.

of these directories starts out empty, other than the fact that Library maintains a local copy of your system settings. We'll talk about how and why you fill them momentarily. First, let's look at how to access your bundle; later, we'll discuss how to access other directories and also how to manipulate files. At the end of the section, we'll put everything together with a concrete example.

8.3.1   *Accessing your bundle*

In previous chapters, we've shown how easy it is to add files to your project. You drag the file into Xcode, and everything is correctly set up so that the file will become part of your program when it compiles. As you now know, that means the file is copied into your application bundle.

For many bundled files, you don't have to worry about anything beyond that. For example, when you work with picture files, you enter the name of the file in Xcode, and the SDK automatically finds it for you. But if you want to access a file that doesn't have this built-in link, you need to do a bit more work.

Whenever you're working with the filesystem on the iPhone or iPad, access is abstracted through objects. You send messages that tell the SDK what area of the filesystem you're looking for, and the SDK then gives you precise directory paths. The benefit of this abstraction is that Apple can reorganize the filesystem in future releases, and your program won't be affected at all.

The first files you'll want to access will probably be in your bundle: files that you included when you compiled your program. Accessing a bundle file is usually a two-step process, as shown in this database example (which we'll return to in the next section):

```
NSString *paths = [[NSBundle mainBundle] resourcePath];
NSString *bundlePath = [paths stringByAppendingPathComponent:dbFile];
```

In this example, `mainBundle` returns the directory path that corresponds to your application's bundle, and `resourcePath` expands that to be the directory path for the resources of your program (including, in this case, a database, but this could be anything else you added to your program). Finally, you use `stringByAppendingPathComponent:` to add your specific file to the path. This `NSString` method makes sure a path is constructed using slashes (//) as needed.

The result is a complete path that can be handed to other objects as needed. You'll see how that works with a database in the next section. You can likewise use it for `UImage`'s `imageWithContentsOfFile:` method or `NSFileHandle`'s `fileHandleForReadingAtPath` method. We'll return to the latter shortly.

But there's one fundamental problem with accessing files in the application bundle: you can't modify them. Apple generally suggests that you should treat the application bundle as read only, and there's a real penalty if you don't: your program will stop working because it won't checksum correctly. This means that the application bundle is great for files that don't change, but if you want to modify something (or create something new), you need to use the other directories we mentioned, starting with the Documents folder.

8.3.2 Accessing other directories

When you're working with directories other than the bundle, you have to think about two things: how to access those files and how to move files among multiple directories.

RETRIEVING A FILE

When a file is sitting in your Documents directory, you can retrieve it much as you retrieved files from the bundle directory:

```
NSArray *paths = NSSearchPathForDirectoriesInDomains(NSDocumentDirectory,
    NSUserDomainMask, YES);
NSString *documentsDirectory = [paths objectAtIndex:0];
NSString *docPath = [documentsDirectory
    stringByAppendingPathComponent:dbFile];
```

The magic here occurs in the `NSSearchPathForDirectoriesInDomains` function. The first argument is usually `NSDocumentDirectory` or `NSLibraryDirectory`, depending on which directory you want to get to. The other two arguments should always be the same for the iPhone and iPad. The result is an array of strings, each containing a path. The first path in the `NSArray` is usually the right one, as shown here. You can then use the `stringByAppendingPathComponent:` method, as before, to build the complete path for your file. Voila! You've now used some slightly different methods to access a file in your Documents directory rather than the bundle directory.

COPYING A FILE

There's been a slight disconnect in our discussion of files and directories to date. When you compile your project, all of your files are placed into your application bundle. But if you ever want to edit a file, it must be placed in a different directory, such as Documents. So how do you get a file from one place to the other? You use the NSFileManager:

```
NSFileManager *fileManager = [NSFileManager defaultManager];
success = [fileManager copyItemAtPath:bundlePath toPath:docPath
    error:&error];
```

The file manager is a class that allows you to easily manipulate files by creating them, moving them, deleting them, and otherwise modifying them. As is the case with many classes you've seen, you initialize it by accessing a shared object. You can do lots of things with the file manager, including copying (as you've done here) and checking for a file's existence (which we'll demonstrate shortly). You should look at the NSFileManager class reference for complete information.

As you'll see, the NSFileManager is one of numerous classes that you can use to work with files.

8.3.3 *Manipulating files*

It's possible that after you've built your file path, you'll be ready to immediately read the file's contents, using something like the UIImage methods (which we'll touch on in chapter 13) or the functions related to SQLite (which we'll cover in the next chapter). But it's also possible that you'll want to manipulate the raw files, reading and parsing them in your code, as soon as you've created a file path. There are numerous ways to do this, as shown in table 8.4.

Table 8.4   Ways to manipulate files using the SDK

Class	Method	Summary
NSFileHandle	fileHandleForReadingAtPath: fileHandleForWritingAtPath: fileHandleForUpdatingAtPath:	Class methods that allow you to open a file
NSFileHandle	readDataOfLength:	Returns an NSData containing the specified number of bytes from the file
NSFileHandle	readDataToEndOfFile:	Returns an NSData with the rest of the file's content
NSFileHandle	closeFile:	Closes an NSHandle
NSFileManager	contentsAtPath:	Returns an NSData with the complete file's contents
NSData	initWithContentsOfFile:	Creates an NSData with the complete file's contents
NSData	writeToFile:atomically:	Writes the NSData to a file

Table 8.4 Ways to manipulate files using the SDK *(continued)*

Class	Method	Summary
NSString	stringWithContentsOfFile:encoding:error:	Class method that returns an NSString with the complete file's contents
NSString	initWithData:encoding:	Returns an NSString with the NSData's contents
NSString	writeToFile:atomically:encoding:error:	Writes the NSString to a file

As table 8.4 shows, you can access files in a huge variety of ways after you've created a file path. If you're a C programmer, opening a file handle, reading from that file handle, and finally closing that file handle is apt to be the most familiar approach. Or, you can use a shortcut and go straight to the NSFileManager and have it do the whole process. Even quicker is using methods from NSData or NSString to directly create an object of the appropriate type.

Any of these simpler methods will cost you the ability to step through a file byte by byte, which may be a limitation or a benefit, depending on your program. But with the simpler methods, you need only a single line of code:

```
NSString *myContents = [NSString stringWithContentsOfFile:myFile
    encoding:NSASCIIStringEncoding error:&error];
```

Table 8.4 also lists a few ways to write back to files, including simple ways to dump an NSData object or an NSString object to a file. There are also other ways. When you decide which set of methods you're most comfortable using, you should consult the appropriate class reference for additional details.

When you're working with files, you're likely to be doing one of two things. Either you have files that contain large blobs of user information, or you have files that contain short snippets of data that you've saved for your program. To demonstrate how to use a few of the file objects and methods, you'll tackle the first problem by building a simple notepad prototype.

File content

In this section—and in our next example—we're largely assuming that files contain plain, unstructured text. But this doesn't have to be the case. XML is a great way to store local data in a more structured format. Chapter 14 covers how to read XML and includes an example of reading local XML data.

8.3.4 *Filesaver: a UITextView example*

This program lets you maintain a text view full of information from one session to another. It's relatively basic, but you can imagine how you could expand it to mimic the Notepad program, with its multiple notes, toolbars, navigator, and image background.

The following listing shows this simple filesaver example. The objects, as usual, were created in Xcode: a UIToolBar (with associated UIBarButtonItem) and a UITextView.

Listing 8.4 A prototype notepad program that maintains a text field as a file

```
@implementation filesaverViewController
- (void)viewDidLoad {
    NSArray *paths =
            NSSearchPathForDirectoriesInDomains(NSDocumentDirectory,
            NSUserDomainMask, YES);
    NSString *documentsDirectory =
        [paths objectAtIndex:0];
    filePath = [documentsDirectory
        stringByAppendingPathComponent:
            @"textviewcontent"];
    [filePath retain];
    NSFileManager *myFM =
        [NSFileManager defaultManager];
    if ([myFM isReadableFileAtPath:filePath]) {
        myText.text =
            [NSString stringWithContentsOfFile:filePath
                encoding:NSASCIIStringEncoding error:nil];
    }
    keyboardIsActive = NO;
    [super viewDidLoad];
}
-(IBAction)finishEditing:(id)sender {
    if (keyboardIsActive == YES) {
        [myText resignFirstResponder];
    }
}
- (void)textViewDidBeginEditing:
    (UITextView *)textView {
    if ([myText.text compare:@"Type Text Here."] == NSOrderedSame) {
        myText.text = [NSString string];
    }
    keyboardIsActive = YES;
}
- (void)textViewDidEndEditing:(UITextView *)textView {
    [textView.text writeToFile:filePath atomically:YES
        encoding:NSASCIIStringEncoding error:NULL];
    keyboardIsActive = NO;
}
...
@end
```

❶ Creates file path

❷ Executes Done action

This program shows how easy it is to access files. The hardest part is determining the path for the file, but that involves using the path-creation methods we looked at a few sections back. When you have your path, you save it as a variable so that you won't have to re-create the path later ❶. Next, you use `NSFileManager` to determine whether a file exists. If it does, you can immediately fill your `UITextField` with its content. Finally, you set a `keyboardIsActive` variable, which you update throughout the program.

As we've previously noted, the objects that pull up keyboards are a bit tricky, because you have to explicitly get rid of the keyboard when editing is done. For `UITextFields`, you can turn the Return key into a Done key to dismiss the keyboard; but for a `UITextView`, you usually want the user to be able to enter returns, so you must typically create a bar at the top of the page with a Done button. Figure 8.6 shows this layout of items.

When the user presses Done, the `finishEditing:` method ❷ is called, which resigns the first responder, making the keyboard disappear (unless you're not editing, in which case it closes the program).

The last two methods are defined in the `UITextFieldDelegate` protocol. When editing begins on the text field, the program checks to see if the starting text is still there, and if so clears it. When editing ends on the text field, the content is saved to your file. Finally, the `keyboardIsActive` variable is toggled, to control what the Done button does in each state.

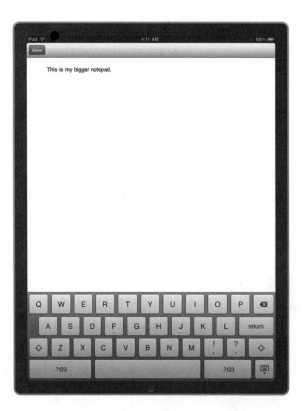

Figure 8.6   The filesaver application with the keyboard activated on both the iPhone and the iPad

As you saw in table 8.4, there are numerous other ways to read files and save them. The methods in listing 8.4 are simple, but they allow you to make good use of your notepad's file.

Files are okay to use for saving one-off data, but if you're storing a lot of really large data, we suggest using a database when it's available. And on the iPhone and iPad, a database is *always* available, as you'll see in chapter 9.

8.4 Summary

In this chapter, we covered a variety of ways that you can import primarily text-based data into your program. User action is one of the most important methods, one well covered by previous sections. In addition to UITextFields, UITextViews, and UISearchBars, many nontextual interface options are available.

Preferences mark the other major way users can influence your program. You can either program them manually or use the System Setting bundle.

Ultimately, user input is somewhat limited on the iPhone because of the slow typing speed. If you're dealing with piles of text, you'll more frequently want to pull that data from an existing resource. The iPad doesn't suffer from this issue, because users can type more quickly on the keyboard.

Files are the traditional way to access large amounts of data. We'll return to files when we deal with photos and sounds in the later chapters. Databases are frequently an easier way to access data, particularly if the data is well organized, as you'll see in chapter 9.

There's only one data-input method that we've largely ignored: the internet. We consider it so important that we'll cover it in chapter 14.

The data-input and -retrieval methods discussed in this chapter and the next will form a foundation for much of the work you do with the iPhone and iPad, because ultimately *everything* is data. You'll need to retrieve data when you work with images and sounds. Similarly, you may want to save data from your accelerometer, from your Core Location, or when you create a graphic. Keep what you've learned here in your back pocket as you move on to the rest of the iOS toolbox.

We're now ready to discuss more advanced data access techniques, including interfacing with the Address Book and saving persistent data with SQLite.

Data:
advanced techniques

9

This chapter covers

- Using SQLite
- Using the Address Book framework
- Using Core Data

In the last chapter, we discussed how information can be saved and retrieved on the iPhone and iPad. Those techniques are great for simple data such as user preferences, but what happens when you want to save more complicated large amounts of data?

Saving large amounts of information to `NSUserDefaults` would be awkward and clunky, and serialization is too slow. The solution is to use a relational database. Apple has provided a couple of options for mass storage using relational databases. These options are SQLite and Core Data. We'll look at both as well as the built-in Address Book framework, which isn't related to data storage but has some complexities of its own.

SQLite is a compact version of MySQL. Even though it doesn't offer as many field types as MySQL, it's still a powerful method of storage. One of the greatest strengths of an SQLite database is its portability. Unlike MySQL, it doesn't require a server in order to run. You can drop the database into your application directory and start using it to store persistent data.

Core Data is a powerful layer that sits on top of an SQLite database. It removes many of the complexities of SQL and allows you to interface with the database in a more natural way. It does this by making the database rows into real Objective-C objects (called *managed objects*) and lets you manipulate them without any knowledge of SQL. We'll be discussing both methods of storage and leave it up to you to decide which works best with your project.

9.1 Using SQLite

Let's look more closely at what SQLite is, look at how to set up and access an SQLite database, and finally explore an example that puts an SQLite database in practice.

The SDK's built-in database is SQLite, a public domain software package. You can find more information on it at www.sqlite.org, including documentation that's considerably more extensive than what we can include here. You need to know the SQL language to use SQLite, and we won't cover SQL syntax here at all. In addition, you must be familiar with the SQLite API. We'll show how to use it for some basic tasks here, but there's a much more extensive reference online.

SQLite has what we find to be two major limitations. First, there's no simple way to create a database. You must create the database by hand for now. Second, SQLite has no object-oriented interface. Instead, you use an API that falls back on C code, which we find less elegant and harder to use than the typical Objective-C class.

Given these limitations, we still think that using an SQL database is a better option than files for most situations, and we highly suggest that you learn enough about SQL to use it comfortably.

9.1.1 Setting up an SQLite database

Prior to using SQLite in your program, you must set up a database that contains all of your tables and the initial data you want. We'll look at the general steps first, and then you'll set up a database that can be used to drive a navigation menu.

CREATING AN SQLITE DATABASE

Creating an SQLite database typically is done from the command line, although it can also be done entirely programmatically. We won't cover programmatic creation of the database here, but you can find documentation on the SQLite site for doing that. The steps for creating a database from the command line are listed in table 9.1.

To show how all this works, you'll put together a data file for a database-driven navigation controller. When we talked about tables in chapters 5 and 7, you created them from arrays and dictionaries. This is a fine technique when you're creating small, stable hierarchies, but what if you want to build something larger or something that can be modified by the user? In those cases, a database is a great backend for a navigation menu.

Table 9.1   Creating an SQLite database from the command line

Step	Description
1. Prepare your table.	Figure out the design of each table in your database. Create a file for the initial data of each table (if any) that has data cells separated by pipes (|) and data rows separated by returns.
2. Create your database.	Start SQLite with this command: `sqlite3 `*`filename`* Use a `CREATE TABLE` command to create each table.
3. Enter your initial info.	Use this command to fill each table: `.import table `*`filename`* Quit SQLite.
4. Add your database to the Xcode.	Inside Xcode, use the Add > Existing Files menu option to add your database to your project.

DESIGNING A NAVIGATION MENU

To support a database-driven menu, we've designed a simple database schema. Each row in the navigation hierarchy is represented by one row in a database. Each of those rows has five elements:

- `catid`—Provides a unique (and arbitrary) ID for an individual row in the menu
- `parentid`—Indicates which row in the database acts as the hierarchical parent of the current row, or lists 0 if it's a top-level row that would appear on the first page of the menu
- `title`—Contains the printed text that will appear in the menu
- `entrytype`—Specifies whether the row is a *category* (which opens a submenu) or a *result* (which performs some action)
- `ordering`—Lists the order in which the rows should appear on an individual page of the menu

Here's an example of what a data file might look like, with the five elements shown in the preceding order:

```
> cat nav.data
1|0|First|category|1
2|0|Third|category|3
3|0|Second|category|2
4|2|Submenu|category|1
5|0|Action #1|result|4
6|1|Action #1B|result|1
```

And here's how you create a table for that data and import it:

```
> sqlite3 nav.db
SQLite version 3.6.12
Enter ".help" for instructions
Enter SQL statements terminated with a ";"
sqlite> CREATE TABLE menu (catid int(5),parentid int(5),title
    varchar(32),entrytype varchar(12), ordering int(5));
sqlite> .import nav.data menu
```

Note that to quit SQLite, type `.quit` and press Enter.

Afterward, you can add your now-complete database to Xcode using the normal procedures, a step that's not shown here. After you've linked in your database the first time, you can go back and make changes to it, and the new version will always be used when you recompile your project.

You now have a ready-to-run database, but you'll still need to prepare your Xcode to use SQLite. We'll look at that next.

9.1.2   Accessing SQLite

You have to link in some additional resources to use SQLite, as is typical for any major new functionality. First, you need to add the framework, which you can find under /usr/lib/libsqlite3.0.dylib, rather than in the standard framework directory. Second, you must add an import of sqlite3.h.

You now have a database that's ready to use, and you've included the functionality that you need to use it. The next step is to access SQLite's functions.

9.1.3   Accessing your SQLite database

SQLite includes approximately 100 functions, about 20 object types, and a huge list of constants. We'll cover the basics that you'll need to access the database you've created. Table 9.2 shows the most critical API commands. They generally revolve around two important concepts: the database handle (which is returned by `sqlite3_open` and is used by everything else) and the prepared statement (which is returned by `sqlite3_prepare` and is used to run queries).

Table 9.2   The most important SQLite API commands

Function	Arguments	Summary
`sqlite3_open`	`filename`, address of database	Opens a database.
`sqlite3_prepare`	`database`, `SQL as UTF-8`, `max length to read`, `address of statement`, `address of unread results`	Turns an SQL statement in UTF-8 format into a pointer to a prepared statement, which can be handed to other functions.
`sqlite3_step`	`prepared statement`	Processes a row of results from a prepared statement, or else returns an error.
`sqlite3_column_int`	`prepared statement`, `column #`	Returns an int from the active row. Several other simple functions similarly return a specific column from the active row.

Table 9.2   The most important SQLite API commands *(continued)*

Function	Arguments	Summary
sqlite3_column_string	prepared statement, column #	Returns a char *, which is to say a string, from the active row. Several other simple functions similarly return a specific column from the active row.
sqlite3_finalize	prepared statement	Deletes a prepared statement.
sqlite3_close	database	Closes a database.

These functions, in order, show the usual lifecycle of an SQLite database:

1   Open the database.
2   Prepare statements, one at a time.
3   Step through a statement, reading columns.
4   Finalize the statement.
5   Close the database.

SQLite includes two convenience functions, sqlite3_exec() and sqlite3_get_table(), that simplify these steps. But the functions are built using the core functionality just mentioned, so that's what we've decided to highlight.

9.1.4   *Building a navigation menu from a database*

Now that you have a basic understanding of the SQLite functions, you can put together a prototype of a database-driven menu navigation system. What you'll do here is by no means complete, but it'll give you a great basis to build on. This example will also be one of the most complex in the book. It includes multiple classes of new objects designed to work either apart (in different programs) or together.

In this section, we'll cover the SKDatabase class (which abstracts database connections), the SKMenu class (which abstracts navigator menu creation), and the Database-ViewController (which transforms a typical table view controller into a database-driven class). In the end, you'll hook everything together with the app delegate.

THE DATABASE CLASS

Because there aren't any preexisting object-oriented classes for the SQLite database functions, any program using a database should start by creating its own. The following listing contains the start of such a class, creating methods for the parts of the API that you'll need to create the database view controller.

Listing 9.1   SKDatabase, a new sqlite3 database class

```
#import "SKDatabase.h"
#import "sqlite3.h"
@implementation SKDatabase
- (id)initWithFile:(NSString *)dbFile {
```

```
    self = [super init];
    NSString *paths = [[NSBundle mainBundle] resourcePath];
    NSString *path = [paths stringByAppendingPathComponent:dbFile];
    int result = sqlite3_open([path UTF8String], &dbh);
    NSAssert1(SQLITE_OK == result, NSLocalizedStringFromTable
        (@"Unable to open the sqlite database (%@).",
        @"Database", @""),
        [NSString stringWithUTF8String:sqlite3_errmsg(dbh)]);
    return self;
}
- (void)close {
    if (dbh) {
        sqlite3_close(dbh);
    }
}
- (sqlite3 *)dbh {
    return dbh;
}
- (sqlite3_stmt *)prepare:(NSString *)sql {
    const char *utfsql = [sql UTF8String];
    sqlite3_stmt *statement;
    if (sqlite3_prepare([self dbh],utfsql,-1,&statement,NULL)==SQLITE_OK) {
        return statement;
    } else {
        return 0;
    }
}
- (id)lookupSingularSQL:(NSString *)sql forType:          ❶ Looks up
    (NSString *)rettype {                                    SQL results
    sqlite3_stmt *statement;
    id result;                                            ❷ Calls prepare
    if (statement = [self prepare:sql]) {                    function
        if (sqlite3_step(statement) == SQLITE_ROW) {
            if ([rettype compare:@"text"] == NSOrderedSame) {
                result = [NSString stringWithUTF8String:
                    (char *)sqlite3_column_text
                        (statement,0)];
            } else if ([rettype compare:@"integer"] == NSOrderedSame) {
                result = (id)sqlite3_column_int
                    (statement,0);
            }
        }
    }
    sqlite3_finalize(statement);
    return result;
}

@end
```

The header file (not shown) includes one variable declaration for the dbh (database handle) variable, the database handle. That's the one variable you want to always have available to your class, because it gives access to the database. Now you're ready to start working on the source code file.

The `initWithFile:` method uses some of the file commands that you learned in the previous section to find the database file, which is in the main bundle (but remember, you'll want to copy this to the Documents directory if you make changes to your database). It then opens the file using `sqlite3_open`, the first of several `sqlite3` API commands. Note that the `NSString` for the path has to be converted with the `UTF8String` method. This must be done throughout the class, because the SQLite API doesn't use the Objective-C classes you're familiar with.

The next few methods are pretty simple. `close` signals the end of the database lifecycle, `dbh` is a getter for the class's one variable, and `prepare` turns an SQL statement into a prepared statement.

The `lookupSingularSQL:` method is where things get interesting, because it shows off the lifecycle of a complete SQL function call ❶. Note that this function allows only a simple SQL call that returns one column from one row of information. That's all you need for the database view controller, but you'll doubtless need more complexity for a larger application.

The function starts by turning the SQL statement into a prepared statement ❷. Then it steps to the first row. Depending on the type of lookup, it fetches either a `string` or an `int`. Finally, it cleans up the statement with a `finalize`.

In a more complex class, you'd doubtless want to write methods that execute SQL calls without any returns, that return multiple columns from a row, and that return multiple rows, but we'll leave that for now (because we don't need any of those features for this example) and move on to the menu class. The SQLite API has more information on these features if you need them.

THE MENU CLASS

The next class, `SKMenu`, acts as an intermediary. At the frontend, it accepts requests for information about the menu that will fill the table view. On the backend, it turns those requests into SQL queries. It's been designed in this way to create an opaque interface: you never have to know that a database is being used, just that the `SKMenu` class returns results for a table view.

The code of `SKMenu` is shown in the following listing. It mainly illustrates how to use the `SKDatabase` class in listing 9.1.

Listing 9.2   `SKMenu`, an interface to the `SKDatabase` class

```
#import "SKMenu.h"
@implementation SKMenu
- (id)initWithFile:(NSString *)dbFile {
    self = [super init];
    myDB = [[SKDatabase alloc] initWithFile:dbFile];
    return self;
}
- (int)countForMenuWithParent:(int)parentid {
    int resultCount = 0;
    NSString *sql = [NSString stringWithFormat:
        @"SELECT COUNT(*) FROM menu WHERE parentid=%i",parentid];
```

❶ **Counts rows in a page**

```
    resultCount = (int)[myDB lookupSingularSQL:sql forType:@"integer"];
    return resultCount;
}
- (id)contentForMenuWithParent:(int)parentid                    ❷ Gets text
    Row:(int)row content:(NSString *)contenttype {                 for row
    NSString *sql = [NSString stringWithFormat:@"SELECT %@ FROM menu WHERE
        parentid=%i AND ordering=%i",contenttype,parentid,row];
    return [myDB lookupSingularSQL:sql forType:@"text"];
}
- (int)integerForMenuWithParent:(int)parentid                   ❸ Gets number
    Row:(int)row content:(NSString *)contenttype {                 for row
    NSString *sql = [NSString stringWithFormat:@"SELECT %@ FROM menu WHERE
        parentid=%i AND ordering=%i",contenttype,parentid,row];
    return (int)[myDB lookupSingularSQL:sql forType:@"integer"];
}
- (void)dealloc {
    [myDB close];
    [myDB release];
    [super dealloc];
}
@end
```

Again, we haven't shown the include file, but it includes one variable, `myDB`, which is a reference to the database object linked to the menu. The `initWithFile:` method initializes `myDB` by creating the database object.

The `countForMenuWithParent:` method is the first one to use the database ❶. It gets a sum of how many menu items there are at a particular level of the menu hierarchy. `contentForMenuWithParent:` ❷ and `integerForMenuWithParent:` ❸ are two other lookup functions. The first looks up database entries that return `strings`, and the second looks up database entries that return `ints`. This is required because, as you'll recall, SQLite has different database lookup functions for each of the variable types.

Finally, the `dealloc` method cleans up the database, first closing it and then releasing the object. It's always important in Objective-C to keep track of which objects are responsible for which other objects. Here, the menu is responsible for the database, so it does the cleanup.

THE DATABASE VIEW CONTROLLER

Now that you have some menu methods that allow a program to figure out the contents of a hierarchy of menus, you can put together your table view controller, which will read that information and fill table views on the fly. The next listing shows how the menu functions are used.

Listing 9.3 `DatabaseViewController`, a database-driven table view controller

```
- (id)initWithParentid:(int)parentid                            ❶ Sets up
    Menu:(SKMenu *)passedMenu {1                                    variables
    if (self = [super initWithStyle:UITableViewStylePlain]) {
        menuparentid=parentid;
        myMenu = passedMenu;
```

```
        }
        return self;
    }

    - (NSInteger)numberOfSectionsInTableView:                    ❷ Counts
        (UITableView *)tableView {                                 sections
        return 1;
    }
    - (NSInteger)tableView:(UITableView *)tableView              ❸ Counts
        numberOfRowsInSection:(NSInteger)section {                 rows
        return [myMenu countForMenuWithParent:menuparentid];
    }

    - (UITableViewCell *)tableView:(UITableView *)tableView      ❹ Draws
        cellForRowAtIndexPath:(NSIndexPath *)indexPath {           cell
        static NSString *MyIdentifier = @"MyIdentifier";
        UITableViewCell *cell = [tableView
            dequeueReusableCellWithIdentifier:MyIdentifier];
        if (cell == nil) {
            cell = [[[UITableViewCell alloc] initWithFrame:CGRectZero
                reuseIdentifier:MyIdentifier] autorelease];
        }
        int thisRow = indexPath.row + 1;
        cell.textLabel.text = [myMenu contentForMenuWithParent:
            menuparentid Row:thisRow
                content:@"title"];
        NSString *cellType = [myMenu contentForMenuWithParent:menuparentid
            Row:thisRow content:@"entrytype"];
        if ([cellType compare:@"category"] == NSOrderedSame) {
            cell.accessoryType = UITableViewCellAccessoryDisclosureIndicator;
        }
        return cell;
    }
    - (void)tableView:(UITableView *)tableView                   ❺ Pops up
        didSelectRowAtIndexPath:(NSIndexPath *)indexPath {         submenu
        int thisRow = indexPath.row + 1;
        NSString *cellType = [myMenu contentForMenuWithParent:menuparentid
            Row:thisRow content:@"entrytype"];
        if ([cellType compare:@"category"] == NSOrderedSame) {
            NSString *thisText = [myMenu contentForMenuWithParent:menuparentid
                Row:thisRow content:@"title"];
            int newParent = [myMenu integerForMenuWithParent:menuparentid
                Row:thisRow content:@"catid"];
            DatabaseViewController *newController =
                [[DatabaseViewController alloc]
                    initWithParentid:newParent Menu:myMenu];
            newController.title = thisText;
            [self.navigationController pushViewController:newController
                animated:YES];
            [newController release];
        }
    }
```

To properly understand how the database view controller works, recall the menu format we introduced a few pages ago. Remember that each row of the menu has an individual ID (the catid) and a parentid that indicates what lies above it in the menu hierarchy. There's also a title, which lists what the menu row says; a category, which indicates whether it leads to a new menu or is an end result; and an ordering variable. You use all that information in putting together your table view.

The database view controller is called multiple times by your project: once per menu or submenu. Each time, the initWithParentid:Menu: method identifies what level of the hierarchy to draw from the menu that's enclosed ❶. For example, if the parentid is 0, the top-level menu is drawn; if the parentid is 2, the menu that lies under entry (catid) 2 is drawn. The sole purpose of the init is to save that information.

You then have to fill in the standard table view controller methods. The count of sections is always 1 ❷. The number of rows is calculated from the database, using the SKMenu's countForMenuWithParent: method ❸ .

tableView:cellForRowAtIndexPath: is the first somewhat complex method ❹. After the standard setup of the cell, the method looks up the title to be placed in the menu row. It then determines whether the menu row is a category; this affects whether the chevron accessory is placed.

Finally, tableView:didSelectRowAtIndexPath: does the fancy work ❺. If the cell isn't a category, it doesn't do anything. (You'll probably change this when creating another program, because you may want results to result in some action; this could be a great place to introduce a new protocol to respond when a result row is selected.)

If the cell *is* a category, magic happens. The database view controller creates a new database view controller, on the fly, using the same old menu. But the current catid becomes the new parentid, which means the new view controller contains all the rows that lie under the current row on the hierarchy. The new database view controller is then placed on the navigator controller's stack, using the navigation methods you learned in chapter 7.

Figure 9.1 shows how all this fits together, using the database you created at the beginning of this section.

There's one thing missing from this example—the app delegate.

THE APP DELEGATE

The app delegate needs to create the Navigator, initialize the menu object, build the first level of the menu hierarchy, and clean things up afterward. Listing 9.4 shows the couple of steps required to do this.

Figure 9.1   This menu was
created directly from a database.

Listing 9.4   The app delegate that glues together these classes

```
- (BOOL)application:(UIApplication *)application
    didFinishLaunchingWithOptions:(NSDictionary *)launchOptions
    (UIApplication *)application {
    myMenu = [[SKMenu alloc] initWithFile:@"nav.db"];
    DatabaseViewController *newController = [[DatabaseViewController alloc]
        initWithParentid:0 Menu:myMenu];
    newController.title = @"DB Menu";
    [self.navigationController pushViewController:newController
        animated:NO];
    [newController release];
    [window addSubview:[navigationController view]];
    [window makeKeyAndVisible];
    return YES;
}
- (void)dealloc {
    [myMenu release];
    [navigationController release];
    [window release];
    [super dealloc];
}
```

The `applicationDidFinishLaunchingWithOptions:` method sets things up. After initializing the menu, it creates the first database view controller and pushes it onto the navigation stack. The `dealloc` method later closes everything out. Note that it releases the menu object, which in turn will close the database and release that, ending the menu's lifecycle.

Not shown here is the Xcode file, which includes one object, a navigation controller. Its standard view controller should be deleted, because you'll be replacing it here.

Though it's relatively basic, you now have a hierarchical menu of tables built entirely from a database.

9.1.5 Expanding this example

This example showed not only how to use databases in a real application but also how to put together a more complex project. Nonetheless, if you wanted to make regular use of the database and menu classes, you'd probably want to expand it more. We've already noted that `SKDatabase` could use more functionality and that the database view controller needs to do something for the `result` pages that it arrives on.

Because this is all database driven, you can also hand off considerable power to the users. It would be easy to expand this example so that users could create their own rows in menus and reorder the existing ones.

With SQLite now covered to the depth we can give it, we'll move on to another major method of data retrieval, one of equal complexity: the Address Book.

9.2 Accessing the Address Book

Like SQLite, the Address Book is too complex to wholly document within the constraints of this chapter. It's made up of two different frameworks—the Address Book framework and the Address Book UI framework—and together they contain over a dozen references. Fortunately, Apple offers an extensive tutorial on the Address Book: "Address Book Programming Guide for iOS."

In this section, we'll provide a basic reference that supplements Apple's own tutorial, but we suggest you read their guide for more extensive information. We'll look at the Address Book frameworks, show how to access the Address Book's properties, and explain how to use the Address Book UI.

9.2.1 An overview of the frameworks

As noted, there are two frameworks for the Address Book. The Address Book framework contains what you'd expect: information on the data types that make up the Address Book and how to access them. The Address Book UI framework contains a bunch of handy interfaces that allow you to hand off the selection and editing of Address Book entries to modal view controllers that Apple has already written.

To use this functionality, you must include one or both frameworks, plus the appropriate include files: AddressBook/AddressBook.h and AddressBookUI/AddressBookUI.h.

Table 9.3 lists many of the most important classes in the frameworks.

Table 9.3   The Address Book classes, the framework they belong to, and what they do

Class	Framework	Summary
ABAddressBook	Address Book	Interface for accessing and changing the Address Book; may not be required if you use the Address Book UI framework
ABNewPersonViewController	Address Book UI	Interface for entering new record manually
ABPeoplePickerNavigationController	Address Book UI	Interface for selecting users and properties
ABPersonViewController	Address Book UI	Interface for displaying and editing records
ABUnknownPersonViewController	Address Book UI	Interface for displaying "fake" contact and possibly adding it to Address Book
ABGroup	Address Book	Opaque type giving access to the records of groups
ABPerson	Address Book	Opaque type giving access to the records of individual people
ABRecord	Address Book	Record providing information on a person or group
ABMultiValue	Address Book	Type containing multiple values, each with its own label; its precise use is defined in ABPerson, where it's applied to addresses, dates, phone numbers, instant messages, URLs, and related names
ABMutableMultiValue	Address Book	An ABMultiValue whose values can be modified

Each of these classes contains numerous functions that can be used to build Address Book projects. We'll talk about a few important functions and point you to the class references for the rest.

9.2.2   *Accessing Address Book properties*

As you'll see shortly, the Address Book and Address Book UI frameworks ultimately provide different ways of accessing the Contacts data information: you might be working with the Address Book programmatically, or a user may be making selections through fancy UIs. Ways to select individual contacts may vary, but after a contact has been selected, you'll generally use the same getter and setter functions to work with that record. These important functions are listed in table 9.4.

Table 9.4 Property setters and getters are among the most important functions in the Address Book.

Function	Arguments	Summary
ABRecordCopyValue	ABRecordRef, property	Looks up a specific property from a specific record
ABRecordSetValue	ABRecordRef, property, value, &error	Sets a property to a value in a record
ABMultiValueGetCount	ABMultiValue	Returns the size of a multivalue (which can contain one or more copies of a record, such as multiple phone numbers)
ABMultiValueCopyLabelAtIndex	ABMultiValueRef, index	Looks up the label of an entry in a multivalue
ABMultiValueCopyValueAtIndex	ABMultiValueRef, index	Looks up the content of an entry in a multivalue
ABCreateMutableCopy	ABMultiValueRef	Creates a copy of a multivalue
ABMultiValueReplaceLabelAtIndex	ABMutableMultiValueRef, label, index	Replaces a label at an index in a multivalue

Generally, when you're using the *getter* functions for contacts in the Address Book, you'll follow this procedure:

1 Select one or more contacts through either the Address Book or the Address Book UI framework.

2 To look at an individual property, like a name or phone number, use ABRecord-CopyValue:

3 If it's a single-value property, you can immediately work with it as a string or some other class.

4 If it's a multivalue property, you need to use the ABMultiValue functions to access individual elements of the multivalue.

We included the *setter* methods in table 9.4 to keep the methods all in one place, but you'll usually only be using the setters if you're working with the Address Book framework, not the Address Book UI framework. Here's how they work:

1 Make changes to individual properties or to multivalues (using the mutable multivalue).

2 Use ABRecordSetValue to save the value to your local copy of the Address Book.

3 Use ABAddressBookSave to save your local changes to the real Address Book database.

We won't cover the setter side of things (which you can find out about in the "Address Book Programming Guide for iOS"), but you'll use many of the getter functions in the next section.

9.2.3   *Querying the Address Book*

Your first exploration of the Address Book will use the plain Address Book framework to access the Address Book and look up many of the values. This is shown in listing 9.5. It centers on a simple application with two objects built in Xcode: a `UISearchBar` and a `UITextView` (with an `IBOutlet` called `myText`).

You haven't used search bars before, but they're a simple way to enter search text. You set the search bar's delegate and then respond to appropriate messages. In this case, your program responds to the `searchBarSearchButtonClicked:` delegate method and then looks up the information that was entered.

Listing 9.5   Looking up information in the Address Book

```
- (void)searchBarSearchButtonClicked:(UISearchBar *)searchBar {
    [searchBar resignFirstResponder];
    ABAddressBookRef addressBook =                              ❶ Copies
        ABAddressBookCreate();                                     Address Book
    CFIndex abPCount =
        ABAddressBookGetPersonCount(addressBook);
    CFIndex abGCount =                                      Searches ❷
        ABAddressBookGetGroupCount(addressBook);          Address Book
    CFArrayRef searchResults = ABAddressBookCopyPeopleWithName(addressBook,
        (CFStringRef)searchBar.text);
    myText.text = [NSString stringWithString:@"Possible Completions:"];
    for (int i=0; i < CFArrayGetCount(searchResults); i++) {
        ABRecordRef thisPerson =                           ❸ Gets personal
            CFArrayGetValueAtIndex(searchResults, i);         record
        myText.text = [myText.text stringByAppendingFormat:@"\n\n%@",
            (NSString *)ABRecordCopyCompositeName
                (thisPerson)];
        CFStringRef thisJob = ABRecordCopyValue(thisPerson,
            kABPersonJobTitleProperty);
        CFStringRef thisOrg = ABRecordCopyValue(thisPerson,
            kABPersonOrganizationProperty);
        if (thisJob != NULL && thisOrg != NULL) {
            myText.text = [myText.text stringByAppendingFormat:
                @"\n%@ of %@",thisJob,thisOrg];
        }                                                  Gets phone ❹
        ABMultiValueRef thisPhones = ABRecordCopyValue(thisPerson,   multivalue
            kABPersonPhoneProperty);
        if (thisPhones != NULL) {
            for (int j = 0; j <ABMultiValueGetCount(thisPhones); j++) {
                myText.text = [myText.text stringByAppendingFormat:
                    @"\n%@: %@", (NSString *)
                        ABMultiValueCopyLabelAtIndex(thisPhones, j),
                    (NSString *)                           ❺ Prints
                        ABMultiValueCopyValueAtIndex         individual
                            (thisPhones, j)];                phone number
            }
        }
    }
    myText.text = [myText.text stringByAppendingFormat:@"\n\nThere are %ld
        records and %ld groups in this address book.",abPCount,abGCount];
```

```
        CFRelease(searchResults);
        CFRelease(addressBook);
}
```

You start by running `ABAddressBookCreate`, which makes a local copy of the Address Book ❶. You'll need to do this whenever you're working manually with the Address Book. After that, you use a few general Address Book functions that let you do things like count your number of contacts and groups. But it's the search function that's most important ❷. This is one of two ways you can extract contacts from the Address Book by hand, the other being `ABAddressBookCopyArrayOfAllPeople`. Note the typing of `searchBar.text` as `CFStringRef`. This is a Core Foundation class equivalent to `NSString *`; you can find more information about the details of Core Foundation in the section "Using Core Foundation."

The preceding steps are the major ones that differentiate working with the Address Book manually from working with it through a UI. With the Address Book framework, your program does the selection of contact records; with the UI framework, the user does it through a graphical interface. Beyond that, things work similarly via either methodology.

When you have a list of contacts, you need to extract individuals from the array ❸. You can then use numerous functions to look at their properties. `ABRecordCopyCompositeName` gives you a full name already put together, and `ABRecordCopyValue` lets you pick out other properties. The list of properties and returned values is in the `ABPerson` reference.

Multivalues are only a little more difficult to use than simple properties. You use `ABRecordCopyValue` as usual ❹, but then you have to work through the entire multivalue, which is effectively an associative array. The easiest thing to do is extract all the individual labels and values ❺. This program displays the slightly awkward label names (for your reference), but you probably won't usually want to show off words like `$!<Mobile>!$`, and it's easy enough to strip them out.

The program ends by cleaning up some of the Core Foundation objects, using the standard Core Foundation memory-management functions. When you run it, this program displays some of the data from names that you search for, as shown in figure 9.2.

You can do lots more with the Address Book, but this should outline the basics of how to access its several classes.

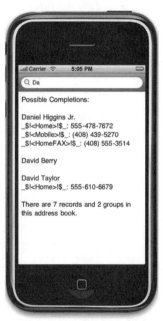

Figure 9.2   As shown here on the iPhone, the Address Book framework gives you low-level access to contact information.

9.2.4   *Using the Address Book UI*

There are definitely times when you'll want to work with the low-level Address Book functions you've seen so far. But you also don't want to reinvent the wheel. If you need to let a user select, edit, or insert a new contact, you don't need to program the UI. Instead, you can use the Address Book UI framework, which has all that functionality preprogrammed.

The Address Book UI framework contains only the four classes that we summarized in table 9.3: ABPeoplePickerNavigationController, ABNewPersonViewController, ABPersonViewController, and ABUnknownPersonViewController. Each of these UI objects is—as the names suggest—a view controller. To be precise, they're highly specialized modal controllers that each assist you in a single Address Book–related task. Each controller also has a delegate protocol, which is how you link to a class that's already pretty fully realized. We'll touch on each of these classes, but we'll give a lot of attention to only the people picker (ABPeoplePickerNavigationController).

THE PEOPLE PICKER VIEW CONTROLLER

To demonstrate the people picker, you'll put together a quick utility with substantially identical functionality to the previous Address Book example. But rather than searching for multiple users using the Address Book framework, the user will instead select a specific user using the Address Book UI framework.

This program is built with a couple of Xcode–created objects. A UIToolBar with a single button allows the user to activate the program via the selectContact: method, and text will once more be displayed in a non-editable UITextView called myText. The program is shown in the following listing.

> **Listing 9.6   People picker: a simple, graphical way to select contacts**

```
-(IBAction)selectContact:(id)sender {
    ABPeoplePickerNavigationController *myPicker =            ❶ Creates
        [[ABPeoplePickerNavigationController alloc]             people picker
            init];
    myPicker.peoplePickerDelegate = self;       ◁─❷ Sets delegate
    [self presentModalViewController:myPicker                 ❸ Displays
        animated:YES];                                          people picker
    [myPicker release];
}
- (BOOL)peoplePickerNavigationController:
    (ABPeoplePickerNavigationController *)peoplePicker
    shouldContinueAfterSelectingPerson:
        (ABRecordRef)thisPerson {
    CFIndex abPCount =                                         ❹ Gets
        ABAddressBookGetPersonCount                              overall
            (peoplePicker.addressBook);                         counts
    CFIndex abGCount =
        ABAddressBookGetGroupCount
            (peoplePicker.addressBook);
    myText.text = [NSString stringWithString:@"Selected Contact:"];
    myText.text = [myText.text stringByAppendingFormat:@"\n\n%@",
        (NSString *)ABRecordCopyCompositeName(thisPerson)];
```

```
    CFStringRef thisJob = ABRecordCopyValue(thisPerson,
        kABPersonJobTitleProperty);
    CFStringRef thisOrg = ABRecordCopyValue(thisPerson,
        kABPersonOrganizationProperty);
    if (thisJob != NULL && thisOrg != NULL) {
        myText.text = [myText.text stringByAppendingFormat:@"\n%@ of
            %@",thisJob,thisOrg];
    }
    ABMultiValueRef thisPhones = ABRecordCopyValue(thisPerson,
        kABPersonPhoneProperty);
    if (thisPhones != NULL) {
        for (int j = 0; j < ABMultiValueGetCount(thisPhones) ; j++) {
            myText.text = [myText.text stringByAppendingFormat:@"\n%@: %@",
                (NSString *)ABMultiValueCopyLabelAtIndex(thisPhones, j),
                (NSString *)ABMultiValueCopyValueAtIndex(thisPhones, j)];
        }
    }
    myText.text = [myText.text stringByAppendingFormat:@"\n\nThere are %ld
        records and %ld groups in this address book.",abPCount,abGCount];
    [self dismissModalViewControllerAnimated:YES];
    return NO;
}
- (BOOL)peoplePickerNavigationController:
    (ABPeoplePickerNavigationController *)peoplePicker
    shouldContinueAfterSelectingPerson:(ABRecordRef)person
    property:(ABPropertyID)property
    identifier:(ABMultiValueIdentifier)identifier {
    return NO;
}
- (void)peoplePickerNavigationControllerDidCancel:
    (ABPeoplePickerNavigationController *)
        peoplePicker {
    [self dismissModalViewControllerAnimated:YES];
}
```

To instantiate a modal view controller, you follow three simple steps that are executed when the user clicks the appropriate button in the toolbar. You create the controller ❶, set its delegate ❷, and use `UIViewController`'s `presentModalViewController: animated:` method to place it at the top of your user's screen ❸. You then don't have to worry about how the modal view controller looks or works; you just have to respond to the messages listed in the protocol reference.

The fully featured interface that's available to you as soon as you pop up the controller is shown in figure 9.3.

You do most of the work in the `peoplePickerNavigationController:should-ContinueAfterSelectingPerson:` method. This is called whenever a user selects an individual contact. Note that you can use a property of the `peoplePicker` variable to access the Address Book ❹, which allows you to use many of the `ABAddressBook` functions without needing to create the Address Book manually. Beyond that, the people picker sends you an `ABRecordRef` for the contact that the user selected; from there, you work with it exactly as you worked with the `ABRecordRefs` you looked up in listing 9.5.

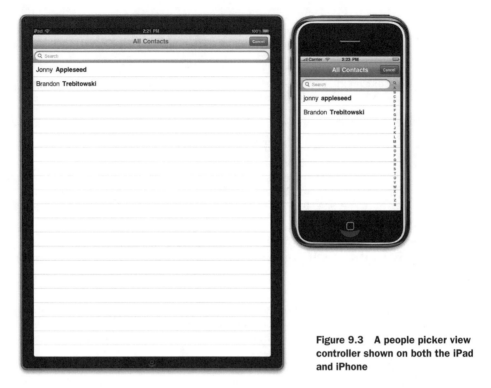

Figure 9.3   A people picker view controller shown on both the iPad and iPhone

In this example, users can only select individual contacts, so when the method is done, you dismiss the modal view controller and then return NO, which tells the people picker that you don't want to take the standard action for selecting the contact (which would be to call up a subpage with all of that contact's properties).

If you wanted to let a user select a specific property from within a contact, you'd fill in the peoplePickerNavigationController:shouldContinueAfterSelecting-Person:property:identifier: method.

The third method defined by the ABPeoplePickerNavigationController protocol is peoplePickerNavigationControllerDidCancel:, which here causes the program to (again) dismiss the people picker.

You can do a little more with the people picker. As we already noted, you could have opted to let a user select an individual property by returning YES for the first shouldContinue method and then filling in the second one. You could also choose the individual properties that display on a contact page. Information on these possibilities is available in the ABPeoplePickerNavigationController and ABPeople-PickerNavigationControllerDelegate class references.

USING CORE FOUNDATION
The Address Book framework is the first framework you've worked with that requires you to use Core Foundation, a non-Cocoa library. This means you have to program slightly differently, as we promised would be the case back in chapter 1. The biggest differences are how variables and memory allocation work.

Core Foundation variables use different classes, such as `CFStringRef` replacing `NSString *`. Remember that the Core Foundation variable types usually have equivalents in Cocoa that you can freely switch between by casting, as is done in listing 9.5 when moving between the Address Book records and the `UITextView` text. When you're using the Core Foundation variables natively, you have to use Core Foundation functions, such as `CFArrayCount`, to deal with them.

You also have to deal with memory management a little differently. Core Foundation memory management uses the same general approach as Cocoa Touch. There's a reference count for each object that's increased when it's created or retained and decreased when it's released. You have to remember slightly different rules for when you have a reference. If you create an object with a function using the word *create* or *copy*, you own a reference to it and must `CFRelease` it. If you create an object in another way, you don't have a reference, and you must `CFRetain` the object if you want to keep it around. Some classes of objects may have their own release and retain functions. The "Memory Management Programming Guide for Core Foundation" tutorial at http://developer.apple.com has more information.

Core Foundation will show up again in chapter 12, where it controls some audio services, and in chapter 13, where it's used for the Quartz 2D graphics package. You can use three other view controllers to allow users to interact with the Address Book, as we'll discuss next.

THE OTHER VIEW CONTROLLERS

The other three view controllers work much like `ABPeoplePickerNavigation-Controller`, with one notable difference: they must each be built on top of a navigation controller. Technically, they're probably not modal view controllers, because they go inside a navigation controller, but you can treat the navigation controller as a modal view controller once everything is loaded up, as you'll see in the example.

The `ABNewPersonViewController` allows a user to enter a new contact. You can prefill some of the info by recording it in an `ABRecordRef` and setting the `displayed-Person` property, but this is purely optional (and probably won't usually be done). After you've created the controller, you need to respond to a method that tells you when the user has entered a new contact. You don't have to do anything with it except dismiss the modal controller, because the controller automatically saves the new contact to the Address Book. You can see what info the user entered, though, and do something with it if you want. The following listing shows how to deploy a new person view on top of a navigation controller and how to respond to its single method.

> **Listing 9.7 Functionality required to call up a new person view controller**

```
-(IBAction)newContact:(id)sender {
    ABNewPersonViewController *myAdder =
        [[ABNewPersonViewController alloc] init];
    myAdder.newPersonViewDelegate = self;
    UINavigationController *myNav = [[UINavigationController alloc]
        initWithRootViewController:myAdder];
```

```
    [self presentModalViewController:myNav animated:YES];
    [myAdder release];
    [myNav release];
}
- (void)newPersonViewController:
    (ABNewPersonViewController *)newPersonViewController
    didCompleteWithNewPerson:(ABRecordRef)person {
    [self dismissModalViewControllerAnimated:YES];
}
```

The other two view controllers work the same way, except for the specifics about what methods each protocol defines.

The `ABPersonViewController` displays the information for a specific user. You'll need to set the `displayedPerson` property to an `ABRecordRef` before you call it up. This `ABRecordRef` might have been retrieved from the Address Book search functions or from the people picker, using the functions we've already discussed. The person view controller can optionally be editable. There's one method listed in the protocol, which activates when an individual property is selected.

Finally, the `ABUnknownPersonViewController` allows you to display the `ABRecord-Ref` defined by `displayedPerson` as if it were a real contact. Optionally, the user can create that information as a new contact, add it to an existing contact, or take property-based actions, like calling a number or showing a URL. It's a great way to give users the option to add contact info for your software company to their Address Book.

You should now understand the basics of how to use the Address Book in your own programs.

9.3   *An introduction to Core Data*

The Core Data framework is a data storage system that was added to the iOS SDK 3.0. It provides a powerful and structured method to save and retrieve persistent data on the iPhone and iPad.

Core Data is based on the design methodology of Model-View-Controller. It's intended as the model and provides such functionality. This allows the data to be completely separate from the views and controllers, giving the developer more control of their application.

Traditionally, when you wanted to save structured data on the device, you looked to such methods as SQLite or serialization. Core Data can be considered a hybrid of these two with some added functionality. It gives you the power of SQL with the simplicity of serialization.

Core Data allows you to take objects you already have in your application and save them directly into a database. You no longer need to do complex queries or make sure that your object property names match up with your database field names. Core Data handles these tasks for you.

Because Core Data is such a large topic, we'll only scratch the surface of what's possible. The next subsections will teach you how to use Core Data by walking you through a simple example of creating a to-do list application. Your application will display a table view of to-do objects that will be saved and retrieved using Core Data.

You'll see how to set up Core Data, how to initialize Core Data objects, how to add those objects to the database, and then how to access and manipulate them. Although this won't be an in-depth discussion about Core Data, it will give you the knowledge necessary to use Core Data for storage in your own applications.

9.3.1 Background information about Core Data

Let's briefly look at the concepts and terminology we'll be using. We'll start by discussing the heart of Core Data, the managed object.

MANAGED OBJECT

A *managed object* is a representation of an object you want to store in a database. Think of it as a record in SQL. It generally contains fields that match up with the properties of an object being saved in your application. After you create a managed object, you must insert it into a managed object context before you can save it to the data store.

MANAGED OBJECT CONTEXT

The managed object context holds all of your managed objects until they're ready to be committed to the database. Inside this context, managed objects can be added, modified, and deleted. This is like a buffer between your application and the database.

MANAGED OBJECT TABLE

This object describes the schema of your database. It's used when interfacing the managed object context with the database. A managed object table contains a collection of entity descriptions. Each of these entities describes a table in your database and is used when mapping managed objects to database entries.

9.3.2 Setting up Core Data in your application

Integrating Core Data into your application is simple. It requires less code than SQLite and offers a much simpler interface. The sample application we'll look at in this section is a basic journal application. It will allow you to post entries and view them by date. To start using the Core Data API, be sure to add CoreData.framework to your project.

The first thing you must do to integrate Core Data is add the data model to your project. The data model file is where you do all the creation of your Core Data database. To add it, choose File > New File. Then, select Data Model under Resource. Name it something appropriate to your application. In this example, name it CDJournal.Xcdatamodel, and click Finish.

Now that you've added the data model to your project, you must define your database entities. Click the Xcdatamodel to open the table editor. Now, follow these steps to add the table for the journal entries:

**Figure 9.4
Entry box**

1 Click the + Add Entity button on the bottom of the editor area. Doing so adds a new entity with a default name. Change the name of this field to Entry. Figure 9.4 shows what this box should look like.

2 Now that you've created an entity named
`Entry`, you must create the properties that
go along with it. To do this, click + in the
Attributes box and add your attribute properties: in this case, `body`, `title`, and `cre-
ationDate`. Notice that you can specify the
type of each property, similarly to how you'd
do it in SQLite. The Property box should
look like figure 9.5.

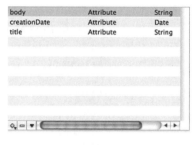

Figure 9.5   Properties of an `Entry`

3 At this point you may also create any other entities needed for your application.
If one entity contains another, you can drag and drop to create relationships.
This is similar to a foreign key in SQL. In this case, you could have authors, and
an author could have many entries.

Now that you've created your database, you must generate the classes that represent
your database objects. This allows you to get a code representation of your entities. To
do this, select the entity in your Xcdatamodel file. Then, choose Editor > Create
NSManagedObject Subclass. Figure 9.6 shows what this menu should look like.
Accept the default path, and click Create. That's it!

When you've completed this process, you should see .h and .m files added to your
project for the entity in your Core Data model. You may now use these class files like

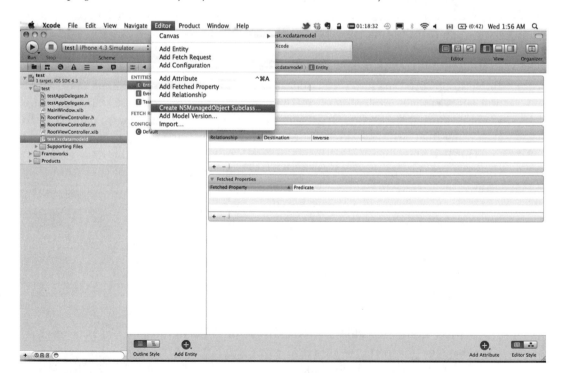

Figure 9.6   Creating a managed object class

any other class in your project. You'll see a little later how they're used to interface with your database.

The last thing you must do to prepare your application is to add the Core Data framework to your project. To do this, in the project editor, select the target; in this case CDJournal is the target. Click Build Phases at the top of the project editor. Open the Link Binary With Libraries section. Then, click the + button and select core-data.framework from the list. Now you're ready to start writing the code to initialize your Core Data model.

9.3.3 Initializing the Core Data objects

As with SQLite, Core Data requires quite a bit of setup before you can get it up and running. Fortunately, the code for doing this is standard and is roughly the same in most situations.

First, you must declare the objects needed by Core Data. As you did with SQLite, you declare them in your application delegate. This lets you send the context to only the classes that need to work with it. The objects you need to declare are `model`, `context`, and `persistent store`. The following listing shows this code.

Listing 9.8 Declaring the Core Data objects

```
#import <CoreData/CoreData.h>

@interface CDJournalAppDelegate : NSObject <UIApplicationDelegate> {
    NSManagedObjectModel *managedObjectModel;
    NSManagedObjectContext *managedObjectContext;
    NSPersistentStoreCoordinator *persistentStoreCoordinator;

    UIWindow *window;
    UINavigationController *navigationController;
}

@property (nonatomic, retain, readonly) NSManagedObjectModel
    *managedObjectModel;
@property (nonatomic, retain, readonly)
    NSManagedObjectContext *managedObjectContext;
@property (nonatomic, retain, readonly)
    NSPersistentStoreCoordinator *persistentStoreCoordiantor;
@property (nonatomic, retain) IBOutlet UIWindow *window;
@property (nonatomic, retain) IBOutlet UINavigationController
    *navigationController;

@end
```

Now that the properties have been declared, they must be initialized. After they're initialized, only the managed object context will be used to interface with the data store. You must add a few methods to your delegate method to initialize all of these properties. They're pretty standard and can be implemented the same way in all your applications. We'll walk you through each of these methods.

The first method is the getter for the `persistentStoreCoordinator`. It's where you'll be loading and initializing the database used by your Core Data application. The next listing shows the code for this method.

Listing 9.9   Setter methods for Core Data objects

```
- (NSPersistentStoreCoordinator *)persistentStoreCoordinator {

    if (persistentStoreCoordinator != nil) {
        return persistentStoreCoordinator;
    }
    NSString *docs = [NSSearchPathForDirectoriesInDomains(
            NSDocumentDirectory, NSUserDomainMask, YES) lastObject];
    NSURL *storeUrl = [NSURL fileURLWithPath: [docs
            stringByAppendingPathComponent: @"CDJournal.sqlite"
    NSError *error = nil;
    persistentStoreCoordinator = [[NSPersistentStoreCoordinator alloc]
    initWithManagedObjectModel:[self managedObjectModel]];

    if (![persistentStoreCoordinator
            addPersistentStoreWithType:NSSQLiteStoreType configuration:nil
            URL:storeUrl options:nil error:&error]) {
            NSLog(@"Unresolved error %@, %@", error, [error userInfo]);
            abort();
    }
    return persistentStoreCoordinator;
}
```

❶ Resolves path to database

❷ Initializes store coordinator

This is a fairly standard getter method. You first check to see if the store coordinator has already been initialized. If so, you return it. This is the case on every call following the first one to this method.

Next, you resolve the path to the database used by your application ❶. As noted before, Core Data is built on top of SQLite. The name of the SQLite database you need to link to is the same as that of your Xcdatamodel file. In this case, it's CDJournal.sqlite.

Finally, you initialize the persistent store coordinator with this path and the managed object model ❷. In the event that an error occurs, the abort methods tell the application to fail and generate an error report. The last line returns a reference to the `persistentStoreCoordinator` object.

The next methods you'll implement are the setters for the `managedObjectContext` and `managedObjectModel` properties. The following code shows how these methods are implemented.

Listing 9.10   Object model and object context getter methods

```
- (NSManagedObjectContext *) managedObjectContext {

    if (managedObjectContext != nil) {
        return managedObjectContext;
    }

    NSPersistentStoreCoordinator *coordinator =
            [self persistentStoreCoordinator];
```

```
    if (coordinator != nil) {
        managedObjectContext = [[NSManagedObjectContext alloc] init];
        [managedObjectContext setPersistentStoreCoordinator: coordinator];
    }
    return managedObjectContext;
}

- (NSManagedObjectModel *)managedObjectModel {

    if (managedObjectModel != nil) {
        return managedObjectModel;
    }
    managedObjectModel = [[NSManagedObjectModel mergedModelFromBundles:nil]
     retain];
    return managedObjectModel;
}
```

Both of these methods check to see if their property has been initialized. If not, they're initialized and returned. The final method you need to implement is applicationWillTerminate. This is where you'll save your managed object context to the data store. You save your context every time the user makes a change to the data. This code is needed in case some unsaved data is lying around when the application exits. The following listing shows the code for this method.

Listing 9.11 Saving the managed object context

```
- (void)applicationWillTerminate:(UIApplication *)application
{
    NSError *error = nil;
    if (managedObjectContext != nil) {
        if ([managedObjectContext hasChanges] &&
            ![managedObjectContext save:&error]) {
                NSLog(@"Unresolved error %@, %@", error,
                        [error userInfo]);
                abort();
        }
    }
}
```

The first thing this method does is check to see if your managedObjectContext is nil. This will most likely never be the case, but it's still good practice to check. Next, you check to see if there are any unsaved changes to the context by calling the hasChanges method. The context will have changes anytime something is added, modified, or deleted.

   If changes are present, the context is saved by calling the save method. Similarly to the code in listing 9.9, you call the abort method in the event of an error in order to generate a crash log. You're now ready to make changes to your data.

9.3.4 *Adding objects to the database*

As you've seen, to work with database objects in SQLite, you must write the raw SQL code. Also, every time you want to add a record, you must write many lines of code that can't be reused in other areas. This is where the true power of Core Data comes in.

In Core Data, you're working with only the class files that were generated from your data model. This allows you to manipulate them as you would any other object in Objective-C. Let's start by looking at the code to add an object to the database. The code for adding a new entity to the database is shown here.

> **Listing 9.12   Adding an entity to the database**

```
Entry * e = (Entry *)[NSEntityDescription
    insertNewObjectForEntityForName:@"Entry"
    inManagedObjectContext:managedObjectContext];

[e setTitle:textField.text];
[e setBody:textView.text];
[e setCreationDate:[NSDate date]];
NSError *error;

if (![managedObjectContext save:&error]) {
    NSLog(@"Error Saving: %@",[error description]);
}
```

As you can see, the only difference here is how you initialize the Entry object. Instead of doing a [[Entry alloc] init], you allow Core Data to create a new object inside the context. After this object has been created, you can begin using its accessor and mutator methods. You can even create your own methods inside these objects and call them.

When you're ready to save your managed object, you call the save method of the managed object context. This causes your changes to be made permanent by writing them to the database.

9.3.5 *Fetching, updating, and deleting objects in Core Data*

To update or delete objects from the database, you must first have them in memory. To do this, you need to fetch them into an array.

Fetching in Core Data is much more elegant than it is in SQL. You tell Core Data what objects you want and how to sort the objects, and it returns them in an array with little code. The code to do a simple fetch on your journal entries and sort them by their creation date is shown here.

> **Listing 9.13   Fetching data**

```
NSFetchRequest *request = [[NSFetchRequest alloc] init];
NSEntityDescription *entity = [NSEntityDescription
    entityForName:@"Entry"
        inManagedObjectContext:managedObjectContext];
        [request setEntity:entity];
        NSSortDescriptor *sortDescriptor = [[NSSortDescriptor alloc]
```

**Creates sort ❶
descriptor
to sort results**

```
        initWithKey:@"creationDate" ascending:NO];
    NSArray *sortDescriptors = [[NSArray alloc]
        initWithObjects:sortDescriptor, nil];
     [request setSortDescriptors:sortDescriptors];
     [sortDescriptors release];
     [sortDescriptor release];
```

Executes request ❷

```
    NSError *error;
    NSMutableArray *mutableFetchResults = [[managedObjectContext
        executeFetchRequest:request error:&error] mutableCopy];
    if (mutableFetchResults == nil) {
        NSLog(@"Error fetching result %@",[error description]);
    }

     [self setEntries:mutableFetchResults];
     [mutableFetchResults release];
     [request release];
```

❸ **Localizes array**

The first step in retrieving results from the database is to create the fetch request. After the request has been created, you must set its entity. The entity represents which object type you're retrieving. In this case, the entity is an `Entry` of your journal.

After your request is created, you must tell it how to sort the results. If you omit this step, the ordering of the results will be undefined. This means the results returned could be in any order. The sort descriptor you create ❶ tells the request to sort the results by the creation date in ascending order. You can sort based on any field in your entity.

The last thing you need to do is execute the request ❷. Notice that the request returns an `NSMutableArray`. This array contains all the objects retrieved from the database in the order specified by the sort descriptor. To keep these results around, you set them to a class variable ❸.

When you have an array of objects on hand, you can begin modifying or deleting them. Let's look at modifying objects. Here's how you update a managed object:

```
- (void) update:(Entry *) entry {
    [entry setTitle:textField.text];
    [entry setBody:textView.text];
    [entry setCreationDate:[NSDate date]];

    NSError *error;
    if (![self.managedObjectContext save:&error]) {
        NSLog(@"Error Saving: %@",[error description]);
    }
}
```

As you can see, the code is almost identical to the code to add a new entry. The only difference is how the entry is retrieved. Instead of letting Core Data allocate a new entry for you, you modify one you already have on hand. Typically, this is first retrieved from the array you created in listing 9.13.

As with updating, you must have a managed object on hand in order to delete it. You can't delete a managed object without first retrieving it. Here's how you delete a managed object from the database:

```
-(void) delete:(Entry *) entry {
    [managedObjectContext deleteObject:entry];

    [entries removeObject:entry];
    NSError *error;
        if (![managedObjectContext save:&error]) {
        NSLog(@"Error deleted entry %@",[error description]);
    }
}
```

The delete method is fairly straightforward. The first thing to do is remove the object from the managed object context. Any time the context is saved after removing the object, it deletes that object from the data store.

Next, you delete the object from the global array of entries so you can reflect the update to the user. If you don't do this, the user may still see the object in a table view, even though it's deleted forever when the application exits.

Finally, you save the context. As with any changes made to the context, saving it makes them permanent.

9.4   *Summary*

As you've seen, you have two powerful options to consider when storing large amounts of data on the iPhone and iPad. SQLite is great for anyone with prior experience with SQL and MySQL. You have the ability to use full SQL syntax to work with the records without having to learn a new design pattern.

Core Data is Apple's response to solving the complexities associated with SQL. You no longer need to know complicated SQL syntax in order to have a fully functional database in your application. Core Data extracts much of the process and gives you high-level objects to work with as you please.

In the next chapter, we'll move away from data storage and work with some of the cool hardware features of the iPhone and iPad. These include the accelerometer, GPS, and compass.

Positioning: accelerometers, location, and the compass

This chapter covers

- Sensing gravity
- Gauging movement
- Determining location and orientation
- Using Core Location

When we first introduced the iPhone and iPad, we highlighted a number of their unique features. Among them were three components that allow the device to figure out precisely where it is in space: a trio of accelerometers or gyroscope, which gives it the ability to sense motion such as shaking or rotation; a locational device (using either GPS or faux GPS), which lets it figure out where in the world it is; and a compass to figure out which direction it's facing.

Other than accessing some basic orientation information, we haven't done much with these features. We'll now dive into these positioning technologies and examine how to use them in your programming.

We'll start with some new ways to look at orientation data and then explain how to use the accelerometers, compass, and GPS in real applications.

10.1 *The accelerometers and orientation*

The easiest use of the accelerometers is to determine the device's current orientation. You already used the view controller's `interfaceOrientation` property, back in chapter 5. As we mentioned at the time, you can also access orientation information through the `UIDevice` object. It can provide more information and real-time access that isn't available using the view controller.

You have two ways to access the `UIDevice` information: through properties and through a notification. Let's examine the orientation property first.

10.1.1 *The orientation property*

The easy way to access the `UIDevice`'s orientation information is to look at its orientation property. You must first access the `UIDevice` itself, which you can do by calling a special `UIDevice` class method, pretty much the same way you access the `UIApplication` object:

```
UIDevice *thisDevice = [UIDevice currentDevice];
```

After you've done this, you can get to the `orientation` property. It returns a constant drawn from `UIDeviceOrientation`. This looks exactly like the results from a view controller's `orientation` property except there are three additional values, shown in table 10.1.

These three additional values are one reason you may want to access the `UIDevice` object rather than examine orientation using a view controller.

Table 10.1 `UIDeviceOrientation` **lists seven types of the device orientation.**

Constant	Summary
`UIDeviceOrientationPortrait`	Device is vertical, right side up.
`UIDeviceOrientationPortraitUpsideDown`	Device is vertical, upside down.
`UIDeviceOrientationLandscapeLeft`	Device is horizontal, tilted left.
`UIDeviceOrientationLandscapeRight`	Device is horizontal, tilted right.
`UIDeviceOrientationFaceUp`	Device is lying on its back.
`UIDeviceOrientationFaceDown`	Device is lying on its screen.
`UIDeviceOrientationUnknown`	Device is in an unknown state.

10.1.2 *The orientation notification*

The `UIDevice` class can also give you instant access to an orientation change when it occurs. This is done through a notification (a topic we introduced in chapter 6). The following code shows how to access this information:

```
[[UIDevice currentDevice]
   beginGeneratingDeviceOrientationNotifications];
[[NSNotificationCenter defaultCenter] addObserver:self
   selector:@selector(deviceDidRotate:)
```

```
   name:@"UIDeviceOrientationDidChangeNotification"
 object:nil];
```

This is a two-step process. First, you alert the device that you're ready to start listening for a notification about an orientation change. This is one of a pair of `UIDevice` instance methods, the other being `endGeneratingDeviceOrientationNotifications`. You generally should leave notifications on only when you need them, because they take up CPU cycles and increase your power consumption.

Second, you register to receive the `UIDeviceOrientationDidChangeNotification` messages, the first live example of the notification methods we introduced in chapter 6. Then, whenever an orientation change notification occurs, the `device-DidRotate:` method is called. Note that you don't receive notification of what the new orientation is; you only know that a change happened. For more details, you have to query the `orientation` property.

You've now seen the two ways in which orientation can be tracked with the `UIDevice` object, providing more information and more rapid notification than you receive when using the view controller. But that only touches the surface of what you can do with the device's accelerometers. It's the raw data about changes in three-dimensional space that you'll really want to access.

10.2 *The accelerometers and movement*

When you use orientation notification, the frameworks do the work for you: they take low-level acceleration reports and turn them into more meaningful events. It's similar to the concept of actions, which turn low-level touch events into high-level control events.

> **WARNING** Accelerometer programs can't be tested on the Simulator. Instead, you need to have a fully provisioned iPhone or iPad to test your code. See appendix C for information about provisioning your device.

Notifications aren't sufficient if you want to program entire interfaces that effectively use the device's movement in three-dimensional space as a new user-input device. For that, you need to access two classes: `UIAccelerometer` and `UIAcceleration`. Let's look at accessing and parsing data from `UIAccelerometer`. Later in the section, you'll use the accelerometers to check for gravity and movement.

10.2.1 *Accessing the UIAccelerometer*

`UIAccelerometer` is a class you can use to receive acceleration-related data. It's a shared object, like `UIApplication` and `UIDevice`. The process of using it is as follows:

```
- (void)viewDidLoad {
   UIAccelerometer *myAccel =
      [UIAccelerometer sharedAccelerometer];
   myAccel.updateInterval = .1;
   myAccel.delegate = self;
   [super viewDidLoad];
}
```

The first step is to access the accelerometer, which you do with another call to a shared-object method. Having this step on its own line is probably unnecessary, because you could perform the other two steps as nested calls, but we find this a lot more readable.

Next, you select your update interval, which specifies how often you receive information about acceleration. This is hardware limited, with a current default of 100 updates per second. That's most likely just right if you're creating a game using the accelerometer, but it's excessive for other purposes. We've opted for 10 updates per second, which is an updateInterval of 0.1. You should always set the lowest acceptable input to preserve power on the device.

Finally, you must set a delegate for the accelerometer, which is how you receive data on accelerometer changes. The delegate needs to respond to only one method, accelerometer:didAccelerate:, which sends a message containing a UIAcceleration object whenever acceleration occurs (to the limit of the updateInterval). Note that the class that utilizes this mechanism needs to declare the UIAccelerometerDelegate protocol in the interface.

10.2.2 Parsing the UIAcceleration

You can use UIAcceleration information to accurately and easily measure two things: the device's relationship to gravity and its movement through three-dimensional space. These are both done through a set of three properties, x, y, and z, which refer to the three-dimensional axes, as shown in figure 10.1.

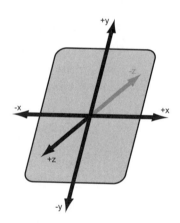

The x-axis measures along the short side of the iPhone or iPad, the y-axis measures along the long side, and the z-axis measures through the device. All values are measured in units of g, which is to say g-force. A value of 1 g represents the force of gravity on Earth at sea level.

The thing to watch for when accessing the accelerometer is that it measures two types of force applied to the device: both the force of movement in any direction *and* the force of gravity, measured in units of g.

Figure 10.1   The accelerometers measure acceleration in three-dimensional space.

That means an iPhone or iPad at rest always shows an acceleration of 1 g toward the Earth's core. This may require filtering if you're doing more sophisticated work.

10.2.3 Checking for gravity

When the accelerometers are at rest, they naturally detect gravity. You can use this feature to detect the precise orientation an iPhone or iPad is currently held in, going far beyond the four or six states supported by the orientation variables.

> ## Filtering and the accelerometer
>
> It may seem that the acceleration data is mushed together, but it's easy to isolate exactly the data you need using basic electronics techniques.
>
> A *low-pass filter* passes low-frequency signals and attenuates high-frequency signals. That's what you use to reduce the effects of sudden changes in your data, such as those caused by an abrupt motion.
>
> A *high-pass filter* passes high-frequency signals and attenuates low-frequency signals. That's what you use to reduce the effects of ongoing forces, such as gravity.
>
> You'll see examples of these two filtering methods in the upcoming sections.

READING ACCELERATION INFORMATION

The following code shows how you can use the accelerometers to modify redBall, a UIImage picture of a red ball initially set in the middle of the screen:

```
- (void)accelerometer:(UIAccelerometer *)accelerometer
    didAccelerate:(UIAcceleration *)acceleration {
    CGPoint curCenter = [redBall center];
    float newX = 3 * acceleration.x + curCenter.x;
    float newY = -3 * acceleration.y + curCenter.y;
    if (newX < 25) newX = 25;
    if (newY < 25) newY = 25;
    if (newX > 295) newX = 295;
    if (newY > 455) newY = 455;
    redBall.center = CGPointMake(newX,newY);
}
```

Any accelerometer program begins with the accelerometer:didAccelerate: method, which you access by setting the current program as a delegate of the Accelerometer shared action. You then mark the current position of the redBall.

To access the accelerometer, all you do is look at the x and y coordinates of the UIAcceleration object and prepare to modify the redBall's position based on those. The acceleration is multiplied by 3 here to keep the ball's movement from being snail-like. There's also a z property for the third axis and a timestamp property indicating when the UIAcceleration object was created, none of which you need in this example. Movement has a limited effect on the example anyway, because an abrupt movement doesn't change the ball's slow roll much.

After acquiring your gravitic information, you make sure the 50 x 50 red ball stays within the bounds of the screen. If you wanted to be fancy, you could introduce vectors and bounce the ball when it hits the edge, but that's beyond the scope of this example. After that check, you move the ball. Figure 10.2 shows what this program looks like on the iPad.

With a minimal amount of work, you've created a program that's acted on by gravity. This program could easily be modified to act as a leveler tool for pictures (by having it move along only one of the three axes) or could be turned into a game

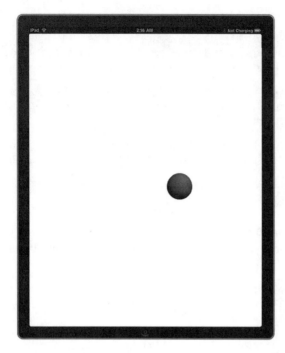

Figure 10.2   Gravity test as shown on the iPad. The ball falls as if pulled by gravity and responds accordingly to changes in the orientation of the device.

where a player tries to move a ball from one side of the screen to the other, avoiding pits on the way.

Now, what would it take to make this example *totally* functional by filtering out all movement? The answer, it turns out, is not much more work at all.

FILTERING OUT MOVEMENT

To create a low-pass filter that lets through gravitic force but not movement, you need to average out the acceleration information you're receiving, so that at any time the vast majority of your input is coming from the steady force of gravity. This is shown in the following code, which modifies the previous example:

```
gravX = (acceleration.x * kFilteringFactor)
    + (gravX * (1 - kFilteringFactor));
gravY = (acceleration.y * kFilteringFactor)
    + (gravY * (1 - kFilteringFactor));
float newX = 3 * gravX + curCenter.x;
float newY = -3 * gravY + curCenter.y;
```

This example depends on three predefined variables: `kFilteringFactor` is a constant set to .1, which means that only 10 percent of the active movement is used at any time; `gravX` and `gravY` each maintain a cumulative average for that axis of movement as the program runs.

You filter things by averaging 10 percent of the active movement with 90 percent of the average. This smoothes out any bumps, which means sudden acceleration is largely ignored. This example does this for the x- and y-axes because that's all that are used in the example. If you cared about the z-axis, you'd need to filter that too.

Afterward, you use the average acceleration instead of the raw acceleration when you're changing the position of the ball. The gravity information can be extracted from what looked like an imposing mass of data with a couple of lines of code.

As you'll see, looking at only the movement is just as easy.

10.2.4 Checking for movement

In the previous example, you isolated the gravitic portion of the accelerometer's data by creating a simple low-pass filter. With that data in hand, it's trivial to create a high-pass filter. All you need to do is subtract the low-pass filtered data from the acceleration value; the result is the pure movement data:

```
gravX = (acceleration.x * kFilteringFactor)
        + (gravX * (1 - kFilteringFactor));
gravY = (acceleration.y * kFilteringFactor)
        + (gravY * (1 - kFilteringFactor));
float moveX = acceleration.x - gravX;
float moveY = acceleration.y - gravY;
```

This filter doesn't entirely stop gravitic movement, because it takes several iterations for the program to cut out gravity completely. In the meantime, the program is influenced by gravity for a few fractions of a second at startup. If that's a problem, you can tell the program to ignore acceleration input for a second after it loads and after an orientation change. We'll show the first solution in the next example.

With that exception, as soon as you start using these new moveX and moveY variables, you're looking at the filtered movement information rather than the filtered gravity information. But when you start looking at movement information, you see that it's trickier to use than gravity information. There are two reasons for this.

First, movement information is a lot more ephemeral. It appears for a second, and then it's gone again. If you're displaying some type of continuous movement, as with the red ball example, you need to make your program much more sensitive to detect the movements. You'd have to multiply the moveX and moveY values by about 25 to see movement forces applied to the ball in any recognizable manner.

Second, movement information is a lot noisier. As you'll see when we look at real movement data, motion occurs in a multitude of directions at the same time, forcing you to parse out the exact information you want.

Ultimately, to interpret movement, you have to be more sophisticated, recognizing what are effectively gestures in three-dimensional space.

10.2.5 Recognizing simple accelerometer movement

If you want to write programs using acceleration gestures, we suggest that you download the Accelerometer Graph program available from Apple's developer site. This is a nice, simple example of accelerometer use; but more important, it also provides you with a clear display of what the accelerometers report as you make different gestures. Make sure you enable the high-pass filter to get the clearest results.

Figure 10.3 shows what the Accelerometer Graph looks like in use (but without movement occurring). As you move the device around, you'll quickly come to see how the accelerometers respond.

Here are some details you'll notice about how the accelerometers report information when you look at the Accelerometer Graph:

- Most gestures cause all three accelerometers to report force; the largest force should usually be in the axis of main movement.
- Even though there's usually a compensating stop force, the start force is typically larger and shows the direction of main movement.
- Casual movement usually results in forces of .1 g to .5 g.
- Slightly forceful movement usually tops out at 1 g.
- A shake or other more forceful action usually results in a 2 g force.
- The accelerometers can show things other than simple movement. For example, when you're walking with an iPhone or iPad, you can see the rhythm of your pace in the accelerometers.

Figure 10.3   The Accelerometer Graph shows movement in all three directions.

All of this suggests a simple methodology for detecting basic accelerometer movement: you monitor the accelerometer over the course of movement, saving the largest acceleration in each direction. When the movement has ended, you can report the largest acceleration as the direction of movement.

The following listing puts these lessons together in a program that could easily be used to report the direction of the device's movement (which you could then use to take some action).

Listing 10.1   Movement reporter that could be applied as a program controller

```
- (void)accelerometer:(UIAccelerometer *)accelerometer
    didAccelerate:(UIAcceleration *)acceleration {
    accelX = ((acceleration.x * kFilteringFactor)       ❶ Gathers
        + (accelX * (1 - kFilteringFactor)))              filtered
    accelY = ((acceleration.y * kFilteringFactor)         info
        + (accelY * (1 - kFilteringFactor)));
    accelZ = ((acceleration.z * kFilteringFactor)
        + (accelZ * (1 - kFilteringFactor)));
    float moveX = acceleration.x - accelX;              ❷ Measures
    float moveY = acceleration.y - accelY;                movement
    float moveZ = acceleration.z - accelZ;
    if (!starttime) {                                   ❸ Marks
        starttime = acceleration.timestamp;               start time
    }
```

```
if (acceleration.timestamp > starttime + 1 &&
    (fabs(moveX) >= .3 ||
     fabs(moveY) >= .3 ||
     fabs(moveZ) >= .3)) {
    if (fabs(moveX) > fabs(moveVector)) {
        moveVector = moveX;
        moveDir = (moveVector > 0 ? @"Right" : @"Left");
    }
    if (fabs(moveY) > fabs(moveVector)) {
        moveVector = moveY;
        moveDir = (moveVector > 0 ? @"Up" : @"Down");
    }
    if (fabs(moveZ) > fabs(moveVector)) {
        moveVector = moveZ;
        moveDir = (moveVector > 0 ? @"Forward" : @"Back");
    }
    lasttime = acceleration.timestamp;
} else if (moveVector && acceleration.timestamp
    > lasttime + .1) {
    myReport.text =
        [moveDir stringByAppendingFormat:
            @": %f.",moveVector];
    moveDir = [NSString string];
    moveVector = 0;
}
}
```

④ Saves largest movements

You start by creating a low-pass filter ❶ and then taking the inverse of it ❷ in order to get relatively clean movement data. Because the data can be a little dirty at the start, you don't accept any acceleration data sent in the first second ❸. You could cut this down to a mere fraction of a second.

You start looking for movement whenever one of the accelerometers goes above .3 g. When that occurs, you save the direction of highest movement ❹ and keep measuring it until movement drops below .3 g. Afterward, you make sure that at least a tenth of a second has passed, so that you know you're not in a lull during a movement.

Finally, you do whatever you want to do with your movement data. This example reports the information in a label, but you'd doubtless do something much more intricate in a live program. Cleanup is required to get the next iteration of movement reporting going.

This sample program works well, unless the movement is very subtle. In those cases, it occasionally reports the opposite direction because of the force when the device stops its motion. If this type of subtlety is a problem for your application, more work is required. To resolve this, you need to make a better comparison of the start and stop forces for movements; if they're similar in magnitude, you'll usually want to use the first force measured, not necessarily the biggest one. But for the majority of cases, the code in listing 10.1 is sufficient. You now have an application that can accurately report (and take action based on) direction of movement.

Together, gravity and force measurement represent the most obvious things that you can do with the accelerometers, but they're by no means the *only* things. We suspect that using the accelerometers to measure three-dimensional gestures will be one of their best (and most frequent) uses as the platform matures.

10.3   *The accelerometers and gestures*

Three-dimensional gestures are one of the coolest results of having accelerometers inside your iPhone or iPad. They let users manipulate your programs without ever having to touch (or even look at) the screen.

To recognize a gesture, you must do two things. First, you must accurately track the movements that make up the gesture. Second, you must make sure that in doing so, you don't recognize a random movement that wasn't intended to be a gesture at all.

Recognizing a gesture requires only the coding foundation that we've discussed already. But we'll show one example that puts that foundation into real-world use by creating a method that recognizes a shake gesture.

10.3.1   *Using accelerometers*

We're defining a *shake* as a rapid shaking back and forth of the device, like you might shake dice in your hand before you throw them. Apple's Accelerometer Graph is a great tool to use to figure out what's going on. It shows a shake as primarily having these characteristics, presuming a program that's running in portrait mode:

- Movement is primarily along the x-axis, with some movement along the y-axis, and even less along the z-axis.
- There are at least three peaks of movement, with alternating positive and negative forces.
- All peaks are at least +/-1 g, with at least one peak being +/-2 g for a relatively strong shake.

You can use the preceding characteristics to define the average requirements for a shake. If you wanted to tighten them up, you'd probably require four or more peaks of movement, but for now, this will do. Alternatively, you might want to decrease the g-force requirements so that users don't have to shake their device quite as much. We've detailed the code that watches for a shake in the following listing.

Listing 10.2   Shake, shake your iPhone

```
- (BOOL)didShake:(UIAcceleration *)acceleration {
    accelX = ((acceleration.x * kFilteringFactor)
        + (accelX * (1 - kFilteringFactor)));
    float moveX = acceleration.x - accelX;
    accelY = ((acceleration.x * kFilteringFactor)
        + (accelY * (1 - kFilteringFactor)));
    float moveY = acceleration.x - accelY;
    if (lasttime && acceleration.timestamp > lasttime + .25) {      ← Waits after ❶ last shake
        BOOL result;
        if (shakecount >= 3 && biggestshake >= 1.25) {
            result = YES;
        } else {
```

```
              result = NO;
        }
        lasttime = 0;
        shakecount = 0;
        biggestshake = 0;
        return result;
    } else {
        if (fabs(moveX) >= fabs(moveY)) {
            if ((fabs(moveX) > .75) && (moveX * lastX <= 0)) {
                lasttime = acceleration.timestamp;
                shakecount++;
                lastX = moveX;
                if (fabs(moveX) > biggestshake) biggestshake = fabs(moveX);
            }
        } else {
            if ((fabs(moveY) > .75) && (moveY * lastY <= 0)) {
                lasttime = acceleration.timestamp;
                shakecount++;
                lastY = moveY;
                if (fabs(moveY) > biggestshake) biggestshake = fabs(moveY);
            }
        }
        return NO;
    }
}
```

❷ **Checks x movement**

❸ **Measures y movement**

In this code, you generally follow the logic you used when viewing the accelerometer graph, although with increased sensitivity, as promised. The `didShake:` method registers a shake if it sees three or more movements of at least .75 g, at least one of which is 1.25 g, with movements going in opposite directions.

You start by removing gravity from the accelerometer data, as you did in previous examples. This time, you don't worry about the quirk at the beginning of data collection; it doesn't register as a shake, because it's a small fraction of a g.

The main work of the function is found in its latter half, which is called whenever movement continues to occur. First, you check whether the strongest movement is along the x-axis ❷. If so, you register the movement if it's at least .75 g and if it's in the opposite direction of the last x-axis move. You do the latter check by seeing if the product of the last two moves on that axis is negative; if so, one must have been positive and the other negative, which means they were opposite each other.

If the strongest move was instead on the y-axis, you check for a sufficiently strong y-axis move that's in the opposite direction as the last y-axis move ❸. We could have written a more restrictive shake checker that only looked for x-axis movement, or a less restrictive checker that also looked for z-axis movement, but we opted for this middle ground.

As long as movement continues without a break of more than a quarter of a second, the `shakecount` continues to increment, but when movement stops ❶, the program is ready to determine whether a shake occurred. You check this by seeing if the shake count equals or exceeds 3 and if the largest movement exceeded 1.25 g. Afterward, all of the variables are reset to check for the next shake.

By building this shake checker as a separate method, you could easily integrate it into a list of checks made in the `accelerometer:didAccelerate:` method. The following code shows a simple use that changes the color of the screen every time a shake occurs. The `nextColor` method can be changed to do whatever you want:

```
- (void)accelerometer:(UIAccelerometer *)accelerometer
    didAccelerate:(UIAcceleration *)acceleration {
    if ([self didShake:(UIAcceleration *)acceleration]) {
        self.view.backgroundColor = [self nextColor];
    }

}
```

We expect that the shake will be the most common three-dimensional gesture programmed into the iPhone or iPad. With this code, you already have it ready to go, though you may choose to change its sensitivity or to make it work in either one or three dimensions.

10.3.2 *Gesture recognizer*

Standard gestures, such as a tap, double tap, a swipe or a pan may be of use, depending on the specifics of your program; you can take the advantage of the gesture API on the standard gestures defined in the iOS platform.

`UIGestureRecognizer` is the base class for the gesture recognizer under iOS. The common gestures are defined as subclasses of `UIGestureRecognizer`:

- `UITapGestureRecognizer`—This class handles single or multiple taps.
- `UIPinchGestureRecognizer`—This class recognizes pinch gestures.
- `UIRotationGestureRecognizer`—This class looks for gestures when the user moves fingers opposite each other in a circular motion.
- `UISwipeGestureRecognizer`—This class detects swipes based on the swipe direction definition, such as from left to right or down.
- `UIPanGestureRecognizer`—This class recognizes the panning/dragging gesture.
- `UILongPressGestureRecognizer`—This class handles the long press gesture.

To create a gesture recognizer, you need to know which view will be the object to monitor for the gesture events. For example, inside the view controller you want to monitor the tap gesture on the view:

```
UITapGestureRecognizer *tap = [[UITapGestureRecognizer alloc]
    initWithTarget:self action:@selector(handleGesture:)];
    [self.view addGestureRecognizer:tap];
    [tap release];
```

With this code, you can create the tap gesture recognizer to the view; when the tap gesture is detected, the method `handleGesture:` will be called to perform the animation or other cool response, depending on the application's specs.

Seems simple, right? Let's practice this new API with other gesture types. For example, we'd like to present an alert view when the user presses the view for longer than 2 seconds.

Fire up the Xcode and create an application with a View-Based Application template. Go to the view controller to add in the long press gesture recognizer, as shown in the following listing.

Listing 10.3 Detect user gesture with long press gesture recognizer

```
- (void)viewDidLoad {
    [super viewDidLoad];
    UILongPressGestureRecognizer *lpress = [[UILongPressGestureRecognizer
     alloc] initWithTarget:self action:@selector(longPressed:)];
    lpress.minimumPressDuration = 2.0;                    Creating long  ❶
    [self.view addGestureRecognizer:lpress];             press recognizer
    [lpress release];
}
                                                              ❷ Display
                                                                 alert view
-(void)longPressed:(UILongPressGestureRecognizer *)sender {
    if ((sender.state == UIGestureRecognizerStateChanged) ||
        (sender.state == UIGestureRecognizerStateEnded)) {
        UIAlertView *alert = [[UIAlertView alloc]
                            initWithTitle:@"Long Press"
                            message:@"Would you like to quit now?"
                        delegate:nil
                    cancelButtonTitle:@"OK"
                            otherButtonTitles:nil];
        [alert show];
        [alert release];
    }
}
```

In the `viewDidLoad` method, you created the long press recognizer ❶ and then defined the minimum press duration as 2 seconds; by default, this value is 0.5. When the user presses the view up to 2 seconds, the method `longPressed` ❷ gets called.

Inside the gesture recognizer, the gesture lookup is continuous. The `UIGesture-Recognizer`'s state will be switched among `UIGestureRecognizerStatePossible`, `UIGestureRecognizerStateBegan`, `UIGestureRecognizerStateChanged`, `UIGesture-RecognizerStateEnded`, `UIGestureRecognizerStateCancelled`, `UIGestureRecognizer-StateFailed`, and `UIGestureRecognizerStateRecognized`. Inside our response function, you'll present the alert view only when the gesture recognizer's state is ended or changed. Without this condition, you might see the alert view pop up two times in a row, which isn't desirable during the application runtime.

For now, we've covered all of the main points of the accelerometers: orientation, gravity, movement, and gestures. In iOS 4, the Core Motion framework is available for raw data access on the accelerometer and gyroscope. This framework is useful when you're combining the 3D model into your app. We're not going to cover the details in this book.

We're now ready to dive into the other major positioning-related tool, and one that we find a lot easier to program because the results are less noisy: Core Location.

10.4   *All about Core Location*

We have only one unique feature left to look at: the device's ability to detect a user's location.

> **WARNING** You can only minimally test Core Location using the Simulator. Longitude and latitude work, but they always report Apple's Cupertino head-quarters. Altitude isn't displayed. For most realistic testing—particularly including distance or altitude—you must use a provisioned device.

There are three ways available on iOS to detect current location: cell phone towers, wi-fi, and, most accurately, GPS. Its accuracy could vary from a few blocks' radius to a few miles, even in an urban area. The iPhone 4 (also iPad 3G, iPhone 3G, and 3GS) has a built-in GPS, but it still has limitations. The iPhone's antenna power is limited, which affects accuracy, and accuracy is further limited by concerns about power usage. As a result, even if you have an iPhone with a built-in GPS, the device makes preferential use of cell tower data and provides information about GPS locations using the minimal number of satellite contacts possible (although that minimum partially depends on an accuracy requirement that you set).

With all that said, the iPhone 4 provides better location information. But it may not be entirely accurate; in particular, altitude seems to be the least reliable information. The wi-fi–only iPad can determine your location based only on its IP address, making it the least accurate.

We offer this preamble both to describe how the location information is created and to introduce a bit of skepticism about the results. What you get should be good enough for 99 percent of your programs, but you don't want to do anything mission critical unless you're careful.

The good news is that you don't have to worry about which type of device a user owns. The Core Location API works identically whether they have a built-in GPS or not. Better, because GPS consumes a lot of power, you'll learn how to save users' battery life in chapter 21 by using the background location service available in the Core Location API. In this section, we'll examine the location classes and how to use the compass. You'll also build two applications: one that finds the current location and distance traveled and one that incorporates an altitude measurement.

10.4.1   *The location classes*

Location awareness is built into two API classes and one protocol. `CLLocationManager` gives you the ability to access location information in a variety of ways. It includes a delegate protocol, `CLLocationManagerDelegate`, which defines methods that can tell you when new location information arrives. Finally, the location information appears as `CLLocation` objects, each of which defines a specific location at a specific time.

Table 10.2 describes the most important properties associated with each of these classes. For more details, you should, as usual, consult the Apple class references. You should examine a number of additional properties and methods to aid with determining location (particularly for the `CLLocation` class), but we're staying with the basics here.

Table 10.2   The most important methods and properties for accessing location information

Method/Property	Type	Summary
Class: `CLLocationManager`		
delegate	Property	Defines the object that responds to `CLLocationManagerDelegate`
desiredAccuracy	Property	Sets the desired accuracy of location as a `CLLocationAccuracy` object
distanceFilter	Property	Specifies how much lateral movement must occur to cause a location update event
location	Property	Specifies the most recent location
startUpdatingLocation	Method	Starts generating update events
stopUpdatingLocation	Method	Stops generating update events
startUpdatingHeading	Method	Starts generating heading update events
stopUpdatingHeading	Method	Stops generating heading update events
headingFilter	Property	The minimum angle required to generate heading events
headingAvailable	Property	Returns `true` if heading events can be generated
Class: `CLLocationManagerDelegate`		
locationManager:didUpdateToLocation: fromLocation:	Method	Delegate method that reports whenever an update event occurs
locationManager:didFailWithError:	Method	Delegate method that reports whenever an update event fails to occur
Class: `CLLocation`		
altitude	Property	Specifies the height of the location in meters
coordinate	Property	Returns the location's coordinates as a `CLLocationCoordinate2D` variable
timestamp	Property	Specifies an `NSDate` of when the location was measured

Generally, location information is generated much like accelerometer information. You access a shared object (`CLLocationManager`) and set some standard properties for how you want it to work, including how often to update (`distanceFilter`). As with the accelerometer, you also have to explicitly turn on location updating (`startUpdating-Location`). Afterward, you keep an eye on certain methods (as defined by `CLLocation-ManagerDelegate`). These methods generate an object (`CLLocation`) when the location changes; you read the object to get the specifics.

With those generalities out of the way, let's see how `CLLocation` works in a real example.

10.4.2 *An example using location and distance*

This section shows an example of using Core Location to record a starting location, monitor the current location, and calculate the distance between them. As usual, the foundation of this program is built in Xcode. Figure 10.4 displays the general setup.

There are three labels: `startLabel` (at the top) and `endLabel` (at the bottom) each display information about a location; `distanceLabel` shows the distance between the two. There are two controls: a button control instantly updates the current location, and a segmented control chooses between miles and kilometers. They're each linked to an `IBAction`, which executes a method that you'll meet in the code.

The following listing shows the code. This is the first of two longer examples in this chapter.

Figure 10.4   This simple utility shows off locations and distance.

Listing 10.4   An application of Core Location for distances

```
- (void)viewDidLoad {
    [super viewDidLoad];
    myLM = [[CLLocationManager alloc] init];
    myLM.delegate = self;
    myLM.desiredAccuracy =
        kCLLocationAccuracyNearestTenMeters;
    myLM.distanceFilter = 100;
    [myLM startUpdatingLocation];
}
- (void)locationManager:(CLLocationManager *)manager
    didUpdateToLocation:(CLLocation *)newLocation
    fromLocation:(CLLocation *)oldLocation {
    if (startLoc == nil) {
        startLoc = newLocation;
        [self updateLocationFor:startLabel toLocation:newLocation];
        [startLoc retain];
    }

    [self updateLocationFor:endLabel
        toLocation:newLocation];
    [self updateDistanceLabel:newLocation];
}
- (IBAction)setEnd:(id)sender {
    [myLM stopUpdatingLocation];
    [myLM startUpdatingLocation];
}
- (IBAction)controlChange:(id)sender {
    if (myLM.location) {
        [self updateDistanceLabel:myLM.location];
    }
}
- (void)updateDistanceLabel:(CLLocation *)newLocation {
    if (startLoc != nil) {
        CLLocationDistance traveled
            = [startLoc distanceFromLocation:newLocation] / 1000;
        if (segmentControl.selectedSegmentIndex == 1) {
            traveled *= .62;
        }
        distanceLabel.text = [NSString stringWithFormat:@"%5.1f",traveled];
    }
}
- (void)updateLocationFor:(UILabel *)thisLabel
    toLocation:(CLLocation *)newLocation {
    CLLocationCoordinate2D curCoords = newLocation.coordinate;
    thisLabel.text = [NSString stringWithFormat:
        @"Lat: %2.4f; Long: %2.4f",curCoords.latitude,curCoords.longitude];
}
```

❶ Starts location updates

❷ Waits for updates

❸ Forces location update

❹ Forces label update

❺ Updates distance label

❻ Updates location label

This program generally follows the broad outline of steps that we've already discussed, but we'll go through each step in turn.

Make sure to add the Core Location framework to your project and import Core-Location/CoreLocation.h in all the files in which you intend to utilize location services. After that, you begin by initializing a CLLocationManager object and then set some standard properties—here a `delegate`, the `desiredAccuracy`, and the `distanceFilter`. The desired accuracy of tens of meters and the update interval of every 100 meters may be more than this particular application requires, but you can tune these in your projects as seems appropriate. Remember that demanding more accuracy and updating more frequently will decrease the battery life of your user's iPhone or iPad. Finally, you start the `CLLocationManager` running ❶.

The `locationManager:didUpdateToLocation:fromLocation:` method is the workhorse of this program ❷. It should be called shortly after the `LocationManager` starts updating and every time the user walks 100 meters or so. First, it saves the current location as the starting location the first time it's called, updating the `startLabel` at the same time. Then, every time it runs, it updates the `endLabel` and the `distance-Label`. Note that you don't have to use the `LocationManager`'s `location` property here (or at almost any other time in the program), because this method always provides the current location of the device; it seems to do so well before the `location` property is updated, based on our own tests. Caveat programmer.

The next few methods have to do with I/O. The method `setEnd:` is run whenever the button control is pushed, to update the current location ❸. Unfortunately, there's no particularly clean way to ask for an update, so you must stop and start the location updates, as shown here. Letting the user force a location update is particularly important if you're using a high `distanceFilter` or if you're trying to measure altitude changes. In the altitude example in the next section, you'll see an alternative way to do this, where the location manager usually isn't running at all. The `controlChange:` method is run whenever the segmented control is updated ❹. It updates the `distanceLabel`. Note that this is the one time when you depend on the `location` property, because there isn't a location event when you change the button.

The last few methods are utilities. The `updateDistanceLabel:` method makes use of an interesting `CLLocation` method that we haven't discussed, `distanceFrom-Location:` ❺. This measures the true distance between two locations, using complex calculations that correctly account for the curvature of the Earth. The method also converts meters to kilometers and alternatively converts them to miles, depending on the status of the segmented control. Finally, `updateLocationFor:toLocation:` updates either the `startLabel` or the `endLabel` by extracting the latitude and longitude coordinates from the `CLLocation` object it's passed ❻.

The result is a program that can show a simple distance traveled in a single direction. If we were going to improve it, we'd probably save the starting location to a file and perhaps even make it possible to record multiple trips. But for the purposes of showing how Core Location works, this is sufficient.

There's one thing that the example didn't show: how to measure altitude. It's another `CLLocation` property, but you'll write another short program to highlight this part of Core Location.

10.4.3 *An example using altitude*

Altitude is as easy to work with as longitude and latitude. It's another property that can be read from a CLLocation object. The biggest problem is that it isn't available to all users. The Simulator and the original iPhone don't support altitude.

Apple suggests using the following code to determine whether altitude is unavailable:

```
if (signbit(newLocation.verticalAccuracy)) {
```

If its return is nonzero, you need to discontinue checking for altitude information.

Even if a user has an iPhone or an iPad 3G, you must watch out for two other gotchas. First, altitude information can be 10 times more inaccurate than the rest of the location information. Adjust your desiredAccuracy accordingly. Second, remember that the Core Location information updates only when you move a certain distance, as determined by the distanceFilter, in a nonvertical direction. This means you need to allow the user to update the distance by hand rather than depending on automatic updates.

Listing 10.5 repeats the techniques you used previously, applying them to altitude. It also shows another useful integration of user input with a slightly more complex program. As usual, its core objects are built in Xcode: three UILabels, one UIText-Field, two UIImageViews, and a UIActivityIndicatorView. The last is the most interesting, because you haven't seen it before; we'll talk about it in our quick discussion of the code. You should be able to pick out all of the objects other than the activity indicator in figure 10.5, which follows the code.

Listing 10.5   Keeping track of a mountain climb with your iPhone

```
@implementation altitudeViewController
- (void)viewDidLoad {
    destinationHeight.returnKeyType = UIReturnKeyDone;
    myLM = [[CLLocationManager alloc] init];
    myLM.delegate = self;
    myLM.desiredAccuracy = kCLLocationAccuracyBest;
    savedDestinationHeight = 0;
    [super viewDidLoad];
}
- (BOOL)textFieldShouldReturn:(UITextField *)textField {
    [textField resignFirstResponder];
    return YES;
}
-(IBAction)changeDestination:(id)sender {
    savedDestinationHeight = [destinationHeight.text intValue];
    [self resetGPS:sender];
}
-(IBAction)resetGPS:(id)sender {
    if (savedDestinationHeight) {
        [myLM startUpdatingLocation];
        [myActivity startAnimating];
```

❶ Responds to text field

❷ Requests location updates

❸ Animates activity icon

```
        }
    }
- (void)locationManager:(CLLocationManager *)manager
        didUpdateToLocation:(CLLocation *)newLocation              ④ Receives
        fromLocation:(CLLocation *)oldLocation {                      location update

        if (savedDestinationHeight) {                              ⑤ Shows
            if (signbit(newLocation.verticalAccuracy)) {             altitude failure
                heightLabel.text = [NSString stringWithString:@"?? m."];
            } else {                                          ◁──⑥ Reports altitude info
                int currentHeight = 395 -
                    ceil((float)newLocation.altitude/savedDestinationHeight *
                        (401-65));
                heightLabel.text = [NSString stringWithFormat:@"%6.2f m.",
                    newLocation.altitude];
                heightButton.center = CGPointMake(106,currentHeight);
                heightLabel.center = CGPointMake(220,currentHeight);
            }
            [myLM stopUpdatingLocation];
            [myActivity stopAnimating];
        }
    }
    ...
@end
```

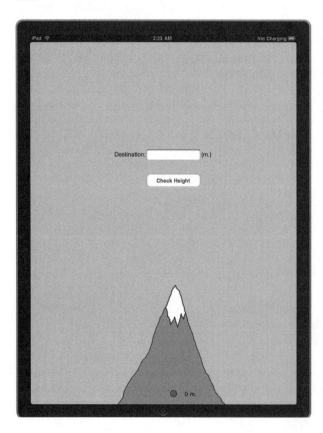

Figure 10.5   An altitude program measures how high you've climbed on a mountain of your choice.

Much of this code combines two SDK elements that you've already met: the flourishes necessary to make a `UITextField` work and the protocols you must follow to use a location manager. You can see both of these elements in the `viewDidLoad:` method, which sets up the text field's return key and then starts the location manager. Note that you don't start the location manager updating; you can't depend on it to update when you're measuring only vertical change, so it's best to have the user do it by hand. Next, you finish the text field's functionality with the `textFieldShouldReturn:` method, which you've met before.

This project contains two controls that can generate actions. When the text field is adjusted ❶, the project saves that destination height for future calculation and then updates the current height using the `resetGPS:` method. The latter method is also used when the Check Height button is pressed. Figure 10.5 shows these input devices for clarity.

Note that `resetGPS:` does two things. First, it starts the location update ❷, which you turn on only for brief, one-time uses. In addition to being more appropriate for monitoring altitude, this also helps save energy. Second, it starts your activity indicator ❸. This object is created visually, where you should mark it with the `hidesWhen-Stopped` property. The view is automatically hidden so it doesn't appear when the program is loaded. As a result, there's nothing on the screen until you start the animation, at which time a little activity indicator appears and continues animating until it's stopped (which you'll see in a minute).

The heavy lifting is done when the location manager reports back its information ❹. In this section, you check whether you're getting altitude information ❺. If you are ❻, you move the dot image and update its height label. To finish, you turn off the location update and then stop the animation of the activity indicator, which makes it disappear.

Voila! You have a working altitude monitor (if you have an iPhone 4, iPhone 3G, 3GS, or iPad 3G) and a nice combination of a few different SDK elements.

10.4.4 Using the compass

In addition to knowing your location, the iPhone 4 and 3GS have the ability to know what direction you're heading. This is because the iPhone 4 and 3GS have a built-in magnetic compass.

With the addition of the `CLHeading` class to the Core Location framework, you can now determine your magnetic heading as well as your true heading. The magnetic heading uses the built-in magnetometer and points to magnetic north, whereas the true heading uses your current location and points to true north.

Let's first examine the properties of the `CLHeading` class. Table 10.3 describes each of these properties.

In addition to these properties, you have access to the raw geomagnetic data. These properties include the raw x, y, and z data, which you can use individually.

Table 10.3   Properties of `CLHeading` used for determining the device's heading

Property	Description
magneticHeading	The heading that points to magnetic north. This value uses the built-in magnetometer and contains a value from 0 to 360.
trueHeading	Represents the heading that points to geographic north. This property relies on the current location and so isn't always guaranteed to be valid. It ranges from 0 to 360.
headingAccuracy	This value represents the error in degrees of the magneticHeading. A low value means the heading is relatively accurate. A negative value means the heading is invalid and can't be trusted.
timestamp	The timestamp when the heading was found.

Accessing the compass information is similar to accessing the GPS information. You first get a reference to the `CLLocationManager` object, and then you may begin collecting data:

```
- (void) viewDidLoad {
    CLLocationManager * locationManager = [[[CLLocationManager alloc] init]
    autorelease];
    if (locationManager.headingAvailable == YES) {
        locationManager.delegate = self;
        [locationManager startUpdatingHeading];
    }
}
```

You first create a new `CLLocationManager` to interact with the location data. The next line is required to ensure that the device supports the compass. The only devices that return `YES` here are the iPhone 4 and 3GS and iPads. If this fails, it's a good idea to notify the user that their device doesn't support the compass. You then start the compass and begin sending data to the `CLLocationManagerDelegate`. In this case, the delegate is set to the caller class. Alternatively, if it's only going to work when certain sensors are available, you can also define the hardware in the info.plist. For example, in order to make sure the Augmented Reality app will only run on the devices with magnetometer and GPS, you can add `UIRequiredDeviceCapabilities` key to your app's info.plist. The App Store will make sure that only the devices with a magnetometer and GPS will be able to download your app.

10.4.5 *Retrieving data from the compass*

To retrieve data from the compass, you must implement the `CLLocationManager-Delegate` method `locationManager:didUpdateHeading:`. This method is called automatically every time the compass heading changes on the device. The heading variable passed into this method contains all the data as described in table 10.3. Here's an example of how to implement this method:

```
- (void)locationManager:(CLLocationManager *)manager
    didUpdateHeading:(CLHeading *)heading {
    self.heading = heading;
}
```

This example isn't too exciting because it only localizes the `heading` variable to the `heading` class property. This is useful because you can now use the heading in other places in the code. The two most important properties of this `heading` variable are `magneticHeading` and `trueHeading`.

These variables are of the type `CLLocationDirection`, which is a `typedef double`. This value ranges from 0 to 360 degrees. A reading of 0 degrees means the device is pointing north, 90 means east, 180 south, and 270 west. If this value is ever negative, that means it's invalid.

Although the compass is a simple addition, it offers much power and flexibility within your applications. The addition has allowed for development of interesting apps, including navigation systems, augmented reality apps, and many others that depend on the user's orientation.

10.4.6 *Core Location and the internet*

In this section, you've seen a few real-world examples of how to use location information in meaningful ways, but you'll find that you can make much better use of the information when you have an internet connection. When you do, you can feed longitudes and latitudes to various sites. For example, you can pull up maps with a site like Google Maps. You can also improve on the altitude information by instead requesting the geographic altitude of a location using a site like GeoNames. This won't be accurate if your user is in an airplane or a tall office building, but for the majority of situations, it'll be better than what the device can currently deliver. See chapter 14 for some examples of using Core Location with the internet.

10.5 *Summary*

In this chapter, we've covered three of the most unique features available to you as an iOS programmer.

The accelerometers can give you access to a variety of information about where a device exists in space. By sensing gravity, you can easily discover precise orientation. By measuring movement, you can see how the device is being guided through space. Finally, you can build more complex movements into three-dimensional gestures, such as a shake.

We've talked about the touch screen when discussing input, but the accelerometers and gyroscopes provide another method for allowing users to make simple adjustments to a program. We can imagine game controls and painting programs built entirely around the accelerometers.

The internal GPS can give you information about longitude, latitude, and altitude. The horizontal information is the most reliable, although it's more useful when you connect to the internet. Altitude information isn't available to everyone, and even if it is, it has a higher chance of being incorrect, so use it with caution.

The compass gives you complete information about the user's heading. It lets you determine exactly which way the device is facing and allows for a large variety of new application types.

In the next chapter, we'll talk about media, highlighting pictures, videos, and sounds.

Media: images and the camera

11

This chapter covers

- Accessing and manipulating images
- Using the camera
- Creating a simple collage application
- Using AirPrint for images

So far, our focus has mainly been on text. Sure, we've displayed the occasional UIImage, such as the mountain drawing in the previous chapter, but we've considered only the simplest means for doing so.

The iPhone, iPod Touch, and iPad offer an experience that's potentially much richer and more engaging. Cameras, a microphone, a complete library of photos, and a speaker are just some of the utilities built into these devices. Less the camera, the first-generation iPad contains all the aforementioned libraries. In this chapter and the next, we'll look at these features as part of a general exploration of media. We'll provide deep coverage of images as well as how to use the camera.

More complex questions are beyond the scope of this chapter. We're saving the topic of image editing for a later chapter, when we look at the graphic libraries.

11.1   *An introduction to images*

We've touched on using images a few times, beginning in chapter 3, where one of the earliest SDK
examples included an image. You've created a
`UIImageView` in Xcode, attached it to a filename,
and not worried about the details.

We're now ready to consider the details. We'll
look at some of the options available when you dive
into Xcode.

When you look more closely, you'll discover that
using images is a two-step process. First, you load
data into a `UIImage`, and then you make use of that
`UIImage` via some other means. There are two
major ways to use `UIImage`s, as shown in figure 11.1.

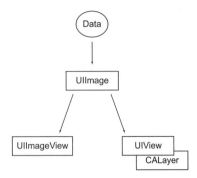

**Figure 11.1   Images can be shown in
`UIImageViews` or in `UIViews`.**

We're going to explore the primary method of displaying images, using
`UIImageView`, in this section, and in section 11.2 we'll examine the more complex
means available for drawing images onto the back layer of a `UIView`.

11.1.1   *Loading a UIImage*

The `UIImage` class offers seven different ways to create an instance of an image. The
four factory methods are probably the easiest to use, and they're the ones we've listed
in table 11.1. You can also use some equivalent `init` methods if you prefer.

The image data can be of several file types, including BMP, CUR, GIF, JPEG, PNG,
and TIFF. In this book, we use mostly JPEGs (because they're small) and PNGs (because
they look good and are accelerated on the hardware). You can also create a `UIImage`
from a Quartz 2D object; this is the SDK's fundamental graphics package, which we'll
talk about more in chapter 13. To support the retina display, the system uses the suffix
of the image filename to load the best-matching image. For example, if you have two
image files for one icon, one standard image and one higher-resolution image for retina display, name the standard file icon.png and HD version file icon@2x.png. During
the loading time, the `UIImage` class will handle which image to load automatically. If
you don't have this HD version image file, the `UIImage` class will load the standard file
and scale it up to fit in the higher-resolution screen display.

Table 11.1   Class methods for creating a `UIImage`

Class method	Summary
`imageNamed:`	Creates a `UIImage` based on a file in the main bundle. In iOS 4 and later, you may omit the filename's extension.
`imageWithCGImage:`	Creates a `UIImage` from a Quartz 2D object. This is the same as `initWithCGImage:`.

Table 11.1 Class methods for creating a `UIImage` (continued)

Class method	Summary
`imageWithContentsOfFile:`	Creates a `UIImage` from a complete file path that you specify, as discussed in chapter 8. This is the same as `initWithContentsOfFile:`.
`imageWithData:`	Creates a `UIImage` from `NSData`. This is the same as `initWithData:`.

After you import an image into your program, you can display it. If you're going to stay entirely within the simple methods of UIKit, you should use the `UIImageView` class to display the image.

11.1.2 Drawing a UIImageView

You've already used the `UIImageView` in your programs when displaying pictures. We're now ready to talk about the details of how it works.

You can initialize a `UIImageView` two ways. First, you can use the `initWithImage:` method, which allows you to pass a `UIImage`, as follows:

```
UIImage *myImage1 = [UIImage imageNamed:@"sprou11.jpg"];
UIImageView *myImageView =
    [[UIImageView alloc] initWithImage:myImage1];
[self.view addSubview:myImageView];
```

Alternatively, you can use a plain `initWithFrame:` method and modify the object's properties by hand. Table 11.2 shows a few of the properties and methods you're most likely to use when doing more extensive work with a `UIImageView`.

To load a normal image, you can use the `image` property, but there's usually little reason to use it rather than the `initWithImage:` method—unless you're dynamically changing your image. If you want to create a set of images to animate, it's useful to take advantage of the other `UIImageView` methods and properties.

Table 11.2 A few properties and methods of note for `UIImageView`

Method or property	Type	Summary
`animationDuration`	Property	Specifies how often an animation cycles
`animationImages`	Property	Identifies an `NSArray` of images to load into the `UIImageView`
`animationRepeatCount`	Property	Specifies how many times to run an animation cycle
`image`	Property	Identifies a single image to load into a `UIImageView`
`startAnimating:`	Method	Starts the animation
`stopAnimating:`	Method	Stops the animation

You can load an array of images into a `UIImageView`, declare how fast and how often they should animate, and start and stop them as you see fit. A simple example of this is shown in the following listing.

Listing 11.1   Using `UIImageView` to animate images

```
- (void)viewDidLoad {
    UIImage *myImage1 =
        [UIImage imageNamed:@"sproul1.jpg"];
    UIImage *myImage2 =
        [UIImage imageNamed:@"sproul2.jpg"];
    UIImage *myImage3 =
        [UIImage imageNamed:@"sproul3.jpg"];
    UIImage *myImage4 =
        [UIImage imageNamed:@"sproul4.jpg"];
    UIImageView *myImageView =
        [[[UIImageView alloc]
            initWithFrame:[[UIScreen
                mainScreen] bounds]];
    myImageView.animationImages =
        [NSArray arrayWithObjects:myImage1,
        myImage2,myImage3,myImage4,nil];
    myImageView.animationDuration = 4;
    [myImageView startAnimating];
    [self.view addSubview:myImageView];
    [myImageView release];
    [super viewDidLoad];
}
```

This code first loads the images, then creates a `UIView`, and finally starts the animation. Taking advantage of `UIImageView`'s animation capability is one of the main reasons you may want to load images by hand.

11.1.3   Modifying an image in UIKit

You've seen how to create images and load them into image views programmatically. The next thing to do is to start modifying them.

Unfortunately, you have only a limited ability to do so while working with `UIImage-View`. You can make *some* changes, based on simple manipulations of the view. For example, if you resize your `UIImageView`, it automatically resizes the picture it contains. Likewise, you can decide where to draw your `UIImageView` by setting its frame to something other than the whole screen. You can even layer multiple images by using multiple `UIImageViews`.

This starts to get unwieldy quickly, though, and you can't do anything fancier, like transforming images or modifying how they stack through blending or alpha transparency options. To do that sort of work (and to stack graphics, not just views), you need to learn about Core Graphics.

`UIImage` offers some simple ways to access Core Graphics functionality that doesn't require going out to the Core Graphics framework (or learning about contexts or the other complexities that underlie its use). We'll talk about those briefly here, but for the most part, Core Graphics will wait for the next chapter, which concentrates on the entire Quartz 2D graphics engine.

11.2　Drawing simple images with Core Graphics

Although it doesn't give access to the entire Core Graphics library of transformations and other complexities, the `UIImage` class includes five simple methods that take advantage of the way Core Graphics works. They're described in table 11.3.

Table 11.3　Instance methods for drawing a `UIImage`

Method	Summary
`drawAsPatternInRect:`	Draws the image inside the rectangle, unscaled, but tiled as necessary
`drawAtPoint:`	Draws the complete unscaled image with the `CGPoint` as the upper-left corner
`drawAtPoint:blendMode:alpha:`	A more complex form of `drawAtPoint:`
`drawInRect:`	Draws the complete image inside the `CGRect`, scaled appropriately
`drawInRect:blendMode:alpha:`	A more complex form of `drawInRect:`

The trick is that these methods *can't* be used as part of `viewDidLoad:` or whatever other method you usually use to load up your objects. That's because they depend on a graphical *context* to work. We'll talk about contexts more in chapter 13; for now, keep in mind that a graphical context is a destination you're drawing to, like a window, a PDF file, or a printer.

On the iPhone and iPad, `UIViews` automatically create a graphical context as part of their `CALayer`, which is a Core Animation layer associated with each `UIView`. You can access this layer by writing a `drawRect:` method for the `UIView` (or rather, for a new subclass that you've created). You usually have to capture a special context variable to do this type of work, but the `UIView` methods take care of this for you, to keep things simple.

Here's how to collage together a few pictures using this method:

```
- (void)drawRect:(CGRect)rect {
    UIImage *myImage1 = [UIImage imageNamed:@"sproul1.jpg"];
    UIImage *myImage2 = [UIImage imageNamed:@"sproul2.jpg"];
    UIImage *myImage3 = [UIImage imageNamed:@"sproul3.jpg"];
    [myImage1 drawAtPoint:CGPointMake(0,0) blendMode:kCGBlendModeNormal
        alpha:.5];
    [myImage2 drawInRect:CGRectMake(10, 10, 140, 210)];
    [myImage3 drawInRect:CGRectMake(170, 240, 140, 210)];
}
```

Note that the `drawAtPoint:` method gives you access to more complex possibilities, such as blending your pictures (using Photoshop-like options such as color dodge and hard light) and making them partially transparent. Here you're using a normal blend but only 50 percent transparency (hence the use of the `drawAtPoint:` method). Using singular draw commands is simpler than going through the effort of creating multiple `UIImageView` objects.

There's still a lot that you can't do until we dive fully into the Core Graphics framework; but for now you have some control, which should be sufficient for most common media needs. If you need more control, skip right ahead to chapter 13.

We've talked a lot about images, and we've presumed so far that you're loading them from your project's bundle. But what if you want to let a user select photographs? That's the topic of the next section.

11.3 Accessing photos

You can use the SDK to access pictures from the photo library or the camera roll. You can also allow a user to take new photos. This is all done with the `UIImagePicker-Controller`, another modal controller that manages a fairly complex graphical interface without much effort on your part. Figure 11.2 shows what it looks like.

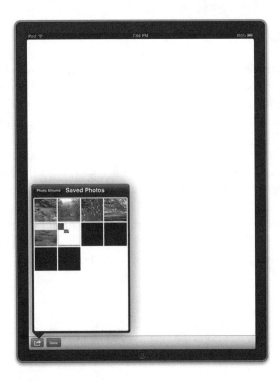

Figure 11.2   The image picker is another preprogrammed controller for your use.

11.3.1 *Using the image picker*

By default, the `UIImagePickerController` lets users access the pictures in their photo library. You load the `UIImagePickerController` by creating the object, setting a few variables, and presenting it. On the iPhone, you present it as a modal view controller; on the iPad, you need to display it in a `UIPopoverController`. Make sure your class implements the `UIImagePickerControllerDelegate` protocol in order to use its methods.

To display the picker on the iPhone, you can use the following code snippet:

```
UIImagePickerController *myImagePicker =
    [[UIImagePickerController alloc] init];
myImagePicker.delegate = self;
myImagePicker.allowsImageEditing = NO;
[self presentModalViewController:myImagePicker animated:YES];
```

As we mentioned, the iPad requires that you display the `UIImagePickerController` inside a `UIPopoverController`. One great thing about this is that you can specify the location on the screen in which the picker appears. The following code displays the `UIImagePickerController` on the iPad:

```
UIImagePickerController *myImagePicker =
      [[UIImagePickerController alloc] init];
   myImagePicker.delegate = self;
   myImagePicker.allowsEditing = NO;

   UIPopoverController *popover = [[UIPopoverController alloc]
      initWithContentViewController:myImagePicker];
   [popover presentPopoverFromRect:CGRectMake(0,0,320,480)
      inView:self.view permittedArrowDirections:
      UIPopoverArrowDirectionAny animated:YES];
```

After you've created your `UIImagePickerController`, you need to have its delegate respond to two methods: `imagePickerController:didFinishPickingMediaWith-Info:` and `imagePickerControllerDidCancel:`. For the first method, you dismiss the modal view controller (or hide the popover on the iPad) and respond appropriately to the user's picture selection; for the second, you only need to dismiss the controller.

Overall, the `UIImagePickerController` is easy to use because you're mainly reacting to a picture that was selected. Section 11.4 presents a complete example of its use.

11.3.2 *Taking photos*

As we noted earlier, the `UIImagePickerController` has three possible sources, represented by these constants:

- `UIImagePickerControllerSourceTypePhotoLibrary`—A picture from the photo library
- `UIImagePickerControllerSourceTypeSavedPhotosAlbum`—A picture from the camera roll
- `UIImagePickerControllerSourceTypeCamera`—A new picture taken by the camera

You should always make sure that the source is available before you launch a UIImage-PickerController, although this is most important for the camera. You can confirm that the source exists with the isSourceTypeAvailable: class method:

```
if ([UIImagePickerController
     isSourceTypeAvailable:UIImagePickerControllerSourceTypeCamera]) {
```

After you've verified the existence of a source, you can tell the image picker to use it with the sourceType property. For example, to use the camera, do the following:

```
myImagePicker.sourceType = UIImagePickerControllerSourceTypeCamera;
```

Note that pictures taken in a program go only to that program. If you want them to go into the photo album, your program has to save them there (as we'll discuss momentarily).

> **NOTE** In our experience, the camera is a bit of a resource hog. More than anything else, this means you need to think about saving your program's state when using the camera, because it could cause you to run out of memory.

We'll present an example of using the camera in section 11.4.

11.3.3 *Saving to the photo album*

You may wish to save a new photograph to the photo album, or you may wish to place a graphic created by your program there. In either case, you use the UIImageWriteTo-SavedPhotosAlbum function. It has four variables: the first lists the image, and the other three reference an optional asynchronous notification function to call when the save has been completed. Usually you call the function like this:

```
UIImageWriteToSavedPhotosAlbum(yourImage,nil,nil,nil);
```

If you instead want to take advantage of the asynchronous notification, look at the UIKit function reference, which is where this function is hidden, or look at the example in chapter 13.

You can use this function (and a bit of trickery) to save the CALayer of a UIView to your photo album, which, for example, lets you save the draw commands that you wrote straight to the CALayer earlier. This again depends on graphical contexts, which we'll explain in the next chapter, but here's how to do it:

```
UIGraphicsBeginImageContext(myView.bounds.size);
[myView.layer renderInContext:UIGraphicsGetCurrentContext()];
UIImage *collageImage = UIGraphicsGetImageFromCurrentImageContext();
UIGraphicsEndImageContext();
UIImageWriteToSavedPhotosAlbum(collageImage,nil,nil,nil);
```

In order for this to work correctly, you must add the Quartz Core framework to your project.

With all the fundamentals of images now covered, we're ready to put them together in our big example for this chapter. It's a program that collages together multiple pictures, first selecting them with a UIImagePickerController, then allowing them to be moved about with a `UIImageView`, and finally drawing them to a `CALayer` that can be saved.

11.4   Collage: an image example

The collage program depends on three objects. The `collageViewController`, as usual, does most of the work. It writes out to a `collageView` object, which exists mainly as a `CALayer` to be written upon. Finally, you'll have a `tempImageView` object that allows the user to position an image after it's been selected but before it's permanently placed.

For this example, the code will be written to deploy the collage application to the iPhone. To learn how to port it to the iPad, be sure to read appendix D; it contains step-by-step instructions for porting this app as well as your own apps to the iPad.

11.4.1   The collage view controller

The collage view controller is built with a few objects: the view controller itself; a toolbar called `myTools`, which will be filled over the course of the program; and the `collageView` `UIView` class, which exists as its own class file and is referred to in the program as `self.view`. You also need to add the Quartz Core framework to your project because you'll use the save-picture trick that we just discussed.

The next listing shows the complete view controller, which is the most extensive file in this program.

Listing 11.2   A view controller, which manages most of the collage's tasks

```
@implementation collageViewController
- (void)viewDidLoad {
    UIBarButtonItem *picButton = [[UIBarButtonItem alloc]
        initWithBarButtonSystemItem:UIBarButtonSystemItemAction target:self
        action:@selector(choosePic:)];
    UIBarButtonItem *camButton = [[UIBarButtonItem alloc]
        initWithBarButtonSystemItem:UIBarButtonSystemItemCamera target:self
        action:@selector(takePic:)];
    UIBarButtonItem *saveButton = [[UIBarButtonItem alloc]
        initWithBarButtonSystemItem:UIBarButtonSystemItemSave target:self
        action:@selector(savePic:)];
    picButton.style = UIBarButtonItemStyleBordered;
    camButton.style = UIBarButtonItemStyleBordered;
    if ([UIImagePickerController
        isSourceTypeAvailable:UIImagePickerControllerSourceTypeCamera]) {
            origToolbar = [[NSArray alloc] initWithObjects:
                picButton,camButton,saveButton,nil];
    } else if ([UIImagePickerController
isSourceTypeAvailable:UIImagePickerControllerSourceTypePhotoLibrary]) {
            origToolbar = [[NSArray alloc] initWithObjects:
                picButton,saveButton,nil];
    } else {
        exit(0);
    }
    [myTools setItems:origToolbar animated:NO];
    [picButton release];
```

```
    [camButton release];
    [super viewDidLoad];
}
-(IBAction)choosePic:(id)sender {
    UIImagePickerController *myImagePicker =
        [[UIImagePickerController alloc] init];
    myImagePicker.delegate = self;
    myImagePicker.allowsImageEditing = NO;
    [self presentModalViewController:myImagePicker animated:YES];
}
-(IBAction)takePic:(id)sender {
    UIImagePickerController *myImagePicker =
        [[UIImagePickerController alloc] init];
    myImagePicker.sourceType = UIImagePickerControllerSourceTypeCamera;
    myImagePicker.delegate = self;
    myImagePicker.allowsImageEditing = NO;
    [self presentModalViewController:myImagePicker animated:YES];
}
- (void)imagePickerController:(UIImagePickerController *)picker
    didFinishPickingImage:(UIImage *)image
    editingInfo:(NSDictionary *)editingInfo {
    [self dismissModalViewControllerAnimated:YES];
    [picker release];
    float percentage = [self scaleImage:image] / 2;
    startingSize = CGSizeMake(image.size.width*percentage,
        image.size.height*percentage);
    myImageView = [[tempImageView alloc]
        initWithFrame:CGRectMake(80,115,
            startingSize.width,startingSize.height)];
    myImageView.image = image;
    myImageView.userInteractionEnabled = YES;
    [self.view addSubview:myImageView];
    [myTools setItems:[NSArray arrayWithObject:[[UIBarButtonItem alloc]
        initWithBarButtonSystemItem:UIBarButtonSystemItemDone target:self
        action:@selector(finishPic:)]] animated:YES];
    mySlider = [[UISlider alloc] initWithFrame:CGRectMake(90,415,210,44)];
    mySlider.value = .5;
    [mySlider addTarget:self action:@selector(rescalePic:)
        forControlEvents:UIControlEventValueChanged];
    [self.view addSubview:mySlider];
}
- (void)imagePickerControllerDidCancel:
    (UIImagePickerController *)picker {
    [self dismissModalViewControllerAnimated:YES];
    [picker release];
}
-(void)rescalePic:(id)sender {
    myImageView.frame = CGRectMake(myImageView.frame.origin.x,
        myImageView.frame.origin.y,
        startingSize.width * mySlider.value * 2,
        startingSize.height * mySlider.value * 2);
}
-(void)finishPic:(id)sender {
    [self.view addPic:myImageView.image at:myImageView.frame];
    [myImageView removeFromSuperview];
    [myImageView release];
```

❶ Responds to image selection

❷ Responds to picker cancellation

```
    [mySlider removeFromSuperview];
    [mySlider release];
    [myTools setItems:origToolbar animated:NO];
}
-(void)savePic:(id)sender {
    UIGraphicsBeginImageContext(self.view.bounds.size);
    myTools.hidden = YES;
    [self.view.layer renderInContext:UIGraphicsGetCurrentContext()];
    UIImage *collageImage = UIGraphicsGetImageFromCurrentImageContext();
    myTools.hidden = NO;
    UIGraphicsEndImageContext();
    UIImageWriteToSavedPhotosAlbum(collageImage,nil,nil,nil);
}
-(float)scaleImage:(UIImage *)image {
    float toSize = 1.0;
    if (image.size.width * toSize > 320) {
        toSize = 320 / image.size.width;
    }
    if (image.size.height * toSize > 460) {
        toSize = 460 / image.size.height;
    }
    return toSize;
}
// ...
@end
```

Although long, this code is simple to follow in bite-size chunks. It starts with `viewDid-Load:`, which sets up the `UIToolBar`. You can't efficiently fill the `UIToolBar` in Xcode because you'll be changing it based on the program's state. You place buttons on the toolbar that call three methods: `choosePic:`, `takePic:` (when a camera's available), and `savePic:`.

`choosePic:` and `takePic:` are similar methods. Each calls up the image picker controller, but the first one accesses the photo library and the second one lets the user take a new picture. The wonder of these modal controllers is that you don't have to do a thing between the time when you create the picker and the point at which the user either selects a picture or cancels.

When the user selects a picture, `imagePickerControl:didFinishPickingImage:editingInfo:` is called ❶, returning control to your program. Here you do four things:

1 Dismiss the modal view controller.

2 Look at the picture you've been handed, and resize it to fill a quarter or less of the screen.

3 Instantiate the image as a `tempImageView` object, which is a subclass of `UIImageView`.

4 Change the toolbar so a Done button is available, along with a slider.

At this point, the user can do three things:

- Use `UITouches` to move the image view (which is covered in the `tempImageView` class, because that's where the touches go, as you saw in chapter 6).

- Use the slider to change the size of the picture.
- Tap Done to accept the image size and location.

The results of what can be produced are shown in figure 11.3.

Note that if the user instead cancels the image picker, your `imagePicker-`
`ControllerDidCancel:` method correctly shuts down the modal controller ❷.

The `UISlider` is hooked up to the `rescalePic:` method. It redraws the frame of
the `UIImageView`, which automatically resizes the picture inside. Meanwhile, the Done
button activates the `finishPic:` method. This sends a special `addPic:at:` message to
the `collageView`, which is where the `CALayer` drawing is done, and which we'll return
to momentarily. `finishPic:` also dismisses the `UISlider` and the `tempImageView` and
resets the toolbar to its original setup.

That original toolbar has one more button that we haven't covered yet: Save. It
activates the `savePic:` method, which saves a `CALayer` to the photo library. Note that
this method temporarily hides the toolbar in the process. Because the toolbar is a subview of the `UIView`, it would be included in the picture if you didn't do this.

The last method, `scaleImage:`, is the utility that sets each image to fill about a
quarter of the screen.

This code has two dangling parts: the methods in the `tempImageView`, which allow
a user to move the `UIImageView`, and the methods in the `collageView`, which later
draw the image into a `CALayer`.

**Figure 11.3 The collager displays
many photos simultaneously.**

11.4.2 *The collage temporary image view*

The tempImageView class has only one purpose: to intercept UITouches that indicate that the user wants to move the new image to a different part of the collage. This simple code is shown in the following listing.

Listing 11.3 Moving a temporary image by touches

```
- (void) touchesMoved:(NSSet *)touches withEvent:(UIEvent *)event {
    UITouch *thisTouch = [touches anyObject];
    CGPoint thisPoint =                                    ❶ Determines
        [thisTouch locationInView:self];                     position in view
    float newX = thisPoint.x+self.frame.origin.x;         ❷ Calculates overall
    float newY = thisPoint.y+self.frame.origin.y;           position
    if (newX < 0) {
        newX = 0;
    } else if (newX > 320) {
        newX = 320;
    }
    if (newY < 0) {
        newY = 0;
    } else if (newY > 416) {
        newY = 416;
    }
    self.center = CGPointMake(newX,newY);
}
```

This is similar to the touch code that you wrote in chapter 6. Recall that locationIn-View: ❶ gives a CGPoint internal to the view's coordinate system and needs to be converted ❷ into the global coordinate system of the application.

In testing, we discovered that when run on an iPhone (but not in the iPhone Simulator), the result is sometimes out of bounds; you need to double-check the coordinates before you move the temporary image view.

11.4.3 *The collage view*

Last up we have the collageView, which is the background UIView that needs to respond to the addPic:at: message and draw on the CALayer with drawRect:. The code to do this is shown in the following listing.

Listing 11.4 Background view managing low-level drawing when an image is set

```
-(void)addPic:(UIImage *)newPic at:(CGRect)newLoc {
    if (! myPics) {
        myPics = [[NSMutableArray alloc] initWithCapacity:0];
        [myPics retain];
    }
    [myPics addObject:[NSDictionary dictionaryWithObjectsAndKeys:
        newPic,@"picture",
        [NSNumber numberWithFloat:newLoc.origin.x],@"xpoint",
        [NSNumber numberWithFloat:newLoc.origin.y],@"ypoint",
        [NSNumber numberWithFloat:newLoc.size.width],@"width",
```

```
            [NSNumber numberWithFloat:newLoc.size.height],@"height",
                nil]];
        [self setNeedsDisplay];
    }
- (void)drawRect:(CGRect)rect {
    if (myPics) {
        for (int i = 0 ; i < myPics.count ; i++) {
            UIImage *thisPic = [[myPics objectAtIndex:i]
                objectForKey:@"picture"];
            float xpoint = [[[myPics objectAtIndex:i]
                objectForKey:@"xpoint"] floatValue];
            float ypoint = [[[myPics objectAtIndex:i]
                objectForKey:@"ypoint"] floatValue];
            float height = [[[myPics objectAtIndex:i]
                objectForKey:@"height"] floatValue];
            float width = [[[myPics objectAtIndex:i]
                objectForKey:@"width"] floatValue];
            [thisPic drawInRect:CGRectMake(xpoint,ypoint,width,height)];
        }
    }
}
```

This code is broken into two parts. The `addPic:at:` method saves its information into an instance variable, adding a `myPics` dictionary to the `NSMutableArray`. Note that you have to convert values into `NSNumber`s so that you can place them in the dictionary. This method then calls `setNeedsDisplay` on the view. You should *never* call `drawRect:` directly. Instead, when you want it to be executed, call the `setNeedsDisplay` method, and everything else will be done for you.

   `drawRect:` is called shortly afterward. It reads through the whole `NSMutableArray`, breaks it apart, and draws each image onto the `CALayer` using the techniques you learned earlier.

   We haven't shown the few header files and the unchanged app delegate, but this is everything important needed to write a complete collage program.

11.4.4 *Further exploration of this example*

This was one of our longer examples, but it could still bear some expansion to turn it into a fully featured application.

   First, it's a little unfriendly with memory. It would be better to maintain references to filenames, rather than keep the `UIImage`s around. In addition, the `NSArray` that the `CALayer` is drawn from should be saved out to a file so it won't get lost if memory is low. But the program as it exists should work fine.

   The program could be made more usable. An option to crop the pictures would be nice, but it may require access to Core Graphics functions. An option to move pictures around after they've been locked in would be relatively simple: you could test for touches in the `collageView` and read backward through the `NSArray` to find which object the user was touching. Reinstantiating it as a `UIImageView` would then be simple.

11.5 Printing images

AirPrint comes with iOS 4.2 and is available to both the iPhone and iPad. The AirPrint user interface on the iPhone and iPad is shown in figure 11.4. Generally, the print button is bar button item. When the user taps the Print button, the view controller to assign the printing task will present as a modal view controller on the iPhone and a popover view on the iPad. Once the print task is assigned, it will be printed right away or it will wait in the print queue. Users can check on the status by accessing the Print Center under the multitasking UI.

AirPrint is handled by the iOS system's UIKit, and no extra framework is required for the project.

The `UIWebView`, `UITextView`, and data such as `UIImage` and PDF files are print ready and can be handled by the print controller directly.

In this section you'll learn how to print an image from the application with the `UIPrintInteractionController` on the iPhone and iPad. Before we start coding, let's examine the printing workflow.

11.5.1 Printing workflow

Inside the AirPrint API, you can create the `UIPrintInteractionController` and present it as a modal view controller in the iPhone or a popover view on the iPad. It works the same as the system printing UI, as shown in figure 11.4.

`UIPrintInteractionController` is the key class in iOS for printing. You can create a printing user interface by calling the following code:

```
UIPrintInteractionController *controller = [UIPrintInteractionController
    sharedPrintController];
```

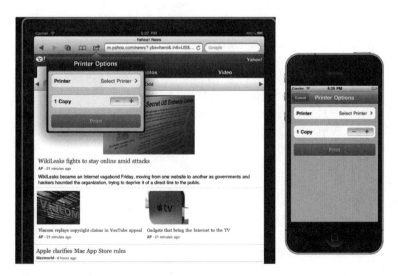

Figure 11.4 Printing UI on the iPad and iPhone

To make sure the print view controller is available in the current system, you can use the method [UIPrintInteractionController isPrintingAvailable] to check the availability.

Next, you need to define or customize the print task by setting the properties of the controller. There are some important properties for the controller listed in table 11.4.

In order to define the printInfo, you need to create an instance of UIPrintInfo. UIPrintInfo is a class that allows you to customize the printing job's information. UIPrintInfo includes properties such as the print-job name, the printer identifier, the orientation of the printed content, the duplex mode, and the kind of content (general, photo, or grayscale).

Similar to the UIImagePickerController, make sure you are implementing the UIPrintInteractionController's delegate method to handle the callback messages. For example, when the print task is assigned, show an alert view to notify the end user.

Table 11.4   A few properties in UIPrintInteractionController

Property	Summary
printingItem	A single UIImage, NSData, NSURL, or ALAsset object containing or referencing image data or PDF data.
printInfo	A UIPrintInfo object to customize the printItem.
printingItems	An array of objects either containing or referencing image data or PDF data. These objects are directly printable.
printFormatter	A UIPrintFormatter object handles the printing format.
printPageRender	An instance of a custom class of UIPrintPageRenderer draws each page of printable content partially or entirely.

In order to present the print view controller on the iPhone, you must create the completion handler and present it with method presentAnimated:completionHandler:; on the iPad, present the popover controller with the method presentFromBarButtonItem:animated:completionHandler:.

11.5.2   Simulating printing

Luckily, the iOS SDK after 4.2 comes with the Air-Print simulator app for Mac OS in case you don't have a printer for testing. You can find this print simulator app at <Xcode>/Platforms/iPhoneOS.platform/Developer/Applications/Printer Simulator, as shown in figure 11.5.

Figure 0.1   Printer Simulator under the iOS SDK

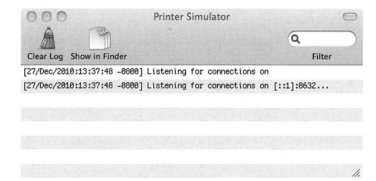

Figure 11.6 Printer Simulator screenshot

Launch the Printer Simulator app on your Mac. You will see a message similar to the one shown in figure 11.6.

With the Printer Simulator running, you can test the printing tasks directly from the iOS Simulator. Now we will start coding for printing.

11.5.3 Creating a demo app-printing image

In this section, we will create a simple view-based application for the iPhone and iPad containing an image in the center, which will print when the user taps the Print button.

Fire up Xcode and create a new project with View-Based Application template under iOS. Name it iPrint. Drag a photo you would like to print to this project's Resources folder.

Select the iPrintViewController header file and add in the changes shown in the following listing.

Listing 11.5 iPrintViewController header file

```
#import <UIKit/UIKit.h>
@interface iPrintViewController :
UIViewController<UIPrintInteractionControllerDelegate> {
    IBOutlet UIBarButtonItem *printButton;
    IBOutlet UIImageView *myPhoto;
}
-(IBAction)printPhoto:(id)sender;
@end
```

With the image view, Print button, and `printPhoto:` method added, let's drag and hook up the two subviews to iPrintViewController's nib file visually. Connect the method `printPhoto:` to the Print button's action.

Now add in the following code to the view controller's implementation file to complete the print task.

Listing 11.6 iPrintViewController implementation file

```
#import "iPrintViewController.h"
@implementation iPrintViewController
```

```
@synthesize myPhoto;
@synthesize printButton;

- (void)viewDidLoad {
    [super viewDidLoad];
    if (![UIPrintInteractionController isPrintingAvailable]) {
            UIAlertView *alert = [[UIAlertView alloc] initWithTitle:@"Sorry"
                          message:@"Printing is not available on your device!"
                          delegate:nil
                          cancelButtonTitle:@"OK"
                          otherButtonTitles:nil];
            [alert show];
            [alert release];
    }
}

-(IBAction)printPhoto:(id)sender {
    UIPrintInteractionController *controller = [UIPrintInteractionController
sharedPrintController];
    controller.delegate = self;
    UIPrintInfo *printInfo = [UIPrintInfo printInfo];
    printInfo.outputType = UIPrintInfoOutputPhoto;
    printInfo.jobName = @"iPrint Photo";
    controller.printInfo = printInfo;
    controller.printingItem = myPhoto.image;
    controller.showsPageRange = YES;
    void (^completionHandler)(UIPrintInteractionController *,
        BOOL, NSError *) = ^(UIPrintInteractionController *pic,
                            BOOL completed, NSError *error) {
            if (!completed && error)
                NSLog(@"FAILED! due to error in domain %@ with error code
                    %u",error.domain, error.code);
    };
    if (UI_USER_INTERFACE_IDIOM() == UIUserInterfaceIdiomPad) {
            [controller presentFromBarButtonItem:printButton animated:YES
             completionHandler:completionHandler];
    } else {
            [controller presentAnimated:YES
             completionHandler:completionHandler];
    }
}

-(void)printInteractionControllerDidFinishJob:(UIPrintInteractionController*)
printInteractionController {
    UIAlertView *alert = [[UIAlertView alloc]
                          initWithTitle:@"Congrats"
                          message:@"Your photo is ready to pick up!"
                          delegate:nil
                          cancelButtonTitle:@"OK"
                          otherButtonTitles:nil];
    [alert show];
    [alert release];
}

- (void)didReceiveMemoryWarning {
    [super didReceiveMemoryWarning];
}
```

Print view controller availability ❶

Print button tapped ❷

Print button tapped ❷

Print job finished ❸

```
- (void)viewDidUnload {
    self.printButton = nil;
    self.myPhoto = nil;
}

- (void)dealloc {
    [myPhoto release];
    [printButton release];
    [super dealloc];
}

@end
```

In the `viewDidLoad:` method, you first check the availability of the print view controller ❶. If it's not currently available on iOS, an alert view will pop up to notify the user. The print job is defined in the `printPhoto:` method ❷. First, create the print view controller, and then define the delegate and the print info. In this example, the printing item is the image from the image view. Then, define the block for the completion handler. You want to monitor the error message in this example:

```
void (^completionHandler)(UIPrintInteractionController *, BOOL, NSError *) =
^(UIPrintInteractionController *pic, BOOL completed, NSError *error) {
    if (!completed && error)
        NSLog(@"FAILED! due to error in domain %@ with error code %u",
        error.domain, error.code); };"
};
```

On the iPad, the print view controller will show as a popover controller from the bar button; on the iPhone, the print view controller will present as a modal view controller.

When the printing job is finished, the `delegate:` method ❸ will be called, so you notify the user with an alert view. That's all!

11.5.4 *Launching the printer app on the Simulator*

Now save all the changes. Before you build and run this iPrint app, make sure the printing simulator app is running. When the app is launched in the Simulator, tap the Print button. You will see that the simulator printer is available on the print view controller, as shown in figure 11.7.

You can play around with this app. For example, you can set the print info's property to change the content to grayscale. Even better, you can change the input image to one of the photos from the photo library.

That's all! Now you've learned how to print out image with AirPrint and test it in iOS.

Figure 11.7   iPrint app running on the Simulator for the iPhone and iPad

11.6   *Summary*

Dealing with media is a huge topic that probably could fill a book on its own. Fortunately, there are relatively easy (if limited) ways to utilize each major sort of media. In
this chapter, we discussed the various ways to manage and manipulate images on the
iPhone and iPad. We first discussed how to load them from disk. This includes images
saved in an application's directory as well as from the camera roll.

   We also showed you how the `UIImagePickerController` can be slightly modified
to allow the user to take a photo and use it in an application.

   You've seen how all these pictorial fundamentals work together, so we're now ready
to move on to the next major types of media: audio and video.

Media: audio
and recording

12

This chapter covers
- Accessing the iPod library to play music
- Recording audio from the built-in microphone
- Playing sounds
- Recording, playing, and accessing video

In the previous chapter, we discussed the basics of images. This chapter will detail how to play and record various types of audio and video. This will include how to play back audio items in the user's iPod library as well as how to record to and play from the user's video library.

To further demonstrate these concepts, you'll create two sample applications. The first application is a simple media player that lets the user choose a song from their iPod library and play it back within the application. The next will be a simple recording and playback application that lets the user record audio of an arbitrary length and play it back.

12.1   *Playing audio from the iPod library*

You may wonder: why do you want to play music from the iPod music library. Many people bought their fancy new iPhones for the sole purpose of combining their electronics (cell phone, iPod, GPS, camera, and so on).

Apple saw the need for such control within an application and provided the Media Player framework to allow you to retrieve items from the iPod media library as well as play them.

There are many reasons why you'd want to have control over the iPod in your applications. You may want to allow the user to use their personal music instead of your game music, or you may want to create a "Name That Tune" sort of game that uses songs from the user's iPod library. Apple has now made it simple to access and play these items. We'll look at how to retrieve items from the media library, how to get information about an item, and how to play an item, and we'll put it all together in a concrete example at the end of the section.

12.1.1   *Retrieving audio items from the iPod media library*

Retrieving items from the iPod media library is similar to retrieving photos from the photo library. The process is as follows:

1   Display the MPMediaPickerController in the current view.
2   Select media items from the iPod library.
3   A callback method in the MPMediaPickerControllerDelegate is called with the media items.

The following example demonstrates how to display the MPMediaPickerController to select media items:

```
MPMediaPickerController  *picker = [[MPMediaPickerController alloc]
    initWithMediaTypes:MPMediaTypeMusic];
[picker setDelegate:self];

[self presentModalViewController:picker animated:YES];
```

MPMediaPickerController allows you to select multiple items. To enable this feature, you must set the allowsPickingMultipleItems property to YES.

Because MPMediaPickerController is a view controller, it can be displayed any way that you can display a view controller. It can be inside a tab bar view controller, pushed onto a navigation controller stack, or, in this case, presented as the modal view controller. How you choose to display it is up to you. Make sure you choose the method that fits the flow of your application. Figure 12.1 shows what the MPMediaPicker-Controller looks like when displayed.

The media types you select aren't limited to music. You can also select podcasts and audio books. When you initialize a new MPMediaPickerController, you have the option of selecting what type of media is shown by default. In the previous example, the picker will display the user's music library. Following in table 12.1 are the constants you can use to change which library is shown.

Figure 12.1 The MPMediaPickerController

After you've created your MPMediaPickerController, you need to create a delegate to respond to two methods: mediaPicker:didPickMediaItems: and mediaPicker-DidCancel:.

mediaPickerDidCancel: is called when the user presses the Cancel button in the toolbar. Typically, you want to hide the MPMediaPickerController from this method.

Table 12.1 Media constants

Constant	Description
MPMediaTypeMusic	The media type is music, and the picker is limited to the music library.
MPMediaTypePodcast	The media type is a podcast, and the picker is limited to the podcast library.
MPMediaTypeAudioBook	The media type is an audio book, and the picker is limited to the audio book library.
MPMediaTypeAnyAudio	The media type is an unspecified type of audio. The picker isn't limited to any specific audio type.
MPMediaTypeAny	Similar to MPMediaTypeAnyAudio. This allows the picker to pick any audio item from the library.

When a media item has been selected, the `mediaPicker:didPickMediaItems:` method of the delegate automatically is called with an `MPMediaItemCollection` containing the selected item. An `MPMediaItemCollection` is a sorted set of `MPMediaItems`.

12.1.2 *Getting information about an MPMediaItem*

When you select an `MPMediaItem` from the iPod's media library, it comes with all the associated meta-information. To get access to this information, you call the `valueFor-Property:` method of the `MPMediaItem` with a given key. The complete list of keys can be found in the API documentation for `MPMediaItem`. Table 12.2 provides a short list of some of the more common keys.

Table 12.2   Common `MPMediaItem` keys

Constant	Description
`MPMediaItemPropertyMediaType`	Corresponds to one of the media types discussed in table 12.1
`MPMediaItemPropertyAlbumTitle`	The title of the album that the media item belongs to
`MPMediaItemPropertyArtist`	The artist of the current media item
`MPMediaItemPropertyPlaybackDuration`	An `NSInteger` that represents the length in seconds of the current media item
`MPMediaItemPropertyArtwork`	The artwork image for the media item

Other properties you have access to include genre, composer, duration, track and disc number, album artwork, rating, lyrics, last played date, and play and skip counts.

Now that you know how to select media items from the iPod library, playing these items is fairly easy.

12.1.3 *Playing media items using MPMusicPlayerController*

The class used to play media items is `MPMusicPlayerController`. It gives you total control over the built-in iPod on the device.

When initializing a new `MPMusicPlayerController`, you have two options for interacting with the iPod. The first way limits the iPod playback to your application. When you choose this method of playback, the iPod will stop playing as soon as your application exits. The other allows you to invoke the global iPod application. Exiting your application won't cause the iPod to stop playing. The following code snippet details how to initialize the `MPMusicPlayerController`:

```
MPMusicPlayerController *player =
    [MPMusicPlayerController applicationMusicPlayer];
```

By using the `applicationMusicPlayer` method of `MPMusicPlayerController`, you're limiting the media playback to your application. Using this method doesn't affect the device's iPod state in any way. If you want to use the main iPod application for media playback, you use the iPodMusicPlayer method.

After you've initialized the MPMusicPlayerController, you need to tell it which items you want it to play. You do so with the setQueueWithItemCollection: method. This method takes an MPMediaItemCollection as an argument. Conveniently enough, an MPMediaItemCollection is available to you when the MPMediaPicker-Controller selects an item. Here's an example detailing how to set up the media player to play items selected from the user's media library:

```
- (void)mediaPicker: (MPMediaPickerController *)mediaPicker
    didPickMediaItems:(MPMediaItemCollection *)mediaItemCollection {
  [player setQueueWithItemCollection:mediaItemCollection];
}
```

After you set up the MPMusicPlayerController, quite a few settings are available to further control the iPod (see table 12.3).

Table 12.3   Common iPod control properties

Constant	Description
currentPlaybackTime	The current playback time in seconds.
nowPlayingItem	A reference to the currently playing item in the queue.
playbackState	The current playback state of the media player. The states are stopped, playing, paused, interrupted, seeking forward, and seeking backward.
repeatMode	The repeat mode of the player. The repeat modes are default, none, one, and all.
shuffleMode	The shuffle mode of the player. The shuffle modes are default, off, songs, and albums.
volume	The volume of the player. This is a float value between 0.0 and 1.0.

See the documentation for the names of the constants for playbackState, repeat-Mode, and shuffleMode.

The MPMusicPlayerController provides a full set of methods that you'd expect to control the playback of the iPod. Table 12.4 provides a complete list of these methods as well as their descriptions.

Table 12.4   Playback control methods for MPMusicPlayerController

Method	Description
play	Starts or resumes the iPod's playback of the current media item.
pause	Pauses the playback if the player is currently playing.
stop	Stops the playback if the player is currently playing.
beginSeekingForward	Moves playback forward at a faster than normal rate.

Table 12.4   Playback control methods for `MPMusicPlayerController` (continued)

Method	Description
`beginSeekingBackward`	Moves playback backward at a faster than normal rate.
`endSeeking`	Stops seeking and resumes playback.
`skipToNextItem`	Starts playback of the next media item in the playback queue. This method ends playback if it's already at the last item in the queue.
`skipToBeginning`	Starts playback of the current media item at the beginning.
`skipToPreviousItem`	Starts playback of the previous media item in the playback queue. This method ends playback if it's already at the first item in the queue.

As you can see, the API gives you quite a bit of control over the iPod. With all of these controls, you're able to create fully featured media playback applications. In the next section, we'll show you how to put it all together, and you'll create a simple media player application.

12.1.4 *Example: creating a simple media player application*

You've already written most of the code needed to create a simple media player application. This example will demonstrate how to use the `MPMediaPickerController` to find media and then play it using the `MPMusicPlayerController`.

Make sure you're testing directly on your device, because the Simulator doesn't have an iPod application. Testing from the Simulator will yield an error when trying to display the picker.

CREATING A VIEW-BASED APPLICATION

You'll start the application from the View-Based Application template provided by Apple. This template creates an application delegate as well as a view controller. The View-Based Application is perfect, because you'll only need to add three buttons to the view. Name the application iPodTest.

ADDING THE NEEDED FRAMEWORKS

This project requires one more framework beyond the defaults provided by the View-Based Application template: `MediaPlayer.framework`. To add it, right-click Frameworks and select Add; then, select Existing Frameworks. Search for `Media-Player.framework` and select it.

SETTING UP THE IBACTIONS

Before you create the interface, you need to create the actions that the buttons will connect to. Open iPodSampleViewController.h, and add the code in the next listing.

Listing 12.1   iPodSampleViewController.h

```
#import <UIKit/UIKit.h>
#import <MediaPlayer/MPMusicPlayerController.h>
#import <MediaPlayer/MPMediaPickerController.h>
```

```
  @interface iPodTestViewController :
   UIViewController<MPMediaPickerControllerDelegate> {
    MPMusicPlayerController * player;
    MPMediaPickerController * picker;
}
- (IBAction) pickMedia:(id) sender;
- (IBAction) playMedia:(id) sender;
- (IBAction) stopMedia:(id) sender;

@end
```

The first import is added by default. The next two are needed to access the music player and media picker. They contain all the classes and methods that you'll be referencing.

Looking at the class signature for `iPodTestViewController`, you see that it implements the `MPMediaPickerControllerDelegate` interface. This means the class is the

delegate for the `MPMediaPickerController`. It receives all the actions sent by the media picker and allows you to respond to them.

After declaring the media player and media picker, you declare the `IBActions`. These actions are hooked up to the `UIButtons` on the interface. As you can see, you implement only two of the nine methods found in `MPMusicPlayerController`. Because the rest of the methods are similar, we'll leave implementing them up to you.

CREATING THE INTERFACE

Open iPodTestViewController.xib for editing. Drag three `UIButtons` from the library onto your view, and title them `Pick Media`, `Play`, and `Stop`. Connect each of them to its corresponding `IBAction` by right-clicking it and dragging to the File's Owner icon. The interface should look like figure 12.2.

Next you will need to edit the view controller implementation file and add the code that will control this interface

WRITING THE CODE

Open iPodTestViewController.m, and add the code in the following listing.

Figure 12.2
A simple media player interface

Listing 12.2   iPodTestViewController.m

```
#import "iPodTestViewController.h"

@implementation iPodTestViewController

- (void)viewDidLoad {
    player = [MPMusicPlayerController iPodMusicPlayer];
```

```
    picker = [[MPMediaPickerController alloc]
        initWithMediaTypes:MPMediaTypeAnyAudio];
    [picker setDelegate:self];
    [super viewDidLoad];
}

- (void )mediaPicker: (MPMediaPickerController *)mediaPicker
    didPickMediaItems:(MPMediaItemCollection *)mediaItemCollection {
    [player setQueueWithItemCollection:mediaItemCollection];
    [self dismissModalViewControllerAnimated:YES];
}

- (IBAction) pickMedia:(id) sender {
    [self presentModalViewController:picker animated:YES];
}

- (IBAction) playMedia:(id) sender {
    [player play];
}

- (IBAction) stopMedia:(id) sender {
    [player stop];
}

- (void)dealloc {
    [super dealloc];
    [player release];
    [picker release];
}

@end
```

You begin by initializing the media player and picker. Because the player is being initialized with the iPodMusicPlayer method, the application uses the global iPod player
when playing media items. The media picker is initialized with the MPMediaType-
AnyAudio constant; this lets the user select any sort of audio media from the iPod
library. Finally, you set the class as the delegate to the MPMediaPickerController so
you can respond to its actions.

The mediaPicker method is called automatically whenever the user selects an
audio item from the iPod library. It receives an MPMediaItemCollection, which contains the audio item to be played. The next line takes this collection and adds it to the
iPod media collection's queue. To hide the picker, you call dismissModalView-
ControllerAnimated.

The pickMedia method displays the media picker on top of the current view. The
playMedia and stopMedia methods are fairly self-explanatory because they only control the media player. Use these methods as a template for implementing other media
player controls on your own.

Finally, you need to make sure to release objects that you allocate. Doing so
ensures that your application doesn't use more memory than it needs and runs as efficiently as possible.

In the next section, we'll discuss how to let users record audio files.

12.2 Recording audio

In this section, you'll learn how to record audio by building a demo app with AVFoundation framework.

AVFoundation framework is really easy to use for a simple audio recording or playing task. You can find all the classes for recording audio in the AV Foundation framework. In order to use these classes, you must add AVFoundation.framework to your project. We'll look at how to initialize and control the audio reader and also how to respond to its associated events.

12.2.1 Initializing the audio recorder

When you're initializing a new AVAudioRecorder object, you should avoid using the default constructor init. This is to reduce complexity, because this class requires quite a bit of configuration. The constructor you should use is initWithURL:settings: error. It allows you to specify the location on disk to record the audio to as well as provide various audio settings.

The first parameter is the location where the recording will be stored. Although it's expressed as an NSURL, it's really a local path that points to a location on disk. In most cases, you'll want to store recordings in the Documents directory.

The next parameter is an NSDictionary that contains the settings for the recording. Table 12.5 lists some of the settings that you may want to consider when setting up your recorder.

Table 12.5 Basic audio settings for AVAudioRecorder

Setting key	Description
AVSampleRateKey	A sample rate, in Hertz, expressed as an NSNumber floating-point value.
AVFormatIDKey	A format identifier. A common value for this is kAudioFormatAppleLossless.
AVNumberOfChannelsKey	The number of channels expressed as an NSNumber integer value. You can set this value to 1.
AVEncoderAudioQualityKey	A key that refers to the quality of the audio being played.

You can specify quite a few other settings when creating your recorder. All of these settings are optional and have default values; you can use them to fine-tune your audio recording. The next listing demonstrates how to build an AVAudioRecorder object with some basic settings.

Listing 12.3 Initialization code for AVAudioRecorder

```
NSString * filePath = [NSHomeDirectory()
    stringByAppendingPathComponent:@"Documents/recording.caf"];
```

```
NSDictionary *recordSettings =
 [[NSDictionary alloc] initWithObjectsAndKeys:
 [NSNumber numberWithFloat: 44100.0], AVSampleRateKey,
 [NSNumber numberWithInt: kAudioFormatAppleLossless],AVFormatIDKey,
 [NSNumber numberWithInt: 1], AVNumberOfChannelsKey,
 [NSNumber numberWithInt: AVAudioQualityMax], AVEncoderAudioQualityKey,nil];
AVAudioRecorder * soundRecorder =
   [[AVAudioRecorder alloc] initWithURL: [NSURL fileURLWithPath:filePath]
   settings: recordSettings
   error: nil];
```

Note the `filePath`. This is an `NSString` that points to a file named recording.caf in the Documents directory. This path is converted to an `NSURL` during the construction of the recorder.

12.2.2 *Controlling the audio recorder*

After you construct an `AVAudioRecorder`, you have quite a bit of control over it. Table 12.6 lists all the methods you can call on a recorder to control the recording session.

The following code shows how to make a simple `toggleRecord` method that can be used as an `IBAction` for a button. The code assumes you've created a few global properties. Theses properties include `recording` of type `BOOL` and `soundRecorder` of type `AVAudioRecorder`:

```
- (IBAction) toggleRecord:(id) sender {
 if (recording) {
   [soundRecorder stop];
 } else {
   [soundRecorder record];
 }
 recording = !recording;
}
```

Table 12.6   Methods to control audio recording

Method	Description
- (BOOL)prepareToRecord	Creates the recording file on disk at the specified URL path. This method also prepares the system for recording.
- (BOOL)record	Starts or resumes recording. This method implicitly calls the `prepareToRecord` method.
- (BOOL)recordForDuration: (NSTimeInterval)duration	Starts the recorder and records for a specified amount of time.
- (void)pause	Pauses a recording. To resume recording, call the `record` method again.
- (void)stop	Stops the recording and closes the audio file.
- (BOOL)deleteRecording	Deletes the current recording. For this method to work, the recording must be stopped.

When `toggleRecord` is called for the first time, `record` is set to `NO`. This starts the audio recording and sets the `recording` property to `YES`. The system creates the recording file and begins receiving input from the built-in microphone. If the device's headset is plugged in, the system uses the headset's microphone instead.

The second time `toggleRecord` is called, the recorder stops recording. This closes the audio file and allows it to be played. The `recording` property is also set to `NO`.

12.2.3 Responding to AVAudioRecorder events

Like many API classes, `AVAudioRecorder` sends messages to a delegate. To respond to delegate actions from the `AVAudioRecorder`, your class must implement the `AVAudio-RecorderDelegate`. Table 12.7 describes the methods that can be implemented.

Table 12.7 `AVAudioRecorderDelegate` methods

Method	Description
- (void)audioRecorderDidFinishRecording: (AVAudioRecorder *)recorder successfully:(BOOL)flag	Called when the recorder finishes recording. This method is passed a reference to the recorder and a Boolean value that's YES if it was successful.
-(void)audioRecorderEncodeErrorDidOccur: (AVAudioRecorder *)recorder error:(NSError *)error	Called when an error occurs during recording.
- (void)audioRecorderBeginInterruption: (AVAudioRecorder *)recorder	Called when the recording is interrupted. The most common interruption is when the user gets an incoming call while recording.
- (void)audioRecorderEndInterruption: (AVAudioRecorder *)recorder	Called when the interruption ends. An example is pressing Ignore in response to an incoming call.

As with most delegate classes, it's important to implement all of these methods in your class. Doing so ensures that your application responds correctly in any circumstance.

Now that you know how to record audio, the next step is to play it back. The next section will discuss the method for playing your recordings as well as any other audio files in your application.

12.3 Playing sounds

Prior to the release of the iOS 3.0 API, playing audio files was a fairly complex task. There were functions to simplify the process, but they were limited to 30 seconds and didn't support simultaneous playback. To achieve this functionality, you had to use some relatively low-level audio libraries. These include Audio Queue Services, Audio File Stream Services, Audio File Services, OpenAL, Audio Session Services, and more.

The aforementioned audio libraries are powerful but are no longer needed. The `AVAudioPlayer` has replaced all of them and is now recommended by Apple for all audio playback. According to the API documentation of the AVAudioPlayer, "Apple recommends that you use this class for audio playback unless your application requires stereo positioning or precise synchronization, or you are playing audio captured from a network stream."

The AVAudioPlayer class provides a fully featured interface for playing and managing audio. Following is a list of some of the features available in AVAudioPlayer:

- Plays sounds of any length
- Loops sounds
- Plays sounds simultaneously
- Controls the playback level for each sound
- Seeks, which allows you to do fast forward and rewind
- Obtains and displays metering data about levels, peaks, and so on

Let's look at how to use the AVAudioPlayer. Later in the section, we'll also explain how to vibrate an iPhone.

12.3.1 *Initializing the AVAudioPlayer*

The AVAudioPlayer provides two methods for initialization. The first method is init-WithData:error. This method initializes the player with an NSData object containing the audio data to be played. The second parameter is a reference to an NSError for error reporting. This method is useful when you have audio data on hand and don't need to load it from disk.

The second method of initialization is initWithContentsOfURL:error. This method will probably be more useful unless you're working on an audio-editing application. The first parameter is an NSURL containing the location of the audio file. You'll need to build an NSURL from the path to your audio file. Here's an example of initializing an AVAudioPlayer using the initWithContentsOfURL:error method:

```
NSString * filePath = [NSHomeDirectory() stringByAppendingPathComponent:
                        @"Documents/recording.caf"];

AVAudioPlayer *newPlayer = [[AVAudioPlayer alloc] initWithContentsOfURL:
                            [NSURL fileURLWithPath:filePath] error: nil];
newPlayer.delegate = self;
```

This example initializes an audio player with a file named recording.caf located in the Documents directory. Like the AVAudioRecorder, this variable is of the type NSURL.

After building a new AVAudioPlayer object, you need to set its delegate to respond to its actions. In this example, the delegate is assigned to the calling class.

12.3.2 *The AVAudioPlayerDelegate*

The delegate for the AVAudioPlayer is similar to the delegate for the AVAudio-Recorder. It responds to exactly the same events, replacing recorder with player. Table 12.8 discusses these events.

Table 12.8 `AVAudioPlayerDelegate` methods

Method	Description

`- (void)audioPlayerDidFinishPlaying:`
`    (AVAudioPlayer *)player`
`    successfully:(BOOL)flag`
	Called when the player finishes playing. This method is passed a reference to the player and a Boolean value that's YES if it was successful.

`- (void)audioPlayerDecodeErrorDidOccur:`
`    (AVAudioPlayer *)player`
`    error:(NSError *)error`
	Called when an error occurs during audio play-back.

`- (void)audioPlayerBeginInterruption:` `    (AVAudioPlayer *)player`	Called when the player is interrupted. The most common interruption is when the user gets an incoming call while playing.
`- (void)audioPlayerEndInterruption:` `    (AVAudioPlayer *)recorder`	Called when the interruption ends. An example is pressing Ignore in response to an incoming call.

As you can see, there's nothing new here. These delegate methods are as expected and should all be implemented in your delegate class.

12.3.3 *Controlling the AVAudioPlayer*

One useful thing Apple did with the `AVAudioPlayer` was to allow it to be controlled like a music player. It contains all the methods you'd expect and then some. These include `play`, `pause`, and `stop`. You can also seek by modifying the `currentTime` property.

One additional method you may find useful is `prepareToPlay`. This method pre-loads the player's buffer with the audio data so that it's ready to play when the `play` method is called. It minimizes the lag between initializing the player and playing the audio.

An example usage is in a video game. You want to preload all the audio for a given level before the user starts playing. That way, when the user attacks an enemy, the attack sound plays right away rather than after the user has already defeated the enemy.

You need to consider quite a few other properties when coding an `AVAudioPlayer`. Here's a list of these properties along with their descriptions:

- `playing`—A Boolean value that's YES when the player is currently playing a sound file. This property is read-only.
- `volume`—The relative volume of this sound. The value is a `float` and ranges from 0.0 to 1.0.
- `numberOfLoops`—The number of times to loop the sound. The default value for this is 0, which means to play the sound once. Setting this value to a positive number loops the sound that many times. To loop the sound indefinitely until the stop method is called, set this value to any negative number.
- `numberOfChannels`—The number of audio channels in the sound. This property is read-only.

- duration—The total length in seconds of the sound file. This property is read-only.
- currentTime—The current playback time of the sound. This file can be used to "seek" or fast-forward and rewind.
- URL—An NSURL with the location of the sound file.
- data—An NSData object containing the audio data for the sound file.
- meteringEnabled—A Boolean value that determines if metering is currently enabled. When this is set to YES, you have access to some metering data associated with the sound. By default, this property is set to NO.

These properties make it simple to manage and control audio objects. You no longer need advanced knowledge of audio programming to integrate sounds into your applications. This code shows how to play back the recording you created in the previous section:

```
NSString * filePath = [NSHomeDirectory() stringByAppendingPathComponent:
                        @"Documents/recording.caf"];

AVAudioPlayer *newPlayer = [[AVAudioPlayer alloc] initWithContentsOfURL:
                            [NSURL fileURLWithPath:filePath] error: nil];
newPlayer.delegate = self;
[newPlayer play];
```

Again, you resolve the URL from the file path and pass it to the player. Next, the delegate is set to the caller class. Finally, play is called to start the audio playback.

Vibrating the iPhone

One cool feature of the API related to audio programming is vibrating the iPhone. It's related because it uses the system's audio interface. The API used is a C interface found in the Audio Toolbox framework. It's a really powerful API on iOS. We will cover details on Audio Toolbox framework in Chapter 22 for background audio.

You can find the function for vibrating the device in AudioToolbox/AudioServices.h. Make sure you add the `AudioToolbox.framework` to your project and import AudioToolbox/AudioServices.h. Here's the single line of code needed to vibrate the iPhone or iPad:

```
AudioServicesPlaySystemSound(kSystemSoundID_Vibrate);
```

Place that line of code in any method that needs to vibrate the phone. It's short and easy to use.

12.4 *Example: creating a simple audio recording/playback application*

Years ago, little electronic devices, commonly available in grocery stores, allowed you to press a button, record some audio, and play it right back. In this section, you'll create an application that will function similarly to one of these devices.

The interface for the application is fairly simple. It contains only a Record button and a Play button. When the user presses the Record button, they must hold it down for as long as they'd like to record. When they release the button, the recorder stops. The user then presses the Play button to play back the audio they just recorded.

12.4.1 Creating a view-based application

As you did in the last example, start by creating a new view-based application. You need this template, because it provides a single view along with the application's delegate. Name the project `TalkBack`.

12.4.2 Adding the needed frameworks

You'll need to add two additional frameworks to the project in order for it to function. The first framework you need is `AVFoundation.framework`. This contains all the s`AVAudioRecorder` and `AVAudioPlayer` classes and methods you'll be using. The next framework is `CoreAudio.framework`; it contains a constant that's needed in the application.

12.4.3 Setting up the IBActions

The application will need to respond to three events. The first is when the user initially pushes the Record button; this event should initialize the recorder and start the recording. The second event occurs when the user releases the Record button; this should stop the recorder. Finally, the third event occurs when the user presses the Play button; this should play back the recorded audio. You need to write the method signatures for each of these methods in the header file. The following listing contains the code inside TalkBackViewController.h.

Listing 12.4   TalkBackViewController.h

```
#import <UIKit/UIKit.h>
#import <AVFoundation/AVAudioRecorder.h>
#import <AVFoundation/AVAudioPlayer.h>
#import <CoreAudio/CoreAudioTypes.h>

@interface TalkBackViewController :
    UIViewController<AVAudioPlayerDelegate,AVAudioRecorderDelegate> {
    AVAudioRecorder * recorder;
}

- (IBAction) record: (id) sender;
- (IBAction) recordStop: (id) sender;
- (IBAction) play: (id) sender;
@end
```

This code import the APIs you use, declares an `AVAudioRecorder`, and then declares the `IBActions`. Now that you've set up the `IBActions`, you need to create the interface.

12.4.4 Creating the interface

Open TalkBackViewController.xib, and add two
UIButtons to the view. Title one `Record` and the
other `Play`. You can place them anywhere on the
view, which should look like figure 12.3.

The Record button will have both the `record`
and `recordStop` methods connected to it, but
they'll be connected to different selectors. Click
the Record button, and open the connection
inspector. Drag from the Touch Down action to
the File's Owner object, and select Record.
Doing so invokes the `record` method when the
button is first touched. Next, drag the Touch Up
Inside action to the File's Owner object, and
select `recordStop`. This will execute after the
button has been released. This way, the application will start recording when the Record button
is pressed and keep recording until it's released.

Now, click the Play button and open the
connection inspector. Drag from Touch Up
Inside to the File's Owner object, and select the
Play action.

**Figure 12.3   The talkback interface: a
simple record/playback application**

12.4.5 Setting up the audio recorder
and implementing the IBActions

Now that the interface is set up and the connections have been made, it's time to
implement these actions. The next listing contains the code that you need to add to
TalkBackViewController.m.

Listing 12.5   TalkBackViewController.m

```
#import "TalkBackViewController.h"

@implementation TalkBackViewController

- (void)viewDidLoad {
  [super viewDidLoad];
  NSString * filePath = [NSHomeDirectory()
    stringByAppendingPathComponent: @"Documents/recording.caf"];

NSDictionary *recordSettings =
[[NSDictionary alloc] initWithObjectsAndKeys:
[NSNumber numberWithFloat: 44100.0],AVSampleRateKey,
[NSNumber numberWithInt: kAudioFormatAppleLossless],AVFormatIDKey,
[NSNumber numberWithInt: 1], AVNumberOfChannelsKey,
[NSNumber numberWithInt: AVAudioQualityMax],AVEncoderAudioQualityKey,nil];
```

```
recorder = [[AVAudioRecorder alloc]
  initWithURL: [NSURL fileURLWithPath:filePath]
  settings: recordSettings error: nil];

recorder.delegate = self;


}

- (IBAction) record: (id) sender {
  [recorder record];
}

- (IBAction) recordStop: (id) sender {
  [recorder stop];
}

- (IBAction) play:(id) sender {
  NSString * filePath = [NSHomeDirectory()
  stringByAppendingPathComponent: @"Documents/recording.caf"];

  AVAudioPlayer * player = [[AVAudioPlayer alloc] initWithContentsOfURL:
    [NSURL fileURLWithPath:filePath] error: nil];
  player.delegate = self;
  [player play];
}

- (void)dealloc {
  [super dealloc];
  [recorder release];
}
```

@end

You perform all the setup for the AVAudioRecorder in the viewDidLoad method. This
is so the recorder is available for recording when the user presses the Record button.

The next few methods are straightforward. record starts the recorder when the
button is pressed, and recordStop stops recording when the button is released. The
play method builds a new AVAudioPlayer and initializes it with the audio file you just
recorded. After the player is initialized, the play method is called to start playback.

As always, you should be a good steward of the iPhone's memory: make sure you
release the recorder when you've finished using it. The application should be ready to
launch.

Next, we'll look at how to work with video.

12.5 Recording, playing, and accessing video

At the time of writing, the iPhone 4, iPod Touch 4th Generation, and the iPad 2 have
two built-in video cameras. This allows users to easily record video and save it to their
media library. The code for recording video is almost identical to the code to show the
camera in chapter 11, but it does have a few required checks.

The following listing shows the code for bringing up the video camera interface.

Listing 12.6 Displaying the video camera

```
-(void) showVideoCamera {                                        ❶ Is camera
if ([UIImagePickerController                                         available?
isSourceTypeAvailable:UIImagePickerControllerSourceTypeCamera]) {
myImagePicker.sourceType = UIImagePickerControllerSourceTypeCamera;
} else {
    NSLog(@"Camera not supported");
return;
}
NSArray *media = [UIImagePickerController availableMediaTypesForSourceType:
UIImagePickerControllerSourceTypeCamera];                        Gets list of
                                                                 supported
if([media containsObject:kUTTypeMovie]) {                      ❷ media types
    myImagePicker.mediaTypes = [NSArray
arrayWithObjects: kUTTypeMovie,nil];
    [self presentModalViewController:myImagePicker animated:YES];
                                                                 Shows
} else {                                                         video
    NSLog(@"Video not supported");                             camera ❸
}
}
```

The first thing you do is check to see if the device has camera support ❶. In two cases, this returns false. The first is when the when the video camera is not available on the device. The other case is that the camera is damaged on the current device.

Next, you check to see what media types the camera supports ❷. In this case, you look for the media type kUTTypeMovie. If this is found, the camera supports video. You set the media type of the picker to kUTTypeMovie to tell it to display the video camera. By default, it's set to kUTTypeImage, which specifies photos, so it's necessary that you set it. The camera control interface will allow the user to switch between the front facing camera and rear camera.

Finally, you display the video camera on the screen ❸. One great feature that Apple added is the ability to edit the video on the fly. This is easy to integrate in the code. Add this line prior to displaying the video camera:

```
myImagePicker.allowsEditing = YES;
```

This great one-liner from Apple adds a ton of functionality. After the user finishes recording the video, the delegate method didFinishPickingMediaWithInfo: for the picker is called. The dictionary passed to this method contains a system path URL to the video file that was just recorded. The following code shows how to use this path to retrieve and play back the video:

```
- (void)imagePickerController:(UIImagePickerController *)picker
    didFinishPickingMediaWithInfo:(NSDictionary *)info {

    NSURL * pathURL = [info objectForKey: UIImagePickerControllerMediaURL];
    MPMoviePlayerController * player =
        [[MPMoviePlayerController alloc] initWithContentURL:pathURL];
    [player play];
}
```

The first thing this method does is retrieve the path URL from the info dictionary. The path URL is the object stored with the key `UIImagePickerControllerMediaURL`. Next, an `MPMoviePlayerController` is allocated with the contents of the path URL. This loads the video and prepares it to play. The last thing to do is call the `play` method, and the video begins.

12.6 Summary

Even novice programmers can now achieve audio recording and playback. With the AV Foundation frameworks, writing fully featured audio applications is a breeze.

The `MPMediaPickerController` provides a method for accessing the user's iPod media library. Using this in conjunction with the `MPMusicPlayerController` gives you the ability to create applications in which the user has complete control over the audio being played.

In addition to discussing how to play music from the user's iPod library, we covered how to play audio from within your own application. This can be anything from simple sounds to recordings made with the `AVAudioRecorder`. The `AVAudioPlayer` makes audio playback a simple and painless task.

Although we've only begun to scratch the surface of audio management, you now have the tools necessary to integrate audio into any application. In iOS 4.0, you can also enable background audio as part of its multitasking features. You will learn the details in Chapter 22.

Graphics: Quartz, Core Animation, and OpenGL

13

This chapter covers

- Using Quartz 2D for drawing
- Understanding context, paths, and state
- Using Core Animation
- Learning about OpenGL ES

As you saw in chapter 11, creating and displaying images often isn't enough. In games and other more complex programs, you'll also want to manipulate those images in various ways at runtime. In iOS there are two major ways to do this.

The first is through Quartz 2D, a two-dimensional drawing library that allows for complex line drawings, much as Canvas did on the web. It's also the heart of the Core Graphics frameworks. We already touched on Quartz in chapter 11, when you drew images straight to the `CALayer` of a `UIView`; it will be the focus of the majority of this chapter. Quartz also supports Core Animation functions, which we'll address somewhat more briefly.

The second major way to manipulate images is through the OpenGL ES API. This cross-platform API, originally developed by Silicon Graphics, could be the topic of its own book, so we'll only show you how to get started with it.

But most of this chapter will be about Quartz. We'll look at drawing paths, setting the graphical state, and more advanced drawing techniques. We'll dive into Quartz immediately.

13.1 An introduction to Quartz 2D

Quartz 2D is a two-dimensional drawing library that's tightly integrated into iOS. It works well with all the relevant frameworks, including Core Animation, OpenGL ES, and the UIKit.

Fundamentally, Quartz's drawings depend on three core ideas: context, paths, and state, each of which will be the topic of a future section:

- *Context* is a description of where the graphics are being written to, as defined by a `CGContextRef`. You'll usually be writing to a `UIView` or to a bitmap.
- *Layers* are a little less important for this overview, but they're where Quartz drawing occurs. They can be stacked one on top of another, creating a complex result. When working with the iPhone or iPad, you'll often only have a single layer associated with each of your UIKit objects.
- *Paths* are what you'll typically draw in Quartz. These are collections of lines and arcs that are drawn in advance and then are painted to the screen by either stroking or filling the path in question (or, possibly, by clipping it).
- *State* saves the values of transformations, clipping paths, fill and stroke settings, alpha values, other blending modes, text characteristics, and more. The current state can be stored with `CGContextSaveGState` and restored with `CGContext-RestoreGState`, allowing for easy switching among complex drawing setups.

Quartz is built on the older Core Foundation framework that you've met a few times over the course of this part of the book. This means you'll need to use older styles of variables to integrate with Cocoa Touch using toll-free bridging, and to respect Core Foundation's memory-management techniques.

If you need more information about any Quartz topic, see the "Quartz 2D Programming Guide" at Apple's developer website. It's a fine introduction to Quartz, although not as focused as you'd probably like, a deficiency that we'll correct in this chapter.

Using Quartz requires little special setup. It can be easily integrated into any template and any project you want. Be sure to include the Core Graphics framework and the CoreGraphics/CoreGraphics.h include file before you get started.

With that said, we're ready to dive into our first major Quartz topic: the context.

13.2   *The Quartz context*

A *graphical context* is a description of *where* Quartz writes to. This could include a printer, a PDF file, a window, or a bitmap image. On the iPhone and iPad, you're only likely to use two of these possibilities.

Most frequently, you'll work with the graphical context that's automatically associated with the `CALayer` (Core Animation layer) of each `UIView`. That means you can use Quartz to draw to most UIKit objects. To do so, you override the `drawRect:` method and, inside the object in question, use `UIGraphicsGetCurrentContext` to retrieve the current context.

You may alternatively create a bitmap context in order to create or modify an image that you'll use elsewhere in your program. You do this by using the `UIGraphicsBeginImageContext` and `UIGraphicsEndImageContext` functions.

You can use a variety of Core Graphics functions to access other sorts of contexts—types that you won't usually use on an iPhone or iPad. The functions required to capture a PDF context are one such example. These have two deficits you should be aware of: they depend more heavily on the Core Foundation frameworks, and they use Quartz's inverted coordinate system.

One thing to note about graphical contexts is that they're created in a stack: when you create a new context, it's pushed on top of a stack, and when you've finished with it, it's popped off. This means that if you create a new bitmap context, it's placed on

---

Warning: inverse coordinate system ahead

By now, you should be familiar with the standard iOS coordinate system. It has the origin at upper left on the screen, with the main axes running to the right and down. Quartz's default coordinate system is inverted, with the origin at lower left and the main axes running right and up.

This isn't *usually* a problem. The Cocoa Touch methods you use to create and write to graphical contexts usually transform Quartz's default coordinates so that they look like iPhone coordinates to you.

Once in a while, though, you'll run into a situation where you'll draw to a UI-derived context and find your content flipped upside down (and in the wrong position). This is a result of accessing Quartz in a way that hasn't been transformed.

As of this writing, we're aware of two situations where you'll have to correct Quartz's coordinate system by yourself, even when using one of the UI-derived contexts: if you import images using the native Quartz functions (as opposed to the `UIImage` methods you saw in chapter 11), and if you write text. We'll talk about each of these when we get to them.

Personally, we consider these coordinate inversions bugs, and it's our expectation that they'll eventually be corrected.

If you create a context without using Cocoa Touch, expect *everything* to be inverted. This is something that we don't expect to change in the future.

top of any existing context, such as the one associated with your `UIView`, and stays there until you've finished with the bitmap.

Table 13.1 lists these context-related functions, including both the standard UI context functions and the older Core Graphics function you're most likely to use—for PDFs.

Table 13.1 Methods for graphical context creation

Function	Arguments	Summary
`UIGraphicsGetCurrentContext`	(none)	Returns the current context, which is usually the context of the current UIKit object but can also be a context that you create by hand
`UIGraphicsBeginImageContext`	`CGSize`	Creates a bitmap context
`UIGraphicsEndImageContext`	(none)	Pops a bitmap context off the stack
`UIGraphicsGetImageFrom-CurrentImageContext`	(none)	Returns a bitmap as a `UIImage *`; used with a bitmap context only
`CGPDFContextCreate`	`CGDataConsumerRef, CGRect, CGDictionaryRef`	Creates a PDF context

We won't cover PDFs in this book, but we'll look at how to use each of the UIKit context styles, starting with the `UIView`.

13.2.1 Drawing to a UIView

In chapter 11, we offered an introductory example of how to write to a `UIView` graphical context using the `drawRect:` method. That example was somewhat simplified because the UIKit draw-image commands mostly hide the idea of graphical contexts from you. They automatically write to the current context, which inside `drawRect:` is the context related to the `UIView`. For most other functions, you need to do a bit more work: retrieving the graphical context and passing that context along to any drawing commands that you use.

Here's how to draw a simple abstract face using this technique:

```
- (void)drawRect:(CGRect)rect {
    CGContextRef ctx = UIGraphicsGetCurrentContext();
    CGContextBeginPath(ctx);
    CGContextAddArc(ctx,110,50,30,0,2*M_PI,1);
    CGContextAddArc(ctx,210,50,30,0,2*M_PI,1);
    CGContextAddArc(ctx,160,110,15,0,2*M_PI,1);
    CGContextAddArc(ctx,160,210,25,0,2*M_PI,1);
    CGContextFillPath(ctx);
}
```

This example is fairly simple. You create a `UIView` subclass, and then you go to its `drawRect:` method. Once there, you capture the current context and use it to do whatever Quartz 2D drawing you desire.

The function calls won't be familiar to you, but they're calls to draw a bunch of circles; we'll discuss them in the next section. As shown in figure 13.1, the art ends up looking oddly abstract, which shows how Quartz draws continuous paths. You see lines connecting one circle to the next, as if the pencil never comes off the page, a topic we'll talk about more in the next section.

Leaving aside those specifics for a moment, this shows one of the two ways you can use all the Quartz functions described in this chapter: by painting a `UIView`. And remember that a `UIView` can be almost any UIKit object, due to inheritance.

Drawing to a `UIView` allows for on-screen picture creation, but you can also draw pictures without displaying them immediately. That's done with a bitmap.

Figure 13.1   The iPhone does abstract art.

13.2.2 *Drawing to a bitmap*

The main reason to create a bitmap rather than draw directly to a view is to use your graphic several times in your program—perhaps all at the same time. For example, Apple offers a sample program that draws the periodic table by creating a standard bitmap that's used for all the elements and then repeating it. You might similarly create billiard balls using bitmaps if you were programming a billiards game. In chapter 10, you could have used Quartz to create the dots that you used in the gravity and altitude programs as bitmaps, so that you didn't have to separately create them outside the program.

The process of creating a bitmap and turning it into a `UIImage` is relatively simple. You create a graphical context, draw in that context, save the context to an image, and close the context. The following code shows how to create a red dot image like the one you used in earlier programs:

```
- (void)viewDidLoad {
    [super viewDidLoad];
    UIGraphicsBeginImageContext(CGSizeMake(20,20));
    CGContextRef ctx = UIGraphicsGetCurrentContext();
    CGContextBeginPath(ctx);
    CGContextAddArc(ctx,10,10,10,0,2*M_PI,1);
    CGContextSetRGBFillColor(ctx, 1, 0, 0, 1);
    CGContextFillPath(ctx);
    UIImage *redBall =
        UIGraphicsGetImageFromCurrentImageContext();
    UIGraphicsEndImageContext();
    UIImageView *redBallView = [[UIImageView alloc] initWithImage:redBall];
    redBallView.center = CGPointMake(160,330);
    [self.view addSubview:redBallView];
}
```

Again, this example is simple. You could do this work anywhere you wanted, but we've elected to use the `viewDidLoad` setup method. To start the process, you create an image context, which is to say a bitmap, and you immediately retrieve that context's variable for use. Following that, you do whatever drawing work you want. When you've finished, you turn the bitmap into a `UIImage` and close out your context. You can then manipulate the image as you see fit; here it's turned into a `UIImageView`.

You now know two ways to use contexts in the Quartz environment. With that in hand, you're ready to dive straight into what Quartz can do, starting with paths, which are the foundation of most Quartz work.

13.3 Drawing paths

The *path* is what Quartz draws. If you've worked with Canvas, this will look familiar, because both libraries use the same drawing paradigm. A path is a set of lines, arcs, and curves that are all placed continuously within a graphical context. You only *paint* a path when it's complete, at which point you can choose to either fill it or stroke it.

Many of the functions required to define and draw paths are listed in table 13.2. `CGContextMoveToPoint` is the one function that deserves some additional discussion. As you'll recall, we said that a path is a continuous series of lines and arcs that you draw without picking the pen up off the paper. But there *is* a way to pick up the pen, and that's with the `CGContextMoveToPoint` function, which is vital when you want to draw unconnected objects as part of a single path.

Table 13.2   A variety of simple drawing functions that allow for vector-based graphics

Function	Arguments	Summary
CGContextBeginPath	context	Creates a new path.
CGContextAddArc	context, x, y, radius, startangle, endangle, clockwise	Creates an arc, with the angles defined in radians. A line is drawn to the start point if there are previous entries in the path and from the end point if there are additional entries. The more complex functions `CGContextAddArcToPoint`, `CGContextAddCurveToPoint`, and `CGContextAddQuadCurveToPoint` allow for the creation of tangential arcs, Bezier curves, and quadratic Bezier curves.
CGContextAddEllipseInRect	context, CGRect	Creates an ellipse that fits inside the rectangle.
CGContextAddLineToPoint	context, x, y	Creates a line from the current point to the designated end point. The more complex `CGContextAddLines` function allows the addition of an array of lines.
CGContextAddRect	context, CGRect	Creates a rectangle. The more complex `CGContextAddRects` function adds a series of rectangles.
CGContextMoveToPoint	context, x, y	Moves to the point without drawing.

For example, to avoid drawing a line between the first two circles in the earlier abstract-art example, you can use the following code:

```
CGContextAddArc(ctx,110,50,30,0,2*M_PI,1);
CGContextMoveToPoint(ctx, 240, 50);
CGContextAddArc(ctx,210,50,30,0,2*M_PI,1);
```

After drawing the first circle, you move your virtual pencil to the point where you begin drawing the arc of the second circle, which is 240, 50.

The rest of the functions are largely self-explanatory. You already saw the arc commands in some of the earlier examples, and the others work in similar ways. For more information about the more complex functions, look at the CGContext class reference.

We'll move on from these simple drawing commands to the question of what you do once you have a path. You have several options, beginning with the simple possibility of closing it and drawing it.

13.3.1 Finishing a path

As we've already noted, the path functions define the points and lines that make up a drawing. When you have that in hand, you have to do something with it. There are three main choices: stroke the path, fill the path, or turn it into a clipping path. These functions are all listed in table 13.3.

You'll usually either stroke (outline) a path or fill it when you've finished. You used a fill in each of the previous examples, but a stroke could be substituted; the difference is that the circles wouldn't be filled in.

A clipping path is a bit more complex, in that you don't draw something on the screen. Instead, you define an area, which corresponds to the area inside the path that you'd have filled in, and you only show later drawings that appear inside that clipping path. We'll talk about clipping paths more, and show an example, when we get to graphical states. For now, note that you create them from paths. Creating reusable paths

Table 13.3   Functions for finishing a path

Function	Arguments	Summary
CGContextClosePath	context	Draws a line from the end point of your path to the start point, and then closes it. This is an optional final command that's usually used when you're stroking a path.
CGContextFillPath	context	Closes your path automatically, and paints it by filling it in. CGContextEOFillPath is an alternative that does the filling in a slightly different way.
CGContextStrokePath	context	Paints your path by stroking it.
CGContextClip	context	Turns the current path into a clipping path.

So far, you've created paths by drawing them directly to a context, be it a UIView or a bitmap. But it's also possible to create reusable paths that you can quickly and easily apply later. This has many of the same advantages as creating a bitmap: you get reusability and multiplicity. Reusable paths are particularly useful in animations and programs where you use the same graphic on multiple pages.

To create reusable paths, you use the CGPath commands rather than the CGContext commands. There are equivalents to many of the simple CGContext functions, as shown in table 13.4.

Table 13.4 CGPath commands and their CGContext equivalents

CGPath function	CGContext function
CGPathCreateMutable	CGContextBeginPath
CGPathAddArc	CGContextAddArc
CGPathAddEllipseInRect	CGContextAddEllipseInRect
CGPathAddLineToPoint	CGContextAddLineToPoint
CGPathAddRect	CGContextAddRect
CGPathMoveToPoint	CGContextMoveToPoint
CGPathCloseSubpath	CGContextClosePath

When you're working with reusable paths, you first use the CGPathCreateMutable function to create a CGPathRef, and then you use CGPath commands to add lines or arcs to that CGPathRef. The reusable path can include multiple, discrete subpaths that don't have to connect to each other. You can end one subpath and start another with the CGPathCloseSubpath function.

Note that no painting functions are associated with the reusable paths. That's because they're storage devices. To use one, you add it to a normal path with the CGContextAddPath function, which draws your stored path to your graphical context, where it abides by the normal rules.

The following code uses a mutable path to replace the CGContext commands that you previously used to draw an abstract face. A more realistic example would probably hold onto the path for use elsewhere; you release it here as a reminder of how Core Foundation memory management works:

```
- (void)drawRect:(CGRect)rect {
    CGMutablePathRef myPath = CGPathCreateMutable();
    CGPathAddArc(myPath,NULL,110,50,30,0,2*M_PI,1);
    CGPathMoveToPoint(myPath,NULL, 240, 50);
    CGPathAddArc(myPath,NULL,210,50,30,0,2*M_PI,1);
    CGPathAddArc(myPath,NULL,160,110,15,0,2*M_PI,1);
    CGPathAddArc(myPath,NULL,160,210,25,0,2*M_PI,1);

    CGContextRef ctx = UIGraphicsGetCurrentContext();
    CGContextBeginPath(ctx);
    CGContextAddPath(ctx,myPath);
```

```
        CGContextStrokePath(ctx);
        CFRelease(myPath);
    }
```

Of note here is the `NULL` that's constantly being sent as a second argument to the `CGPath` commands. This argument is intended to be a `CGAffineTransform` variable. It allows you to apply a transformation to the element being drawn, which is something we'll discuss shortly.

Now that we've looked at two different ways to create complex paths, we'll take a step back and look at how to draw much simpler objects in a simpler way.

13.3.2 *Drawing rectangles*

Drawing paths takes some work, but if you want to draw a rectangle, Quartz makes it easy. All you have to do is use one of a few functions listed in table 13.5. These functions take care of the path creation, drawing, and painting for you in a single step.

Table 13.5 **Specific functions allow you to draw rectangles**

Function	Arguments	Summary
CGContextClearRect	context, CGRect	Erases a rectangle.
CGContextFillRect	context, CGRect	Draws a filled rectangle. The more complex variant `CGContextFillRects` allows you to fill a whole array of rectangles.
CGContextStrokeRect	context, CGRect	Draws a stroked rectangle.
CGContextStrokeRectWithWidth	context, CGRect, width	Draws a stroked rectangle, with the stroke being the designated width.

The `CGContextClearRect` function can be particularly useful for erasing a window when you're ready to draw something new to it. Now that we've told you how to draw objects in the simplest way possible, we're ready to move on and discuss how to draw objects in more complex ways—by modifying state.

13.4 *Setting the graphical state*

The graphical state is *how* Quartz draws. It includes a variety of information such as what colors are used for fills or strokes, which clipping paths constrain the current drawing path, what transformations are applied to the drawing, and a number of other less-important variables.

State is maintained in a stack. You can save a state at any time; it doesn't change how things are being drawn, but it does push that current state onto the top of a stack for later retrieval. Later, you can restore a state, which pops the top state off the stack, putting things back to how they were before the last save. We've mentioned these functions before, but we've also listed them here in table 13.6.

Table 13.6 State-related functions that help define how you draw

Function	Arguments	Summary
CGContextSaveGState	context	Pushes the state onto a stack
CGContextRestoreGState	context	Pops the state off a stack

As we've already noted, you can store a *lot* of things in graphical state. We'll cover many of them here, starting with colors.

13.4.1 Setting colors

In Quartz, you select colors by setting the fill color, the stroke color, or both in the current graphic state. After you've done this, any fill or stroke commands following the color commands appear in the appropriate colors. Note that color is irrelevant while you're drawing the individual elements of a path—the color commands apply only to the painting of the complete path at the end.

You can select colors from a variety of *color spaces*, which are different ways to choose colors. They include RGB (red-green-blue), RGBA (red-green-blue-alpha), CMYK (cyan-magenta-yellow-black), and CGColor (the underlying Core Graphics color model). On the iPhone and iPad, you'll usually either use the RGBA color space or use a command that lets you select a color using standard UIKit methods. Table 13.7 lists the four most relevant of these functions.

Table 13.7 The most important of numerous coloring functions

Function	Arguments	Summary
CGContextSetRGBFillColor	context, red, green, blue, alpha	Sets the fill to the RGBA value
CGContextSetRGBStrokeColor	context, red, green, blue, alpha	Sets the stroke to the RGBA value
CGContextSetFillColorWithColor	context, CGColor	Sets the fill to the CGColor
CGContextSetStrokeColorWithColor	context, CGColor	Sets the stroke to the CGColor

The two RGB functions allow you to set a color using values from 0 to 1 for each of red, green, blue, and alpha transparency (opacity). You saw an example of this earlier:

```
CGContextSetRGBFillColor(ctx, 1, 0, 0, 1);
```

The last two functions in table 13.7 allow you to set the color using any CGColor, and you'll understand how useful that is when you realize that you can read a CGColor property from any UIColor you create:

```
CGContextSetFillColorWithColor(ctx, [[UIColor redColor] CGColor]);
```

Given that you're already familiar and comfortable with the UIColors, we expect that this latter function will be a popular one.

Having now covered the main ways to apply colors to your graphical state, we're ready to move on to the next topic: how to change how you draw through graphical state transformations.

13.4.2 *Making transformations*

Transformations modify how you draw to your graphic context. They do this by changing the grid on which you're drawing by moving its origin, rotating, or resizing.

Why would you want to do these transformations?

- They can be useful for drawing photographs (or other images), because they allow you to scale or rotate the picture.
- They can make it a lot easier to do certain types of mathematical drawing. For example, it's probably easier to draw a symmetric mathematical construct if you have your origin in the center of the screen rather than in the upper-left corner.
- They can allow you to flip your screen if you end up in a context (or using a function) with an inverse coordinate system.

CTM TRANSFORMATIONS

The simplest way to apply a transformation is to use one of the functions that modify the current transformation matrix (CTM), which is a matrix that's applied to all drawing done in your current graphical state. These functions are described in table 13.8.

Table 13.8   CTM transformation functions that allow you to change how you draw

Function	Arguments	Summary
CGContextRotateCTM	context, radian rotation	Rotates the grid
CGContextScaleCTM	context, x-scale, y-scale	Scales the grid
CGContextTranslateCTM	context, x-change, y-change	Moves the origin

There are two gotchas that you should watch for.

First, note that the ordering of transformations is somewhat pickier than the ordering of color commands. You need to start your transformation *before* you add the relevant lines to your path, and you need to maintain it until *after* you paint that path.

Second, although these transformations can be applied in any sequence, order matters. Following are two transformation commands that can be applied together:

```
CGContextTranslateCTM(ctx, 100, 100);
CGContextRotateCTM(ctx, .25*M_PI);
```

These functions move a drawing 100 to the right and 100 down and rotate it by 45 degrees. Figure 13.2 shows the untransformed picture (which you've seen before), the results if these commands are applied with the translation before the rotation, and the results if they're applied in the opposite order.

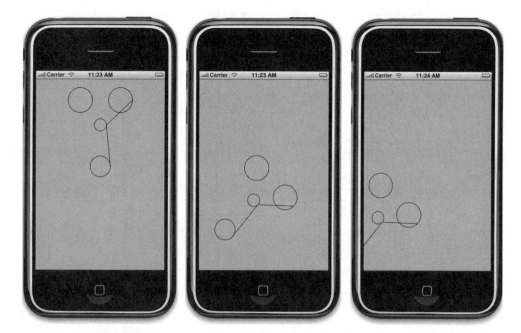

Figure 13.2 As these variant transformations show, order matters. The left picture is untransformed, the middle one is translated and then rotated, and the right one is rotated and then translated.

Clearly, you need to be careful and think about ordering when you're applying CTM transformations.

But CTM transformations aren't the only way to change your drawing space.

AFFINE TRANSFORMATIONS

Just as you can create a reusable path and then apply that to the context with the CGContextAddPath function, you can also create a reusable transformation matrix (using the affine transformation functions) and then apply that to the context with the CGContextConcatCTM function. This is managed by a set of six core functions, listed in table 13.9. Half of them create a new matrix, applying a transformation at the same time, and the other half apply a transformation to an existing matrix. The last function is the one that applies an affine transformation to your current graphical state.

Table 13.9 Affine transformations for creating reusable transformations

Function	Arguments	Summary
CGAffineTransformMake-Rotation	radian rotation	Makes an array with the rotation
CGAffineTransformMakeScale	x-scale, y-scale	Makes an array with the scale
CGAffineTransformMake-Translation	x-change, y-change	Makes an array with the translation

Table 13.9   Affine transformations for creating reusable transformations *(continued)*

Function	Arguments	Summary
CGAffineTransformRotate	array, radian rotation	Rotates the array
CGAffineTransformScale	array, x-scale, y-scale	Scales the array
CGAffineTransformTranslate	array, x-change, y-change	Translates the array
CGContextConcatCTM	context, array	Applies the transformation

The following code applies a rotation followed by a translation using a reusable affine matrix:

```
CGAffineTransform myAffine = CGAffineTransformMakeRotation(.25*M_PI);
CGAffineTransformTranslate(myAffine, 100, 100);
CGContextConcatCTM(ctx, myAffine);
```

In addition to creating reusable affine transformations, you can also modify the transforms at a much lower level. Any affine transformation is constructed from a 3 x 3 matrix that's then multiplied across the individual vectors of your path using matrix multiplication. If you have specific needs, you can use the CGAffineTransformMake function to create a matrix by hand. Using it looks like this:

```
CGAffineTransform flip = CGAffineTransformMake(1,0,0,-1,0,0);
```

You can find information about how the matrix works and about some other functions in the CGAffine reference.

The next sort of state you may want to change is one that makes fairly large-scale changes to your drawings: the clipping path.

13.4.3 Setting clipping paths

We already spoke about clipping paths in section 13.3. You create a path as usual, but then you clip it, rather than filling it or stroking it. Anything you paint on the screen afterward (within that graphical state) appears only if it's inside the clipping path.

For example, the following code causes later painting to appear only inside a large circle centered on the screen:

```
CGContextBeginPath(ctx);
CGContextAddArc(ctx,160,240,160,0,2*M_PI,1);
CGContextClip(ctx);
```

Figure 13.3 shows what a full-screen image looks like before clipping and after.

As with most of these Quartz functions, you have some opportunities for subtleties when using clipping paths. The CGContext reference offers a few additional functions for creating and modifying clipping paths.

So far, we've discussed all the big-picture options for modifying your graphical state. You can do many smaller things, too.

Figure 13.3   An example of a clipping path in use. The unclipped image is on the left, and the clipped image is on the right.

13.4.4 *Other settings*

A wide variety of additional settings can be used as part of the graphical state. Table 13.10 lists many of the most interesting ones.

Table 13.10   A selection of other ways to change state

Function	Arguments	Summary
CGContextSetAlpha	context, alpha	Sets alpha transparency
CGContextSetBlendMode	context, CGBlendMode	Sets blending to one of almost 30 values, which specify how objects laid on top of each other interact with each other
CGContextSetFlatness	context, flatness	Defines the accuracy of curves
CGContextSetLineCap	context, CGLineCap	Defines how to draw the end of a line
CGContextSetLineDash	context, phase, lengths array, count	Describes how to draw dashes along a stroke
CGContextSetLineJoin	context, CGLineJoin	Defines how lines come together
CGContextSetLineWidth	context, width	Describes the width of a stroke
CGContextSetShadow	context, CGSize, blur	Sets a shadow behind all drawings
CGContextSetShadowWithColor	context, CGSize, blur, color	Sets a colored shadow behind all drawings

You can also find a number of more complex state changes in the CGContext class reference, but we've described the ones you're most likely to use in the course of an average program.

We're drawing to a close on the topic of graphical state, so let's step back for a moment and look at how graphical state works.

13.4.5 *Managing the state*

When you use any of the various functions that modify the graphical state, you're changing how you paint inside your current graphical context. The functions change the colors you're using, they transform your underlying grid, they clip the area you're allowed to paint within, or they make various smaller changes.

You can constantly reset these variables as your needs change, but this can get annoying. That's why you should use the stack of states. It allows you to make many changes to state and then revert to a previous setup that you were happy with. We've already shown the two functions that do this in table 13.6.

Remember to save the state before you make a big change, such as adding a clipping path or running a whole bunch of graphical state functions. Then, restore the state when you've done that. If you want, you can even be clever and slowly build up a set of states in your stack and move back through them appropriately.

You should now understand the three most important elements of drawing with Quartz: contexts, which specify *where* to draw; paths, which specify *what* to draw; and graphical states, which specify *how* to draw. You can do numerous more advanced things in Quartz, and although we won't get to all of them, the next section covers the most interesting ones.

13.5   *Advanced drawing in Quartz*

Quartz has a number of advanced capabilities that go beyond simple line drawings. In this section, we'll look at using gradients, images, and words.

13.5.1 *Drawing gradients*

Gradients are a core part of SDK design, because they're a clearly evident aspect of the standard user interface. Unfortunately, there's no UIKit-level class for creating gradients; instead, you have to fall back on Quartz.

You can create gradients in Quartz in two ways: using a CGShadingRef object or a CGGradientRef object. As is often the case in Core Foundation functions, the difference is in complexity. CGGradientRef allows you to draw simple gradients, and CGShadingRef requires you to define a CGFunctionRef object to precisely calculate how the colors in the gradient are displayed. As you've probably guessed, we'll talk about CGGradientRef here and point you to the Apple class references for CGShadingRef.

Table 13.11 shows the important functions required to draw gradients with CGGradientRef.

Table 13.11 `CGColorSpace`, `CGGradient`, and `CGContext` functions for drawing gradients

Function	Arguments	Summary
`CGColorSpaceCreateWithName`	`color space constant`	Creates a color space by name
`CGGradientCreateWithColors`	`color space, color array, location array`	Creates a gradient using pregenerated colors
`CGGradientCreateWithColorComponents`	`color space, color components array, location array, color count`	Creates a gradient with an array of color parts
`CGContextDrawLinearGradient`	`context, gradient, start CGPoint, end CGPoint, options`	Draws a linear gradient
`CGContextDrawRadialGradient`	`context, gradient, start center, start radius, end center, end radius, options`	Draws a radial gradient
`CGColorSpaceRelease`	`color space`	Frees up a color space object
`CGGradientRelease`	`gradient`	Frees up a gradient object

Drawing a gradient is a four-step process:

1 Define the color space, which you usually do by calling `CGColorSpaceCreate-DeviceRGB` for the iPhone and iPad.

2 Define the gradient by listing colors and where they appear in the gradient, from 0 to 1. You can do this two ways. You can hand off an array of `CGColors` (which may be useful if you want to generate them using `UIColors`), or you can hand off a longer array that defines the colors using another method, such as RGBA.

3 Draw the gradient as a linear gradient (going from point to point) or a radial gradient (going from the center to the edge of a circle).

4 Free up the memory.

The following code shows the steps required to draw a three-color linear gradient that spans an entire iPhone screen:

```
CGColorSpaceRef myColorSpace =
    CGColorSpaceCreateDeviceRGB();
CGFloat components[12] = {1,0,0,1,
    0,1,0,1,
    0,0,1,1};
CGFloat locations[3] = {0,.5,1};
CGGradientRef myGradient =
    CGGradientCreateWithColorComponents(myColorSpace,
        components, locations, (size_t)3);
CGContextDrawLinearGradient(ctx, myGradient, CGPointMake(0,0),
```

```
        CGPointMake(320,480), (CGGradientDrawingOptions)NULL);
CGColorSpaceRelease(myColorSpace);
CGGradientRelease(myGradient);
```

This code steps through the steps we just listed, defining the color space, creating the parts of the gradient, drawing it, and cleaning up after it. As usual, you can find more info about gradients in the `CGGradient` reference. For now, though, we're ready to move on to the next advanced category of Quartz work: images.

13.5.2 *Drawing images*

In chapter 11, you saw one way to work with images, using methods that largely hid the specifics of graphical contexts from you as a programmer. Now that you're fully immersed in Quartz, you can choose to use the Core Graphics functions instead.

THE IMAGE FUNCTIONS

The two major Core Graphics functions for drawing are listed in table 13.12.

Table 13.12   **Two image functions in Quartz**

Function	Arguments	Summary
CGContextDrawImage	context, CGRect, image	Draws an image scaled to fit the rectangle
CGContextDrawTiledImage	context, CGRect, image	Draws an image scaled to fit the rectangle but filling the current clip region

These functions both require a `CGImageRef`, but remember that you can use the `CGImage` property of a `UIImage` to produce one. Alternatively, you can use the commands described in the `CGImage` reference, which offer more precise functionality, to create a new `CGImage`. Our suggestion is to go with what you know, which means using the UIKit methods, unless they can't do what you need.

There's one big gotcha to using the Quartz-related image-drawing functions: they produce a flipped image because they use Quartz's native coordinate system internally. We'll show you how to fix that momentarily.

DRAWING ON A BITMAP

Often, you'll want to turn an image into a bitmap and modify it before displaying it on the screen, most frequently so that you can make multiple uses of the image. We'll offer a quick example of crossing out a picture here.

Part of what's unique about this example is that you can do all your drawing work without ever showing the image to the user (unlike if you were drawing on a `UIView`), thus opening up the possibility of many image-editing functions. When you do decide to display your newly saved image, you'll see results like the image in figure 13.4.

Figure 13.4   **You can change a `UIImage` without showing it to the user.**

The code needed to accomplish this simple crossing out is shown in the next listing.

Listing 13.1 Using bitmaps to edit images

```
UIImage *origPic = [UIImage imageNamed:@"pier.jpg"];
UIGraphicsBeginImageContext(origPic.size);
CGContextRef thisctx = UIGraphicsGetCurrentContext();

CGContextRotateCTM(ctx, M_PI);
CGContextTranslateCTM(ctx, -origPic.size.width, -origPic.size.height);
CGContextDrawImage(ctx,CGRectMake(0,0,origPic.size.width,
    origPic.size.height),[origPic CGImage]);

CGContextSetLineWidth(ctx, 20);
CGContextBeginPath(ctx);
CGContextMoveToPoint(ctx, 0, 0);
CGContextAddLineToPoint(ctx, origPic.size.width,origPic.size.height);
CGContextMoveToPoint(ctx, 0, origPic.size.height);
CGContextAddLineToPoint(ctx, origPic.size.width, 0);
CGContextSetStrokeColorWithColor(ctx, [[UIColor redColor] CGColor]);
CGContextStrokePath(ctx);
UIImage *newPic =
    UIGraphicsGetImageFromCurrentImageContext();
UIGraphicsEndImageContext();
```

❶ Transforms image

❷ Draws on image

The process of modifying an image involves relatively few steps. You start by creating your bitmap context. Next, you apply any transformations that you want to use for the picture ❶. If you want to rotate or scale the original picture, here's where you do it. Likewise, you can use a combination of translations and the context size to easily crop an image. In this example, you flip the picture over by applying a rotation and a translation, to account for the fact that `CGContextDrawImage` produces an inverted picture. (You'll see an alternative way to do this in the next example.)

When your transformations are finished, you can draw your image and then draw whatever you want on top of it ❷ (or modify it in some other way). Finally, you save the new picture.

We'll return to the idea of drawing on pictures in section 13.6 (though we'll do it in a much more interactive way), but in the meantime we're ready to draw words.

13.5.3 Drawing words

Unlike Canvas, Quartz supports drawing words on top of your pictures. The functions required are intricate, though, and we generally suggest using `UILabel` or other UIKit objects and placing them on top of your Quartz objects. But if you need words in Quartz (either because you're interweaving the words with other Quartz content or because you're adding words to a picture), you'll need to use the `CGContext` text options.

The majority of the text-related functions modify the graphical state, as described in table 13.13. The last two functions in the table draw your text.

You can find several other text-related functions in the `CGContext` reference. Most notably, if you need more control over your fonts (and particularly if you want to link

Table 13.13   A variety of functions for drawing text in Quartz

Function	Arguments	Summary
CGContextSelectFont	context, font name, size, text encoding	Sets a font for the graphical state
CGContextSetTextDrawingMode	context, CGTextDrawingMode	Defines how to draw text in the graphical state
CGContextSetTextMatrix	context, affine transform	Places a transformation matrix in the graphical state for drawing *only* text
CGContextSetSetPosition	context, x, y	Sets where to draw in the graphical state
CGContextShowText	context, string, length	Draws the text at the current position
CGContextShowTextAtPoint	context, x, y, string, length	Draws the text at the specified position

up to UIFonts), you should use CGContextSetFont and CGContextSetFontSize instead of the CGContextSelectFont function that's noted here—but keep in mind that you can't use CGContextShowTextAtPoint when you set your font in this alternative way.

Here's a simple example of printing text in Quartz:

```
CGContextSelectFont (ctx, "Helvetica",20,kCGEncodingMacRoman);
CGContextSetTextDrawingMode(ctx, kCGTextFill);
CGAffineTransform flip = CGAffineTransformMake(1,0,0,-1,0,0);
CGContextSetTextMatrix(ctx, flip);
CGContextShowTextAtPoint(ctx, 20, 85, "A Quartz Example", 16);
```

The only thing of note is the creation of the affine transformation matrix, flip. We've already pointed out that the text-drawing functions don't use the iOS coordinate system at present. Instead, they're stored in an inverted manner, so you need to flip them over to use them correctly. (We hope that this changes in some future release of iOS.)

The affine transformation shown here describes the matrix using the CGAffineTransformMake function. It effectively does the same thing as the two-part transformation in listing 13.1. In our view, it's a bit simpler but less clear.

That's only the basics of using text, but it should be enough to get you started when you need to draw in Quartz.

13.5.4   *What we didn't cover*

Quartz 2D is a fully featured drawing and painting language that we can only briefly touch on in this chapter. Among the other topics you may want to research if you're going to do more advanced work with Quartz are patterns, transparency layers, layer drawing, and PDF creation. As we've mentioned previously, Apple's "Quartz 2D Programming Guide" is an excellent introduction to these topics.

We're not quite finished with Quartz. Before we finish this chapter, we'll put together an example that combines some of the Quartz lessons from this chapter with some of the photographic work we covered in chapter 11.

13.6   Drawing on a picture: an example

To put together the lessons we've covered, you'll create a program that allows a user to load up a picture, draw on it, and then save the results. Figure 13.5 shows the intended result.

As usual, you'll begin by building your interface visually, but you have only two simple things to do:

1   Create a `UIButtonBar` with a single action-type button (which is one of the standard styles you can select for a button).
2   Link the existing `UIView` to a new `drawView` class (which should be a `UIView` subclass).

When you get into Xcode, the programming will look a lot like the collage program in chapter 11, but with some nuances related to your greater understanding of Quartz.

You'll do the coding in two parts. The overall structure of the program will go in PhotoDrawViewController.m, and the drawing specifics will go in drawView.m.

Figure 13.5   PhotoDraw can place drawings on pictures.

13.6.1   The PhotoDraw view controller

The view controller manages an image selector as well as several toolbar buttons, including the action button you created, and Save and Cancel buttons that appear later. The code is shown in listing 13.2. We've omitted some of the view controller's overall structure and focused on the code that's involved when the user pushes the action button and activates `choosePic:`.

Listing 13.2   The important bits of a view controller for a PhotoDraw program

```
-(IBAction)choosePic:(id)sender {
    UIImagePickerController *myImagePicker =
        [[UIImagePickerController alloc] init];
    myImagePicker.delegate = self;
    myImagePicker.allowsEditing = NO;
    [self presentModalViewController:myImagePicker animated:YES];
}
- (void)imagePickerController:(UIImagePickerController *)picker
    didFinishPickingImage:(UIImage *)image
```

```
        editingInfo:(NSDictionary *)editingInfo {
        [self dismissModalViewControllerAnimated:YES];
        [picker release];
        [myTools setItems:[NSArray arrayWithObjects:
            [[UIBarButtonItem alloc]
                initWithBarButtonSystemItem:UIBarButtonSystemItemSave
                target:self action:@selector(savePic:)],
            [[UIBarButtonItem alloc]
                initWithBarButtonSystemItem:UIBarButtonSystemItemCancel
                target:self action:@selector(clearDrawing:)],
            nil] animated:YES];
        [(drawView *)self.view drawPic:image];
}
- (void)imagePickerControllerDidCancel:
    (UIImagePickerController *)picker {
        [self dismissModalViewControllerAnimated:YES];
        [picker release];
}
- (void)savePic:(id)sender {
        UIGraphicsBeginImageContext(self.view.bounds.size);
        [myTools removeFromSuperview];
        [self.view.layer renderInContext:UIGraphicsGetCurrentContext()];
        UIImage *finishedPic = UIGraphicsGetImageFromCurrentImageContext();
        UIGraphicsEndImageContext();
        UIImageWriteToSavedPhotosAlbum(finishedPic,self,
            @selector(exitProg:didFinishSavingWithError:contextInfo:),nil);
}
- (void)exitProg:(UIImage *)image didFinishSavingWithError:(NSError *)error
    contextInfo:(void *)contextInfo {
        exit(0);
}
-(void)clearDrawing:(id)sender {
        [(drawView *)self.view cancelDrawing];
}
```

1 ◁— **Finishes image picker**

2 ◁— **Resolves image cancellation**

3 ◁— **Ends program**

This is a fairly simple snippet of code because it shows the view controller acting as a traffic cop, accepting input from controls and sending messages to other objects, which is pretty much the definition of what a view controller should do.

For once, you don't have any setup in viewDidLoad:. Instead, the toolbar initiates your program's actions. At startup, the user has only one choice: to click the action button and start the image picker. When the picker returns, you modify the UIButtonBar to give options for Save and Cancel, and then you send the picture to drawView to be dealt with **1**. Alternatively, you clear away the image picker if the user cancels it **2**.

The save-picture routine works the same way as the one you wrote in the collage program. The only difference is that this one includes a callback, which ends the program after the saving is done **3**. The clear-drawing method, meanwhile, makes a call to the drawView object again.

To learn what's done with the initial picture, how drawing occurs, and what happens when the drawing is cleared, we need to look at this program's other major class.

13.6.2 *The photodraw view*

As you saw in the previous section, the view controller hands off three responsibilities to the view: displaying a picture, responding to touch events, and clearing the drawing. We'll step through these functions one at a time.

Here's what's done when a user picks an image:

```
-(void)drawPic:(UIImage *)thisPic {
    myPic = thisPic;
    [myPic retain];
    [self setNeedsDisplay];
}
```

This routine is simple: it saves the picture to an instance variable and then alerts the UIView that its CALayer must be drawn.

We'll save the CALayer's drawRect: method for last, so we'll look now at how the drawView class interprets touch events. This is shown in the next listing.

Listing 13.3   Recording touch events

```
- (void) touchesBegan:(NSSet *)
    touches withEvent:(UIEvent *)event {
    [myDrawing addObject:[[NSMutableArray alloc] initWithCapacity:4]];
    CGPoint curPoint = [[touches anyObject] locationInView:self];
    [[myDrawing lastObject] addObject:[NSNumber
        numberWithFloat:curPoint.x]];
    [[myDrawing lastObject] addObject:[NSNumber
        numberWithFloat:curPoint.y]];
}
- (void) touchesMoved:(NSSet *)touches
    withEvent:(UIEvent *)event {
    CGPoint curPoint = [[touches anyObject] locationInView:self];
    [[myDrawing lastObject] addObject:[NSNumber
        numberWithFloat:curPoint.x]];
    [[myDrawing lastObject] addObject:[NSNumber
        numberWithFloat:curPoint.y]];
    [self setNeedsDisplay];
}
- (void) touchesEnded:(NSSet *)touches
    withEvent:(UIEvent *)event {

    CGPoint curPoint = [[touches anyObject] locationInView:self];
    [[myDrawing lastObject] addObject:[NSNumber
        numberWithFloat:curPoint.x]];
    [[myDrawing lastObject] addObject:[NSNumber
        numberWithFloat:curPoint.y]];
    [self setNeedsDisplay];
}
```

The overall concept here is simple. You maintain an NSMutableArray called myDrawing as an instance variable. Within that, you create a number of NSMutable-Array subarrays, each of which contains an individual path. You set up a new subarray when a touch starts and then add the current point when the touch moves or ends.

The result is an array that contains a complete listing of all touches. But again, you'll have to wait to see how that's drawn.

It's notable that you tell drawView to draw (via the setNeedsDisplay method) both when a touch moves *and* when it ends. That's because whenever the touch moves, you want to provide instant gratification by drawing what the user has sketched out so far. When the touch ends, you do the same thing.

The following method clears all current drawings. Its functionality is obvious now that you know that the list of drawings is held as an array:

```
-(void)cancelDrawing {

    [myDrawing removeAllObjects];
    [self setNeedsDisplay];
}
```

At this point, the drawView object is maintaining two different instance variables: myPic contains the current picture, and myDrawing contains an array of paths. Putting them together into a coherent whole requires using some of the Quartz functions we discussed in the last two chapters. The results are shown in the next listing.

Listing 13.4   Drawing from user-created variables

```
- (void)drawRect:(CGRect)rect {
    float newHeight;
    float newWidth;
    if (!myDrawing) {
        myDrawing = [[NSMutableArray alloc] initWithCapacity:0];
    }
    CGContextRef ctx = UIGraphicsGetCurrentContext();
    if (myPic != NULL) {
        float ratio = myPic.size.height/460;
        if (myPic.size.width/320 > ratio) {
            ratio = myPic.size.width/320;
        }
        newHeight = myPic.size.height/ratio;
        newWidth = myPic.size.width/ratio;                          ❶ Draws image
        [myPic drawInRect:CGRectMake(0,0,newWidth,newHeight)];          to context
    }
    if ([myDrawing count] > 0) {
        CGContextSetLineWidth(ctx, 5);
        for (int i = 0 ; i < [myDrawing count] ; i++) {
            NSArray *thisArray = [myDrawing objectAtIndex:i];
            if ([thisArray count] > 2) {
                float thisX = [[thisArray objectAtIndex:0] floatValue];
                float thisY = [[thisArray objectAtIndex:1] floatValue];
                CGContextBeginPath(ctx);                         ❷ Starts drawing path
                CGContextMoveToPoint(ctx, thisX, thisY);
                    for (int j = 2; j < [thisArray count] ; j+=2) {
                        thisX = [[thisArray objectAtIndex:j] floatValue];
                        thisY = [[thisArray objectAtIndex:j+1] floatValue];
                        CGContextAddLineToPoint(ctx, thisX,thisY);
                    }
                                                            Adds line ❸
```

```
            CGContextStrokePath(ctx);
        }
    }
  }
}
```
◁┐ **Strokes**
❹ **path**

The bulk of this method is spent iterating through the information you saved in other methods. Four Quartz functions do the drawing work. First, you draw the selected image. You go back to using the UIKit methods from chapter 11 ❶ so the image doesn't end up upside-down. Then, you begin working through the myDrawing array. Each subarray results in your program beginning a new path ❷ and moving to the start. As you move through the array, you add lines ❸. Finally, when a subarray is complete, you stroke the path ❹.

The result allows for drawing simple lines on a picture, which can then be saved, as you saw back in the view controller.

But is it possible to do more with this example? As usual, the answer is, yes.

13.6.3 Expanding on the example

If you want to expand this example into a more complete application, you can take several routes. The first and most obvious expansion is to select a color before drawing a line. The hard part is creating a color picker, although you can make a standalone class that you can then reuse elsewhere. With that in hand, it's simple to add a color variable to your line arrays, by always saving it as the 0 element of a subarray.

The program could also benefit from a more sophisticated line-drawing algorithm that tosses out nearby points and smoothes the lines into curves, removing some of the sharp edges that show up in the current program.

In any case, that ends our look at Quartz 2D. There's a lot more you can learn, but you should have the foundation you need to move forward.

Two other ways you can draw using the SDK are Core Animation and OpenGL. We don't have the space in this introductory book to give full attention to either, but we'll introduce them and show you where to go for more information, beginning with Core Animation.

13.7 An introduction to Core Animation

Core Animation is a fundamental technology on the iPhone and iPad. It manages all the nifty scrolls, pivots, zoom-ins, zoom-outs, and other bits of animation that make up the user interface. As you've already seen, many UIKit classes give you an option to use animation or not, usually by having an animated: argument as part of a method.

Core Animation is also tightly integrated with Quartz. As you've seen, each UIView is linked to a graphical layer called the CALayer, which is the *Core Animation* layer. Though you've only used it to depict simple graphics and images so far, you can also use it to manage more complex changes.

But you don't *have* to use Quartz at all to create animations. There's a CALayer behind every UIView; and because almost everything is built on a UIView, you can

Figure 13.6   A jet moves across the screen on an iPhone, thanks to Core Animation.

animate your existing UIViews, possibly including pictures that you've loaded into UIImageViews. For example, figure 13.6 shows how you can use Core Animation to show an approaching plane by moving its UIImageView and turning it opaque as it approaches.

This is the example we'll show later in this section, using two different means to create the animation.

13.7.1 *The fundamentals of Core Animation*

When we speak of animation using Core Animation, we're talking about changing the properties of the CALayer and then smoothly animating those property changes. The CALayer class reference lists which properties can be animated; they include anchor-Point, backgroundColor, opacity, position, transform, and several others. This means you can use Core Animation to animate the position of an object, its color, its transparency, and also its CGAffine transformations.

Before we get further into Core Animation, we want to talk about its fundamentals—those terms and ideas that you'll meet throughout this section:

- *Layer*—This is where animation occurs. You always have one CALayer hooked up to every UIView, accessible via the layer property. You can call up additional layers with a [CALayer layer] class message and then add them to your existing CALayer with the addSublayer: method. Adding layers this way results in inverted coordinate systems. Each layer can be individually animated, allowing for complex interactions between numerous animated properties. You may find it as easy to create a more complex animation by creating multiple UIKit objects (most likely multiple UIImageViews) and animating each one.

- *Implicit animation*—This is the simplest type of animation. You tell the UIView that it should animate and then you change the properties.
- *Explicit animation*—This is an animation created with CABasicAnimation that allows you to more explicitly define how the property change animates.
- *Key-frame animation*—This is an even more explicit type of animation, where you define not only the start and end of the animation but also some of the frames in between.

You can also create much more complex animations, such as redefining how implicit animations work, collecting animations into transactions, and building complex animation layer hierarchies. For more information, look at the "Core Animation Programming Guide" and the "Core Animation Cookbook," both available from Apple.

13.7.2 Getting started with Core Animation

To use Core Animation, make sure you add Quartz Core, the framework required for animation, to your project. You should also include QuartzCore/QuartzCore.h, the main header file for Core Animation.

With that done, you're ready to try the two simplest types of animation: a simple implicit animation and an explicit animation.

13.7.3 Drawing a simple implicit animation

Implicit animations are the simplest type of animation, because they just require starting an animation block and then changing CALayer-level properties. The following code shows a simple example involving a UIImageView called plane that contains a clipart picture of a plane. The image starts at the upper-left corner of the screen with 25 percent opacity and moves downward while growing more opaque:

```
[UIView beginAnimations:nil context:NULL];
CGAffineTransform moveTransform
    = CGAffineTransformMakeTranslation(200, 200);
[plane.layer setAffineTransform:moveTransform];
plane.layer.opacity = 1;
[UIView commitAnimations];
```

Between them, beginAnimations:context: and commitAnimations define an animation block.

Within the block, you set two properties to animate. setAffineTransform: is a special CALayer method that allows the setting of its transform property using an affine transformation matrix, which you're already familiar with; opacity is a more obvious property.

Alternatively, you can pass the implicit animation blocks in class method. The following table contains common animations API in iOS 4:

Table 13.2   Common animations API with blocks arguments in iOS 4

Class method	Details

`+ (void)animateWithDuration:`
`(NSTimeInterval)duration animations:`
`(void (^)(void))animations`
	This method will apply the animation blocks to views without delay and the duration is in seconds.

`+ (void)animateWithDuration:`
`(NSTimeInterval)duration animations:`
`(void (^)(void))animations completion:`
`(void (^)(BOOL finished))completion`
	This method will apply the animation blocks to views and execute the completion handler after the animation.

`+ (void)animateWithDuration:`
`(NSTimeInterval)duration delay:`
`(NSTimeInterval)delay options:`
`(UIViewAnimationOptions)options`
`animations:(void (^)(void))animations completion:`
`(void (^)(BOOL finished))completion`
	This method will apply the animation blocks, options and completion handler to the views. UIViewAnimationOptions options can be defined.

`+ (void)transitionWithView:`
`(UIView *)view duration:`
`(NSTimeInterval)duration options:`
`(UIViewAnimationOptions)options animations:`
`(void (^)(void))animations completion:`
`(void (^)(BOOL finished))completion`
	This method will apply the animation transition from the first view to the second view. For example, the view controller can use this method to transit from the main view to the flip view.

Let's take a look at the previous code example, the plane image starts at the upper-left corner of the screen with 25 percent opacity and moves downward while growing more opaque. Use the animation blocks API, use the default animation duration value, 0.2 second.

```
[UIView animateWithDuration:0.2 animations:^{
  CGAffineTransform moveTransform = CGAffineTransformMakeTranslation(200,200);
  [plane.layer setAffineTransform:moveTransform];
  plane.layer.opacity = 1;
}];
```

With a start of "^", the complier understands the following anonymous blocks of code applying to animations.

As soon as you close out the block, the animation begins. The plane moves and grows more distinct. That's all there is to it!

But sometimes an implicit animation doesn't give you as much control as you want. That's where explicit animations come in.

13.7.4   Drawing a simple explicit animation

When you're working with explicit animations, instead of defining a bunch of changes to a `CALayer` and executing them all, you define animations one by one using the `CABasicAnimation` class. Each of these animations can have its own value for duration, `repeatCount`, and numerous other properties. You then apply each animation to a layer separately, using the `addAnimation:forKey:` method.

The following code executes an animation similar to the previous one but with more control:

```
CABasicAnimation *opAnim = [CABasicAnimation
    animationWithKeyPath:@"opacity"];
opAnim.duration = 3.0;
opAnim.fromValue = [NSNumber numberWithFloat:.25];
opAnim.toValue= [NSNumber numberWithFloat:1.0];
opAnim.cumulative = YES;
opAnim.repeatCount = 2;
[plane.layer addAnimation:opAnim forKey:@"animateOpacity"];
CGAffineTransform moveTransform
    = CGAffineTransformMakeTranslation(200, 200);
CABasicAnimation *moveAnim = [CABasicAnimation
    animationWithKeyPath:@"transform"];
moveAnim.duration = 6.0;
moveAnim.toValue= [NSValue valueWithCATransform3D:
    CATransform3DMakeAffineTransform(moveTransform)];
[plane.layer addAnimation:moveAnim forKey:@"animateTransform"];
```

This example is definitely longer than the implicit animation example, but you get to define the two animations with separate durations, which is the first step to creating a more beautiful and better-controlled animation. Note that you also use yet another way to change an affine transformation matrix into a `Transform3D` matrix of the type used by Core Animation: the `CATransform3DMakeAffineTransform` function.

The code includes a bit of a kludge: to keep the plane opaque through the last 3 seconds, it keeps counting opacity cumulatively, making it climb from 1.0 to 1.75 the second time through. A better solution would create three key frames for `opacity`: .25 at 0 seconds, 1.0 at 3 seconds, and 1.0 at 6 seconds. *That's* why you may want to use a key-frame animation of the sort we alluded to at the start of this section, rather than a basic animation.

These simple methods for using Core Animation can take you far. Look through the `CALayer` class reference for everything you're allowed to animate. For more details, read the two Apple guides we pointed out.

Before we leave graphics behind, we want to touch on one other toolkit: OpenGL.

13.8 An introduction to OpenGL

OpenGL is SGI's standardized 2D and 3D graphical drawing language. The iPhone and iPad more specifically use OpenGL ES, or OpenGL for Embedded Systems, which features a reduced API for use on devices like mobile phones. For full information about using OpenGL, you should pick up a book on the topic or read Apple's "OpenGL ES Framework Reference," which links to the most important documents available from Apple. We'll cover some of the general information you need to access OpenGL through iOS.

iOS manages OpenGL through `EAGL`, a class that interfaces between the device's views and OpenGL's drawing functions. It allows for the writing of OpenGL functions onto an `EAGLView`, which is the `CAEAGL` layer of a `UIView`, showing the same layer-based paradigm you met when using Core Animation.

To simplify your programming of OpenGL projects, Xcode supplies a standard template to use, which sets up all the OpenGL defaults for you. It's the OpenGL ES Application template, the only Xcode template that we have yet to examine. This template includes all the basic setup of OpenGL, which is extensive. That includes the setup of a timer, the creation of frame buffers, and the code needed to draw something. To do basic OpenGL programming, all you have to do is write your code into the `drawView` method of the `EAGLView` class.

Rather than giving a completely insufficient overview of this enormous library, we'll instead point you toward a few bits of sample code. The OpenGL template comes complete with a rotating square as an example. There are also three OpenGL samples currently available from Apple: GLGravity shows simple OpenGL rendering related to accelerometer output, GLSprite demonstrates texturing, and GLPaint explores another way to allow finger painting.

These examples should be sufficient to get you started if you already have a strong basis in OpenGL and need to see how it's integrated into the iPhone and iPad.

13.9 Summary

Graphics are one of the most important elements for making your projects look great. Not only does iOS support high-quality graphics, but it also gives you a wide variety of options, depending on the needs of your program.

Quartz 2D will be your main workhorse for most graphical programs. If you're already familiar with the Canvas library for the web, you'll see that Quartz is similar. You can draw paths and use many graphical state variables to modify exactly how that path is painted.

Core Animation is an expansion to Quartz that was created for the iPhone and iPad. You've already seen it integrated into numerous native programs, and now you can use it yourself. Core Animation is built around the idea of automated animations: you tell it the endpoints, and Core Animation fills in the rest for you. Again, this is much as you may have seen on the web, with the WebKit's various styles of implicit and explicit animation.

OpenGL is a whole new graphics library that has been imported into iOS, much as SQLite is a third-party library that Apple made available to developers. The difference is that Apple has made OpenGL easier to use, thanks to the creation of the EAGL framework. Although this chapter suggests how to get started with OpenGL, the topic is large enough that you'll need to pick up a book to fully explore the topic.

With graphics covered, we need to look at another major topic in the SDK toolkit: the internet. How do you access the Net, and how do you use various protocols that let you access the web's ever-growing social network?

*The web: web views
and internet protocols*

14

This chapter covers

- Using web views
- Parsing XML
- Accessing other protocols

Internet connectivity is an essential feature of modern life, and the iPhone and iPad are so useful because iOS allows for easy internet access. In this chapter, we'll cover the major ways to access the internet from the SDK. You can use a variety of approaches, and we'll outline their hierarchy in the first section. Later in the chapter, we'll look at low-level networking, working with URLs, using the UIWebView, parsing XML, using POST, and accessing the social web using various protocols.

14.1 The hierarchy of the internet

Internet programming involves a hierarchy of protocols. At the lowest level are the sockets you use to connect one computer to another. Above them are a variety of more sophisticated technologies, such as FTP, Bonjour, and HTTP. HTTP is a critical protocol, represented on the iPhone and iPad by both low-level access and the

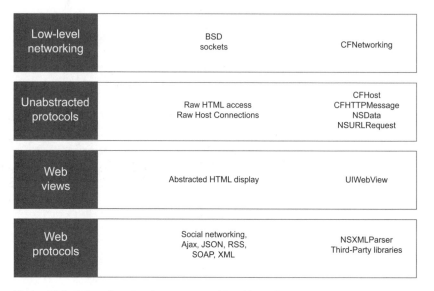

Figure 14.1   Internet protocols are arranged in a hierarchy.

high-level `UIWebView`. Recently, an increasing number of protocols have been built on top of HTTP, forming what we call the *social web*.

This hierarchy of internet protocols is shown in figure 14.1, along with iOS classes of note.

In this chapter, we'll cover all these protocols, starting with the lowest level. But our real focus will be on the higher-level internet and social web protocols, because they're the protocols that are best supported by iOS, and they're the ones you're most likely to want to interact with.

14.2   *Low-level networking*

We've opted not to pay much attention to BSD sockets and the lower-level networking classes, because we expect they'll be of little interest to most application programmers. If you need to work with BSD sockets, you should look at Apple's "Introduction to CFNetwork Programming Guide."

If you need to work with the lower-level protocols, CFNetwork provides a variety of classes that you'll find useful. You can find more information about them in the "Networking & Internet" topic in the Apple docs. In particular, the "CFNetwork Framework Reference" will give you an overview of the various classes. Among the classes are `CFFTPStream`, which lets you communicate with FTP servers; and `CFNetServices`, which gives you access to Bonjour—Apple's service discovery protocol. There are also two low-level HTTP-related classes, `CFHTTPMessage` and `CFHTTPStream`. We'll leave these classes alone, because our HTML work will be related to the higher-level `NSURL`, `NSURLRequest`, `UIWebView`, `NSMutableURLRequest`, and `NSURLConnection` classes.

Rather than skipping over these low-level and unabstracted protocols entirely, we'll look at one of them: CFHost. It's the easiest to work with and perhaps the most immediately useful.

CFHost allows your program to request information about an internet host, such as its name, its address, and whether it's reachable. The following listing shows a sample of how to determine whether a hostname exists.

Listing 14.1 A simple hostname lookup

```
-(IBAction)reportStatus:(id)sender {
    CFStreamError errorTest;
    if (myInput.text) {
        CFHostRef myHost = CFHostCreateWithName(kCFAllocatorDefault,
            (CFStringRef)myInput.text);
        if (myHost) {
            if (CFHostStartInfoResolution(myHost, kCFHostAddresses,
                &errorTest)) {
                myOutput.text = [myInput.text stringByAppendingString:
                    @" COULD be resolved."];
            } else {
                myOutput.text = [myInput.text stringByAppendingFormat:
                    @" could NOT be resolved (Error: %i).",
                        errorTest.error];
            }
        }
        CFRelease(myHost);
    }
}
```

The sample method, reportStatus:, is activated by a button push. It reads a hostname from a UITextField called *myInput* and reports out to a UITextView called *myOutput*.

All uses of the CFHost commands follow the same pattern. First you create a CFHostRef object with CFHostCreateCopy, CFHostCreateWithAddress, or CFHostCreateWithName. Then, you use CFHostStartInfoResolution to request a certain type of information, which can be kCFHostAddresses, kCFHostNames, or kCFHostReachability. This example omits a final step in which you retrieve the information with CFHostGetAddressing, CFHostGetNames, or CFHostReachability—something that isn't necessary here because the point is to see if the request for an address resolves correctly.

You can find more information about these functions, and about how to use a callback function to make the host resolution asynchronous, in the CFHost reference.

We consider this look at low-level networking—and CFHost—an aside, meant only to hint at what's possible if you must do lower-level networking work. Now, we'll move on to higher-level HTML-related network work that's more likely to be the focus of your network programming. The first thing you'll need to know is how to use iOS's URL objects.

14.3 *Working with URLs*

With HTTP being the basis of most internet programming, it shouldn't be a surprise that URLs are a foundational technique for internet-based programming. You'll use them whether you're calling up `UIImageViews`, accessing content by hand, or parsing XML. As a result, we'll spend some time on the two fundamental URL classes: `NSURL` and `NSURLRequest`. We'll also look at how to manipulate HTML data by hand.

14.3.1 *Creating an NSURL*

An `NSURL` is an object that contains a URL. It can reference a website or a local file, as any URL can. You've used it in the past to access Apple's stock page and to load local media files for play.

As noted in the `NSURL` class reference, you can use numerous methods to create an `NSURL`. The most important ones are listed in table 14.1.

Table 14.1   A variety of `NSURL` creation methods

Method	Summary
`fileURLWithPath:`	Creates a URL from a local file path
`URLWithString:`	Creates a URL from a string; equivalent to `initWithString:`
`URLWithString:relativeToURL:`	Adds a string to a base URL; equivalent to `initWithString:relativeToURL:`

When you have an `NSURL` in hand, you can do any number of things with it:

- You can pass it on to functions that require a bare `NSURL`.
- You can query its properties to easily break down the URL into its parts. As usual, you can find a complete list of properties in the Apple reference, but properties like `baseURL`, `fragment`, `host`, `path`, `port`, and `query` may be particularly useful.
- You can use the `NSURL` to load a `UIWebView`.

The first two possibilities require only the use of an `NSURL`; but when you're working with a `UIWebView`, you must first create an `NSURL` and then turn it into an `NSURLRequest`.

> **`NSURL` and `CFURLRef`**
> `NSURL` is a toll-free bridge to `CFURL`, making an `NSURL *` and a `CFURLRef` equivalent. We take advantage of this in chapter 12 when dealing with the `MPMoviePlayer-Controller` and with sounds. Whenever you need to create a `CFURLRef`, you can do so using the standard methods for `NSURL` creation that are described in this chapter.

14.3.2 *Building an NSURLRequest*

The NSURLRequest class contains two parts: a URL and a specific policy for dealing with cached responses. As noted in table 14.2, there are four ways to create an NSURL-Request, although we expect you'll usually fall back on the simple factory method, requestWithURL:.

Table 14.2 The related NSURLRequest init methods

Method	Summary
requestWithURL:	Creates a default request from the URL; equivalent to initWithURL:
requestWithURL:cachePolicy:timeoutInterval:	Creates a request with specific caching choices; equivalent to initWithURL: cachePolicy:timeoutInterval:

By default, an NSURLRequest is built with a caching policy that's dependent on the protocol and a timeout value of 60 seconds, which should be sufficient for most of your programming needs. If you need to get more specific about how things are loaded, you can call requestWithURL:cachePolicy:timeoutInterval:, giving it an NSURLRequestCachePolicy for the policy and an NSTimeInterval for the timeout.

You can also create a more interactive NSURLRequest by using the NSMutableURL-Request class, which allows you to more carefully form and modify the request that you're sending. We'll talk about this in section 14.6, when we examine how to send POST requests.

The NSURLRequest will get you through most web page work. As with the NSURL, you can do a few different things with an NSURLRequest. You can hand it off to a UIImageView, or you can use it to read in the contents of a web page, to later manipulate it by hand.

14.3.3 *Manipulating HTML data by hand*

To read the contents of a web page manually, you need to access an NSURLRequest's properties. Table 14.3 lists some of the most important ones, although, as usual, you can find more information in the class reference.

Table 14.3 NSURLRequest can give access to a page's content.

Property	Summary
allHTTPHeaderFields	Returns an NSDictionary of the header
HTTPBody	Returns an NSData with the body
valueforHTTPHeaderField:	Returns an NSString with the header

Other ways to read HTTP content

If you're not reading data that meets the HTTP protocol, you can't use NSURL-Request's properties to access the data. Instead, you must fall back on other functions that let you read in data from an NSURL.

You've already met functions that read data that follows other protocol specifications, such as the MPMoviePlayerController and the sound players from chapter 12. Similarly, in this chapter we'll talk about an XML parser. All of these classes can read directly from a URL.

If you need to capture raw data that isn't set in HTML, the best way to do so is with an init or factory method that reads from a URL, such as NSData's dataWithContentsOfURL:. We'll look at an example of that in the last section of this chapter.

The catch with these properties is that you can work only with well-defined HTML pages. Most notably, the NSURLRequest properties can't read fragments, such as would be generated by Ajax or JSON, nor can they parse other sorts of content, such as XML or RSS.

You may also discover that you need a more interactive way to deal with HTML data. In this case, you'll probably use an NSURLConnection object; but as with the NSMutableURLRequest, we'll save that for later, because you'll typically need to use it only when you're POSTing information to a web page rather than just retrieving it.

For the moment, we'll put all these complexities aside and look at how to display straight HTML data using the SDK's UIWebView.

14.4   *Using UIWebView*

One of the easiest ways to connect to the internet is to use the UIWebView class, which gives you full access to web pages of any sort. In some ways, this class is of limited utility, because it largely duplicates Safari, and Apple isn't interested in approving applications that duplicate their existing technology. But there are clearly situations where you'll want a program to be able to refer to some specific web pages, and that's what UIWebView is for.

The class is easy to use—we included it in simple examples way back in chapters 3 and 4. The only real complexity is in building an NSURL or NSURLRequest object to get your web view started, but that process follows the methods you've already seen.

14.4.1 *Calling up the web view*

The two main ways to fill a web view once you've created it are listed in table 14.4. Most frequently, you'll start with an NSURLRequest, which you must create using the two-step process we described in the previous section; but you can also load a web view with an NSURL and an NSString. A few other init methods can be found in the class reference.

Table 14.4   Methods for loading `UIWebView`

Method	Summary
`loadHTMLString:baseURL:`	Loads a page from a URL and a string
`loadRequest:`	Loads a page from an `NSURLRequest`

Assuming you use the more common `NSURLRequest` method, you can put together all the lessons you've learned so far, which is just what you did back in chapter 3 when you created your first `UIWebView`:

```
[myWebView loadRequest:
    [NSURLRequest requestWithURL:
        [NSURL URLWithString:url]]];
```

When you have a `UIWebView`, you can start working with it. The five `UIWebView` methods and properties of particular note are summarized in table 14.5.

Table 14.5   Some sterling `UIWebView` options

Method/Property	Type	Summary
`goBack`	Method	Moves back a page; check `canGoBack` property first
`goForward`	Method	Moves forward a page; check `canGoForward` property first
`reload`	Method	Reloads the current page
`scalesPageToFit`	Property	Boolean that determines whether the page is zoomed into a viewport and whether user zooming is allowed

We think the most exciting options are the `goBack`, `goForward`, and `reload` methods, which give you some control over how the `UIWebView` moves among pages. Similarly, the `loadRequest:` method can be continually rerun if you want to move a user through multiple pages, treating the `UIWebView` more like a web slideshow than a browser.

> **WARNING**   In our opinion, the `scalesPageToFit` property doesn't work correctly at the current time. It always scales the page as if the `UIWebView` were full screen, and it leaves a less than optimal view if you create a small `UIWeb-View`, as you'll do in the next example. As of iOS 4.0, this has yet to be resolved.

You must always load `NSURLs` using the `loadRequest:` method of `NSURLRequest` that we've laid out here to load pages into your web views.

14.4.2 Managing the web view delegate

One critical element we haven't discussed previously is that you can set a delegate to manage a few common responses. You must follow the UIWebViewDelegate protocol, which lists four methods, described in table 14.6.

Table 14.6   Managing UIWebViews with delegate methods

Method	Summary
webView:shouldStartLoadWithRequest:navigationType:	Called prior to content loading
webViewDidStartLoad:	Called after content begins loading
webViewDidFinishLoad:	Called after content finishes loading
webView:didFailLoadWithError:	Called after content fails to load

Together with the UIWebView methods, these delegate methods give you considerable power. You can use them to load alternative web pages if the preferred ones don't load. Or, continuing the slideshow analogy, you can use them to continuously load new pages when old ones finish. All those possibilities highlight the ways you may be able to use the UIWebView as more than a Safari clone.

14.4.3 Thumbnails: a web view example

As we've previously stated, UIWebViews are easy to set up, and we're not going to spend a lot of time on a coding sample. Listing 14.2 presents a simple example that creates a set of web page thumbnails, similar to the startup page of the Google Chrome browser. It uses delegates first to get rid of UIWebViews that don't load and later to zoom in on the one the user selects.

You should initially create it visually by laying out four UIWebViews on your interface. Make sure they're set to scale, and set their delegates to be the view controller.

Listing 14.2   A thumbnail web viewer

```
- (void)viewDidLoad {                              ◁   Sets up
    [super viewDidLoad];                          ①   web views
    webArray = [[NSArray alloc]
        initWithObjects:webView1,webView2,webView3,webView4,nil];
    NSString *paths = [[NSBundle mainBundle] resourcePath];
    NSString *filePath = [paths
        stringByAppendingPathComponent:@"weblist.txt"];
    NSString *webList = [NSString stringWithContentsOfFile:filePath
encoding:NSASCIIStringEncoding error:nil];
    NSArray *webListArray = [webList componentsSeparatedByString:@"\n"];
    for (int i = 0 ; i < [webArray count] ; i++) {
        [[webArray objectAtIndex:i] loadRequest:
            [NSURLRequest requestWithURL:
```

```
                    [NSURL URLWithString:
                        [webListArray objectAtIndex:i]]]];
    }
}
- (void)webView:(UIWebView *)webView                          ❷ Resolves
    didFailLoadWithError:(NSError *)thiserror {                    errors
    NSLog(@"Web Thumbs Error: %@",thiserror);
    if (thiserror.code == -1003) {
        [webView removeFromSuperview];
    }
}                                                            ❸ Zooms
- (void)webViewDidFinishLoad:(UIWebView *)webView {              active view
    if (webView.canGoBack == YES) {
        for (int i = 0 ; i < [webArray count] ; i ++) {
            if ([webArray objectAtIndex:i] != webView) {
                [[webArray objectAtIndex:i] removeFromSuperview];
            } else {
                webView.frame = [[UIScreen mainScreen] bounds];
            }
        }
    }
}
```

To start with, you read a set of (exactly) four URLs from a file and use the NSString method componentsSeparatedByString: to turn them into an NSArray that you use to seed your web views ❶. After that, it's a question of responding to delegation messages.

The webView:didFailLoadWithError: method ❷ shows off some valuable techniques for both debugging and error management. You should use NSLog when you want to do a printf-style reporting of runtime variables. It outputs to /var/log/system .log when you run it in the Simulator.

In a UIWebView, two error codes come up with some frequency: -1003 is "Can't find host," and -999 is "Operation could not be completed." This example ignores -999 (which usually means the user clicked a link before the page finished loading); but in the case of a -1003 failure, you dismiss the web view.

Debugging

We haven't talked much about debugging your SDK program in this book, primarily for reasons of space. Here's a short overview of our favorite techniques:

Xcode itself provides the best debugging. Pay careful attention to autocompletion of words and note when an expected autocompletion doesn't occur, because that usually means you didn't set a variable correctly.

Always carefully consider the warnings and errors that appear on compilation.

Finally, after you've finished with your program, you should run it through Instruments to check for memory leaks.

For more information, see "Xcode Debugging Guide," "Debugging with GDB," and "Instruments User Guide," Apple articles that contain comprehensive explanations of those subjects.

Finally, the `webViewDidFinishLoad:` method ❸ zooms in on an individual web view (dismissing the rest) after a user clicks a link and the page loads. Realistically, this should occur whenever the user touches the web view; but we wanted to show the `UIWebView` delegate methods, so we chose this slightly more circuitous route.

And that's it—a simple web thumbnail program, as shown in figure 14.2. It could be improved by giving the user the ability to manage the selected URLs and by polishing the way the user selects an individual page (including an option to return to the thumbnail page afterward). For our purposes, though, it does a great job of demonstrating some of the intricacies of the `UIWebView`.

Before we finish with web views, we'll look at one more example. In chapter 10, we talked about how Core Location would be better served when we got into the world of the internet. In section 14.5.4, we'll look at the first of two Core Location internet examples.

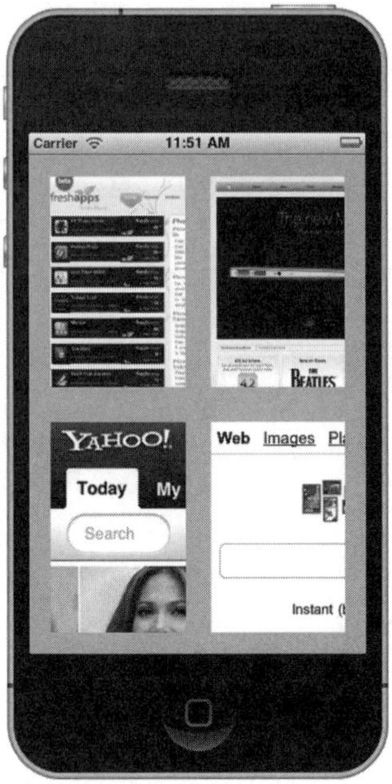

Figure 14.2   As shown on an iPhone, the thumbnail web views load on the screen.

14.5   *Parsing XML*

Extensible Markup Language (XML) is a generalized markup language whose main purpose is to deliver data in a well-formed and organized way. It has some similarities to HTML, and an XML version of HTML has been released, called XHTML.

Because of XML's popularity on the internet, the iOS SDK includes its own XML parser, the `NSXMLParser` class. This is an event-driven API, which means it reports start and end tags as it moves through the document, and you must take appropriate action as it does.

Running the `NSXMLParser` involves setting it up, starting it running, and then reacting to the results. We'll cover that process in the rest of this section. For more information about any of these topics, we suggest reading Apple's "Event-Driven XML

XML and files

When using `NSXMLParser`, you'll probably immediately think about reading data taken from the internet, but it's equally easy to read XML from your local files. You create a path to the file and then use `NSURL`'s `fileURLWithPath:` method, as you've seen elsewhere in this book.

An XML file can be a nice intermediary step between saving data in plain text files and saving it in databases, which were two of the options you saw in chapter 9. Although you're still using files, you can do so in a well-organized manner. You'll see an example of this in section 14.5.3.

Programming Guide for Cocoa," but we'll provide a tutorial on the basics and build an RSS reader. We'll start with the parser class.

14.5.1 *Starting up NSXMLParser*

In order to get started with the `NSXMLParser`, you need to create it, set various properties, and then start it running. The most important methods for doing so are listed in table 14.7.

Table 14.7 Methods to get your `NSXMLParser` going

Method	Summary
initWithContentsOfURL:	Creates a parser from an NSURL
initWithData:	Creates a parser from an NSData
setDelegate:	Defines a delegate for the parser
parse	Starts the parser going

Not listed are a few additional setters that allow the parser to process namespaces, report namespace prefixes, and resolve external entities. By default, these properties are all set to NO; you shouldn't need them for simple XML parsing.

14.5.2 *Acting as a delegate*

There are approximately 14 delegate methods for `NSXMLParser`. They're all optional: you need to write delegates only for things you're watching for.

In this chapter, we'll look at the five most critical methods you'll need to use whenever you're parsing XML. These methods report the start and end of elements, the contents inside, when the XML parsing has ended (unrecoverably!) with an error, and when the XML parsing has ended because it's finished. These are listed in table 14.8.

Generally, when you're parsing XML, you should take the following steps as you move through elements:

1 When you receive the `didStartElement:` method, look at the `NSString` to see what element is being reported, and then prepare a permanent variable to save its content, to prepare your program to receive the information, or both. Optionally, look at the `NSDictionary` passed by the `attributes:` handle and modify things accordingly.

2 When you receive the `foundCharacters:` method, save the contents of the element into a temporary variable. You may have to do this several times, appending the results to your temporary variable each time, because there's no guarantee that all the characters will appear in one lot.

3 When you receive the `didEndElement:` method, copy your temporary variable into your permanent variable, take an action based on having received the complete element, or both.

4 Optionally, when you receive `parserDidEndDocument:`, do any final cleanup.

Beyond that, the `parser:parseErrorOccurred:` method should call up an `NSAlert` or otherwise alert the user to the problem. As we noted, this is only for an unrecoverable problem: the user can't do anything about it without modifying the original XML.

To show how you can use the `NSXMLParser`, the next example involves writing a simple RSS reader. Building an RSS reader on your own will allow you to walk through the basic functionality of `NSXMLParser` using an XML type that's widely available on the internet for testing.

Table 14.8   The five important `NSXMLParser` delegate methods

Method	Summary
`parser:didStartElement:namespaceURI:qualifiedName:attributes:`	Reports the start of an element and its attributes
`parser:foundCharacters:`	Reports some or all of the content of an element
`parser:didEndElement:namespaceURI:qualifiedName:`	Reports the end tag of an element
`parserDidEndDocument:`	Reports the end of parsing
`parser:parseErrorOccurred:`	Reports an unrecoverable parsing error

14.5.3 *Building a sample RSS reader*

Now that you understand the basics of XML, you're ready to put together a sample program that uses `NSXMLParser` in two ways: first to read a text file, and then to read an RSS feed. The results will be output to a hierarchy of tables. The first level of the hierarchy will show all the possible feeds, and the second level will show the contents of individual feeds. An example of the latter sort of page is shown in figure 14.3.

THE TOP-LEVEL TABLE

To start this project, you'll need to create a Navigation-Based Application, which will provide the navigator and initial table setup needed to get this project started. In a more advanced program, you'd give users the opportunity to create a settings file for whichever RSS feeds they want to read. But for the purposes of this example, create an XML settings file called rssfeeds.xml by hand, using the following format:

```
<rdf:RDF xmlns:rdf="http://www.w3.org/1999/02/22-rdf-syntax-ns#"
    xmlns="http://purl.org/rss/1.0/"
    xmlns:dc="http://purl.org/dc/elements/1.1/">
  <feed title="RPGnet News" url="http://www.rpg.net/index.xml" />
  <feed title="RPGnet Columns" url="http://www.rpg.net/columns/index.xml"
      />
</rdf:RDF>
```

For each entry, create a singular `<feed>` element and include `title` and `url` attributes.

Figure 14.3   RSS feeds can easily be placed in table views.

After you've added rssfeeds.xml to your project, you're ready to write the code for the top-level table, which will parse your local XML file and give your user the option to select one of the RSS feeds. The following listing displays this code, which appears in the main view controller.

Listing 14.3   Reading an XML text file

```
- (void)viewDidLoad {
    [super viewDidLoad];                                    ← ❶ Parses XML file
    self.title = @"RSS Feeds";
    rssList = [[NSMutableArray alloc] initWithCapacity:1];
    NSString *paths = [[NSBundle mainBundle] resourcePath];
    NSString *xmlFile = [paths
        stringByAppendingPathComponent:@"rssfeeds.xml"];
    NSURL *xmlURL = [NSURL fileURLWithPath:xmlFile isDirectory:NO];
    NSXMLParser *firstParser = [[NSXMLParser alloc]
        initWithContentsOfURL:xmlURL];
    [firstParser setDelegate:self];
    [firstParser parse];
}
- (void)parser:(NSXMLParser *)parser                        ❷ Reads attribute elements
    didStartElement:(NSString *)elementName
    namespaceURI:(NSString *)namespaceURI
    qualifiedName:(NSString *)qualifiedName
    attributes:(NSDictionary *)attributeDict {
    if ([elementName compare:@"feed"] == NSOrderedSame) {
```

```
        [rssList addObject:[[NSDictionary alloc] initWithObjectsAndKeys:
            [attributeDict objectForKey:@"title"],@"title",
            [attributeDict objectForKey:@"url"],@"url",
            nil]];
    }
}
- (void)parserDidEndDocument:(NSXMLParser *)parser {
    [parser release];
}
- (NSInteger)numberOfSectionsInTableView:
    (UITableView *)tableView {
    return 1;
}
- (NSInteger)tableView:(UITableView *)tableView
    numberOfRowsInSection:(NSInteger)section {
    return [rssList count];
}
- (UITableViewCell *)tableView:(UITableView *)tableView
    cellForRowAtIndexPath:(NSIndexPath *)indexPath {
    static NSString *CellIdentifier = @"Cell";
    UITableViewCell *cell = [tableView
        dequeueReusableCellWithIdentifier:CellIdentifier];
    if (cell == nil) {
        cell = [[[UITableViewCell alloc]
         initWithStyle:UITableViewCellStyleDefault
         reuseIdentifier:CellIdentifier] autorelease];
    }
    cell.textLabel.text = [[rssList objectAtIndex:indexPath.row]
        objectForKey:@"title"];
    cell.accessoryType = UITableViewCellAccessoryDisclosureIndicator;
    return cell;
}
- (void)tableView:(UITableView *)tableView
    didSelectRowAtIndexPath:(NSIndexPath *)indexPath {
    rssViewController *nextController =
        [[rssViewController alloc] initWithURL:
            [[rssList objectAtIndex:indexPath.row] objectForKey:@"url"]];
    nextController.title = [[rssList objectAtIndex:indexPath.row]
        objectForKey:@"title"];
    [self.navigationController pushViewController:nextController
        animated:YES];
    [nextController release];
}
```

❸ Cleans up parser

❹ Calls up RSS view

This example begins by reading in XML from a file ❶. The result is a lot more pleasing than trying to read raw text, as in the thumbnail example earlier in this chapter, so we suggest encoding simple preference files as XML in the future.

Because we designed a simple XML format, where the information is encoded as attributes, you have to watch only one delegate method, didStartElement: ❷. Here you add the information to rssList, an NSMutableArray, for use later. The only other thing you have to do with your XML parser is clean it up when you've finished ❸.

The next few functions are standard table view work, because you define the sections, rows, and cells using the rssList array you created. Finally, you define what happens when the user selects a row ❹, and that's to call up a brand-new type of object, the rssViewController.

THE RSS TABLE

The rssViewController is a subclass of the UITableViewController that displays an RSS feed if initialized with a URL. Listing 14.4 shows the complete contents, much of which are similar to listing 14.3. The biggest differences are in the XML parsing, because an RSS feed is a much more complicated XML format, even when you're using only minimal information from it, as is the case here.

Listing 14.4 Creating a table from an RSS feed

```
- (id)initWithURL:(NSString *)url {                              Parses
    if (self = [super init]) {                               ❶ RSS feed
        feedList = [[NSMutableArray alloc] initWithCapacity:0];
        NSXMLParser *nextParser = [[NSXMLParser alloc]
            initWithContentsOfURL:[NSURL URLWithString:url]];
        [nextParser setDelegate:self];
        [nextParser parse];
    }
    return self;
}
- (void)parser:(NSXMLParser *)parser
    didStartElement:(NSString *)elementName
    namespaceURI:(NSString *)namespaceURI
    qualifiedName:(NSString *)qualifiedName
    attributes:(NSDictionary *)attributeDict {
    if ([elementName compare:@"item"] == NSOrderedSame) {
        currentItem = [[NSMutableDictionary alloc] initWithCapacity:0];
    } else if (currentItem != NULL) {
        currentContents = [[NSMutableString alloc] initWithCapacity:0];
    }
}
- (void)parser:(NSXMLParser *)parser              ❷ Reads
    foundCharacters:(NSString *)string {              content
    if (currentContents && string) {
        [currentContents appendString:string];
    }
}
- (void)parser:(NSXMLParser *)parser              ❸ Finishes
    didEndElement:(NSString *)elementName             reading
    namespaceURI:(NSString *)namespaceURI
    qualifiedName:(NSString *)qName {
    if ([elementName compare:@"item"] == NSOrderedSame) {
        [feedList addObject:currentItem];
        [currentItem release];
    } else if (currentItem && currentContents) {
        [currentItem setObject:currentContents forKey:elementName];
        currentContents = nil;
        [currentContents release];
    }
}
- (void)parserDidEndDocument:(NSXMLParser *)parser {
```

```
        [parser release];
}
- (NSInteger)numberOfSectionsInTableView:(UITableView *)tableView {
    return 1;
}
- (NSInteger)tableView:(UITableView *)tableView
    numberOfRowsInSection:(NSInteger)section {
    return [feedList count];
}
- (UITableViewCell *)tableView:(UITableView *)tableView
    cellForRowAtIndexPath:(NSIndexPath *)indexPath {
    static NSString *CellIdentifier = @"Cell";
    UITableViewCell *cell = [tableView
     dequeueReusableCellWithIdentifier:CellIdentifier];
    if (cell == nil) {
        cell = [[[UITableViewCell alloc]
            initWithStyle:UITableViewCellStyleDefault
            reuseIdentifier:CellIdentifier]
                autorelease];
    }
    if ([[feedList objectAtIndex:indexPath.row] objectForKey:@"title"]) {
        cell.textLabel.text = [[feedList objectAtIndex:indexPath.row]
            objectForKey:@"title"];
    }
    if ([[feedList objectAtIndex:indexPath.row] objectForKey:@"link"]) {
        cell.accessoryType = UITableViewCellAccessoryDisclosureIndicator;
    }
    return cell;
}
- (void)tableView:(UITableView *)tableView
    didSelectRowAtIndexPath:(NSIndexPath *)indexPath {
    UIWebView *thisInfo = [[UIWebView alloc] init];
    [thisInfo loadRequest:[NSURLRequest requestWithURL:
        [NSURL URLWithString:[[feedList objectAtIndex:indexPath.row]
            objectForKey:@"link"]]]];
    thisInfo.scalesPageToFit = YES;
    UIViewController *thisVC = [[UIViewController alloc] init];
    thisVC.view = thisInfo;
    thisVC.title = [[feedList objectAtIndex:indexPath.row]
        objectForKey:@"title"];
    [self.navigationController pushViewController:thisVC animated:YES];
    [thisInfo release];
    [thisVC release];
}
```

4 Calls up web view

The difference in this new table view starts with the fact that you have a custom init function that allows you to start an XML parser running on an RSS feed ❶. In a more polished application, you'd check for the feed's existence, but for this example you can dive right in.

Because this XML file is more complex than the previous one, you can't do all your work in `didStartElement:`. Instead, you use this method as part of a systemic examination of the XML content, by preparing variables, creating a dictionary to hold the contents of a complete RSS item, and initializing a string to hold each individual element.

In `parser:foundCharacters:` ❷, you have to keep appending data to the current element's string, as we promised. The XML parser *will* break the data from an individual element into multiple strings, so you have to be careful about this.

When you've finished ❸, you can add your string to the element's dictionary; and when the element is done, you can add the dictionary to the array of RSS contents that you're maintaining.

From here on, most of the table work is similar to the previous example. You read back through your master array to fill in the contents of the table. The only thing of note comes in the last method ❹, when a user clicks a table row. At this point, you call up a `UIWebView` so the user can hop straight to the RSS feed item they're interested in.

Before we finish with XML entirely, we want to look at one more Core Location example, using GeoNames to read in altitude.

14.5.4 Altitude redux: a Core Location example

GeoNames, which you can find at www.geonames.org, offers a variety of web services related to location. It can give you information about postal codes, countries, addresses, and more. A complete listing of its web services is available at www.geonames.org/export/ws-overview.html.

Most of GeoNames's information is returned in either XML or JSON format, as you prefer. We'll look at the XML interface here. Table 14.9 shows off some of the XML-based GeoNames information that you may find particularly useful.

Table 14.9 GeoNames searches allowable with coordinate information

Information	Summary
`findNearestIntersection`	Returns nearest street intersection in the U.S.
`gtopo30`	Returns altitude of location or -9999 for sea
`srtm3`	Returns altitude of location or -32768 for sea
`timezone`	Returns not only the time zone info but also the current time

We'll use `gtopo30` to follow through on our promise from chapter 10 to look up the altitude from GeoNames based on the location manager's results. This project requires a somewhat complex chaining together of multiple delegate-driving classes, as shown in figure 14.4.

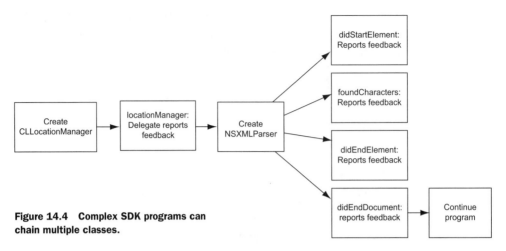

Figure 14.4   Complex SDK programs can chain multiple classes.

The bare skeleton of the code needed to make this work is shown in the following listing.

Listing 14.5   Deriving altitude from GeoNames

```
- (void)locationManager:(CLLocationManager *)manager
    didUpdateToLocation:(CLLocation *)newLocation
    fromLocation:(CLLocation *)oldLocation {          ←─① Prepares XML
    [myLM stopUpdatingLocation];
    [myActivity stopAnimating];
    NSString *gnLookup = [NSString stringWithFormat:
       @"http://ws.geonames.org/gtopo30?lat=%f&lng=%f&style=full&type=XML",
       newLocation.coordinate.latitude,newLocation.coordinate.longitude];
    NSXMLParser *gnParser = [[NSXMLParser alloc]
        initWithContentsOfURL:[NSURL URLWithString:gnLookup]];
    [gnParser setDelegate:self];
    [gnParser parse];
}
- (void)parser:(NSXMLParser *)parser
    didStartElement:(NSString *)elementName
    namespaceURI:(NSString *)namespaceURI
    qualifiedName:(NSString *)qualifiedName          ② Watches for
    attributes:(NSDictionary *)attributeDict {       ←─  gtopo30
    if ([elementName compare:@"gtopo30"] == NSOrderedSame) {
        gnAlt = [[NSMutableString alloc] initWithCapacity:4];
    }
}
- (void)parser:(NSXMLParser *)parser
    foundCharacters:(NSString *)string {             ←─③ Saves altitude
    if (gnAlt && string) {
        [gnAlt appendString:string];
    }
}
- (void)parser:(NSXMLParser *)parser
    didEndElement:(NSString *)elementName
    namespaceURI:(NSString *)namespaceURI
    qualifiedName:(NSString *)qName {                ←─④ Writes altitude
```

```
        if ([elementName compare:@"gtopo30"] == NSOrderedSame) {
           altLabel.text = [NSString stringWithFormat:@"%@ m.",gnAlt];
        }
}
```

In general, this is a simple application of lessons you've already learned. It's also an interesting application of the internet to Core Location.

The only thing particularly innovative comes in the Core Location delegate ❶, where you create a GeoNames URL using the format documented at the GeoNames site. Then you watch the start tags ❷, content ❸, and end tags ❹ and use those to derive altitude the same way that you pulled out XML information when you were reading RSS feeds.

As we mentioned in chapter 10, the result should be an altitude that's much more reliable than what the iPhone and iPad can currently provide, unless you're in a tall building, in an airplane, or hang gliding.

To date, all the examples of web parsing have involved simple GET connections, where you can encode arguments as part of a URL. That won't always be the case on the web; so before we leave web pages behind, we'll return to some basics of URL requests and look at how to POST information to a web page when it becomes necessary.

14.6 POSTing to the web

Many web pages allow you to GET or POST information interchangeably. But in some situations, that's not the case, and you're instead forced to POST (and then to read back the response manually). In this section, we'll look at both how to program a simple POST and how to do something more complex, like a form.

14.6.1 POSTing by hand

When you need to POST to the web, you have to fall back on some HTTP-related low-level commands that we haven't yet discussed in depth, including NSMutableURL-Request (which allows you to build a piecemeal request) and NSURLConnection (which allows you to extract information from the web).

In general, you'll follow this process:

1 Create an NSURL pointing to the site you'll POST to.
2 Create and encode the data you plan to POST, as appropriate.
3 Create an NSMutableURLRequest using your NSURL.
4 Use the NSMutableURLRequest's addValue:forHTTPHeaderField: method to set a content type.
5 Set the NSMutableURLRequest's HTTPMethod to POST.
6 Add your data to the NSMutableURLRequest as the HTTPBody.
7 Create an NSURLConnection using your NSMutableURLRequest.
8 Either immediately capture the return using a synchronous response, or set up a delegate to receive the data as it comes, as defined in the NSURLConnection class reference.
9 Parse the NSData you receive as you see fit.

For a simple synchronous response, the next listing shows how to put these elements together.

Listing 14.6   A simple POSTing example

```
NSURL *myURL = [NSURL URLWithString:@"http://www.example.com"];
NSMutableURLRequest *myRequest = [NSMutableURLRequest
    requestWithURL:myURL];
[myRequest setValue:@"text/xml" forHTTPHeaderField:@"Content-type"];
[myRequest setHTTPMethod:@"POST"];
NSData *myData = [@"someText" dataUsingEncoding:NSASCIIStringEncoding];
[myRequest setHTTPBody:myData];
NSURLResponse *response;
NSError *error;
NSData *myReturn = [NSURLConnection sendSynchronousRequest:myRequest
    returningResponse:&response error:&error];
```

A large number of steps are required to move from the URL through to the data acquisition, just as there were when creating a URL for a simple UIWebView; but when you have them down, the process is easy. The hardest part, as it turns out, often is getting the data ready to POST.

This code works fine for posting plain data to a web page. For example, you could use it with the Google Spell API found at www.google.com/tbproxy/spell to send XML data and then read the results with NSXMLParser.

Things can get tricky if you're doing more intricate work than that, such as POSTing form data.

14.6.2 *Submitting forms*

Sending form data to a web page follows the same process as any other POSTed data, and reading the results works the same way. The only tricky element is packaging the form data so it's ready to use.

The easiest way to work with form data is to create it using an NSDictionary or NSMutableDictionary of keys and values, because that matches the underlying structure of HTML forms. When you're ready to process the data, you pass the dictionary to a method that turns it into NSData, which can be sent as an NSMutableURLRequest body. After you've written this method the first time, you can use it again and again.

The next listing shows how to turn a dictionary of NSStrings into NSData.

Listing 14.7   Creating form data

```
- (NSData*)createFormData:(NSDictionary*)myDictionary
    withBoundary:(NSString *)myBounds {
    NSMutableData *myReturn = [[NSMutableData alloc] initWithCapacity:10];
    NSArray *formKeys = [dict allKeys];
    for (int i = 0; i < [formKeys count]; i++) {
        [myReturn appendData:
            [[NSString stringWithFormat:@"--%@\n",myBounds]
                dataUsingEncoding:NSASCIIStringEncoding]];
        [myReturn appendData:
```

```
            [[NSString stringWithFormat:
                @"Content-Disposition: form-data; name=\"%@\"\n\n%@\n",
                    [formKeys objectAtIndex:i],
                    [myDictionary valueForKey:[formKeys objectAtIndex: i]]]
                dataUsingEncoding:NSASCIIStringEncoding]];
    }
    [myReturn appendData:
        [[NSString stringWithFormat:@"--%@--\n", myBounds]
            dataUsingEncoding:NSASCIIStringEncoding]];
    return myReturn;
}
```

There's nothing particularly notable here. If you have a sufficiently good understanding of the HTML protocol, you can easily dump the dictionary elements into an NSData object. The middle appendData: method is the most important, because it adds both the key (saved in an NSArray) and the value (available in the original NSDictionary) to the HTML body.

Back outside the method, you can add the data to your NSMutableURLRequest just as in listing 14.6, except the content type looks a little different:

```
NSMutableURLRequest *myRequest = [NSMutableURLRequest
    requestWithURL:myURL];
NSString *myContent = [NSString stringWithFormat:
    @"multipart/form-data; boundary=%@",myBounds];
[myRequest setValue:myContent forHTTPHeaderField:@"Content-type"];
[myRequest setHTTPMethod:@"POST"];
[myRequest setHTTPBody:myReturn];
```

Some other types of data processing, such as file uploads, require somewhat different setups, and you'd do well to look at HTML documentation for the specifics; but the general methods used to POST data remain the same.

With POSTing out of the way, we've now covered all of the SDK's most important functions related to the internet. But we want to touch on one other topic before we close this chapter—a variety of internet protocols that you can access through third-party libraries.

14.7 Accessing the social web

Since the advent of Web 2.0, a new sort of internet presence has appeared. We call it the *social web*. This is an interconnected network of web servers that exchange information based on various well-known protocols. If you're building internet-driven programs, you may wish to connect to this web so that your users can become a part of it.

14.7.1 Using web protocols

To participate in the social web, clients need to speak a number of protocols, most of them built on top of HTML. These include Ajax, JSON, RSS, SOAP, and XML. Here's how to use each of them from your iPhone and iPad:

- *Ajax*—Ajax is something that, as it turns out, you can largely ignore. It's usually used as part of a client/server setup, with HTML on the front side, but iOS uses an entirely different paradigm. You can dynamically load material into labels or text views, and you can dynamically call up websites using the XML or HTML classes we've discussed. There's no need for Ajax-type content as long as you have good control over what a server will output. You just need to remember some of the lessons that Ajax teaches, such as downloading small bits of information rather than a whole page.

- *JSON*—JSON is perhaps the most troublesome protocol to integrate. It's important as a part of the social web, because it's one of the standardized ways to download information from a website. It also depends on your iPhone or iPad being able to understand JavaScript, which it doesn't (unless you do some fancy work with DOM and the WebKit, which are beyond the scope of this section). Fortunately, two JSON toolkits are already available: JSON Framework and TouchJSON. We'll look at an example of the latter shortly.

- *RSS*—At the time of this writing, we're not aware of any RSS libraries for the iPhone and iPad. But as we've already demonstrated in this chapter, it's easy to parse RSS using an XML parser.

- *SOAP*—SOAP isn't as popular in the social web as most of the other protocols listed here, but if you must use it, you'll want a library. One SOAP library written for Objective-C (though not necessarily for the iPhone and iPad), is SOAP Client.

- *XML*—XML is, as you've seen, fully supported by iOS. But if you don't like how the default parser works and want an alternative, you should look at TouchXML.

These libraries should all be easy to find with simple searches on the internet, but table 14.10 lists their current locations as of this writing.

Because of its importance to the social web, we'll pay some additional attention to JSON, using the TouchJSON library.

Table 14.10   Download sites for social protocol libraries

Library	Location
JSON Framework	http://code.google.com/p/json-framework/
TouchJSON	https://github.com/TouchCode/TouchJSON
SOAP Client	http://code.google.com/p/mac-soapclient/
TouchXML	https://github.com/TouchCode/TouchXML

14.7.2 *Using TouchJSON*

For this final example, we'll return to Core Location one more time, because GeoNames offers a lot of JSON information. You're going to use GeoNames to display the postal codes near a user's current location. Figure 14.5 shows our intended result by highlighting the postal codes near Apple headquarters, the location reported by the Simulator.

In order to get to this point, you must first install this third-party library and make use of it.

INSTALLING TOUCHJSON

To integrate TouchJSON into your project, you must download the package from Google and move the source code into your project. The easiest way to do this is to open the TouchJSON download inside Xcode and copy the Source folder to your own project. Tell Xcode to copy all the files into your project as well. Afterward, you'll probably want to rename the copied folder from Source to TouchJSON.

Then you need to include the header CJSON-Deserializer.h wherever you want to use TouchJSON.

USING TOUCHJSON

In order to use TouchJSON, you pass the CJSON-Deserializer class an NSData object containing the JSON code. Listing 14.8 shows how to do so. In this example, this work occurs inside a location manager delegate. It's part of a program similar to our earlier GeoNames example, but this time we're looking up postal codes with a JSON return rather than altitudes with an XML return.

Figure 14.5 It's easy to extract data using TouchJSON.

Listing 14.8   Using TouchJSON

```
- (void)locationManager:(CLLocationManager *)manager
    didUpdateToLocation:(CLLocation *)newLocation
    fromLocation:(CLLocation *)oldLocation {
    [myLM stopUpdatingLocation];
    [myActivity stopAnimating];
    NSString *gnLookup = [NSString                              ❶ Grabs the content of the
        stringWithString:@"http://ws.geonames.org/findNearbyPostalCodesJSON"     URL and stores as NSData
            "?lat=37.331689&lng=-122.030731"];
    NSData *gnData = [NSData dataWithContentsOfURL:
        [NSURL URLWithString:gnLookup]];
    NSError *error = nil;
    NSDictionary *dictionary = [[CJSONDeserializer deserializer]
        deserializeAsDictionary:gnData error:&error];
    if(error) {
        postalLabel.text = [NSString stringWithFormat:@"Error: %@",
            [[error userInfo] objectForKey:@"NSLocalizedDescription"]];
    } else {                                                     ❷ Converts the
        NSMutableString *postCodes = [NSMutableString              JSON into an
            stringWithString:@"Nearby post codes are:\n\n"];       NSDictionary
        for (int i = 0 ;
            i < [[dictionary objectForKey:@"postalCodes"] count] ;
            i++) {
            [postCodes appendFormat:@"%@ (%@)\n",
                [[[dictionary objectForKey:@"postalCodes"] objectAtIndex:i]
```

The figure shows an iPhone screen displaying:

Carrier 🔋 1:19 PM

Nearby post codes are:

95014 (Cupertino)
94087 (Sunnyvale)
95015 (Cupertino)
95170 (San Jose)
95129 (San Jose)

```
                  objectForKey:@"postalCode"],
           [[[dictionary objectForKey:@"postalCodes"] objectAtIndex:i]
                  objectForKey:@"placeName"]];
       }
       postalLabel.text = postCodes;
   }
}
```

To access the JSON results, you first retrieve the data from a URL using the dataWith-ContentsOfURL: method ❶, which was one of the ways we suggested for retrieving raw data earlier in the chapter. Then you plug that NSData object into the CJSON-Deserializer ❷ to generate an NSDictionary containing the JSON output.

The TouchJSON classes are much easier to use than the XML parser we met earlier in this chapter. All you need to do is read through the arrays and dictionaries that are output. The downside is that the resulting dictionary may take up a lot of memory (which is why the XML parser didn't do things this way), so be aware of that if you're retrieving particularly large JSON results.

Absent that concern, you should be on your way to using JSON and creating yet another link between your users and the whole World Wide Web.

14.8   Summary

"There's more than one way to do it."

That was the slogan of Perl, one of the first languages used to create dynamic web pages, and today you could use that slogan equally well to describe the iPhone and iPad, two of the popular mobile devices.

We opened this book by talking about the two different ways that you could write apps: using web technologies and using the SDK. We also highlighted two different ways that you could interact with the internet: either as an equal participant—a web-based member of the internet's various peer-to-peer and client/server protocols—or as a pure client that runs its own programs and connects to the internet via its own means.

We've said before that each programming method has its own advantages, and we continue to think that web development is often a better choice when you're interacting with the internet already. But when you need to use other SDK features, the SDK offers some great ways to connect to the web.

As you've seen in this chapter, you have easy and intuitive access to the social web—that conglomeration of machines that's connected via various public protocols. You should have no trouble creating projects that use the HTML and XML protocols, and even further flung protocols like JSON and SOAP are usable thanks to third-party libraries. That'll cover most programmers' needs, but for those of you who need to dig deeper, the SDK has you covered there too, thanks to Core Foundation classes.

In the next chapter, we'll take networking one step further and introduce the Game Kit framework. There, we'll show you how to use Apple's built-in network layers to create a fully functional two-player video game.

Peer-to-peer connections using Game Kit

This chapter covers

- Overview of Game Kit
- Creating peer-to-peer applications using the peer picker
- Building a multiplayer game

Networking has always been a complicated task in any programming language. It normally requires intimate knowledge of sockets, as well as a solid understanding of various network protocols such as TCP/IP and UDP. Apple has simplified this process with the release of the Game Kit framework.

In this chapter, we'll take a tour of the Game Kit framework. Then, we'll examine how to create peer-to-peer applications and a simple multiplayer game.

15.1 Overview of Game Kit

Game Kit is a framework that provides some simple yet powerful classes for accomplishing various networking tasks. These classes are built on top of the Bonjour protocol and do much of the heavy lifting needed for peer-to-peer interaction.

Although the Game Kit framework was primarily intended for game development, it isn't limited to that. Many applications incorporate the Game Kit framework to accomplish network-related tasks. These tasks may be as simple as sharing photos or as complex as multiuser collaboration on a drawing board.

In Game Kit, peers communicate through objects called *sessions*. Each peer creates a session and uses it to discover other sessions. The sessions are also responsible for sending data to and receiving data from each peer.

Three different modes of a session determine how it interacts with peers. The first is server mode. When sessions are in this mode, they advertise their service to everyone on the network. The next is client mode. In this mode, sessions search for servers that are advertising. Finally, there is peer mode. In peer mode sessions play the role of both the client and the server at the same time.

We'll show you how to implement the built-in peer picker in peer mode to establish a connection between two devices. After you've learned the basics, you'll be able to move on and create a fully functional multiplayer application.

15.2 Creating peer-to-peer applications using the peer picker

The peer picker gives you a simple way to connect two devices over Bluetooth or wireless. It involves displaying Apple's built-in Peer Picker view and implementing the delegate methods. This view is easy to use but is somewhat limited. First, it allows a connection only between two peers. You can never have more than two users playing the same game at once. Second, it can't be customized. Although the view looks nice, it may not always fit into the look and feel of your application.

If you find yourself in a situation where you need to connect more than two peers at a time, you must create your own custom peer picker. Because we'll be focusing on using Apple's built-in peer picker, you should refer to the developer documentation titled "Game Kit Programming Guide" if you want more information about creating one.

This section will discuss how to communicate using the peer picker component of the Game Kit framework. We'll use a simple chat application to demonstrate the concepts. You can obtain the full source for the chat application on the book's website.

> **NOTE** You can't test Game Kit applications using the Simulator. To run the examples in this chapter, you must have two devices in hand.

15.2.1 Using Apple's built-in peer picker

Before you can do any programming using Game Kit, you must import the Game Kit framework into your project. After you've imported the framework, you must include the Game Kit/Gamekit.h header file in every project file that you wish to use the Game Kit functionality.

The GKPeerPickerController is simple to implement. You initialize it, set its delegate, and show it. Here's an example of displaying the GKPeerPickerController:

```
-(void)viewDidLoad {
  [super viewDidLoad];
  chatPicker = [[GKPeerPickerController alloc] init];
  [chatPicker setDelegate:self];
  [chatPicker setConnectionTypesMask:GKPeerPickerConnectionTypeNearby];
  peers = [[NSMutableArray alloc] init];
}

-(IBAction) connect {
    [chatPicker show];
}
```

As you can see, it isn't much different than displaying a `UIAlertView` or `UIAction-Sheet`. Here, you initialize the picker inside the `viewDidLoad` method and show it when the user presses a connect button. This allows you to reuse the same picker in case the user wants to find a different peer or needs to reconnect in the event the connection gets dropped. Figure 15.1 shows what the peer-picker interface looks like when it's displayed.

One interesting variable you set is `connectionTypeMask`. It lets the picker know what type of peers it's searching for. The values you can use here are `GKPeer-ConnectionTypeNearby` and `GKPeerConnectionTypeOnline`. The value `GKPeer-ConnectionTypeNearby` is required by any application that wants to use Game Kit; it tells the application to look for peers over Bluetooth as well as the local wireless network. If this value isn't included, your application will throw an exception. The other

Figure 15.1   The peer-picker interface on both the iPhone and iPad. Using Bluetooth, users can connect to other nearby devices and interact in real time.

Table 15.1 `GKPeerPickerControllerDelegate` method descriptions

Delegate Method	Description
`peerPickerController:didSelectConnectionType:`	This optional method is called when the user selects a connection type. As noted previously, the possible connection types are `GKPeerConnectionTypeNearby` and `GKPeerConnectionTypeOnline`.
`peerPickerController:sessionForConnectionType:`	This optional method is called when the controller requests a session. Implementing this method gives you greater control over the session, including the ability to customize the display name and session ID.
`peerPickerController:didConnectPeer:toSession:`	This is an optional method but is expected to be implemented. It's called when a peer connects. At this point, you should dismiss the peer picker and take ownership of the session.
`peerPickerControllerDidCancel:`	This is another optional but expected method that's called when the user cancels the request. At this point, you notify the user that the session was cancelled.

value, GKPeerConnectionTypeOnline, tells the picker that you want to search for peers online. This requires some more complex networking knowledge that's out of the scope of this book.

As usual, you set the delegate of the picker to self. This requires that the class implement the GKPeerPickerControllerDelegate interface. Table 15.1 describes the delegate methods in detail.

Although all the delegate methods are optional, it's a good idea to implement all of them in your application for greater control over the picker's actions. The last thing you do in the viewDidLoad method is to create an NSMutableArray of peers. You add peers to this array as they join. Keeping a reference to all connected peers is necessary when sending data to them. We'll discuss this in greater detail later in this section.

Now that you've created the picker, the next step is to implement these delegate methods. The following listing shows how you can implement each of these delegate methods.

Listing 15.1 `GKPeerPickerControllerDelegate` methods

```
- (void)peerPickerController:(GKPeerPickerController *)picker
    didSelectConnectionType:(GKPeerPickerConnectionType)type{
}

- (void)peerPickerControllerDidCancel:(GKPeerPickerController *)picker{
    NSLog(@"The connection was cancelled");
}

- (void)peerPickerController:(GKPeerPickerController *)picker
```

```
    didConnectPeer:(NSString *)peerID toSession:(GKSession *)session{
    self.chatSession = session;                                Localizes
                                                          session to class  ❶
    self.chatSession.delegate = self;
    [self.chatSession setDataReceiveHandler: self withContext:nil];
    [chatPicker dismiss];
}                                                    ❷  Hides picker
-  (GKSession *)peerPickerController:(GKPeerPickerController *)picker
    sessionForConnectionType:(GKPeerPickerConnectionType)type{          Creates
                                                                        custom
    GKSession* session = [[GKSession alloc]                          ❸  session
      initWithSessionID:@"chatSession" displayName:@"Peer"
      sessionMode:GKSessionModePeer];
    [session autorelease];
    return session;
}
```

The peerPickerController:didSelectConnectionType: method has no use in this application because you have only one connection type. If you added multiple connection types, you'd do an if statement here and handle each connection type accordingly.

The peerPickerControllerDidCancel: method isn't very interesting and is useful only to the developer. This method prints a message to the console notifying you that the connection was cancelled. Normally, you might want to do something like display an UIAlertView to do this.

peerPickerController:didConnectPeer: does three things ❶. First, it sets the incoming session to the class's session property. This lets you use it in other methods. Next, the session's delegate is set to the class. Table 15.2 lists the session delegate methods that can be implemented. Finally, the dataReceiveHandler of the session is set to the class. This allows the class to receive network data sent to the session. In order to use the class as the session's dataReceiveHandler, you must implement the receiveData method. We'll discuss this method a little later in this section.

When the picker has done its job and is no longer needed, you dismiss it ❷. The last method lets you create a custom session ❸ If you didn't implement this method, a default session would be created for you. As you can see, you can specify a custom session ID as well as a display name. The session ID is used to differentiate the application's session from others that might be in the area. The display name is a custom name for a given peer. Think of it as a username.

The next step is to implement the session delegate methods to manage the session.

15.2.2 *Implementing the GKSessionDelegate methods*

To send and receive data with Game Kit, you must implement the delegate methods for GKSession. These methods provide a nice high-level interface for you to use to send data over the network. Your class must also implement the GKSessionDelegate interface. Your application should implement four delegate methods, outlined in table 15.2.

Table 15.2 `GKSessionDelegate` methods

Delegate method	Description
`session:peer:didChangeState:`	Called any time a peer changes state. The five possible states are `GKPeerStateAvailable`, `GKPeerStateUnavailable`, `GKPeerStateConnected`, `GKPeerStateDisconnected`, and `GKPeerStateConnecting`.
`session:didReceiveConnectionRequestFromPeer:`	Called when a peer wants to connect. Apple's documentation suggests that this method can be ignored if you're using the built-in peer picker.
`session:connectionWithPeerFailed:withError:`	Called when a connection error occurs. This method can also be ignored if you're using Apple's peer picker, because it automatically handles it and displays a `UIAlertView`.
`session:didFailWithError:`	Called when an unrecoverable error happens. In this method, you should disconnect all peers and notify the user.

For most applications, you only need to implement the `didChangeState` method. The others are handled automatically. The `didChangeState` method is important for keeping track of all the peers connected. When a peer connects, you should maintain a reference to it by adding it to a global peers array. That way, when it comes time to send data to it, you'll know where to send it. When a peer leaves, you should remove it from the peer array. The following listing details a simple way to implement this method.

Listing 15.2 Implementing the `didChangeState` delegate method

```
- (void)session:(GKSession *)session peer:(NSString *)peerID
    didChangeState:(GKPeerConnectionState)state {
    switch (state)
    {                                                       ❶ Adds peer to
        case GKPeerStateConnected:                              peers list
            [peers addObject:peerID];
            [chatTextArea setText:[NSString stringWithFormat:
                @"%@ has joined the chat.\n",[session displayName]]];
            break;
        case GKPeerStateDisconnected:                       ❷ Removes peer
            [peers removeObject:peerID];                        from peers list
            NSString * text = [chatTextArea text];
            [chatTextArea setText:[NSString stringWithFormat:
                @"%@\n%@ has left the chat.\n",text,
                [session displayName]]];
            break;
    }
}
```

As you can see, this method is relatively simple to implement. You determine the state of the peer with a simple `case` statement. You add code to detect the two most important states, `GKPeerStateConnected` and `GKPeerStateDisconnected`. You should also handle the other states as noted in table 15.2.

In the event that a peer connects, you want to make sure to maintain a reference to that peer's ID ❶. You do this by adding the ID to an array of peer IDs. You'll later use this ID to send data to that specific peer. Note that you update the text of a `UIText-View` to notify the user that a given peer has connected. You can also do this with a `UIAlertView` or else start the game if you're creating a multiplayer game.

The session object contains quite a bit of information about the incoming session. The most important property for the sake of the chat application is the `displayName` field. This lets you display the unique name of a given peer. As you can imagine, almost any multiuser application can benefit from this field.

Finally, you handle the case where a peer disconnects ❷. In the event of a disconnection, you want to remove the peer ID from the array. This ensures that you don't waste any resources sending data to it. Again, you notify the user that the peer has disconnected.

Now that you've implemented the delegate methods, you need a way to send and receive data.

15.2.3 *Sending and receiving data between peers*

When you're sending data from one peer to another, keep in mind that everything you send must be converted to `NSData`. Every one of Apple's built-in objects supports this conversion. You can even convert custom objects to `NSData` using the `NSKeyed-Archiver` class.

The type of data you send over the network is highly dependent on what your application does. For example, if you're creating a real-time game that sends a lot of data quickly, then you probably don't want to send complete objects. In this case, you're better off sending low-level data structures such as a `struct`. Although this method is much faster, it requires that you have a good understanding of some low-level C code. You'll see more about sending `struct`s over the network in the next section.

On the other hand, if your application doesn't rely so much on speed, you can send high-level objects and greatly reduce the complexity of your application. For the simple chat application, you convert strings to `NSData`, send them over the network, and convert them back into strings. In the next listing you'll see how to implement the `receiveData` method as well as the `send` method.

> **Listing 15.3 Implementing the `receiveData` and `send` methods**

```
-(IBAction) send:(id)sender {
    NSData * data = [[sendTextField text]
        dataUsingEncoding:NSASCIIStringEncoding];

    [chatSession sendData:data toPeers:peers
```

```
            withDataMode:GKSendDataReliable error:nil];

        NSString * text    = [chatTextArea text];
        [chatTextArea setText:[NSString stringWithFormat:
            @"%@Me: %@\n",text,[sendTextField text]]];
        [sendTextField setText:@""];
        [sendTextField resignFirstResponder];
}

- (void) receiveData:(NSData *)data fromPeer:(NSString *)peer inSession:
    (GKSession *)session context:(void *)context
{
        NSString * string = [[NSString alloc] initWithData:data
            encoding:NSASCIIStringEncoding];
        NSString * text    = [chatTextArea text];
        [chatTextArea setText:[NSString stringWithFormat:
            @"%@%@: %@\n",text,[session displayName],string]];
}
```

❶ Updates user interface

❷ Converts NSData back to NSString

❸ Updates UI

The first thing you do is convert the `NSString` to `NSData`. This is relatively straightforward because you use the `dataUsingEncoding` method of `NSString`. For almost all strings, the encoding type is `NSASCIIStringEncoding`.

Next, you send the string data to all the connected peers. Only two potential values can be used with the `withDataMode` property: `GKSendDataReliable` and `GKSendDataUnreliable`. The type of data mode you choose depends on the application you're creating. It can even be dependent on the type of data you're sending.

The `GKSendDataReliable` value tells the session to keep sending the data until it's received. It does this by using TCP/IP. The session knows when the data has been received because the receiver sends an acknowledgement back to the sender to confirm. Another benefit of reliable transmission is that the data is always received in order. If you send data packet A and then data packet B, the receiver always gets data packet A before it gets data packet B. The downside of `GKSendDataReliable` is that it's much slower than `GKSendDataUnreliable`. You use this method of sending when you want to ensure the data is received and you don't care about speed. The protocol used when sending data unreliably is UDP. Examples include sending initial game information such as usernames, maps, and stats. This is also good for sending textual data, as in the chat application.

The `GKSendDataUnreliable` value tells the session that you don't care if the data is received or in what order. Choosing this route gives you a big improvement in speed but is a little more complex to use. A good example of when you would use this is in a game where the position of an object changes quite a bit. Say you have a spaceship that moves three pixels, sending its position to the other peer every time it moves one pixel. If the data packet that notifies the peer that the ship has entered the second pixel gets dropped, but the packet at pixel 3 arrives, it's not a problem. This is trivial, and you can move the ship's position from pixel 1 to pixel 3 without the user ever knowing. If too many packets get dropped, your application may experience lag.

Another thing that you must track when sending unreliable data is the ordering of the packets. In the previous example, if the data packet containing position 1 arrives before the packet containing position 3, the ship will appear to go backward if you don't keep track of the ordering. You can manage the data packet ordering by assigning a unique packet number to each of the data packets that get sent. We'll discuss assignment of unique packet numbers in further detail in section 15.3.

Next, in listing 15.3, you update the interface **❶**. As with most chat applications, it appends the text of the user who just wrote the message to their chat window. This allows the user to see the text they just wrote. This section does a couple other things to clean up, such as clearing the text field where the user typed the text as well as hiding the keyboard.

To convert the NSData back into an NSString, you must call the initWithData method of NSString **❷**. Again, you should use NSASCIIStringEncoding for the encoding property. The last thing to do is update the user interface to display the received string. You append to the chat window the received string along with the name of the sender **❸**.

Now that you've seen the basics of connecting two peers, we can show you how to dig deeper and create a fully functional multiplayer application. The next section will discuss how to create a simple multiplayer table tennis application using the Game Kit framework.

15.3 *Example: creating a multiplayer table tennis game*

Although Game Kit is practical in a wide variety of business applications, it was intended for gaming. When using Game Kit for this purpose, you must consider quite a few things. These include game state, multiple packet types, packet frequency, and size. You'll learn about all these topics in the following example.

Basic game development design patterns

Programming games for the iPhone and iPad is different than for other applications. It's often intimidating for new developers to jump right in and start creating them. Luckily, some basic design patterns are commonly used. After you've wrapped your head around these patterns, you'll be able to create a game with any programming language.

Note that games generally follow a Model-View-Controller design. This means the interface code, game logic code, and game objects code are all separate. This approach, although a little challenging to get used to, removes complexity and promotes great code organization.

The driving force behind every game is called the *game loop*. This loop is usually invoked during initialization and periodically updates the game state. The rate at which the loop updates can vary, but it's normally every hundredth of a second. The game loop is responsible for applying the game logic to the game objects and calling the draw methods in the interface to render them to the screen. The entire flow of the game depends on this loop.

(continued)

Along with a game loop, any multiplayer game on the iPhone or iPad needs to implement all the networking methods mentioned in the previous section. The combinations of these provide a great starting point for any game.

One problem in multiplayer games involving the game loop is synchronization. How do you ensure that both players have the same game state? You achieve this by making one of the players a server and the other a client. The server maintains the global game state and sends it to the client. That way, if the client ever gets out of sync, the next message from the server will get it right back on track.

The game you'll create is a simple table tennis clone, where two users hit a ball back and forth trying to get it past their opponent. The player who reaches five points first wins the game. You'll use the Game Kit framework to establish the connection between the players and allow them to send data to one another.

15.3.1 *Starting the GKTennis project*

Begin the project by creating a View-Based Application. Name it `GKTennis`. Make sure you add the Game Kit framework to your application, because you'll use it extensively. You'll need to work with only three files: GKTennisViewController.h, GKTennisViewController.m, and GKTennisViewController.xib.

15.3.2 *Creating the header file*

You'll start by declaring the properties needed for the application in the GKTennisViewController.h header file. The following listing contains this code.

> **Listing 15.4 GKTennisViewController.h**

```
#import <UIKit/UIKit.h>
#import <GameKit/GameKit.h>

typedef struct {
    CGPoint ballPosition;
    CGPoint paddlePosition[2];
    CGPoint ballVelocity;
    int score[2];
} gameInfo;

typedef enum {
    kStateStartGame,
    kStatePicker,
    kStateMultiplayer,
    kStateMultiplayerCointoss,
    kStateMultiplayerReconnect,
    kStateGameOver
} gameStates;

typedef enum {
    NETWORK_COINTOSS,
```

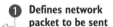 ❶ **Defines network packet to be sent**

```
        NETWORK_MOVE_EVENT,
        NETWORK_BALL_MOVE_EVENT,
        NETWORK_GAME_STATUS
} packetCodes;

typedef enum {
        kServer,
        kClient
} gameNetwork;
```

Implements delegate methods

```
@interface GKTennisViewController : UIViewController
        <GKPeerPickerControllerDelegate,GKSessionDelegate> {
        IBOutlet UIView * paddle_1;
        IBOutlet UIView * paddle_2;
        IBOutlet UIImageView * ball;
```

View outlets

```
        IBOutlet UILabel * score_1_label;
        IBOutlet UILabel * score_2_label;
        IBOutlet UILabel * game_label;
```

Game state properties

```
        NSInteger    gameState;
        NSInteger    peerStatus;

        gameInfogameStatus;
        BOOL         justCollided;
```

Networking properties

```
        GKSession        *gameSession;
        int              gameUniqueID;
        int              gamePacketNumber;
        NSString         *gamePeerId;
}

@property(nonatomic, retain) IBOutlet UIView * paddle_1;
@property(nonatomic, retain) IBOutlet UIView * paddle_2;
@property(nonatomic, retain) IBOutlet UIImageView * ball;

@property(nonatomic, retain) IBOutlet UILabel * score_1_label;
@property(nonatomic, retain) IBOutlet UILabel * score_2_label;
@property(nonatomic, retain) IBOutlet UILabel * game_label;

@property(nonatomic) NSInteger          gameState;
@property(nonatomic) NSInteger          peerStatus;

@property(nonatomic, retain) GKSession      *gameSession;
@property(nonatomic, copy)   NSString       *gamePeerId;

- (void)showPicker;
- (void)sendNetworkPacket:(GKSession *)session packetID:(int)packetID
        withData:(void *)data ofLength:(int)length reliable:(BOOL)howtosend;
- (void) resetBall;
@end
```

We won't go into much detail about what's in the header file right now because we'll discuss each property and method as you implement them in the code. One section of code you may find unfamiliar is the group of structs ❶. Structs are C data structures for organizing variables and are lightweight in terms of size. The first struct maintains most of the information about the state of the game, including the ball position, ball velocity, paddle positions, and scores. You also use it to send over the network in order to update each player on the state of the game. The next `struct` contains all the possible states of the game. You use these states in the game loop to control the flow of the game. Following that is a `struct` containing the various packet types you send over the network. Even though you're sending the same data every time, it's important to distinguish the event that just occurred. We'll explain this in section 15.3.5. Finally, you declare a `struct` that contains two values. This is used to determine which peer is the client and which peer is the server.

Now, you need to create the interface and hook it up to the `IBOutlets`.

15.3.3 *Creating the table tennis interface*

The interface for the table tennis game is simple. It consists of two paddles, a ball, and three labels. Open GKTennisView-Controller.xib to add these interface elements. Figure 15.2 shows how you should set up your view.

For the paddles, drag two `UIViews` onto the main view and resize them to your liking. Set the background color of each one to something different. Now, connect each paddle to its respective `IBOutlet` that was declared in the header file.

To create the ball, drag a `UIImageView` onto the main view. You may either create your own ball image or use the one provided with the source code for this section. Make sure the ball image has been added to the project, and set the `image` property of this view to your ball. Finally, connect the ball to its `IBOutlet`.

Figure 15.2
The `GKTennis` interface

The last things you need to add to the view are three labels. Two of them are for the scores, and the other is for displaying game messages. Set the text of the game label to the string "Touch To Start." After you connect these labels to their `IBOutlets`, save the nib file.

15.3.4 *Game initialization*

Initializing the game is straightforward. You set all the properties to their default values and invoke the main game loop. Also, you must synthesize all the properties you declared in the header file. You don't need to do anything related to the Game Kit at this point. The following listing shows the initialization methods.

Listing 15.5   Game initialization

```
- (void)viewDidLoad {
    [super viewDidLoad];

    self.gameState  = kStateStartGame;

    NSString *uid = [[UIDevice currentDevice] uniqueIdentifier];
```

Gets ❶
device's
UDID

```
    gameUniqueID = [uid hash];

     [self resetBall];

    gameStatus.paddlePosition[0].x =
        gameStatus.paddlePosition[1].x = 320/2;

    [NSTimer scheduledTimerWithTimeInterval:0.01 target:self
        selector:@selector(gameLoop) userInfo:nil repeats:YES];
}
- (void) resetBall {
    gameStatus.ballPosition.x = 320/2;
    gameStatus.ballPosition.y = 480/2;
    float isNegative = random() % 2;
    int direction = (isNegative < 1) ? -1 : 1;
    gameStatus.ballVelocity.x = 4 * direction;
    gameStatus.ballVelocity.y = 4 * direction;
    score_1_label.text = [NSString
     stringWithFormat:@"%d",gameStatus.score[kServer]];
    score_2_label.text = [NSString
     stringWithFormat:@"%d",gameStatus.score[kClient]];
    if(gameSession)
      [self sendNetworkPacket:gameSession packetID:NETWORK_GAME_STATUS
         withData:&gameStatus ofLength:sizeof(gameInfo) reliable:YES];
}
```

② **Resets ball to center**

Invokes game timer **③**

You set the initial game state to kStateStartGame. You'll see this used later in the touchesMoved method to show the picker when the user touches the screen. Next, you get the UDID of the device **①** and store it. The UDID of each device playing is used to determine who is the client and who is the server. Next, you call the method **③** that resets the ball position to the center of the screen. Don't worry about the last line, which sends the network packet—we'll discuss it a little further in this section. Finally, you create a timer that runs the game loop every hundredth of a second **②**.

15.3.5 *Setting up the peer picker and getting connected*

Now that you've initialized the game, it's time to establish a connection to another peer. As you did in the previous section, you need to implement the GKPeerPicker-Controller delegate methods. The next listing shows the implementation of these methods.

Listing 15.6 Setting up the peer picker and responding to its events

```
- (void) showPicker {
    self.gameState = kStatePicker;
    GKPeerPickerController * picker =
       [[GKPeerPickerController alloc] init];
    picker.delegate = self;
    [picker show];
}

- (void)peerPickerControllerDidCancel:(GKPeerPickerController *)picker {

    picker.delegate = nil;
    [picker autorelease];
```

```
        self.gameState = kStateStartGame;
        self.game_label.hidden = NO;
    }

    (GKSession *)peerPickerController:(GKPeerPickerController *)picker
        sessionForConnectionType:(GKPeerPickerConnectionType)type {
        GKSession *session = [[GKSession alloc] initWithSessionID:@"GKTennis"
            displayName:nil sessionMode:GKSessionModePeer];
        return [session autorelease];
    }

    - (void)peerPickerController:(GKPeerPickerController *)picker
        didConnectPeer:(NSString *)peerID toSession:(GKSession *)session {
        self.gamePeerId = peerID;
        self.gameSession = session;
        self.gameSession.delegate = self;
        [self.gameSession setDataReceiveHandler:self withContext:NULL];

        [picker dismiss];
        picker.delegate = nil;
        [picker autorelease];

        self.gameState = kStateMultiplayerCointoss;
    }
```

The showPicker method is called in the touchesMoved method when the state of the game is kStateStartGame. It then shows the peer picker. Notice that you're not releasing the peer picker after showing it, as you would with an alert or action sheet. The reason is that it's up to the delegate methods to release the picker when they finish using it.

The peerPickerControllerDidCancel: method is straightforward. It fires when the user presses the Cancel button on the peer picker. At this point, you set the game state back to kStateStartGame and show the Touch To Start label.

As in the previous section, you create a custom session called GKTennis for the game and return it.

The last method fires when a successful connection has been made to a peer. At this point, you retain the session and peer ID as well as set the delegate to the class. Finally, you hide the peer picker and set the game state to kStateMultiplayer-Cointoss. This state is used in the game loop method to allow the peers to determine who is the client and who is the server. The last methods related to networking that must be implemented are the send and receive methods.

15.3.6 *Implementing the send and receive methods*

The send and receive methods are a crucial part of the application because they do much of the heavy lifting. They're also where most of the complexity associated with networking lies.

You can implement the send method in any number of ways. Apple has created a sample send method in the GKTanks application that can be used in most situations. Here, you take that method and use it directly. In general, send takes in some data, adds a header and packet ID, and sends the data over the network. The following listing shows how this method is implemented.

Listing 15.7 `sendNetworkPacket` method

```
- (void)sendNetworkPacket:(GKSession *)session packetID:(int)packetID
    withData:(void *)data ofLength:(int)length reliable:(BOOL)howtosend {

    static unsigned char networkPacket[1024];
    const unsigned int packetHeaderSize = 2 * sizeof(int);

    if(length < (1024 - packetHeaderSize)) {
        int *pIntData = (int *)&networkPacket[0];            Copies data to  ❶
        pIntData[0] = gamePacketNumber++;                      char array
        pIntData[1] = packetID;
        memcpy( &networkPacket[packetHeaderSize], data, length );

        NSData *packet = [NSData dataWithBytes: networkPacket length:
            (length+8)];
        if(howtosend == YES) {                          ❷ Sends data
            [session sendData:packet toPeers:[NSArray
                arrayWithObject:gamePeerId]
                withDataMode:GKSendDataReliable error:nil];
        } else {
            [session sendData:packet toPeers:[NSArray
                arrayWithObject:gamePeerId]
                withDataMode:GKSendDataUnreliable error:nil];
        }
    }
}
```

This code may look frightening if you're unfamiliar with the C programming language. Although the code is a little complex, you have to write it only once, because most applications can use this method completely unchanged. We'll give you a high-level explanation of what's going on.

First, you declare a char array. You copy data into this array to be sent over the network. Next, you add two `int`s to the header. The first `int` is a unique packet number that gets incremented every time you send a packet. This is useful in the `receive` method in case the packets are received out of order. The second is the type of packet you're sending; you saw the various packet types declared in the header file.

Now, the data you passed in to the `send` method is copied to the packet ❶. Following that, the `char` array is converted to an `NSData` object in preparation to be sent. Finally, the data is sent ❷.

The `receive` method must be implemented in the exact opposite manner. After unpacking the data, `receive` must determine what to do based on the packet ID that was sent. You'll see this handled in the following listing as a `switch` statement.

Listing 15.8 The `receiveData` method

```
- (void)receiveData:(NSData *)data fromPeer:(NSString *)peer
    inSession:(GKSession *)session context:(void *)context {
    static int lastPacketTime = -1;
    unsigned char *incomingPacket = (unsigned char *)[data bytes];
    int *pIntData = (int *)&incomingPacket[0];
```

```
int packetTime = pIntData[0];
int packetID = pIntData[1];
if(packetTime < lastPacketTime && packetID != NETWORK_COINTOSS) {
    return;
}

lastPacketTime = packetTime;
switch( packetID ) {                              ① Determines client
    case NETWORK_COINTOSS:                           and server
    {
        int coinToss = pIntData[2];
        if(coinToss > gameUniqueID) {
            self.peerStatus = kClient;
        }
        self.game_label.hidden = YES;
    }
    break;                                        ② Updates
    case NETWORK_GAME_STATUS:                        game state
    {
        gameInfo *gs = (gameInfo *)&incomingPacket[8];
        memcpy( &gameStatus, gs, sizeof(gameInfo) );
        score_1_label.text = [NSString
            stringWithFormat:@"%d",gameStatus.score[kServer]];
        score_2_label.text = [NSString
            stringWithFormat:@"%d",gameStatus.score[kClient]];
    }
        break;                                    ③ Updates
    case NETWORK_MOVE_EVENT:                          paddle location
    {
        gameInfo *gi = (gameInfo *)&incomingPacket[8];
        gameStatus.paddlePosition[1-self.peerStatus].x =
            gi->paddlePosition[1-self.peerStatus].x;

    }
        break;                                    ④ Updates
    case NETWORK_BALL_MOVE_EVENT:                     ball location
    {
        gameInfo * gi = (gameInfo *)&incomingPacket[8];
        gameStatus.ballPosition.x = gi->ballPosition.x;
        gameStatus.ballPosition.y = gi->ballPosition.y;
        gameStatus.ballVelocity.x = gi->ballVelocity.x;
        gameStatus.ballVelocity.y = gi->ballVelocity.y;
        break;
    }
    }
}
```

As noted before, the first part of this method reverses what you did in the send method: it converts the NSData back into an array of chars and retrieves the header data. Next, you determine whether the packet number is less than the number of the previous packet. If so, you ignore it because you're interested in only the most recent data.

If the packet is current, you use a switch statement to determine what to do with the data. The switch statement is based on the packet ID specified in the header file.

At the beginning of the game, players send a coin-toss packet that contains their UDID. The code compares the UDIDs and determines who is the client and who is the server ❶.

The next packet type is the game status packet. This type of packet is sent reliably and is used when you want to push the entire state of the game from the server to the client ❷. When this packet is sent, the client will memcpy its contents to its local copy of the game state.

The next packet is sent every time a player moves their paddle ❸. You use `1-self.peerStatus` to set the position of the opponent.

The final packet denotes the ball's location ❹. It's sent every time the ball collides with the wall or a paddle.

Now that all the heavy lifting is out of the way, it's time to implement the game loop method.

15.3.7 *The game loop*

The game loop is the driving force behind the application. This method is called frequently and is responsible for modifying game variables, updating the interface, and making sure the peers are in sync. Your game loop will generally be the largest method in your application. The next listing shows the code used for the game loop.

Listing 15.9 The game loop

```
-(void) gameLoop {

    switch (self.gameState) {
        case kStatePicker:
        case kStateStartGame:
            break;
        case kStateMultiplayerCointoss:
        {
            [self sendNetworkPacket:self.gameSession
                packetID:NETWORK_COINTOSS withData:&gameUniqueID
                ofLength:sizeof(int) reliable:YES];
            self.gameState = kStateMultiplayer;
        }
            break;
        case kStateMultiplayer:                          ⟵──❶ Detects collision
        {
            BOOL collision = NO;
            if(self.peerStatus == kServer) {
                CGPoint bottomRight =
                    CGPointMake(ball.frame.origin.x +
                    ball.frame.size.width, ball.frame.origin.y +
                    ball.frame.size.height);

                if(gameStatus.ballPosition.y <= 0 ) {
                    gameStatus.score[kClient]++;
                     [self resetBall];
                    return;
                }
```

```
        if(gameStatus.ballPosition.y >= 480 ) {
            gameStatus.score[kServer]++;
            [self resetBall];
            return;
        }

        if(ball.frame.origin.x <= 0 || bottomRight.x >= 320) {
            gameStatus.ballVelocity.x *= -1;
            collision = YES;
        }

        if(collision)
              [self sendNetworkPacket:gameSession
              packetID:NETWORK_BALL_MOVE_EVENT
              withData:&gameStatus
              ofLength:sizeof(gameInfo)
              reliable:NO];

        if((CGRectIntersectsRect(ball.frame, paddle_1.frame) ||
           CGRectIntersectsRect(ball.frame, paddle_2.frame)) &&
           !justCollided) {
            gameStatus.ballVelocity.y *= -1;
            collision = YES;
            justCollided = YES;
            [self performSelector:@selector(resetCollision)
                withObject:nil afterDelay:1.0];
        }

        paddle_2.center = CGPointMake(gameStatus.paddlePosition[1-
            self.peerStatus].x, paddle_2.center.y);
    } else {
        paddle_1.center = CGPointMake(gameStatus.paddlePosition[1-
            self.peerStatus].x , paddle_1.center.y);
    }
    gameStatus.ballPosition.y = gameStatus.ballPosition.y +
        gameStatus.ballVelocity.y;
    gameStatus.ballPosition.x = gameStatus.ballPosition.x +
        gameStatus.ballVelocity.x;

    ball.center = CGPointMake(gameStatus.ballPosition.x,
        gameStatus.ballPosition.y );
    if(gameStatus.score[kServer] >= 5) {
        self.game_label.text = @"Player 1 wins!";
        self.game_label.hidden = NO;
        self.gameState = kStateGameOver;
          [self sendNetworkPacket:gameSession
              packetID:NETWORK_GAME_STATUS
              withData:&gameStatus
              ofLength:sizeof(gameInfo)
                        reliable:YES];
        return;
    }

    if(gameStatus.score[kClient] >= 5) {
        self.game_label.text = @"Player 2 wins!";
        self.game_label.hidden = NO;
        self.gameState = kStateGameOver;
```

2 Updates ball position for other peer

3 Updates local ball position

4 Checks winning conditions

```
            [self sendNetworkPacket:gameSession
                packetID:NETWORK_GAME_STATUS
                withData:&gameStatus
                ofLength:sizeof(gameInfo)
                reliable:YES];
            return;
        }
    }
        break;
    default:
        break;
    }
}
```

The first case occurs only once per game, when the game is in the coin-toss state. In this state, each player sends their UDID to the other. Immediately after this, the game state is set to multiplayer, and the game begins.

The next case gets into the game logic ❶. You first determine whether you're in the game loop of the client or the server. Following that is collision detection to determine if the ball hits a paddle, a side wall, or a back wall to score a point. Note that you set the collision Boolean to NO. You use this to determine when to send the ball's location to the other peer ❷. Because both peers are running different timers, there's a good chance that the ball's location could get out of sync. To combat this, the server sends the ball's current position to the client every time the ball collides with something.

One thing you may think of doing here is sending the ball's position on every step of the timer. This would be a bad approach, because it would quickly flood the network, causing poor performance for the client. You must always be clever about when to send network packets. Try to send them as far apart as possible while still maintaining synchronization between the peers. For the example, you send a packet every time the ball changes direction, which is about once every half second.

Both the client and the server update the position of the ball on the screen ❸. Following this, the winning conditions are checked to see if either player has scored five points ❹. If this is the case, you end the game.

Although the code for this game loop could be improved quite a bit to make the game more interesting, it does a good job of showing when to send network packets. Because you send network data only when the ball collides with something, this loop may run a couple hundred times before the client is updated. The last part of the game involves user interaction by implementing the touchesMoved method.

15.3.8 User interaction

As with most applications, you'll handle the user interaction by implementing the touchesBegan and touchesMoved methods. In these methods, you'll capture the user's touch location, move the paddle to that location, and send that location to the other peer. The following listing shows the code for these methods.

Listing 15.10   Methods for user interaction

```
-(void) touchesBegan:(NSSet *)touches withEvent:(UIEvent *)event {
    [self touchesMoved:touches withEvent:event];
}

-(void) touchesMoved:(NSSet *)touches withEvent:(UIEvent *)event {

    switch (self.gameState) {                         ◁┐   Determines
        case kStateStartGame:                          ❶   game state
        {
            self.game_label.hidden = YES;
            [self showPicker];
        }
            break;                                Captures touch  ❷
        case kStateMultiplayer:                          location;
        {                                            moves paddle
            UITouch * t = [[event allTouches] anyObject];    ◁┘
            CGPoint paddlePoint = [t locationInView:self.view];

            if(self.peerStatus == kServer) {
                paddle_1.center = CGPointMake(paddlePoint.x,
                    paddle_1.center.y);
                gameStatus.paddlePosition[self.peerStatus].x =
                    paddle_1.center.x;
            } else {
                paddle_2.center = CGPointMake(paddlePoint.x,
                    paddle_2.center.y);
                gameStatus.paddlePosition[self.peerStatus].x =
                    paddle_2.center.x;              Sends network packet to  ❸
            }                                          update other player
            [self sendNetworkPacket:gameSession        ◁┘
                packetID:NETWORK_MOVE_EVENT withData:&gameStatus
                ofLength:sizeof(gameStatus) reliable: NO];
        }
            break;
        case kStateGameOver:
            exit(0);
            break;
        default:
            break;
    }
}
```

The first thing you see is common in many applications. Because the `touchesBegan`
and `touchesMoved` methods do the exact same thing, you have one call the other.

As in most of the game methods, the game state is determined at the beginning of
this method ❶. That's because you want to do different things based on the state of
the game. If you're at the beginning of the game, and the user taps the screen, the
method `showPicker` is called to display the peer picker to the user. At that point, the
Game Kit code takes over until a connection is established.

You next get the location on the screen where the user touched ❷. The x coordinate of this touch is used to move the player's paddle. As the user drags their finger on
the screen, their paddle moves along with it.

After each movement of the paddle, you must notify the other player of its new location ❸. Notice that you send the data unreliably; this is because you're sending so many packets to the other user that you don't care if they don't receive a few of them.

The game you've just created is nowhere near complete, but it provides you with enough code to understand how Game Kit should be used in a multiplayer game. You could take this game further by adding better graphics as well as basic physics for the collisions.

15.4 Summary

The Game Kit framework provides a high-level interface to create fully networked applications. It handles every step of the process, including finding peers, establishing a connection, and transferring various types of data between them.

You must implement three things when creating any application that uses Game Kit for networking. The first is the set of delegate methods for the peer picker. These methods respond to various events, including finding peers and selecting which ones you want to connect to. The next thing is the set of delegate methods for the session. These methods allow you to create custom sessions as well as keep track of all the sessions currently connected. The last methods you must consider are send and receive. They're responsible for all the data that's transferred over the network.

As you saw in section 15.3, Game Kit is easy to integrate into a game application. You can use the basic Game Kit methods along with a game loop to create a simple template for any multiplayer game.

With the networking code behind you, you're ready to learn how to communicate with the mother ship. The next chapter will discuss how to use the Event Kit.

Using Event Kit
on the iPhone and iPad

16

This chapter covers

- Overview of the Event Kit frameworks
- Adding an event programmatically
- Using Event Kit view controllers
- Fetching events by using Grand Central Dispatch

With the Calendar app in iOS 4, iPhone or iPad owners can easily consolidate their Gmail account, Microsoft Exchange account, Mobile Me account, and other calendar accounts on the same device. The Calendar's database can be accessed within your application through Event Kit frameworks. The Event Kit frameworks are made up of two frameworks: the Event Kit framework and the Event Kit UI framework. Together, they help your application access the Calendar's database from a high level. Previously, in chapter 9, we covered the Address Book frameworks on iOS. The Event Kit frameworks are quite similar to the Address Book API in a way.

Imagine you can build a birthday event planner application and have every friend's birthday party plan automatically added to the Calendar's database by clicking one button. In this chapter, we'll first provide some basic references on the Event Kit framework with the Birthday application, and then we'll show another Event application to fetch and display the existing events from the Calendar's database to the table view controller, with the help of the Event Kit UI framework. Finally, with the help of Grand Central Dispatch (GCD) from iOS 4, we'll demonstrate an improved technique for fetching data from Calendar's database.

16.1 An overview of the Event Kit frameworks

Calendar apps coming with iOS on iPhone and iPad are convenient for several reasons (see figure 16.1). They allow users to check out their schedule on the go and consolidate all the information into one Calendar database.

In order to access the Calendar database, Apple provides a convenient API in iOS 4 called Event Kit. There are two frameworks for Event Kit, as we mentioned earlier. The Event Kit framework gives you access to insert and delete an event in the Calendar's database. It's high-level API access to the Calendar database, and the best part is that any changes made to the Calendar will be synced automatically, so you can have peace of mind when you're writing the code for Calendar access. The Event Kit UI framework provides the handy interfaces to display and edit the Calendar's database with the same view controller you're already familiar with by using the Calendar app on the iPhone or iPad.

16.1.1 Adding Event Kit frameworks to your project

In order to use the Event Kit frameworks, you first need to add the existing frameworks `EventKit.framework` and `EventKitUI.framework` into the project. Head over to Xcode, highlight the top-level Project node in the project navigator tree, and on the right side view choose a target; then select the Build Phases tab. Under this tab is

Figure 16.1 Calendar app on iPhone and iPad

an entry called Link Binary with Libraries. Click the + button, and you'll see a window with the entire list of available frameworks under the current SDK, as shown in figure 16.2. Navigate to `EventKit.framework` and click the Add button. You'll see a new framework added to your project. Repeat the same process for `EventKitUI.framework`.

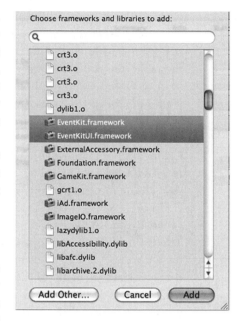

After adding the required frameworks into the project, you also need to include two files to the header file you wish to use Event Kit, as follows:

```
#import <EventKit/EventKit.h>
#import <EventKitUI/EventKitUI.h>
```

With the Event Kit frameworks added into the project, you can start to use them for accessing Calendar's database from the application. First, we'll look at the Event Kit classes.

Figure 16.2   Add the Event Kit framework from the project panel.

16.1.2 *Event Kit classes*

Inside the powerful Event Kit API are a handful of classes that are like useful friends; figure 16.3 gives you a general idea about the relationships among these important classes.

As you can see from figure 16.3, `EKEventStore` is the key object here, and it's the connection to the Calendar database. You can use the following code snippet to initialize an `EKEventStore` object for Calendar data access:

```
EKEventStore *store = [[EKEventStore alloc] init];
```

Note that this initial method may consume a lot of time, so it's a good practice to keep around that `EKEventStore` object in your program for all data access.

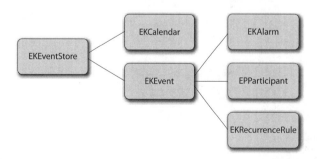

**Figure 16.3
The Event Kit class structure**

EKEvent is the object representing an event, which includes some import properties, as listed in table 16.1.

Table 16.1 EKEvent's property table

Property	Details
title	Title of the event; NSString type
location	*Location of the event;* NSString *type*
allday	BOOL type, indicating the event is an all-day event
startDate	Start date of the event
endDate	End date of the event
calendar	Calendar for a new event, EKCalendar type
attendees	Array of participants
alarms	Array of EKAlarm objects
eventIdentifier	Unique identifier for an event; NSString type

After the EKEventStore object is initialized, the Calendar is ready for you to add or delete events. You can create an event object and add it to the Calendar's database programmatically. Alternatively, you can use the Event Kit UI framework for event view controllers, which is a great choice for calendaring related user interaction. The Event Kit UI framework contains two types of view controllers for manipulating events:

- EKEventViewController—Use if you have an existing event you want to display or allow the user to edit
- EKEventEditViewController—Use if you allow the user to create, edit, or delete events

We'll talk about how to do this in section 16.3. Next, let's look at how to add a new event to Calendar programmatically with the Event Kit framework.

16.2 Adding new events to Calendar programmatically

At the beginning of this chapter, we mentioned a birthday application example. In this section, you'll build a small application that you can use to add a friend's birthday party planner into Calendar's database by clicking a button. The user interface looks like figure 16.4.

Let's get started.

Figure 16.4   Birthday application launching on the iPhone and IPad

16.2.1 *Adding Event Kit frameworks to the Birthday application*

Fire up Xcode, and create a new project from the iOS application template: select View-Based Application, and select Device Family of iPhone. Name the application `Birthday`. Add the Event Kit and Event Kit UI frameworks to the project (as shown in figure 16.2); then include them in BirthdayViewController.h, as noted in section 16.1.1. Add a new method to the view controller:

```
-(IBAction)addEventToCalendar:(id)sender;
```

Click `BirthdayViewController`'s nib file to bring up the Interface Builder. You want to throw in a button for adding a new event to Calendar; don't forget to hook up the button to the method you created for adding an event.

Go back to Xcode, and select Birthday under Targets. Navigate to Project > Upgrade Current Target for iPad, and create the universal application for the iPhone and iPad.

16.2.2 *Adding an event to Calendar*

Now it's time to add code to BirthdayViewController.m. The process to create a new event and add it to the Calendar database is shown in the following listing.

> **Listing 16.1   Adding a new event to Calendar's database**

```
-(IBAction)addEventToCalendar:(id)sender
{
EKEventStore *store = [[EKEventStore alloc] init];
```
❶ Init event store

```
EKEvent *myEvent = [EKEvent eventWithEventStore: store];
myEvent.title = @"Amy's Birthday";
myEvent.location = @"BBQ House";
myEvent.startDate = [NSDate dateWithTimeIntervalSinceNow:60*60*24];
myEvent.endDate = [NSDate dateWithTimeIntervalSinceNow:60*60*26];
myEvent.calendar = store.defaultCalendarForNewEvents;
EKAlarm *reminder = [EKAlarm alarmWithRelativeOffset:-2*60*60];
[myEvent addAlarm:reminder];
NSError *error;
BOOL saved = [store saveEvent:myEvent span:EKSpanThisEvent
              error:&error];
if (saved) {
  UIAlertView *alert = [[UIAlertView alloc] initWithTitle:@"Amy's Party"
                        message:@"Saved to Calendar" delegate:self
                        cancelButtonTitle:@"Right On!"
                        otherButtonTitles:nil];
        [alert show];
        [alert release];
    }
}
```

❷

Create new event

⟵**❸** **Save event**

First, you initialize the event store with `[[EKEventStore alloc] init]` **❶**. Then, you create a new event from the event store with `[EKEvent eventWithEventStore: store]` **❷**, followed by setting properties for the birthday party's title, location, start-Date, endDate, and default Calendar and configuring a reminder alarm that will trigger two hours before the event's start time. In the code, the start time is 24 hours from now and the event will end after 2 hours. Finally, you save that event to the event store with method `[store saveEvent:myEvent span:EKSpanThisEvent error:&error]` **❸** and give feedback to the user when the event is saved to Calendar successfully. That's all you need to do to add a new event.

> **NOTE** At the time of writing, the iOS SDK doesn't include the Calendar app on the Simulator. In order to test this application, you need to use a real device: your iPhone, iPod Touch, or iPad.

Build and run this application on your device. You should have a Birthday application similar to the one shown in figure 16.4. Click the Add to Calendar button to add a new event to Calendar. You should see the alert view informing you that the new birthday party event was added to Calendar successfully.

Go to the Calendar application on your device. You should see the new event appear on your schedule for tomorrow (figure 16.5).

You've learned how to create a new event and add it to the Calendar database. Next, we'll discuss how to add or edit an event by using the Event Kit UI framework.

Figure 16.5 The Birthday application successfully added the new event to the Calendar.

16.3   *Creating an event with the Event Edit view controller*

Previously, we focused on how to add a new event to Calendar's database programmatically. With the Event Kit UI framework, you can use the modal view controller to allow the user to add and edit events with a few lines of codes. As explained in section 16.1, `EKEventEditViewController` is for new events, whereas `EKEventViewController` is for existing events. First, let's learn how to create a new event from `EKEventEditView-Controller`.

Follow the same steps as in section 16.2.1 and add the Event Kit frameworks to a simple view-based project. With the necessary frameworks included, the project is ready for the Event Edit view controller.

In order to allow the user to add a new event to the calendar you'll use the `EKEventEditViewController` and `EKEventEditViewController`'s delegate. The Event Edit view controller must contain the `eventStore` property. The `eventStore` is an `EKEventStore` object representing the Calendar database. In the code example, you'll use the default Calendar to save the new event.

The Event Edit view controller can be presented as a modal view controller; the delegate method `eventEditViewController:didCompleteWithAction:` lets you dismiss the Event Edit view controller once the user finishes editing or cancels the current work:

```
- (void)eventEditViewController:(EKEventEditViewController *)controller
didCompleteWithAction:(EKEventEditViewAction)action {
    [self dismissModalViewControllerAnimated:YES];
}
```

Now let's continue the example. Add the Event Edit view controller to the `Simple-EventViewController` in the application.

In the header file, add `EKEventEditViewDelegate` and a new method for event editing, as shown in the following listing.

Listing 16.2 `SimpleEventViewController` header file

```
#import <UIKit/UIKit.h>
#import <EventKitUI/EventKitUI.h>
#import <EventKit/EventKit.h>
@interface SimpleEventViewController : UIViewController
<EKEventEditViewDelegate> {
    EKEventStore *eventStore;
    EKCalendar *defaultCalendar;
}
@property (nonatomic, retain) EKEventStore *eventStore;
@property (nonatomic, retain) EKCalendar *defaultCalendar;

-(IBAction) addEvent:(id)sender;
@end
```

The code in listing 16.2 is similar to the header file in the birthday party planner in section 16.2. Make sure you have a button linked to the `addEvent` method from Interface Builder. Next, add the code from the following listing to implement the Event Edit view controller

Listing 16.3 Using EventEditViewController and delegate to add a new event

```
@implementation SimpleEventViewController
@synthesize eventStore;
@synthesize defaultCalendar;

- (void)viewDidLoad {                                            ❶ Init Event Store
    self.eventStore = [[EKEventStore alloc] init];                  and Calendar
    self.defaultCalendar = [self.eventStore defaultCalendarForNewEvents];
    [super viewDidLoad];
}

- (void)dealloc {                                               ❷ Release
    [eventStore release];                                          memory
    [defaultCalendar release];
    [super dealloc];
}
                                                               ❸ Create
-(IBAction) addEvent:(id)sender {                                  event
    EKEventEditViewController *addController =
     [[EKEventEditViewController alloc] initWithNibName:nil bundle:nil];
    addController.eventStore = self.eventStore;
    addController.editViewDelegate = self;
    [self presentModalViewController:addController animated:YES];
    [addController release];
}
- (void)eventEditViewController:(EKEventEditViewController *)controller
        didCompleteWithAction:(EKEventEditViewAction)action {
    NSError *error = nil;                                    Dismiss view
    EKEvent *thisEvent = controller.event;                controller ❹
```

```
    switch (action) {
        case EKEventEditViewActionCanceled:
            break;
        case EKEventEditViewActionSaved:
                [controller.eventStore saveEvent:thisEvent
    span:EKSpanThisEvent error:&error];
            break;
        default:
            break;
    }

    [controller dismissModalViewControllerAnimated:YES];
}
```

The access to Calendar's database is done by a few lines of code. You initialize the event store `[[EKEventStore alloc] init]` and define Calendar for data access `[self.eventStore defaultCalendarForNewEvents]` ❶. As mentioned earlier, it's a good practice to keep one event store around for all the data access. `dealloc` ❷ reminds you to release the memory when the view controller is released. The new thing you learned for using Event Edit view controller is all in `addEvent` ❸ and the delegate method `-(void)eventEditViewController:(EKEventEditViewController *)controller didCompleteWithAction:(EKEventEditViewAction)action` ❹. You define the Event Edit view controller's event store and delegate and then present the modal view controller `[self presentModalViewController:addController animated:YES]` ❸. When the user finishes editing the new event, the method `[controller dismissModalViewControllerAnimated:YES]` ❹ will dismiss the edit view and save the new event to the Calendar.

Now let's build and run it. When the application launches, click the Add button to present the Event Edit view controller. As you can see in figure 16.6, the new event's Title, Location, Starts, Ends, Repeat, and Alert options are editable.

Congrats! You just created a new event and saved it successfully to the local Calendar with the Event Kit UI framework! Now let's talk about how to fetch the existing events from the Calendar's database.

16.4   *Fetching events*

Previously, you learned how to create an event with `EKEventEditViewController`. The next step is to get the existing events from Calendar's database.

First, you need to learn how to access Calendar's database to fetch the existing events. It's time to introduce a new friend, the predicate.

Figure 16.6
`EventEditViewController`
presented as a modal view controller

16.4.1 Fetching events with the predicate

A common task is to find out all the events within a certain time period. For example, the user wants to figure out what's on their Calendar for the next 24 hours. This task can be defined as a predicate in the following listing. Once you have the predicate, you can use a method called `eventsMatchingPredicate` in the event store to search for qualified events; the return of the search results will be an array of existing events.

> **Listing 16.4 Using `NSPredicate` to search for existing events in the device's Calendar**

```
NSDate *startDate = [NSDate date];
NSDate *endDate = [NSDate dateWithTimeIntervalSinceNow:60*60*24];
EKEventStore *defaultCalendar = [[EKEventStore alloc] init];
NSArray *calendarArray = [NSArray arrayWithObject:defaultCalendar];
NSPredicate *predicate =
  [defaultCalendar predicateForEventsWithStartDate:startDate       ❶ Create
  endDate:endDate calendars:calendarArray];                           predicate
NSArray *events = [defaultCalendar                               ❷ Store data
  eventsMatchingPredicate:predicate];                              to array
```

> **TIP** Because the `eventsMatchingPredicate` method is running synchronously, you may not want to run it on your application's main thread because that would block the UI until the operation is done. For example, if you're fetching events from last month, you may want to have a spinner animation indicating the waiting time. The background thread will take care of the data fetching asynchronously. We'll cover how to do this with GCD in the next section.

You create the predicate with the method `[defaultCalendar predicateForEventsWithStartDate:startDate endDate:endDate calendars:calendarArray]` ❶. In the events array from `[defaultCalendar eventsMatchingPredicate:predicate]` ❷, each object is an object of `EKEvent`.

The application you're about to build will show you how to fetch all the existing events in your Calendar from the app and display the `events` array as the table view's data. Each of the rows in the table view will be an event's title. When you select a row by tapping, the event's detail view controller will get pushed onto the navigation controller's stack. Sound good?

16.4.2 Displaying events with Event view controller

Let's create a new project with the Navigation-based application template. Name it `Event`. First, let's add the two Event Kit frameworks into the project. You learned how to do so in section 16.1.

Inside the `RootViewController`, define that the table view's data equals the `events` array from Calendar's database. Single-click the file RootViewController.h, and add the changes from the following listing.

Listing 16.5 `RootViewController`'s header file

```
#import <UIKit/UIKit.h>
#import <EventKit/EventKit.h>
#import <EventKitUI/EventKitUI.h>
@interface RootViewController : UITableViewController {
    EKEventStore *eventStore;
    EKCalendar *defaultCalendar;
    NSArray *events;
}
@property (nonatomic, retain) NSArray *events;
@property (nonatomic, retain) EKEventStore *eventStore;
@property (nonatomic, retain) EKCalendar *defaultCalendar;

-(NSArray *)fetchEventsForTommorrow;
@end
```

The method in listing 16.5 is for the table view's data, which will be fetched by predicate from Calendar's database.

Now you'll implement the RootViewController.m file. First, fetch the events array before the table view is loaded inside the method viewWillAppear:; then store the data in the events array.

Single-click the file RootViewController.m, and then add the new method from the next listing.

Listing 16.6 Fetch tomorrow's events from Calendar and display the details

```
#import "RootViewController.h"
@implementation RootViewController
@synthesize events;
@synthesize eventStore, defaultCalendar;

-(NSArray *)fetchEventsForTommorrow {                        ❶ Fetch data
    NSDate *startDate = [NSDate date];                          with predicate
    NSDate *endDate = [NSDate dateWithTimeIntervalSinceNow:60*60*24];
    NSArray *calendarArray = [NSArray arrayWithObject:defaultCalendar];
    NSPredicate *predicate = [self.eventStore
                        predicateForEventsWithStartDate:startDate
                        endDate:endDate calendars:calendarArray];
    NSArray *eventList = [self.eventStore
                        eventsMatchingPredicate:predicate];
    return eventList;
}

- (void)viewWillAppear:(BOOL)animated {
    [super viewWillAppear:animated];
    self.title = @"Event List";
    self.eventStore = [[EKEventStore alloc] init];
    self.defaultCalendar = [self.eventStore defaultCalendarForNewEvents];
    self.events = [NSArray arrayWithArray:[self fetchEventsForTommorrow]];
}

- (NSInteger)numberOfSectionsInTableView:(UITableView *)tableView {
    return 1;
}
```

```
- (NSInteger)tableView:(UITableView *)tableView
    numberOfRowsInSection:(NSInteger)section {
    return [events count];
}

- (UITableViewCell *)tableView:(UITableView *)tableView
        cellForRowAtIndexPath:(NSIndexPath *)indexPath {
    static NSString *CellIdentifier = @"Cell";
    UITableViewCell *cell = [tableView

    dequeueReusableCellWithIdentifier:CellIdentifier];

    if (cell == nil) {
      cell = [[[UITableViewCell alloc]
            initWithStyle:UITableViewCellStyleDefault
            reuseIdentifier:CellIdentifier] autorelease];
    }
    EKEvent *myEvent = (EKEvent *)[self.events
        objectAtIndex:indexPath.row];
    cell.textLabel.text = myEvent.title;
    return cell;
}

- (void)tableView:(UITableView *)tableView didSelectRowAtIndexPath:
    (NSIndexPath *)indexPath {
  EKEvent *selectEvent = (EKEvent *)[self.events
    objectAtIndex:indexPath.row];
  EKEventViewController *eventViewController = [[EKEventViewController
    alloc] init];
  eventViewController.event = selectEvent;
  eventViewController.allowsEditing = NO;
  [self.navigationController pushViewController:eventViewController
    animated:YES];
  [eventViewController release];
}
```

❷ Display event's title *(annotation pointing to `cell.textLabel.text = myEvent.title;`)*

❸ Event view controller *(annotation pointing to `eventViewController` code block)*

The method fetchEventsForTommorrow ❶ fetches the events from the Calendar data-base and returns them as an array. It's called in the method viewWillAppear. Each time the Root view controller's view appears, it will fetch the next day's events from the device's Calendar and store the data into the array eventList. With the events data in an array, you define the total number of rows as the count of events. Then you get the event in each row in ❷ and pass the event's title to the cell's text. The code in ❸ is almost self-explanatory. You get the selected event, define the event on the view controller, and present the Event view controller by pushing it on the Navigation controller. (We covered the view controllers in chapter 6.) Save all the changes, and build the application.

You may define the Event view controller's property allowEditing = YES. Doing so will allow the user to edit the existing event.

Save all the changes. Try to build and run the app on your device. You should be able to fetch all the existing events for the next day. The app launches in table view format, as shown in figure 16.7. As you can see inside my Calendar, I have a few events coming up. Tap each event; the details appear in the Event view controller.

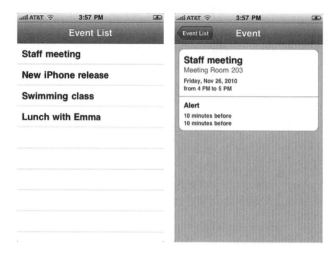

Figure 16.7   Fetching and displaying events from the device's Calendar database

> **TIP**   Make sure you have some events scheduled in Calendar during the test. That's how the application will get the events' data.

In this section, you learned how to fetch existing events from the Calendar database and then how to display the events' details in the application with the Event view controller. As noted, the fetching method isn't performed asynchronously. In the next section, you'll use an improved method and use Grand Central Dispatch to fetch the existing events asynchronously.

16.5   *Fetching events with GCD*

Grand Central Dispatch (GCD) was introduced in Mac OS X Snow Leopard as a comprehensive library for concurrent code execution on multicore hardware technology. Now it's available on iOS 4 as a C API. Although multicore isn't available on most current iOS devices (the iPad 2 has a multicore processor), GCD helps the application to run faster, more efficiently, and asynchronously. Concurrency is an advanced topic, and we don't plan to dive into this concept in this chapter. You can find more information on the Concurrency Programming Guide from the iOS developer website. Let's look at GCD and use it to fetch events.

16.5.1   *Grand Central Dispatch overview*

GCD is available to any application, and there's no need to add in any other framework. Imagine that you have queues of operations, and each queue is running in its own thread separately on the system. You don't have to worry about when to run the time-consuming operations. The system will take care of the order and make sure that the queue's operations get done.

In order to keep the application running responsively, the key concept is *don't block the main thread.* Throw the time-consuming tasks, such as fetching a list of events from the Calendar's database or downloading an image file from the internet, to the background thread. Then update the UI after the work in the background is done and the data is ready to display.

How do you accomplish this task with GCD? As it turns out, it's pretty easy. Call the method `dispatch_async()` to submit a queue of operations (a block of code) to the main queue and execute the task on a dispatch queue asynchronously; then tell the system to update the UI. You've already learned how to use blocks in the Core Animation API in chapter 13.

The definition for `dispatch_async()` is listed as

```
void dispatch_async( dispatch_queue_t queue,
dispatch_block_t block);
```

How do you create a queue or get the main queue? Here are some common methods related to GCD:

- *Creating a queue*—dispatch_queue_t dispatch_queue_create(const char *label, NULL);
- *Releasing a queue*—void dispatch_release(dispatch_queue_t);
- *Getting the main queue*—dispatch_queue_t dispatch_get_main_queue();

Don't forget to release the queue when it's created with the method `dispatch_queue_create()`.

With GCD and blocks in hand, how can you improve the code in section 16.4? You want to create a queue for the fetching-events operations and let the system decide when to run this queue, followed by updating the UI in the main thread.

16.5.2 *Fetching events with GCD*

Let's use GCD and blocks to fetch the whole month of events and update the table view display. You'll re-create the Events application from section 16.4 but use the method in the following listing to fetch events with GCD.

Listing 16.7   Fetching events with GCD

```
-(void)fetchEventsForNextMonth {
NSDate *startDate = [NSDate date];
NSDate *endDate = [NSDate dateWithTimeIntervalSinceNow:60*60*24*30];
NSPredicate *predicate = [self.eventStore
                        predicateForEventsWithStartDate:startDate
                        endDate:endDate
                        calendars:eventStore.calendars];
dispatch_queue_t fetching_queue =                            ❶ Define
  dispatch_queue_create("Fetching events", NULL);              custom queue
dispatch_async(fetching_queue, ^{                           ❷ Fetch events
  NSArray *eventList =
  [self.eventStore eventsMatchingPredicate:predicate];
  dispatch_async(dispatch_get_main_queue(), ^{              ❸ Update UI
    [self.events addObjectsFromArray:eventList];
    [self.tableView reloadData];
    });
```

```
    });
dispatch_release(fetching_queue);                    <———④  Release queue
}
```

In listing 16.7, you first create the custom queue ❶. Then the GCD function starts ❷. The block of operations will first execute the custom task to fetch events from the Calendar database on the dispatch queue. When the `eventList` array is ready, you want to update the table view's UI with the new data on the main queue dispatch. The block ❸ first updates the `events` array and then reloads the table view's data. Finally, don't forget to release the queue ❹. Follow the design flow; GCD will automatically finish the task and provide a quick response asynchronously.

As you can see from the example, with a few lines of code, you manage to perform a task in the background and update the UI when the new data is ready. That's the power of GCD and blocks.

16.6   *Summary*

The Event Kit framework provides an interface for accessing Calendar events on a user's device. You can use this framework to get existing events and add new events to the user's Calendar. In this chapter, you learned how to accomplish this task both with the Event Kit UI view controllers and programmatically. With GCD, the application's performance is greatly improved, especially when fetching events from Calendar's database asynchronously.

Calendar events can also include alarms to notify the user of the upcoming events. Similar to the alarms, the local notifications provide an alert view but with more interesting features. In the next chapter, we'll tackle the local notifications and push notifications.

17

Local and Push notification services

As mobile devices become more popular, developers must face new and exciting challenges. One of these major challenges has been around since the dawn of mobile software. It's related to background processes. All the previous chapters we have been focusing on the foreground activities. When the application is active and running, it's easy to interact with users. However, what shall we do when the application is not in the foreground. What is the best way to update application data and notify users to launch the application without the user explicitly running the application? Local and Push notifications are Apple's solution on iOS 4. In this chapter we'll look at Apple's local and push notification system, how to use local notifications, how to prepare an application to work with push notifications, and how to create a notification provider on a server. First though, let's examine what exactly local and push notifications are.

17.1   *What are local and push notifications?*

At the beginning of this chapter, we briefly discussed that we would like to have the local and push notifications to notify end users when the application is not running on the foreground. First let's take a closer look at what notifications are. On iOS 4, the notifications may include the sound, a short message, and badge the application's icon. For example, in figure 17.1 you will find the common user interface for local and push notifications.

There are two notification methods in iOS 4: local and push notifications. On the first glance, they are similar. Both may come with the alert sound, short custom message body and badge number on the icon. What's the difference?

Push notification is a notification sent remotely by Apple's Push Notification service to the device that your application is running on. A classic example of the problem of presenting the user with real-time data updates is an instant messenger program. Instant messaging allows users to send quick chat messages to their contacts who are online.

Suppose that a contact isn't online, so they can't receive the chat messages. In order to maintain constant communication, you must stay online indefinitely. One way to solve this problem on a mobile device is to run the chat client in the background and pulling data from server even after the user has exited the application.

Figure 17.1   **Local and push notifications with custom message and badge number**

This allows the chat client to periodically ping the server to check whether the user has received any new chat messages.

The elegant solution that Apple came up with is called push notification. A push notification is a simple message that originates at a push provider, containing information related to a specific program. These messages can contain any number of things, including a message, a sound file to play, a badge count, and any custom key-value pair needed for an application. Figure 17.1 shows an example of what a push notification might look like for an application. As you can see in the figure, the push notification looks similar to a text message. It contains a title, a message, and buttons. The title is the title of the application that the push notification is related to. When the user taps the View button, the iPhone or iPad launches the application that invoked the push notification.

It should become apparent how this approach solves the issue of background processing for most applications. In the case of an instant message program, users can opt to stay online via the chat server. That way, they can exit the application and the server can push notifications any time they receive a new chat message. Users don't have to waste system memory having their chat client run in the background, pinging the server for new messages. Push notifications are simple to include in your applications, because little code is required. One challenge is the fact that in addition to enabling your applications for push notifications, you must also create a push provider. We'll discuss both of these aspects of the system and show you how to create a full system for sending and receiving push notifications.

Push notification has been a great service since iOS 3, but it only works when the iPhone or iPad is connected to the internet. With local notifications available in iOS 4, it's much easier to handle local reminders for your To-Do list application or fire up an alert for your timer application locally on the iPhone, iPod Touch, or iPad. In this chapter we will work on how to implement a custom local notification in the Alarm application. Using local notifications, you need to define exactly when the alarm should trigger, so the event has to be predefined. However in some occasions, for example, you may want to notify your users about the latest score from ESPN or a new game application you just created is available in the App Store, you won't be able to forecast the date or message ahead of time. How can you notify your users in this situation? The solution is push notification. We will cover this topic later in this chapter. First, let's start coding with local notifications.

17.2   *Implementing local notifications on Timer application*

In this section, we will cover how to fire up a countdown local notification with sound and badge count. Let's start by creating a new project. In Xcode, select **New Project...** from the File menu. When the new project assistant comes up, choose view-based application, the target is iPhone, and name the new application **Alarm**.

By default, the app's icon is a white square. Let's change the icon to be a better looking clock image as we see in figure17.1. There will be a button on the AlarmView-

Controller's nib file. When you tap on the button, the `createAlarm` method will be called and schedule a local notification based on the count down timer. The UI is similar to figure 17.2.

We are going to create our very first local notification in the application. Single-click `AlarmView-Controller.h`, and add in the methods to create the alarm and respond to the date picker:

```
#import <UIKit/UIKit.h>
@interface AlarmViewController : UIViewController {
IBOutlet UIDatePicker *myPicker;
NSTimeInterval myTimer;
}
-(IBAction)createAlarm;
-(IBAction)datePickerValueDidChange:(id)sender;
@end
```

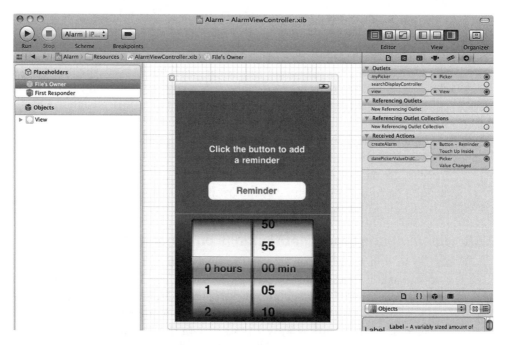

**Figure 17.2
The AlarmViewController.xib
under Interface Builder**

Double-click the AlarmViewController's nib file, drag and add the button and date picker to the view as figure 17.3 demonstrates.

Select our new button, bring up the attributes inspector, change the text and font color; click the File's Owner icon next to the view, keep the mouse button down. Drag away toward to the View's button. When the actions options appear, choose *Touch up*

Figure 17.3   The screenshot of the AlarmViewController.xib with button and date picker connected to action methods under Interface Builder

inside. By doing so, we connect the method `createAlarm` to button's event *Touch up inside.* Follow the same step to link the method `datePickerValueDidChange` to UIPickerView's event *Value Did Change.*

Next, single-click the AlarmViewController.m file, and add listing17.1. We want to display an alert view message: *Wake up right now,* the action button will be "view details", and add a badge count on the Icon to inform user there is one notification from this application.

Listing 17.1 Creating a custom local notification based on the count down timer

```
-(IBAction)createAlarm {                          Cancel previous notification  ❶
[[UIApplication sharedApplication] cancelAllLocalNotifications];
    NSDate *itemDate = [NSDate dateWithTimeIntervalSinceNow:myTimer];

    UILocalNotification *localNotification = [[UILocalNotification alloc]
    init];
    if (localNotification == nil)                              Create local
          return;                                           notification  ❷
localNotification.fireDate = itemDate;
localNotification.timeZone = [NSTimeZone defaultTimeZone];
localNotification.alertBody = [NSString stringWithFormat:
@"Wake up right now!"];
localNotification.alertAction = @"View Details";
    localNotification.soundName = UILocalNotificationDefaultSoundName;
    localNotification.applicationIconBadgeNumber = 1;
    [[UIApplication sharedApplication]
scheduleLocalNotification:localNotification];             Schedule
    [localNotification release];                        ❸ notification
}

-(IBAction)datePickerValueDidChange:(id)sender {          ❹ Timer from
    myTimer = myPicker.countDownDuration;                     picker
}
```

Let's take a look at the code. Inside the method `createAlarm`, we first use `cancelAllLocalNotifications` ❶ to cancel all the previous local notifications to reset the system, and then define the starting date based on the count down timer. We create a localNotification object ❷, define the fire date, with a custom message "Wake up right now." custom the notification's action button and the alarm sound. More we defined the badge count to 1 on the application's icon; use `scheduleLocalNotificaiton` ❸ to schedule the localNotification for this application. In `datePickerValueDidChange` ❹, we simply read out the count down timer from the date picker's value.

The local notification methods are straightforward. You can play with the property settings to custom the notification on your own.

One more thing, we need to reset the badge number back to 0 when the application is launched again. Let's next add in the new changes to the appdelegate.m file. Inside the method `application:didFinishLaunchingWithOptions:` add the reset as highlighted in the code snippet below:

```
- (BOOL)application:(UIApplication *)application
didFinishLaunchingWithOptions:(NSDictionary *)launchOptions {
    [window addSubview:viewController.view];
```

```
    [window makeKeyAndVisible];
    application.applicationIconBadgeNumber = 0;
    return YES;
}
```

That's all we need to do for setting up a timer based local notification. Build and Run, you will have the application launching in the simulator. When you set the timer value and click the button, it will automatically schedule a local notification for you.

Now it's time to take a break and go back to the home screen, drink a cup of coffee. Soon the local notification will work though the application is not running in foreground, you will see an message on the home screen similar to figure 17.1; that's the local notification, as defined in the notification's badge number property, there will be a badge count showing up on the app's icon. When you click on the button options "view details", the alarm app will launch automatically.

So far it's pretty amazing, right? You've already learned how to implement local notifications. It's time to move to the next part: push notifications.

17.3   *An overview of Apple's push notification system*

Push notifications rely on one specific service provided by Apple. This service is called Apple Push Notification Service (APNS). APNS is a web service that every provider must communicate with in order to send notifications to a client device. Devices establish a connection to this service and receive messages from it when they're available. If a device isn't running the application that received the notification, it's prompted with an alert window containing information pertaining to the state of the application. Figure 17.4 shows the complete cycle of a push notification that we'll discuss in this section.

Push notifications originate in what Apple calls the *push notification provider*. The provider is a server created by the developer of an application. These providers are often used in conjunction with applications that depend on the web to get new data to use.

When something changes on the provider, data must be generated and sent to the APNS. This data, called the *payload*, is in the format of a JSON dictionary. JSON is an acronym that stands for *JavaScript Object Notation*. It's a simple format that allows associative arrays to be transferred between applications regardless of their implementation language. The following code shows an example of the JSON data that is sent to APNS:

```
{
"aps":{"alert":"This is a message","badge":11,"sound":"default"}
}
```

Figure 17.4   The lifecycle of
a push notification

Table 17.1　Push data descriptions

Data	Description
Alert	The text message that appears to users when they aren't running the application that received the notification.
Badge	The number to display on the icon of the application receiving the notification. If you choose to omit this value, the badge number is set to 0 and isn't displayed.
Sound	The sound file in your application to be played when the notification arrives. This file must be in a specific format, as discussed later in this section.

This format isn't much different from a dictionary. You first have a key named *aps* that has a value of an associative array. Within this array, you see the various types of data that you can send to Apple. Table 17.1 lists all of these data types as well as their descriptions.

In addition to the `aps` dictionary, you can also send a dictionary containing your own custom data. Here's an example of a notification containing the standard data as well as a custom dictionary:

```
{
"aps":{"alert":"Hello World","badge":1,"sound":"default"},
"foo":{"bar":1,"baz":"Custom text"}
}
```

Notice that you add a new dictionary with the key `foo`. You can assign this dictionary to strings, numbers, and even other dictionaries. This one contains a key named *bar* that has the value 1 and a key named *baz* that has the value of "Custom text". Using this technique, you can customize the data that is sent to your application.

After the payload has been created, you must establish a secure connection to APNS. This is done using an SSL certificate, which you'll create in section 17.5. The SSL certificate also contains other data that APNS uses to identify which application is receiving the notification. After APNS receives the payload and device token, it attempts to send a push notification to the given device. But sometimes the notification isn't received.

If APNS tries to send a notification to a device and fails, it queues up the notification until a connection can be established. One of the main reasons for failed deliveries is a device that doesn't have an internet connection. This happens when a device is off or is out of range for cell and wi-fi service. When a connection is established, all of the stored-up notifications are sent to the device.

If a device receives more than one push notification at a time, only the most recent one is displayed. Although the other messages can still play a sound and modify the badge number, their alert messages are hidden from view and aren't shown again.

You'll see in section 17.5 that a device will handle notifications differently depending on whether the application is running. The next section will walk you through all the steps necessary to get your application ready to receive and process push notifications.

17.4 Preparing your application to use push notifications

Leave it to Apple to make the preparation more complex than the coding. You'll find that you spend more time creating and uploading the signing certificates than writing the code to receive push notifications. You begin by setting up the signing certificates.

17.4.1 Setting up your application certificate

You must have a valid Apple iOS developer account to test push notifications. We'll show you how to generate two items that are required. The first item you'll generate is a special provisioning profile. This profile will be used to sign the application when deploying it to your device. The second is a client SSL certificate. The push provider will use this to establish a connection with Apple's push notification servers.

Start by logging into your iOS developer account. Then, open the program portal, and navigate to the App IDs tab. If you haven't already done so, you'll need to add your application bundle identifier to this list. The format for this should be reverse domain—for example, com.rightsprite.pushtest. Make sure you don't use any wild-cards, because the system must be able to uniquely identify your application.

After you've added your application, you must configure it to receive push notifications. You have the option to configure the app for development as well as production. It's always good practice to use the development certificate when testing and switch to the production certificate when you're ready to submit to the app store. Figure 17.5 shows what this section should look like.

Figure 17.5   Configuring the app to receive push notifications

Click the Configure button. The following screen gives you the option to configure either the development or the production certificate. For this example, you'll configure the debug certificate, but the steps for both are exactly the same. Figure 17.6 shows what this process looks like.

As you may have guessed, this process is similar to creating any other provisioning profile. After completing this step, you need to download this certificate and install it in your keychain by double-clicking it.

17.4.2 Setting up your provisioning profile

Now that you've created the signing certificate, you need to create the provisioning profile to allow the application to be installed. Again, you don't want to use your generic developer certificate. You must generate a new certificate that is specific to your app's full bundle id.

Go to the Provisioning tab. Because you created a push certificate for debug, you must also create a debug provisioning profile. Had you created a production certificate, you would need to create an app store or ad hoc certificate. Click the New Profile button on the Development tab.

Figure 17.6 Wizard to create a push certificate

As you may have seen before, you need to set up quite a few options. The first is the profile name. This can be anything you want, but your best bet is to be descriptive. Name the profile something of the format "(*application name*) Debug". Next, you'll select the certificate that the profile will use.

If you're a single user, you should see only your certificate in the list. But if you're on a team, you should see a certificate for every one of your team members. Check the boxes of the teammates who will be testing the push notifications. Note that when you're creating a build for the app store, you'll select your distribution certificate.

Following the certificate, you need to select the app id that the profile will be used for. This corresponds to the app id created in section 17.4.1. Finally, you must select the devices the provisioning profile will work on. Figure 17.7 shows an example of what this form looks like when it's complete.

After you create this profile, you need to download and install it. That's about it for the certificate creation. We'll now discuss how to implement the methods in your client application to enable and receive push notifications.

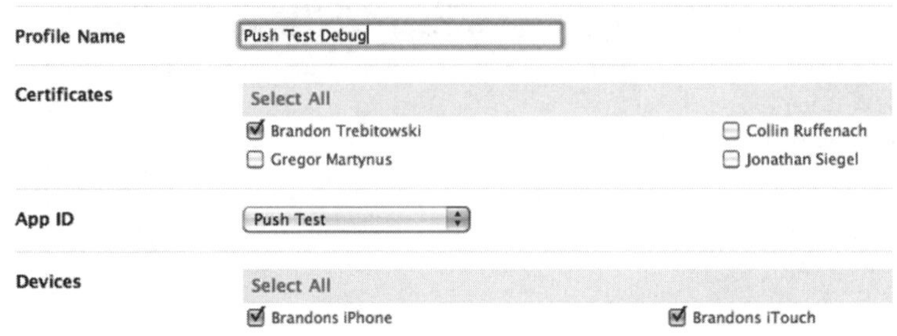

Profile Name	Push Test Debug	
Certificates	Select All	
	☑ Brandon Trebitowski	☐ Collin Ruffenach
	☐ Gregor Martynus	☐ Jonathan Siegel
App ID	Push Test	
Devices	Select All	
	☑ Brandons iPhone	☑ Brandons iTouch

Figure 17.7 Provisioning profile form

17.4.3 *The code for handling push notifications*

As we mentioned earlier, the code to handle push notifications is simple. You need to implement only three methods. We'll walk through each of these methods and discuss their use.

The first method is `application:didFinishLaunchingWithOptions:`. This method is already implemented for you in any application that you create. You need to add one line of code that tells your application to register for push notifications. The following code shows you how to do this:

```
- (BOOL)application:(UIApplication *)application
    didFinishLaunchingWithOptions:(NSDictionary *)launchOptions
    [[UIApplication sharedApplication]
        registerForRemoteNotificationTypes:( UIRemoteNotificationTypeAlert
        |UIRemoteNotificationTypeBadge | UIRemoteNotificationTypeSound)];
}
```

As you may have seen, your application will have other setup tasks in this method; we just wanted to show you the line of code that must be added to register for push notifications. This code tells the device that this application wants to receive push notifications in the form of alerts, badge numbers, and sounds. You can omit any of these properties if you choose not to send them.

You may wonder why you must do this more than once. The reason is that the token generated when you set up push notifications isn't guaranteed to be the same. You must touch base with Apple every time the application launches, to make sure everything is correct to receive notifications.

As you may have guessed, you must implement some delegate methods to react to events generated by this registration call. The following code shows a simple implementation of these methods:

```
- (void)application:(UIApplication *)app
didRegisterForRemoteNotificationsWithDeviceToken:(NSData *)devToken {
    [self sendProviderDeviceToken: devToken];
}

- (void)application:(UIApplication *)app
```

```
    didFailToRegisterForRemoteNotificationsWithError:(NSError *)err {
    NSLog(@"Error in registration. Error: %@", err);
}
```

The first method fires upon successful registration for push notifications. When you register to receive push notifications, your application communicates with Apple and receives back a unique device token. This token is used in all push communication with your device.

Notice that you call a method called `sendProviderDeviceToken:` in the class. This is a custom method you should create to send the device token to your push provider. You can do this via a web service interaction, as discussed in chapter 14. We'll discuss a simple method for creating a push provider in the next section.

The method `didFailToRegisterForRemoteNotificationsWithError:` is for error handling. It fires when there is an error registering for push notifications. If this method is called, your signing certificate is probably invalid, or the device doesn't have an internet connection. Make sure you put some code in this method to notify the user that there was a problem registering for notifications and they won't receive any at this point.

Now that the application has registered to receive push notifications, the next step is to handle the notifications when they come in. Apple gives you a few methods that let you control what happens when the user clicks the View button on the notification alert.

The first way to handle an incoming push notification is to implement the code in the `application:didFinishLaunchingWithOptions:` method. You should go this route if the notification was used to open the application and didn't pass any additional data. The following code shows a simple way to respond:

```
- (BOOL)application:(UIApplication *)application
    didFinishLaunchingWithOptions:(NSDictionary *)launchOptions
    application.applicationIconBadgeNumber = 0;
    [self getUpdatedDataFromServer];
}
```

The first and most important thing you must do here is to reset the badge number to 0. If you don't do this, the badge count will stay at whatever number was sent by the push notification. After that, you should perform any updates that are needed. The previous code assumes that some data has changed on the server and calls a method to download the updated data.

If the notification contains a custom dictionary, you must use the `application:didFinishLaunchingWithOptions:` method. The `options` variable is an `NSDictionary` containing the custom values passed in.

In the event that the user is currently running the application, you must implement the `application:didReceiveRemoteNotification:` method. It's called automatically and passed a dictionary containing all the standard information, including badge number, message, sound, and any custom dictionaries sent to the device.

After implementing the aforementioned methods, your application should be ready to receive push notifications. One final step in preparation is to format any audio files that will be played in response to a push notification.

17.4.4 Preparing audio files

As noted before, when a push notification is received, it can invoke the playback of an audio file included with your application. There are many interesting scenarios in which different audio files may be appropriate. For example, during a chess match, if a player receives a notification informing them that it's their turn, the system might play the default audio file. But if they receive a notification related to a piece being captured, the system might play some sort of battle sound effects. The more creative you get with this, the more value you add to your application.

The first thing to note when considering the audio file to play is the fact that the file must be stored in your application's main bundle directory. This is the root folder in which your applications files are stored. Your audio file could be any format but based on best practice, AIFF, WAV or CAF format is recommended and is limited to 30 seconds. In order to convert the audio file to one of these formats, use the `afconvert` command on your Mac.

To do this, open the terminal and navigate to the directory containing the audio file you wish to convert. Next, type the `afconvert` command followed by `-f caff -d LEI16 {INPUT} {OUTPUT}`. The following shows an example of using this command to convert the file track2.mp3 to track2.caf (see figure 17.8):

```
/usr/bin/afconvert -f caff -d LEI16 track2.mp3 track2.caf
```

Now that your application is ready to receive push notifications, we can discuss a method for creating a push notification provider using the PHP programming language.

17.5 Creating a push notification provider in PHP

Push notification providers can be implemented in many different ways. Plenty of open source scripts are available for you to use in your applications; but we'll show you a simple way to implement your own using PHP. This book isn't about PHP development, so

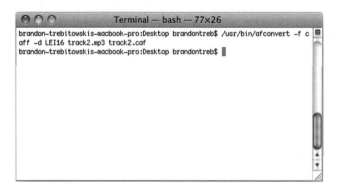

Figure 17.8 Converting audio files in the terminal

we won't go into much detail about the code. But we'll explain the process at a high level to help you understand it. The first step is to create an SSL certificate.

17.5.1 *Creating the SSL certificate*

Before you can begin coding, you must generate an SSL certificate to communicate with Apple. You'll create this certificate in the terminal using your push certificate and the private key that you generated in section 17.4.

Here are the steps required to generate this certificate:

1 Open your keychain.
2 Click My Certificates.
3 Click the arrow next to the Apple Development Push Services certificate, to expand it.
4 Ctrl-click the certificate, and select Export (see figure 17.9). Save this certificate as apns_cert.p12.
5 Do the same thing with the private key, and name it apns_key.p12. Note that you'll be prompted for a password when exporting. Make it something simple, because you'll need it later.
6 You need to merge the key and the certificate and convert the merged file to the .pem format. This allows your PHP application to load it. Open the terminal,

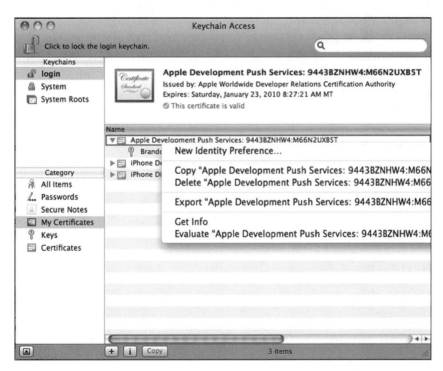

Figure 17.9   Exporting your Apple developer certificate

navigate to the location of your certificate and key, and type the following commands:

```
openssl pkcs12 -clcerts -nokeys -out apns_cert.pem -in apns_cert.p12
openssl pkcs12 -nocerts -out apns_key.pem -in apns_key.p12
```

7 To remove the passphrase on your apns_key.p12 file, type the following command:

```
openssl rsa -in apns_key.pem -out apns_key_unenc.pem
```

8 The last thing you need to do is merge these two files using the `cat` command. Type the following command into the terminal:

```
cat apns_cert.pem apns_key_unenc.pem > apns.pem
```

Make sure you keep track of all these files, because you may need to do this again if you change your APNS provider server.

NOTE   This process is exactly the same for development and production.

Now that you've generated this certificate, upload it to the server, and place it in the directory where you'll be putting the provider script.

17.5.2 *Implementing the PHP push notification provider*

A quick Google search reveals that quite a few free libraries are available to help you interface with Apple's push servers. Although it's recommended that you use a pre-made solution, we'll show you how to write your own.

The code for sending a push notification to Apple's server is simple. You need to make an SSL connection and send the data in the form of JSON. As we mentioned in section 17.3, JSON data is a form of a dictionary. Apple uses this data to create an NSDictionary that is sent to the device.

The following listing shows the code in PHP to send a push notification to Apple.

Listing 17.2   PHP code to send a push notification

```php
<?php
$message     = "Text to send";
$badgeCount = 1;
$sound = "default";
$payload['aps'] = array('alert' => $message,
    'badge' => $badgeCount,
    'sound' => $default);

$payload = json_encode($payload);

$deviceToken =
    'c902XXX556dc5581f2750XXX97ea8c496XXXa613fafXXX50cb356749XXX07cf1';

$apnsHost = 'gateway.sandbox.push.apple.com';          ◁┐  Establishes
$apnsPort = 2195;                                      ❶  connection
$apnsCert = 'apns-dev.pem';

$streamContext = stream_context_create();
stream_context_set_option($streamContext, 'ssl', 'local_cert', $apnsCert);
```

```
$apns = stream_socket_client('ssl://' . $apnsHost . ':' . $apnsPort,
    $error, $errorString, 2, STREAM_CLIENT_CONNECT, $streamContext);
$apnsMessage = chr(0) . chr(0) . chr(32) . pack('H*', str_replace(' ', '',
    $deviceToken)) . chr(0) . chr(strlen($payload)) . $payload;

fwrite($apns, $apnsMessage);

fclose($apns);
?>
```

Converts data into format required by Apple ❷

The first thing you see is a declaration of all the data that will be sent in the payload. This includes the text, badge count, and sound to play. If you specify a custom sound in your application, make sure it's in the correct format, as discussed in 17.4.2. Following this, you create the payload and convert it into the JSON format. You also see a declaration for the device token to which you'll send a notification.

Normally, you'll want to send data to every device that has registered for notifications. To achieve this, you must store the device tokens in a database when they're sent to you from your application. Then, you use a loop in your server code to send notifications to each token in the system.

Next, you establish a connection stream with Apple ❶. Notice that you connect to Apple's sandbox server. This is because you chose to send messages in debug mode. You should switch to Apple's production server when you're ready to submit your app to the store. Note the $appCert variable: this is the name of the SSL certificate you uploaded to the server. The code uses this certificate to establish a secure connection to Apple.

The next section is a little tricky ❷: it converts the packet to be sent into the binary interface required by Apple. You can find more information about this format in the documentation for push notifications. Finally, you write the data to the stream and close it.

The code for this provider is by no means complete for production. You must make several improvements. The first includes making a way for devices to send their tokens to your server. You need some sort of endpoint that takes a device token as a POST or GET request and stores it into a database. Also, you need to loop over these tokens and send out push notifications to everyone to which you intend to send a push notification. Finally, you need to create an interface to your provider that sends notifications when certain actions occur. These actions may be anything from a text message to notifying the user that it's their turn to move in a game.

17.6 Summary

In this chapter, we started by introducing the notifications and the system behind both local and push notifications. Now, you've learned how to create a local notification inside the alarm application, then get the application ready for Apple's push notification service. As you've seen, local and push notifications offer a simple solution to a complex problem. They give developers the ability to notify users while the application is running in the background and conserving the system resources on the iPhone and iPad.

Apple has provided a robust service that you can use free of charge. This service is the centerpiece of the entire push notification system and lets you send simple messages from a provider to a specific device with little delay.

The communication is done using a simple data format known as JSON. The JSON format allows you to send text messages, badge counts, sounds, and even custom data from your provider to any device with your application installed.

In order to receive push notifications, applications must be prepared and signed with a special signing certificate generated on Apple's website. You must create a signing certificate for use in development mode as well as debug mode when testing push notifications in your application. This certificate is used in conjunction with your private key to create the SSL certificate needed to communicate with Apple's servers.

The last thing to keep in mind when creating a push notification system is the architecture of your provider. We showed you how to create a simple provider using a few lines of PHP code. You may choose to use this as the core code of your system, or you can select from a growing number of open source solutions. In the next chapter, we'll discuss the MapKit framework, which offers an easy way to integrate fully functional and customizable maps into your application, complete with custom annotations.

The Map Kit framework

18

This chapter covers

- Adding a map to an application
- Reverse geocoding
- Annotating the map

With the Map Kit framework, you can add fully functional and customizable google maps to your application. This framework provides you with a simple view that you can add anywhere you want a map to appear.

In addition to adding the map, you can add custom annotations such as pins to show more information about a specific location. In this chapter we will look at how to add a map to an application first, then use the other functions available in Map Kit to find out the address and put the annotations on the map. Let's get started!

18.1 Adding a map view to an application

Adding a map view to an application is similar to adding any other view. You can either do it through Interface Builder or programmatically. The choice is up to you, depending on how you like to work with UI elements. We'll show you both methods.

The view that displays a map is called `MKMapView`. This class contains quite a bit of functionality including how to display the map, annotations, and user location.

We'll first discuss how to add an MKMapView through Interface Builder. After you add the map to the view, you'll connect it to an IBOutlet and set its delegate class.

18.1.1 Adding the map using Interface Builder

In this section we will build a View-based application containing the map view and name it SimpleMap. Before you start coding the MKMapView, you must first import Map-Kit.framework to your project. It provides all the libraries you need to work with maps.

To add a map to your view, your must first create an MKMapView IBOutlet in the class that will be using the map. The following listing shows how to include the MapKit to the header file in the view controller and define the outlet for the map view.

Listing 18.1 View Controller header file with map view

```
#import <UIKit/UIKit.h>
#import <MapKit/MapKit.h>

@interface SimpleMapViewController : UIViewController<MKMapViewDelegate> {
    IBOutlet MKMapView * theMap;
}

@property (nonatomic, retain) IBOutlet MKMapView * theMap;
@end
```

The first thing we want to point out is that you must import the MapKit.h header file. It's included in MapKit.framework and is needed for all Map Kit interaction. Second, your class implements the MKMapViewDelegate interface. It will allow this class to become the delegate of the MKMapView and receive messages from it. We'll discuss the delegate methods in detail later in this section. In addition to making a property, you should also synthesize the map property in the .m file.

Now that the IBOutlet has been declared, you need to add the MKMapView to the view in the nib file. To do this, open the nib file associated with the class that contains your IBOutlet. Select MKMapView from the Object Library, and drag it on to your view. Figure 18.1 shows what this object should look like.

When you drag the map onto your view, you can move and resize it however you like. Now that it's been added, you must connect it to the IBOutlet. To do this, click the file's owner object and open the Connection Inspector. Drag from the map outlet to the map view to make the connection.

The last thing you need to do is set the delegate of the MKMapView. To do this, right-click the map, and drag to the file's owner object. It

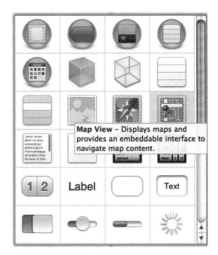

Figure 18.1 Adding an MKMapView to your view

should pop up a bubble that reads *delegate*. Click the word *delegate* to make the connection. Figure 18.2 shows what the Connection Inspector should look like after you've completed all these steps.

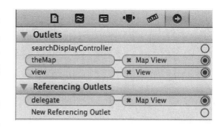

Figure 18.2 Connection Inspector for the **MKMapView** connections

As you can see, adding an MKMapView is very similar to adding UILabels, UITextFields, and other view elements. Next, we'll show you how to add one programmatically.

18.1.2 *Adding the map view programmatically*

As noted before, whether you add the map visually or with code is up to you. It depends completely on your preferences and organizational technique. The following example demonstrates how to add an MKMapView to your view controller's view using code:

```
- (void)viewDidLoad {
    [super viewDidLoad];

    MKMapView * map = [[MKMapView alloc] initWithFrame:
    CGRectMake(0, 0, 320, 480)];
    map.delegate  = self;
    [self.view addSubview:map];
}
```

This code is quite short. You create the map using a frame, set its delegate to your class, and add it to your class's view. As with any other view, modifying the frame passed to the map will alter its size and position.

18.1.3 *Controlling the map*

By default, a map gives the user some control. Without any additional code, they can scroll all over the world by scrolling the map. The map also lets users zoom in and out by using the pinch and tap gestures.

To navigate a map programmatically, you must specify a region. Doing this lets you move the map to a specified location. You also can set the zoom level.

Let's examine the region properties and methods for navigating a map. Table 18.1 discusses them and their uses.

Table 18.1 MKMapView region properties and methods for navigating the map

Task	Type	Description
region	Property	A property of type MKCoordinateRegion. This is made up of two float values for latitude and longitude and a float value for span. The span represents the zoom level. The larger the span, the lower the zoom level.

Table 18.1   `MKMapView` region properties and methods for navigating the map *(continued)*

Task	Type	Description
`setRegion:animated:`	Method	Sets the region on the map with the option to use an animation. If `animated` is set to `YES`, the map animates to the new location.
`centerCoordinate`	Property	Sets the coordinates on which to center the map without changing the current zoom level.
`setCenterCoordinate:animated:`	Method	Sets the coordinates on which to center the map without changing the current zoom level. Allows you to animate the map to the new coordinate.
`regionThatFits:`	Method	Adjusts the aspect ratio of the region so that is fits in the map's frame.

Continue with our app SimpleMap. In this section, we want to add a button titled Apple inside the view controller's nib file. When the user taps on the button, it will move the map's center from the current location to Apple's headquarters in Cupertino. The method in listing 18.2 shows how to create an `MKCoordinateRegion` and move the map to display it on the screen. Connect the bar button's action to the method - `(IBAction) apple:(id) sender` under the interface builder.

Listing 18.2   Controlling the zoom in and center on the map view

```
- (IBAction) apple:(id) sender {
    CLLocationCoordinate2D coords;
    coords.latitude  = 37.33188;
    coords.longitude = -122.029497;
    MKCoordinateSpan span = MKCoordinateSpanMake(0.002389, 0.005681);

    MKCoordinateRegion region = MKCoordinateRegionMake(coords, span);
    [theMap setRegion:region animated:YES];
}
```

The first thing you see here is the creation of a `CLLocationCoordinate2D`. This is a `struct` that holds two doubles for latitude and longitude. Next, you assign them to the Apple coordinates using the WGS 84 reference frame.

Following the coordinates, you create a span using the `MKCoordinateSpanMake` method. An `MKCoordinateSpan` is a `struct` made of two doubles that represent a delta for latitude and longitude. The span represents the amount of area to view and is used when setting the zoom level. A larger number tells the map to show a larger view area, resulting in the map zooming out. Similarly, a smaller number tells the map to show less area and causes it to zoom in.

After the coordinates and span have been initialized, you can create a region using the `MKCoordinateRegionMake` method. Finally, you set the region of the map to your newly created one and animate the transition.

In addition to controlling the map's location, you can control how the user can interact with it. Table 18.2 details these properties.

Table 18.2 `MKMapView` **user interaction properties**

Task	Description
`mapType`	The type of map to be displayed. The possible options for this variable are `MKMapTypeStandard`, `MKMapTypeSatellite`, and `MKMapTypeHybrid`. Updating this property automatically causes the map to change its view.
`zoomEnabled`	Determines if the user is able to zoom in. If set to `NO`, the map is fixed to a specific span.
`scrollEnabled`	When set to `YES`, the user is able to scroll around the map. If set to `NO`, the map becomes fixed on one location.

As we've mentioned, the `mapType` property allows you to display the map in three different ways. Most likely, you'll want to make this configurable by the user, because preferences vary about how the map should display. In the SimpleMap's view controller, let's add in a segmented controller to the navigation bar as shown in Figure 18.3. There are three choices for map type. We will use this segmented controller to allow user change the map type. Now let's add a new function to the view controller in charge of the segmented controller's action - (IBAction) changeMapType:(id)sender; Make sure it's connected to the segmented controller under the nib file. Then define the function inside the view controller's implementation file as below:

```
- (IBAction) changeMapType:(id)sender {
        UISegmentedControl *control = (UISegmentedControl *)sender;

        [self.theMap setMapType:control.selectedSegmentIndex];
}
```

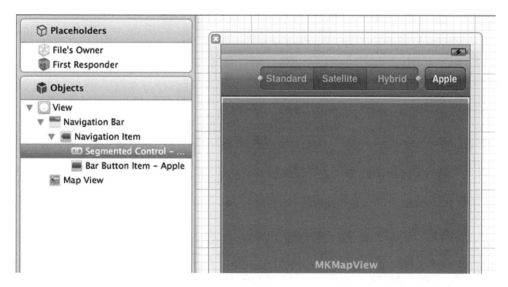

Figure 18.3   Layout of MKMapView with segmented controller set up with appropriate options in Interface Builder

Figure 18.4 `mapTypes`: **(from left to right)** `MKMapTypeStandard`, `MKMapTypeSatellite`, `MKMapTypeHybrid`

Build and launch the app after all the changes you will see the difference between the map types as shown in figure 18.4. As you can see, you have quite a bit of control over how the map looks. The standard map view looks much like a road map that you use for navigation. This is often the most useful of the map types.

The other two are similar. The only difference between them is the road names that appear in the hybrid view in addition to the satellite photos.

Now that you have a grasp of the basic map controls, we'll discuss something a little more interesting: reverse geocoding.

18.2   *Reverse geocoding*

Reverse geocoding is the process of finding an address, an area, or other information about a given location based on its latitude and longitude. Apple has provided a simple interface for retrieving this information.

The class used for reverse geocoding is called `MKReverseGeocoder`. It's a powerful class with a simple interface. In addition to its `init` method, it only has two other methods and two properties. Table 18.3 lists these and explains their use.

Table 18.3 `MKReverseGeocoder` **class methods and properties**

Task	Type	Description
`delegate`	Property	Specifies the delegate of the reverse geocoder. The delegate receives messages from the geocoder, including errors and location information.
`coordinate`	Property	The coordinate for which the reverse geocoder is retrieving data.
`start:`	Method	Invokes the reverse geocoding. When this method completes, it calls one of the two delegate methods for this class.
`querying`	Property	A Boolean variable to indicate whether the reverse geocoder is currently retrieving data.
`cancel:`	Method	Cancels the request for data.

To create a new `MKReverseGeocoder` object, you must call its `initWithCoordinate` method. This method sets the geocoder's coordinate property to the incoming value and prepares it to receive the data. The following code shows how to initialize an `MKReverseGeocoder` given the center of a map:

```
- (IBAction) getAddress:(id) sender {
    MKReverseGeocoder * geoCoder = [[MKReverseGeocoder alloc]
        initWithCoordinate:theMap.centerCoordinate];
    [geoCoder setDelegate:self];
    [geoCoder start];
}
```

You need to make sure you set the geocoder's `delegate` property to something that implements the `MKReverseGeocoderDelegate` protocol. Otherwise, you won't see the data that gets received.

Only two methods must be implemented as part of the `MKReverseGeocoder-Delegate` protocol: `reverseGeocoder:didFindPlacemark:` and `reverseGeocoder:didFailWithError:`.

The `didFailWithError` method is similar to any other error delegate method. It's passed a reference to the geocoder as well as an error object containing information about the failure.

There are two cases for a failure. The first occurs when the device isn't connected to the internet. Because information is retrieved from Google's web servers, a device must be connected to the internet to be able to access it. The second case for failure occurs when no data is available for the given coordinate. This may occur when the user requests information about a remote location or the ocean.

Upon a successful retrieval of data, the `didFindPlacemark` method is called with a reference to the geocoder and an `MKPlacemark` object. An `MKPlacemark` is a simple object that contains specific information about a given location. This information is stored inside a property called `addressDictionary`. In addition to this dictionary, all the values are parsed out and put into their own properties of the class. Here's some simple code to output the placemark data in the form of an `NSDictionary`:

```
-(void)reverseGeocoder:(MKReverseGeocoder *)geocoder
    didFindPlacemark:(MKPlacemark *)placemark {
    NSLog(@"%@",placemark.addressDictionary);
}
```

Figure 18.5 shows the output of the method.

As you can see, the dictionary contains quite a bit of information about a location in Glendale, Arizona. In addition to this dictionary, all these keys are made available through properties of an `MKPlacemark`. For example, if you just want to output the country, you can call `placemark.country`, and it will return the string "US".

Keep in mind that Google limits the number of reverse geocode lookups. This is often believed to be by IP address. Make sure you save the retrieved data in order to cut down on duplicated calls.

Now that you've seen how to retrieve data for a specific location, we'll show you how to drop pins on the map to display that data.

Figure 18.5   Reverse geocoder output

18.3   *Annotating the map*

As you may have seen with applications such as Maps, developers can annotate an MKMapView. By dropping "pins" on the map, you can display additional information to the user about a given location. This may be anything from geographic details to the spot where they parked their car.

Apple gives you considerable control when creating annotations for the map. You can use the built-in pins or create your own. We'll explore both methods and show you how to annotate a map using the MKAnnotationView class.

At first glance, the design pattern used when annotating a map seems strange. But when you start writing code for it, you'll quickly understand why it's needed. You add an annotation to the map by calling the addAnnotation method of MKMapView. This adds the annotation to a queue to be displayed on the map. When the map needs to display the annotation, it calls the `viewForAnnotation` method in the delegate class. This is where you tell the map how to display your annotation.

Apple recommends that you add all your annotations at once, even if they won't be seen. They aren't added to the map until they're needed in the view. This saves memory, because the map reuses each of the annotation UI elements.

18.3.1 Adding basic map annotations

If you only plan to display simple pins in your application, the basic map annotations are the way to go. They're simple to use, and you can quickly integrate them with any application. The example code in this section uses the code you created in the reverse geocoding section as a base.

The first thing you must do when annotating a map is make the calling class implement the `MKMapViewDelegate` protocol. To add annotations to the map, you need to implement only one of the delegate methods. The following listing shows how you can use the reverse geocoder code to drop a pin at the center of the map.

Listing 18.3 Dropping a pin on the center of the map

```
- (IBAction) dropPin:(id) sender {                          ⟵ Starts
    MKReverseGeocoder * geoCoder = [[MKReverseGeocoder alloc]    geocoder
        initWithCoordinate:theMap.centerCoordinate];            when button
    [geoCoder setDelegate:self];                                is pressed
    [geoCoder start];
}
                                                           ❶ Adds placemark
- (void)reverseGeocoder:(MKReverseGeocoder *)geocoder     ⟵   to map
    didFindPlacemark:(MKPlacemark *)placemark {
    [mapView addAnnotation:placemark];
}

- (void)reverseGeocoder:(MKReverseGeocoder *)geocoder     ⟵ Handles errors
    didFailWithError:(NSError *)error {
    UIAlertView * alert = [[UIAlertView alloc] initWithTitle:@"Error"
                    message:@"Unable to get address"
                    delegate:nil
                    cancelButtonTitle:@"OK"
                    otherButtonTitles:nil];
    [alert show];
    [alert release];
}

- (MKAnnotationView *)mapView:(MKMapView *)mapView viewForAnnotation:(id
    <MKAnnotation>)annotation {                                    ⟵

    MKPinAnnotationView *aView = [[MKPinAnnotationView alloc]
            initWithAnnotation:annotation reuseIdentifier:@"location"];
    aView.animatesDrop = YES;                            Tells map how to
    return aView;                                        display annotation
}
```

As you can see, you add little code to the geocoder example to annotate the map. In the first new code, `MKPlaceMark` conforms to the `MKAnnotation` protocol and can be

Figure 18.6   Annotated map

used to add an annotation to the map ❶. In this case, it uses the address as the title of the annotation. When the geocoder finds a location, it adds it to the map using the `addAnnotation` method of your `MKMapView` object.

Now that the annotation has been added, the map queries your delegate to find out how to display it. In this case, you create a new object of type `MKPinAnnotationView`. This is a simple view, similar to the one used in the Maps application that comes on the iPhone. When you tap the pin, it displays the address of the location in a pop-up. Figure 18.6 shows what the annotated map should look like after dropping a pin.

All the data for the pin, including how the pin looks, is fully customizable. We'll discuss how to do this customization in the next section.

18.3.2   *Adding custom map annotations*

Adding a custom annotation isn't much different than creating custom `UITableView-Cells`. You create a view that extends the parent and return that in the `viewFor-Annotation` method. In this case, the parent is `MKAnnotationView`.

Before we dive into the code for creating your own view, let's discuss some of the properties available for use in customization. Table 18.4 details some of the important `MKAnnotationView` properties associated with customization.

Table 18.4 `MKAnnotationView` properties

Property	Description
`enabled`	A Boolean value that determines whether an annotation is enabled. If this is set to `NO`, the annotation won't respond to various events such as touching.
`image`	The graphic representing the annotation. The `MKPin-AnnotationView` is a view with the graphic set to an image of a pin. This is probably the most useful property in customization.
`highlighted`	You should never manually set this property. It's set by the map view and is accessed by calling `isHighlighted`. It's set to `YES` when the user touches the annotation.
`centerOffset`	Tells the annotation where to center. By default, it centers on the point on the map. This property is useful when you want to change where the annotation is with respect to the map point.
`calloutOffset`	Determines the offset of the callout when the user taps the annotation. By default, this is (0,0) and is placed on the top center point of the annotation's frame.
`canShowCallout`	Determines whether the annotation shows the callout when the user taps it.
`rightCalloutAccessoryView`	View on the right side of the callout. Usually used to display additional information or link to another place in the app. This is usually a `UIButton` with type `UIButtonTypeDetailDisclosure`.
`leftCalloutAccessoryView`	View on the left side of the callout. Usually used to display additional information or link to another place in the app.

As you can see, Apple gives you considerable control over annotations while preserving their basic use. Note that `MKPinAnnotationView` is an `MKAnnotationView` with the `image` property set to an image of a pin.

To create your own `MKAnnotationView`, you'll also need to create a class that implements the `MKAnnotation` protocol. The `MKAnnotation` object will be used to populate the information for the `MKAnnotationView`.

In the following example, you'll plot custom views for the locations of Google and Apple on an `MKMapView`. After the map has been added to your view, you must create the `MKAnnotation` object. The next listing shows the code for the header file.

Listing 18.4 MyAnnotation.h

```
#import <MapKit/MapKit.h>

typedef enum AnnotationType {
    Apple,
    Google
} AnnotationType;

@interface MyAnnotation : NSObject<MKAnnotation> {
    CLLocationCoordinate2D coordinate;
```

❶ **Struct containing types of annotations**

❷ **Declares class properties**

```
        NSString * title;
        NSString * subtitle;
        AnnotationType annotationType;
}

@property (nonatomic, readonly) CLLocationCoordinate2D coordinate;
@property (nonatomic, retain) NSString * title;
@property (nonatomic, retain) NSString * subtitle;
@property (nonatomic) AnnotationType annotationType;

- (id)initWithCoords:(CLLocationCoordinate2D) coords
    andType:(AnnotationType) type;

@end
```

❸ **Declares init method**

Because your map will have different annotations, you must come up with a way to specify which image to display. One solution is to give your annotations a type. In this case, the possible types are Google and Apple. You define an enum that differentiates the annotation types **❶**.

The most important code for this class implements the MKAnnotation protocol **❷**. To fulfill the requirements of being an MKAnnotation, your class must have a read-only property named coordinate. This is the coordinate location of the annotation on the map and will be used to determine where to display it.

Because the coordinate property is defined to be read-only, you need a way to set it. The best way to do this is to set it in the class init method. The code defines the init method that you use to build your objects **❸**. It takes a coordinate and an annotation type.

In addition to the coordinate property, you can optionally define title and subtitle properties for your MKAnnotation. These are displayed in the callout when the user taps your annotation. The implementation of this class is fairly simple and is shown in the following listing.

Listing 18.5   MKAnnotation.m

```
@implementation MyAnnotation

@synthesize title;
@synthesize subtitle;
@synthesize annotationType;

- (id)initWithCoords:(CLLocationCoordinate2D) coords
    andType:(AnnotationType) type {
    if(self = [super init]) {
        coordinate = coords;
        self.annotationType = type;
    }
    return self;
}

- (CLLocationCoordinate2D) coordinate {
    return coordinate;
}

- (void) dealloc {
```

Initialization method

Getter method for coordinate property

```
        [title release];
        [subtitle release];
        [super dealloc];
}
```

Notice that you don't synthesize the `coordinate` property. This is because it's read-only and is set only when the object is initialized. As noted earlier, this is the only required method in this class.

Now that you've created your custom `MKAnnotation` object, you need to create the view that will use it. The view must be a subclass of `MKAnnotationView` and doesn't have any required methods or properties. Note that it's a standard view, so you can add any UI components to it that you want. The header file for your view looks like this:

```
#import <MapKit/MapKit.h>
#import "MyAnnotation.h"
@interface MyAnnotationView : MKAnnotationView{
}
- (id)initWithAnnotation:(id )annotation reuseIdentifier:
    (NSString *)reuseIdentifier;
@end
```

Notice that you import MyAnnotation.h. You'll need this in your `init` method to determine the type of annotation to be displayed. Other than that, there should be nothing new here. The next listing shows this class's implementation.

Listing 18.6 MyAnnotationView.m

```
#import "MyAnnotationView.h"
@implementation MyAnnotationView

- (id)initWithAnnotation:(id )annotation reuseIdentifier:
    (NSString *)reuseIdentifier {
    MyAnnotation * myAnnotation = (MyAnnotation*)annotation;

    if([myAnnotation annotationType] == Apple) {
        self = [super initWithAnnotation:myAnnotation
                    reuseIdentifier:reuseIdentifier];
            self.image = [UIImage imageNamed:@"sign-apple.png"];
    } else if([myAnnotation annotationType] == Google) {
        self = [super initWithAnnotation:myAnnotation
                    reuseIdentifier:reuseIdentifier];
        self.image = [UIImage imageNamed:@"sign-google.png"];
    }

    return self;
}
@end
```

First, you cast the incoming annotation to the type you declared earlier. This lets you access the `annotationType` property. Based on this type, you set the `image` property of your `MKAnnotationView`.

You may be tempted to set the frame of your view here. This isn't needed because the frame is automatically changed based on the size of the image.

After these classes have been created, integrating them into your map is simple. You must first add the annotations to the map, similarly to the next listing.

Listing 18.7   Adding custom annotations to the map

```
- (void)viewDidLoad {
    [super viewDidLoad];

    CLLocationCoordinate2D coords;
    coords.latitude  = 37.331689;
    coords.longitude = -122.030731;
    MKCoordinateSpan span = MKCoordinateSpanMake(0.011209, 0.22597);

    MKCoordinateRegion region = MKCoordinateRegionMake(coords, span);
    [theMap setRegion:region animated:YES];

    CLLocationCoordinate2D appleCoords;
    appleCoords.latitude = 37.331689;
    appleCoords.longitude = -122.030731;
    MyAnnotation * apple = [[MyAnnotation alloc] initWithCoords:
            appleCoords andType:Apple];
    [apple setTitle:@"Apple Inc."];
    [apple setSubtitle:@"Cupertino, CA"];
    [theMap addAnnotation:apple];
    [apple release];

    CLLocationCoordinate2D googleCoords;
    googleCoords.latitude = 37.421793;
    googleCoords.longitude = -122.084434;
    MyAnnotation * google = [[MyAnnotation alloc] initWithCoords:
            googleCoords andType:Google];
    [google setTitle:@"Google Inc."];
    [google setSubtitle:@"Mountain View, CA"];
    [mapView addAnnotation:google];
    [google release];
}
```

Annotations:
- **Centers map over point of interest**
- ❶ **Gets coordinates for annotation**
- **Creates annotation and sets properties**

As you can see, adding custom annotations to the map isn't much different than adding a standard annotation. You set up the coordinates to denote the location of your annotation ❶, and then you initialize the MKAnnotation with these coordinates along with the type of annotation to be displayed.

Next, you set the title and subtitle. As previously noted, these properties are displayed on the annotation's callout when the user taps it. Finally, you add the annotation to the map by calling the addAnnotation method of the MKMapView.

Now that the annotations have been added to the map, the last thing you must do is implement the viewForAnnotation delegate method of the MKMapViewDelegate:

```
- (MKAnnotationView *)mapView:(MKMapView *)mapView viewForAnnotation:(id
    <MKAnnotation>)annotation {
    MyAnnotationView *aView = [[MyAnnotationView alloc]
            initWithAnnotation:annotation reuseIdentifier:@"location"];
    [aView setEnabled:YES];
    [aView setCanShowCallout:YES];
    return aView;
}
```

This code is similar to the code you saw earlier for this method. The only difference is, you create your custom annotation view rather than the built-in pin annotation view. This lets you display custom annotations when the map asks for them. Figure 18.7 shows what the map looks like with custom annotations.

18.4 Summary

You've now seen how easy it is to integrate fully functional maps into any application. The Map Kit framework is powerful but simple to use.

To add a map to any application, drag and drop it onto your view in Interface Builder and connect it using an IBOutlet. This gives you complete control over the look, feel, and behavior of the map.

If you require additional data to be added to the map, the Map Kit framework provides a great mechanism for adding annotations. These can either be the built-in pins or completely customized to suit your application's needs.

In the next chapter, we'll discuss the Store Kit framework and how to integrate it with your applications. It may seem complex to use, but it can be a great way to make a profit in the App Store. You'll use it to support in-app purchases.

Figure 18.7 `MKMapView` **with custom annotations**

In-app purchasing
using Store Kit

19

This chapter covers

- Setting up a sandbox testing environment
- Creating a simple store

This chapter will be structured a little differently than ones prior. Rather than going over the Store Kit API, we'll demonstrate the topics for creating an in-app store by walking through a basic example. We'll look at how to set up a sandbox testing environment (to mimic selling actual items) and work through how to build the store interface.

The Store Kit API allows you to sell various items within your application. The items sold are called *products*. These products may be virtual goods, services, or even subscriptions. All transactions are processed securely through iTunes without the user ever having to enter their payment information on the device. There are countless ways to add a store to your application, and how you do so depends entirely on your needs. In this chapter, we'll discuss one of those ways and give you the tools to implement your own store.

The example store you'll be creating will let users purchase iPhone backgrounds on their phone. Users will browse through the available products and purchase the ones they want to keep. When a background has been purchased, it will be saved to the user's camera roll so the user can use it on their device.

19.1 Setting up a sandbox testing environment

Prior to building a store into your application, you must set up the products and testing environment on iTunes Connect. This will allow you to simulate payment processing without charging your iTunes account each time.

The major prerequisite for setting up products is that you must first add the application you want to test with to iTunes Connect at http://itunesconnect.apple.com. To do this, you must go through all the steps to create a new app under Manage your applications. Keep in mind that you shouldn't upload a binary, so your application isn't accidently submitted to Apple before it's ready.

The sample application we've uploaded for this test is called RS Wallpaper. It has the bundle identifier com.rightsprite.wallpaper. You'll want to change this to something unique to you. It's important to use this reverse domain style when adding your bundle ID, because this is what iTunes uses to recognize your application for in-app purchase. For example, if your website is www.foobar.com, and your application is called baz, your bundle identifier should be com.foobar.baz.

19.1.1 Creating an iTunes test user

In order to test in Apple's sandbox (testing) environment, you must first set up a test iTunes account in iTunes Connect. The sandbox account functions exactly like a live one except that it doesn't bill your iTunes account. Attempting to log into the sandbox with your normal iTunes account will cause your iTunes account to become invalid.

To create a test user, navigate to the Manage Users section in iTunes Connect. Figure 19.1 shows what this link looks like.

When you're inside, iTunes Connect asks what type of user you want to create. Make sure you select In App Purchase Test User, as shown in figure 19.2.

In App Purchase Test User

Figure 19.2   In App Purchase Test User

Figure 19.1   Managing users in iTunes Connect

Fill out the information and click Save.

First Name :

Last Name :

Email Address :

Password :

Confirm Password :

Secret Question :

Secret Answer :

Date of Birth : Month ⬍ Day ⬍

Select iTunes Store : Select ⬍

Figure 19.3   The form to add a new test user

This user is created for the sole purpose of testing the sandbox store. Apple is picky about the information you use here, so be sure you don't use the information from your current iTunes account. If you don't have a ton of email addresses to test with, a good trick is to use Gmail. If you have a Gmail account, you can add +1, +2, and so on after your existing address to a create new one. For example, if your email address is manningreader@gmail.com, you can register for new accounts with the address manningreader+1@gmail.com, and all the mail will forward to manningreader@gmail.com.

After you click the Add New User button, you're presented with the form shown in figure 19.3.

A new test user must be created for each territory you want to test with. For example, if you want to test products in the U.S. App Store and the Chinese App Store, you'll need to create two separate users. That way, each user will see their localized version of your product. If you don't specify, your purchase will be available in all the app stores. After you've added all your test users, navigate back to the iTunes Connect homepage.

19.1.2 Adding products

You can sell three types of products in your store:

- *Consumable*—A product that is purchased every time the user needs it. An example of a consumable product might be a power-up in a video game.
- *Non-consumable*—A product that a user purchases only once and gets to keep. An example is a downloadable song or image.
- *Subscription*—Consumable or non-consumable. This gives you the ability to let users renew their subscriptions as frequently as you want. Because this is the case, Apple doesn't provide a record of whether a subscription is valid. You must provide this on your own server.

For this example, you'll create non-consumable products. After the user has purchased a background, they will forever have access to it without any additional charge. Follow these steps:

1 Select Manage Your In App Purchases from the iTunes Connect homepage, as shown in figure 19.4.

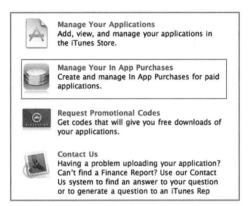

Figure 19.4   Choosing Manage Your In App Purchases in iTunes Connect

2 On the next screen, click the Create New button, as shown in figure 19.5. You see all the applications you've added to iTunes Connect.

Figure 19.5   Click the Create New button.

3 Select the application that will be using in-app purchasing. Doing so takes you to a page where you'll add your first product.

4 You need to fill out three sections. The first contains the pricing details and product type. Figure 19.6 shows the information to add for one of the example background products.

The first field is Reference Name. This is a plain text name that identifies the product in iTunes Connect; it's only for your reference and is never seen by the user.

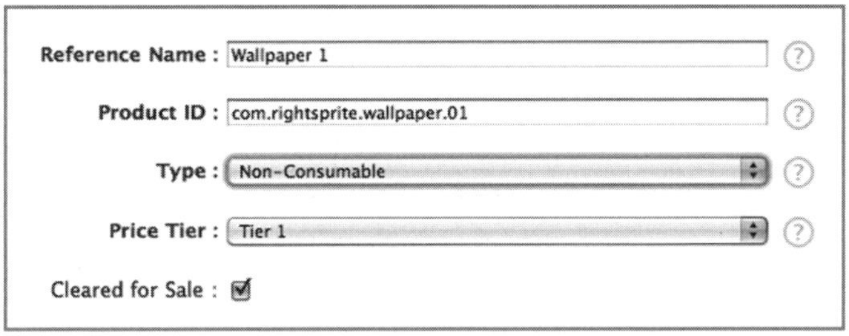

Reference Name :	Wallpaper 1	?
Product ID :	com.rightsprite.wallpaper.01	?
Type :	Non-Consumable	?
Price Tier :	Tier 1	?
Cleared for Sale :	☑	

Figure 19.6   Setting up wallpaper product pricing in iTunes Connect

The Product ID is similar to your application identifier and must be unique for each product. You'll use this identifier to look up products in the store code later in the chapter.

For the Type value, choose Non-Consumable. This is the most appropriate for the type of application you're creating.

Finally, set the price tier and clear the product for sale. Apple provides a link so that you see what price corresponds with which tier. For this example, use Tier 1, which is $.99.

5 In the next section, you create the product title and description. You need to create a localized name and description for every language in which you intend to offer your product. Figure 19.7 shows the information you should add for the first test product.

You don't have to add a localized name and description for every language, but doing so is a good idea if you want to increase profits in countries that don't speak English.

6 In the last section, you can add a screenshot. This is important only when you're ready to submit the in-app purchase to Apple for approval, so you can do it later.

7 Click the Save button.

You need to add a separate product in iTunes Connect for each thing you want to sell. For this example, add two more products. You can call your products whatever you want, but make sure you keep their product IDs consistent with your application. In this case, use the IDs com.rightsprite.wallpaper.02 and com.rightsprite.wallpaper.03. After you submit all of your products, your in-app purchase screen should look something like figure 19.8.

Note that Apple must approve your products before you can sell them in your application. When you've fully tested your products, you must come back to this screen and approve each product. Then, they will go into review by Apple. The review process for products is similar to the review process for applications and follows the same guidelines as to what's appropriate. It can take several days for your products to be approved.

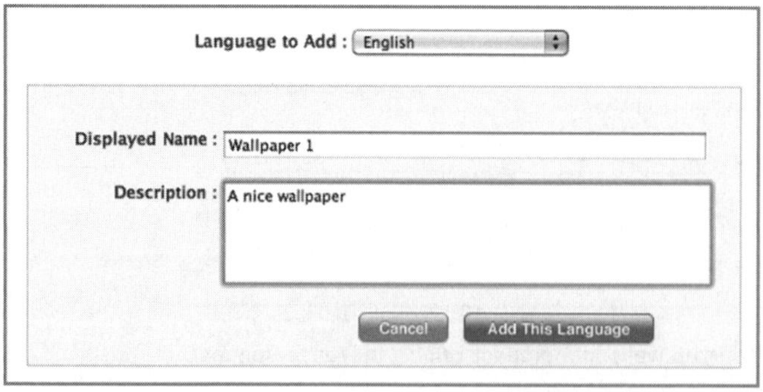

Figure 19.7   Creating a test product name and description in iTunes Connect

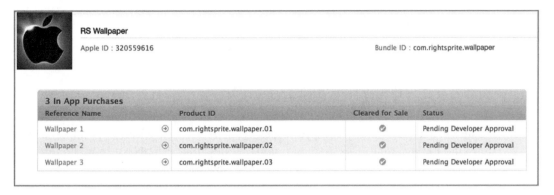

| 3 In App Purchases | | | | |
Reference Name		Product ID	Cleared for Sale	Status
Wallpaper 1	⊕	com.rightsprite.wallpaper.01	⊘	Pending Developer Approval
Wallpaper 2	⊕	com.rightsprite.wallpaper.02	⊘	Pending Developer Approval
Wallpaper 3	⊕	com.rightsprite.wallpaper.03	⊘	Pending Developer Approval

Figure 19.8   Your in-app purchase list in iTunes Connect

19.2   *Creating a simple store interface*

Generally, you'll add a store to an existing application to improve functionality. This is why, for this example, you'll create a basic store without any additional bells and whistles. It will use the Navigation-Based Application template and display a list of products in a `UITableView`. Check out figure 19.9 for an idea of what the application will look like.

19.2.1   *Creating the demo app*

To get started, open Xcode and create a new navigation-based project. Name the project WPStore. Then, add the Store Kit framework to your project by right-clicking Frameworks and selecting Existing Framework from the menu that displays.

Now, you need to declare the class properties and methods that will be used in the application. Open RootViewController.h, and add the code in the following listing.

Figure 19.9   The wallpaper store interface as shown on the iPhone

Listing 19.1   RootViewConroller.h

```objc
#import <StoreKit/StoreKit.h>

@interface RootViewController : UITableViewController
<SKProductsRequestDelegate,SKPaymentTransactionObserver> {
    NSMutableArray * products;
    NSMutableArray * transactionHistory;
}

@property (nonatomic, retain) NSMutableArray * transactionHistory;
```

```
- (void) requestProductData;
- (void) completeTransaction: (SKPaymentTransaction *)transaction;
- (void) restoreTransaction: (SKPaymentTransaction *)transaction;
- (void) failedTransaction: (SKPaymentTransaction *)transaction;
- (void) recordTransaction:(SKPaymentTransaction * )transaction;
- (void) provideContent:(NSString * )productIdentifier;

@end
```

The first thing you see here is that the class imports the Store Kit header file. This gives you access to all the objects and properties needed for the application to implement a store. Following that, the class signature states that the class implements the SKProductsRequestDelegate and SKPaymentTransactionObserver protocols. We'll explain what each of these does further on in this section.

The class has two properties. The first is an NSMutableArray of products. This is the product array that populates the UITableView. The other property stores transaction history when a user purchases items. The last bit of code declares the methods you're using in the class. We'll explain these methods in detail when you implement them in this section.

19.2.2 Adding Store Kit interface

Now that you've created the header file, you're ready to implement the initialization method. Open RootViewController.m, and add the code in the following listing to the viewDidLoad method.

Listing 19.2   viewDidLoad method of RootViewController.m

```
#import "RootViewController.h"
#import "WallpaperViewController.h"

@implementation RootViewController

@synthesize transactionHistory;

- (void)viewDidLoad {                                    Sets payment ❶
    [super viewDidLoad];                                 observer to class

    [[SKPaymentQueue defaultQueue] addTransactionObserver:self];  ⟵

    products = [[NSMutableArray alloc] init];    ⟵— Initializes products array

    NSArray *paths = NSSearchPathForDirectoriesInDomains
                (NSDocumentDirectory, NSUserDomainMask, YES);
    NSString *documentsDirectory = [paths objectAtIndex:0];
    NSString * path = [documentsDirectory stringByAppendingPathComponent:
            @"history.plist"];
                                                          Builds path to
    self.transactionHistory =                    Initializes  transaction
    [NSMutableArray arrayWithContentsOfFile:    transaction  history file ❷
            path];                               history

    if(!transactionHistory) {
        NSMutableArray *_transactionHistory = [[NSMutableArray alloc]
                init];
        self.transactionHistory = _transactionHistory;
```

```
        [_transactionHistory release];
    }

    [self requestProductData];
}
```

The first thing you may notice is you import a file called WallpaperViewController.h. Don't worry about it at the moment; you'll create it later in the section.

You add the class as the transaction observer ❶. This means the class implements the SKPaymentTransactionObserver protocol as well as the delegate methods. The methods that must be implemented for this protocol are completeTransaction, restoreTransaction, and failedTransaction. These methods are called in response to various actions received from the Store Kit framework.

Next, you retrieve the transaction history. Whenever transactions are made, it's a good idea to store them somewhere in your application or on a server. You store the products that are purchased in a simple plist file and attempt to load the plist file into memory ❷. If no history exists, this array is initialized to be empty.

The last line in the code starts the process of retrieving your products from Apple. Although you don't do it here, it's a good idea to display a loading message to the user at this point while they wait for the product list to download. The next listing shows the code for this method.

Listing 19.3 Requesting product information

```
- (void) requestProductData {
  SKProductsRequest *request= [[SKProductsRequest alloc]
   initWithProductIdentifiers:[NSSet setWithObjects:
      @"com.rightsprite.wallpaper.01",
      @"com.rightsprite.wallpaper.02",
      @"com.rightsprite.wallpaper.03",nil]];
  request.delegate = self;
  [request start];
}
- (void)productsRequest:(SKProductsRequest *)request
  didReceiveResponse:(SKProductsResponse *)response{

  NSArray *myProducts = response.products;
  for(SKProduct * product in myProducts) {
    [products addObject:product];
  }

  [request autorelease];
  [self.tableView reloadData];
}
```

You start by creating the product request. Notice that these are the product IDs you registered in section 19.1.2. You're basically asking iTunes for information about the products with these identifiers. If you wanted to make your application a little more dynamic, you could load the identifier list from a server. We won't go into detail about that because it's out of the scope of this book.

After the request has been created, the code starts the process of retrieving the product information from iTunes. When the information has been retrieved, the delegate method `didReceiveResponse` is called with the data. You loop over the products and add them to the global products array. That way, you can populate the `UITableView` with their names and descriptions.

Finally, you reload the `UITableView` with the product data. The last thing you need to do to see the product list is to implement the delegate methods for the `UITableView`. Add the code from the following listing to your RootViewController.

Listing 19.4   Delegate methods for `UITableView`

```
- (NSInteger)tableView:(UITableView *)tableView
    numberOfRowsInSection:(NSInteger)section {
    return [products count];
}

- (UITableViewCell *)tableView:(UITableView *)tableView
    cellForRowAtIndexPath:(NSIndexPath *)indexPath {

    static NSString *CellIdentifier = @"Cell";

    UITableViewCell *cell = [tableView
        dequeueReusableCellWithIdentifier:CellIdentifier];
    if (cell == nil) {
        cell = [[[UITableViewCell alloc]
          initWithStyle:UITableViewCellStyleSubtitle
          reuseIdentifier:CellIdentifier] autorelease];
    }

    SKProduct * product = [products objectAtIndex:indexPath.row];
    cell.textLabel.text = [NSString stringWithFormat:@"$%.2f %@",
            product.price.doubleValue, product.localizedTitle];
    cell.detailTextLabel.text = product.localizedDescription;
    cell.accessoryType = UITableViewCellAccessoryDisclosureIndicator;

    return cell;
}
```

This code is straightforward: you've already seen how to populate a `UITableView` from an `NSArray`. Note that you populate the cell's text label and detail text label from the localized product information.

At this point, you should be able to see your list of products when you run the application. If you intend to test now, make sure you comment out the line to import WallpaperViewController.h, because you haven't yet created it.

19.2.3   *Creating individual wallpaper product*

The next step is to display the wallpapers to the user when they tap on a row in the table. This will allow them to see the wallpaper as well as purchase it. Before you create the view controller you'll use, let's implement the `didSelectRowAtIndexPath` method of the `UITableView` to push the new view onto the navigation stack. The next listing details this code.

Listing 19.5　`didSelectRowAtIndexPath` method for the `UITableView`

```
- (void)tableView:(UITableView *)tableView
    didSelectRowAtIndexPath:(NSIndexPath *)indexPath {

    SKProduct * product = [products objectAtIndex:indexPath.row];

    WallpaperViewController * wpViewController = [[WallpaperViewController
    alloc] initWithNibName:@"WallpaperViewController" bundle:
    [NSBundle mainBundle]];

    wpViewController.product = product;

    [self.navigationController pushViewController:wpViewController
            animated:YES];

    [wpViewController release];
}
```

You first get the product associated with the selected row. This is then passed to the `WallpaperView-Controller` class after initialization. The `Wallpaper-ViewController` uses this product to determine which wallpaper image to display. Finally, the view is pushed onto the navigation view stack.

You'll now create the `WallpaperViewController`. Figure 19.10 shows what its view will look like.

To create this object, add a new `UIViewController` subclass called `WallpaperViewController` to your project. Make sure you select the With XIB for User Interface check box.

Before creating the interface, you need to create the `IBOutlets` and `IBAction`. Open WallpaperView-Controller.h, and add the code in the following listing.

Figure 19.10　Previewing the product in the wallpaper view

Listing 19.6　WallpaperViewController.h

```
#import <UIKit/UIKit.h>
#import <StoreKit/StoreKit.h>

@interface WallpaperViewController : UIViewController {
    IBOutlet UIImageView * imageView;
    SKProduct * product;
}

@property (nonatomic, retain) IBOutlet UIImageView * imageView;
@property (nonatomic, retain) SKProduct * product;

- (IBAction) buttonClicked:(id) sender;

@end
```

As you may have guessed, you only need an `IBOutlet` for the `UIImageView` that will display the selected wallpaper. You set its `image` property from the `product` property after the view has been initialized.

In addition to the `IBOutlet`, you create an `IBAction` that responds when the user presses the Purchase button. As you'll see later in this section, this will initiate the in-app purchasing process.

After you've created this header file, open WallpaperViewController.xib and add a `UIImageView` and a `UIButton`. Finally, connect the `UIImageView` to your `IBOutlet` and the `touchUpInside` method of the `UIButton` to your `IBAction`.

19.2.4 Store Kit Payment

The code for this class is simple. Open WallpaperViewController.m, and implement the methods in the following listing.

Listing 19.7   WallpaperViewController.m

```
#import "WallpaperViewController.h"

@implementation WallpaperViewController

@synthesize product;
@synthesize imageView;

- (void)viewDidLoad {                                              ❶ Sets image
    [super viewDidLoad];                                             property of
    imageView.image = [UIImage imageNamed:[NSString                 imageView
        stringWithFormat:@"%@.jpeg",self.product.productIdentifier]];
}

- (IBAction) buttonClicked:(id) sender {
    SKPayment *payment = [SKPayment paymentWithProductIdentifier:
    self.product.productIdentifier];
    [[SKPaymentQueue defaultQueue] addPayment:payment];
}
```

You set the `image` property of the `UIImageView` to a JPEG with the same name as the product identifier ❶. To make things easy, you name each of the images you're selling based on their product identifiers. For example, the three images in the sample code are named com.rightsprite.wallpaper.01.jpeg, com.rightsprite.wallpaper.02.jpeg, and com.rightsprite.wallpaper.03.jpeg. If you didn't want to name your images this way, you could store a mapping of product IDs to image names in a plist file.

When the user presses the Purchase button, the code creates a new `SKPayment` object and queue in the global payments queue. Because `SKPaymentQueue` is a singleton class, payments can be queued from anywhere in your code. All you need is the product identifier of the product being purchased.

After the payment has been queued, Store Kit takes over and begins processing it. Figure 19.11 shows the alert that pops up when you press the Purchase button.

When the user presses the Buy button, Store Kit notifies your transaction observer class about the status of payment via the delegate methods you declared in listing 19.1.

We'll now discuss how to implement those methods and deliver the purchased content to the user.

Add the code from the next listing to the file RootViewController.m.

Listing 19.8 Delegate methods for Store Kit

```
- (void)paymentQueue:(SKPaymentQueue *)queue updatedTransactions:(NSArray
    *)transactions
{
    for (SKPaymentTransaction *transaction in transactions)
    {
        switch (transaction.transactionState)
        {
            case SKPaymentTransactionStatePurchased:
                [self completeTransaction:transaction];
                break;
            case SKPaymentTransactionStateFailed:
                [self failedTransaction:transaction];
                break;
            case SKPaymentTransactionStateRestored:
                [self restoreTransaction:transaction];
            default:
                break;
        }
    }
}
```

Store Kit calls this method after the user has tried to purchase an item, and it's used as a controller based on the status of the purchase. A purchase has three potential states:

- SKPaymentTransactionStatePurchased Occurs when the transaction was successful. At this point, you should deliver the content to the user and record the transaction history.

- SKPaymentTransactionStateFailed The transaction may fail for a number of reasons, including insufficient funds or a network error. If this is the case, you need to notify the user that their purchase wasn't completed.

- SKPaymentTransactionStateRestored Occurs when the user has already purchased an item. If this is the state of the transaction, you should deliver the content to the user as if it was a new transaction.

Now that you've implemented this driver method, you need to implement each of the response methods that it calls. Add the code from the following listing to your RootViewController.m file.

Figure 19.11 A purchase confirmation as shown on the iPhone

Listing 19.9   Store Kit response methods

```
- (void) completeTransaction: (SKPaymentTransaction *)transaction
{
    [self.navigationController popViewControllerAnimated:YES];
    [self recordTransaction: transaction];
    [self provideContent: transaction.payment.productIdentifier];
    [[SKPaymentQueue defaultQueue] finishTransaction: transaction];
}

- (void) restoreTransaction: (SKPaymentTransaction *)transactionB
{
    [self completeTransaction:transaction];
}

- (void) failedTransaction: (SKPaymentTransaction *)transaction
{
    if (transaction.error.code != SKErrorPaymentCancelled)
    {
        UIAlertView * alert = [[UIAlertView alloc]
            initWithTitle:@"Error in purchase"
            message:transaction.error.description delegate:nil
            cancelButtonTitle:@"Ok" otherButtonTitles:nil];

        [alert show];
        [alert release];
    }
    [[SKPaymentQueue defaultQueue] finishTransaction: transaction];
}
```

Completes transaction and delivers content ◁

Restores transaction ◁

Notifies user that transaction failed ◁

As we stated before, the actions for completing and restoring transactions are usually similar. For the example, you have `restoreTransaction` call `completeTransaction` to save lines of code.

When a purchase is successful, Store Kit notifies the user via a `UIAlertView`. Figure 19.12 shows what this view looks like in the application.

The process you should follow when completing a transaction is usually the same in every application. You call a series of methods to record the history, provide the content to the user, and finalize the transaction. Listing 19.10 details each of these methods. To record the transactions, you keep a plist file on disk containing the product identifiers of every product purchased by the user. Although you don't do much with the recorded transaction information in this application, it's good practice to track it.

Figure 19.12   A successful purchase confirmation as shown on an iPhone

Listing 19.10   Recording transactions and delivering content

```
- (void) recordTransaction:(SKPaymentTransaction * )transaction {

    if([self.transactionHistory containsObject:
            transaction.payment.productIdentifier]) return;        ① Saves history
                                                                       to disk
    NSArray *paths = NSSearchPathForDirectoriesInDomains(
            NSDocumentDirectory, NSUserDomainMask, YES);
    NSString *documentsDirectory = [paths objectAtIndex:0];
    NSString * path = [documentsDirectory
            stringByAppendingPathComponent:@"history.plist"];
    [self.transactionHistory
            addObject:transaction.payment.productIdentifier];
    [self.transactionHistory writeToFile:path atomically:YES];
}                                                                  ② Saves image
                                                                      to user's
- (void) provideContent:(NSString * )productIdentifier {              camera roll
    UIImageWriteToSavedPhotosAlbum([UIImage imageNamed:[NSString
        stringWithFormat:@"%@.jpeg",productIdentifier]],self,
        @selector(image:didFinishSavingWithError:contextInfo:),nil);
}

- (void)image:(UIImage *)image didFinishSavingWithError:(NSError *)error
    contextInfo:(void *)contextInfo {
                                                                Notifies user ③
    UIAlertView * alert = [[UIAlertView alloc]
        initWithTitle:@"Purchase Complete"
        message:@"The wallpaper has been saved to your camera roll."
        delegate:nil cancelButtonTitle:@"Ok" otherButtonTitles:nil];
    [alert show];
    [alert release];
}
```

The code first checks to see if the user has already purchased the given item. If so, you don't need to double-record it. After that, you resolve the path to the file history.plist in the application's documents directory and write the history to it ①.

When you're creating a store in an application, the provideContent method varies depending on what type of content you're selling. In the case of the wallpaper sale application, you need to save the purchased wallpaper from the application's directory to the user's camera roll. You can do this using the UIImageWriteToSavedPhotosAlbum method ②. After this method completes, it calls the selector you passed in, which notifies the user that the wallpaper was saved to their device ③. The user now has full access to that wallpaper via their camera roll.

The last method in ③ shows what to do if an error occurs. It's important to notify the user that their payment wasn't processed. Otherwise, you'll have unhappy customers thinking they paid for something and it wasn't delivered.

19.3   *Summary*

In this chapter, you've seen one way to implement a store for non-consumable goods. You provided a simple store interface that lets users browse, purchase, and save wallpapers on their iPhones.

Stores can come in many different varieties to suit your needs. Almost anything can be considered a product to be sold in a store. Be creative, and utilize this opportunity to make some extra income off your application.

When adding a store to your application, always think about how it will affect development time. Be sure to submit your in-app purchase products as soon as you consider them ready, so the review process doesn't slow down your deployment.

Finally, keep functionality in mind. Don't make your application entirely dependent on in-app purchases. Be sure to offer some value for the users who download it and choose not to purchase your products. Make sure you structure your store in such a way that it adds to your application rather than being the focus of it.

In the next chapter, we'll discuss how to make money with iAd.

Making money with iAd

This chapter covers

- Creating a banner ad in your application
- Responding to a user's interaction, such as screen rotation
- Handling ad downloading errors
- Going live with iAd

You may remember the popular quotation from the movie *Jerry Maguire*: "Show me the money!" Let's talk about making money. We covered the majority of the iOS 4 frameworks in the previous 19 chapters. You may have a plan to get your app-design business started. Sure, there are a lot of ways to make money with your applications. You can build a paid app, a free app with an app purchase, or a totally free app with some advertisements; when users see and interact with the ads inside your app, you'll get paid. How much money can you make? The answer will be based on how many active users you have for your apps and, in turn, how many ads you've served and the reaction of your users. Apple will sell and distribute the ads through the iAd service; as a developer, you'll keep 60% of the total revenue from iAd (at the time of writing).

If you decide to go for the advertisement option, there's a good chance you'll consider the iAd framework in iOS 4. In this chapter, we'll cover how to integrate banner ads into your application, how to implement screen-rotation support for iAd, and how to handle ad-downloading errors. At the end of the chapter, we'll cover how to enable iAd through iTunes Connect.

20.1 Adding a banner ad into your application

Before you start to code, let's spend some time together on the banner advertisement structure. First, you need to provide some space for the banner image view in your application's user interface, roughly 10% of the screen size. For example, the banner view under portrait mode on iPhone is 320 x 50 points (pt) in size, and portrait mode on the iPad is 768 x 66 pt. Ad sizes based on device and screen orientation are described in detail in table 20.1.

Table 20.1   iAd banner view size table

Device	Screen orientation	Banner size (width x height in points)
iPhone	Portrait	320 x 50
iPhone	Landscape	480 x 32
iPad	Portrait	768 x 66
iPad	Landscape	1280 x 66

The iAd framework provides a convenient way to display that image banner view through `ADBannerView`. `ADBannerView` will make sure that the advertisements are automatically loaded from the iAd Network and presented in your application properly. When an end user or customer taps a banner image view, the current advertisement will begin its animation. A full-screen view controller will appear and interact with user gestures. The full-screen view controller could be a mini-application, which is a rich media advertisement based on HTML5; it may contain other features, such as the ability to use maps and purchase directly from iTunes. The customer can return to the app interface by tapping the Close button on the top-left corner of the screen.

Where is the advertisement from? It's from the iAd service running on Apple's ad servers. The good news is that you don't need to worry about how the banner image was downloaded. That's what the iAd framework is for. In this section, you'll create a demo app with an ad banner view added to the view hierarchy.

20.1.1 Creating a simple app for the ad banner view

To start your money-making journey, you need to have a simple app to get your business going. Let's use a simple application in the app template. Keep one important rule in mind: you need to have a view controller to display the banner view. In this section, you'll use a view-based application for the iAd demonstration. It will give you a nice, simple view controller to display the `AdBannnerView`.

Fire up Xcode, and create a new project. When the project template opens, under iOS Application, choose View-Based Application. The product is iPhone. Name it MyApp. Now you have the basic view controller for the banner ad. Single-click the Classes folder on the Groups & Files panel. You're going to use MyAppViewController as the parent view controller for the banner display.

Do you remember how to add a new framework into your app? (You can refer to chapter 16 for details.) You need to add the iAd framework into the app. Head back to Xcode. Highlight the top-level Project node in the Projects tree, and on the right side, choose a Target; then select the Build Phases tab. Under this tab is an entry called Link Binary with Libraries. Click the + button next to it, and you'll see a window with the entire list of available frameworks under the current SDK. Navigate to `iAd.frame-work`, and click the Add button. Now the iAd framework is added to the app.

In order to have this simple app running on both the iPhone and iPad, go to Xcode 4 and select MyApp project node in the Navigation View. The editor view will display the project summary. Select MyApp target, and choose Universal for Devices option. Now you have the universal app for the iAd banner demonstration.

20.1.2 Adding the banner view to the view controller

It's time to add in the banner view. Single-click the MyAppViewController.h file, and add the header file for iAd framework:

```
#import <iAd/iAd.h>
```

Single-click the MyAppViewController.m file. Add the code in the following listing to make a simple banner ad.

Listing 20.1 Creating the banner view inside the view controller

```
#import "MyAppViewController.h"

@implementation MyAppViewController

- (void)viewDidLoad {
    [super viewDidLoad];
    ADBannerView *adView = [[ADBannerView alloc]           ❶ Create
      initWithFrame:CGRectZero];                               ADBannerView
    adView.currentContentSizeIdentifier =                  ❷ Define
      ADBannerContentSizeIdentifierPortrait;                  content size
    [self.view addSubview:adView];                         ❸ Add adView to
}                                                             current view
-(BOOL)shouldAutorotateToInterfaceOrientation:
  (UIInterfaceOrientation)interfaceOrientation {
    return (interfaceOrientation ==
            UIInterfaceOrientationPortrait);
}                                                          ❹ Define interface
...                                                           orientation
- (void)dealloc {
    [super dealloc];
}

@end
```

Let's go through the changes. Inside the `viewDidLoad` method, you create a banner view ❶, and then you define the content size to be portrait (320 x 50 on iPhone, 768 x 66 on iPad) ❷. Finally, you add the banner view to the view controller's view hierarchy ❸. In order to define the interface orientation as portrait mode only, you define the interfaceOrientation ❹. Save all the changes.

Click Build and Run on the Simulator. You should see the app running with a nice test banner on the top of the screen. Make sure your laptop is connected to the internet, because the test banner in figure 20.1 will work only when there's an internet connection.

As we mentioned in the beginning of the chapter, the banner view will respond to the user's action. Click the banner view; are you getting the text shown in figure 20.2 on your Simulator now? Congrats! As you can tell from the message, you have the test advertisement running successfully.

Click the top-left button to close the full-screen view controller. Now you have the banner view running smoothly in the app when it's under portrait mode only. What if the user rotates the device from portrait mode to landscape mode? We'll look into this scenario in the next section.

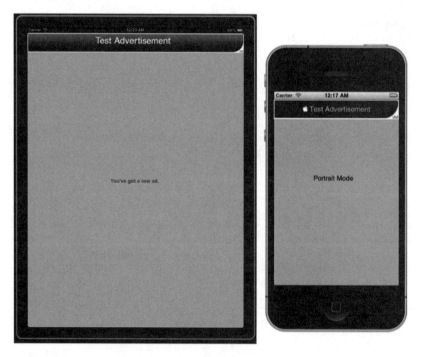

Figure 20.1   A successful demonstration of a test iAd banner view inside the view controller

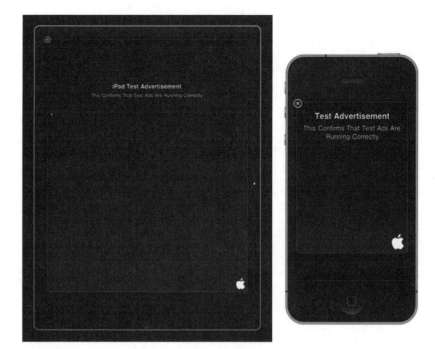

Figure 20.2   Full-screen view controller presented when the user taps the banner ad

20.2 *Supporting both portrait mode and landscape mode*

Previously we talked about how to integrate the portrait-mode banner ad. It turns out that when the device is in landscape mode, you can change the banner view size from 320 x 50 to 480 x 32 on the iPhone and from 768 x 66 to 1024 x 66 on the iPad. In this section, we'll cover how to change banner size dynamically when the user rotates the iPhone or iPad.

In order to make the app more responsive, let's add a text label in the center of the screen. Go back to Xcode, single-click the MyAppViewController.h file, and add the following changes.

Listing 20.2   Adding the text label and banner view in MyAppViewController.h
---

```
#import <UIKit/UIKit.h>
#import <iAd/iAd.h>
@interface MyAppViewController : UIViewController {
      ADBannerView *adView;
      IBOutlet UILabel *textLabel;                          Show current
                                                            device interface
}
@property (nonatomic, retain) ADBannerView *adView;
@end
```

This text label will be updated to show you the current device orientation. Save the changes, and follow up with the new code in the MyAppViewController.m file in the following listing. Single-click the MyAppViewController.m file, and implement the changes.

Listing 20.3 Presenting the banner view dynamically when the orientation changes

```
#import "MyAppViewController.h"

@implementation MyAppViewController
@synthesize adView;                                          Define ❶
                                                             content size
- (void)viewDidLoad {
    [super viewDidLoad];
    self.adView = [[ADBannerView alloc] initWithFrame:CGRectZero];
    self.adView.requiredContentSizeIdentifiers =
      [NSSet setWithObjects: ADBannerContentSizeIdentifierPortrait,
        ADBannerContentSizeIdentifierLandscape, nil];
    self.adView.autoresizingMask =
      UIViewAutoresizingFlexibleWidth | UIViewAutoresizingFlexibleHeight |
      UIViewAutoresizingFlexibleBottomMargin;
    [self.view addSubview:adView];                          Autoresize ❷
}                                                           view to top

- (void)willRotateToInterfaceOrientation:
    (UIInterfaceOrientation)toInterfaceOrientation
    duration:(NSTimeInterval)duration
{
    if (UIInterfaceOrientationIsLandscape(
      toInterfaceOrientation)) {
        self.adView.currentContentSizeIdentifier =          ❸ Landscape
          ADBannerContentSizeIdentifierLandscape;              mode
        textLabel.text = @"Landscape Mode";
    } else {
        self.adView.currentContentSizeIdentifier =
          ADBannerContentSizeIdentifierPortrait;            ❹ Portrait
        textLabel.text = @"Portrait Mode";                     mode
    }
}

- (BOOL)shouldAutorotateToInterfaceOrientation:
    (UIInterfaceOrientation)interfaceOrientation {          ❺ Support all
    return YES;                                                directions
}

- (void)viewDidUnload {                                     ❻ Release
    self.adView = nil;                                         banner view
}

- (void)dealloc {
    [adView release];
    [super dealloc];
}

@end
```

Save the changes. Let's spend some time examining listing 20.3. You create a banner view ❶ and define the size to include both portrait mode and landscape mode. Then you add autoresizing and position the banner view during the runtime ❷. Inside the method `willRotateToInterfaceOrientation`, you change the banner view's size dynamically according to the new device interface. Next, you change the banner to landscape mode ❸ and update the `textLabel`'s text to indicate that the current banner size will be in landscape mode. Then you define the banner to portrait mode and update the `textLabel`'s text to indicate that the new banner size will be portrait mode ❹. Remember that you define `interfaceorientation` to be portrait mode only: you change it here to support all directions ❺. You release the banner view in the memory because you're a good citizen ❻.

Don't forget to create the `textLabel` inside the nib file. Double-click the MyApp-ViewController.xib file. Fire up the library, drag a `UILabel` onto the view, and place the label in the center. Double-click the label you just created, and change the text to `Portrait Mode`. Bring up the Connection Inspector (View menu > Utilities > Connections Inspector), click the File's Owner icon in the MyAppViewController.xib file window to have the `textLabel` showing in the outlets, and then hook up the `textLabel` with the label you just created. When everything is finished, you should see a user interface similar to the one in figure 20.3.

Under the text label's Size tab, you can set the label's positioning to be the center of the view. Save all the changes. Now you're ready for the test run.

Click Build and Run on the Simulator. With everything running smoothly, you should be able to see the screen shown in figure 20.4 under portrait mode; and when you rotate the Simulator to landscape mode (press Command-left arrow on the keyboard, or choose Hardware menu > Rotate Left), the banner view is changed to the landscape size.

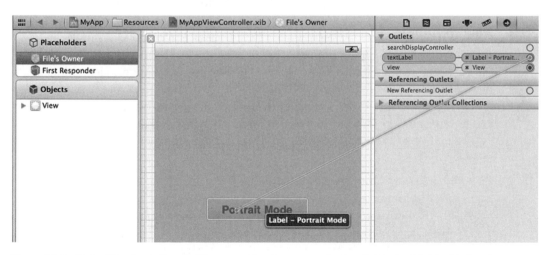

Figure 20.3 MyAppViewController.xib file, connecting the `textLabel` outlet to the label inside the view

Figure 20.4 Dynamically update the banner view size to support both portrait mode and landscape mode.

Looking good! So far you've learned how to create a banner view inside the universal app with the iAd framework. We also looked into how to define the banner size dynamically when the device changes its interface orientation. Now let's tackle another issue you may face in the real world: what if the iPhone or iPad has no wi-fi connection?

As we mentioned earlier, the banner ad is downloaded from the iAd Network. You won't have a banner-ad view when no connection is available. It's a bad user experience to have some sort of gray view on the top or bottom of the screen, with nothing showing up. Maybe you can try to hide the banner when there's no ad or an error occurs. We'll discuss this technical problem in the following section.

20.3 *How to handle advertisement downloading errors*

As we mentioned in the beginning of this chapter, the iAd banner is downloaded from the iAd Network somewhere in the cloud. When no connection or no ad is available, a download error will occur. Here we'll revisit MyApp from section 20.2 to demonstrate how to hide the banner view when an error occurs during advertisement downloading and how to show the banner view with animation when a new advertisement arrives.

`ADBannerViewDelegate` provides you with some helpful methods for these common events:

- When a new advertisement is loaded:

  `-(void)bannerViewDidLoadAd:(ADBannerView *)banner`

- When an error occurs or advertisements are not available:

  `-(void)bannerView:(ADBannerView *)banner`
  `    didFailToReceiveAdWithError:(NSError *)error`

In this section, we'll cover how to handle the ad-downloading error with the `ADBannerViewDelegate` methods.

20.3.1 *Adding a delegate to ADBannerView's view controller*

In Xcode, single-click the MyAppViewController.h file, and add the `ADBannerView-Delegate` to the header file as follows:

```
@interface MyAppViewController : UIViewController <ADBannerViewDelegate> {
```

Now you'll add the new changes to the MyAppViewController.m file. Single-click the MyAppViewController.m file, define the adView's delegate as `self` in the `viewDidLoad` method, and hide the banner view, as shown in the following listing.

Listing 20.4   Creating `ADBannerView` and assigning delegate to view controller

```
- (void)viewDidLoad {
    [super viewDidLoad];
    self.adView = [[ADBannerView alloc] initWithFrame:CGRectZero];
    self.adView.requiredContentSizeIdentifiers = [NSSet
      setWithObjects: ADBannerContentSizeIdentifierPortrait,          ❶ Hide
      ADBannerContentSizeIdentifierLandscape, nil];                      banner
    self.adView.hidden = YES;                                          ◁ view
    self.adView.frame = CGRectOffset(adView.frame, 0,
      -adView.frame.size.height);                           ◁──❷ Offset frame
    self.adView.delegate = self;
    self.adView.autoresizingMask = UIViewAutoresizingFlexibleWidth |
      UIViewAutoresizingFlexibleHeight |
     UIViewAutoresizingFlexibleBottomMargin;

    [self.view addSubview:adView];
}
```

The view controller now has the delegate methods ready to implement. Notice that you hide the banner view when you create the banner ❶. Then you offset the banner's frame height ❷ to prepare for the banner view's slide in animation. We'll cover two methods in this section: when a new advertisement is loaded, you'll load the banner view with animation; when an error occurs during the loading time, you'll hide the banner view with the method `bannerView:didFailToReceiveAdWithError`.

Add the two `ADBannerView` delegate methods to the MyAppViewController.m file, as shown in the following listing.

Listing 20.5   Implementing the delegate methods for `ADBannerView`

```
- (void)bannerView:(ADBannerView *)banner
    didFailToReceiveAdWithError:(NSError *)error {        ❶ Error occurred
    if (!self.adView.hidden) {                               in banner view
        [UIView beginAnimations:@"animateAdBannerSlideOut"
          context:NULL];
        banner.frame = CGRectOffset(banner.frame, 0,
          -banner.frame.size.height);
        [UIView commitAnimations];
        self.adView.hidden = YES;                        ❶ Error occurred
        textLabel.text = @"Sorry, no ad.";                  in banner view
    }
}
```

```
- (void)bannerViewDidLoadAd:(ADBannerView *)banner {
    if (self.adView.hidden) {
        [UIView beginAnimations:@"animateAdBannerSlideIn"
          context:NULL];
        banner.frame = CGRectOffset(banner.frame, 0,
          banner.frame.size.height);
        [UIView commitAnimations];
        self.adView.hidden = NO;
        textLabel.text = @"You've got a new ad.";
    }
}
```

❷ New ad arrived in banner view

You use the `ADBannerView`'s delegate method ❶ to hide the banner view when an error occurs inside the banner view and add the animation to slide out the banner when a new ad is loaded. Meanwhile, you update the `textLabel`'s text to give a hint as to what's going on with the banner view. With the next method ❷, you define the banner view to appear when a new advertisement is loaded and update the `textLabel`'s text to "You've got a new ad." Pretty easy, right?

Next, let's test the delegate methods with the application running under the Simulator.

20.3.2 *Simulating event handling*

Save all the changes, click Build, and run the project on the Simulator. With an internet connection, you'll see the screen shown in figure 20.5 on the Simulator when you get a new test advertisement. The animation effect is kind of cool, right?

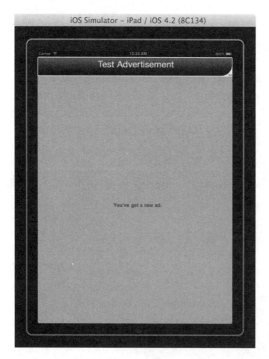

Figure 20.5   The banner view delegate method notifies you when there's a new advertisement on the iPad.

Figure 20.6 Hide the banner view when there's an error in the banner view.

Turn off the internet connection (Apple's iAd test environment will send you the error example from time to time even with the wi-fi connection). You'll have a hidden banner view and a message saying "Sorry, no ad," as shown in figure 20.6.

With the error handling, MyApp's user interface makes the default error banner view unnoticeable. Instead of showing a gray empty banner as in figure 20.7, you have a much better user experience with a few lines of code from listing 20.5.

Some other delegate methods are worth mentioning here. When a user taps on the banner view, before the full-screen view controller presents, it calls the delegate's `bannerViewActionShouldBegin:willLeaveApplication:` method. If your app is a game, you may want to save the current status or pause the game before the user leaves the application's interface, so when the user comes back, the app can continue running without losing all the data. When the user dismisses the full-screen modal view controller, another method, `bannerViewActionDidFinish:`, gets called. Inside this method, you can restart the game or continue to run the app before the full-screen view controller appears.

Let's review the new methods you've added in this part. You assigned the delegate to the view controller `self` when you first created the banner view; then you saw how

Figure 20.7 Default banner view when an error occurs during advertisement downloading

to hide the banner view when an error occurs in the delegate method `bannerView didFailToReceiveAd:WithError:`. You can test the app on the device now: try it by either disabling wi-fi and 3G data on the device or by disabling networking entirely by setting the device to Airplane Mode in the Settings app. The banner view will be hidden as defined in the delegate method.

You've done enough testing. What if you want to go live and publish the application with the iAd Network? We'll talk about this next.

20.4   *Going live with the application*

So far, you've tested the view-based application MyApp with test advertisements from the iAd Network service. You may wonder when you can see some real advertisements instead of the test ads. Well, it turns out the iAd Network will send test advertisements to MyApp under the entire testing process, which means under Simulator, under developer builds on the device, under ad hoc distribution builds to beta testers, and so on. The live ads will be available to MyApp only when the distribution build is submitted to the App Store. When end users download your app from the App Store, they'll see the live ads automatically displayed.

First, go to the iPhone Developer Program portal, and open the iTunes Connect Online Application. You need to accept the contract for iAd. Once your contract is ready, you can submit the final distribution build to the App Store. To receive advertisements from the iAd Network, you first need to enable the iAd service for the application you're submitting, as shown in figure 20.8.

When you have at least one application with iAd enabled, there should be a new iAd Network item available on your iTunes Connect page, as shown in figure 20.9.

Click iAd Network. You can use this page to manage the ads that appear in your apps. You can also monitor the ads' performance in your apps. For example, you can

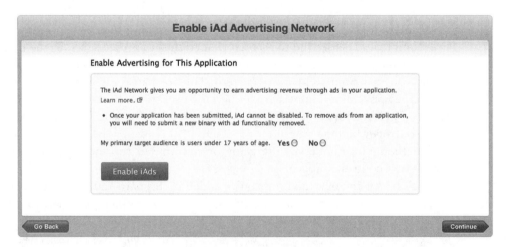

Figure 20.8   Enable the iAd Advertising Network for your application during the new application submission.

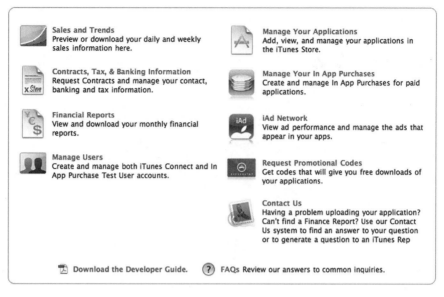

Figure 20.9 Your iTunes Connect page will include the iAd Network when the iAd's contract is accepted.

find out ad revenue, key metrics, and ad performance by app or country, as shown in figure 20.10.

Another important feature on this page is that you can add exclusions for each app. You can add certain keywords, Apple IDs, or URLs to make sure ads from your

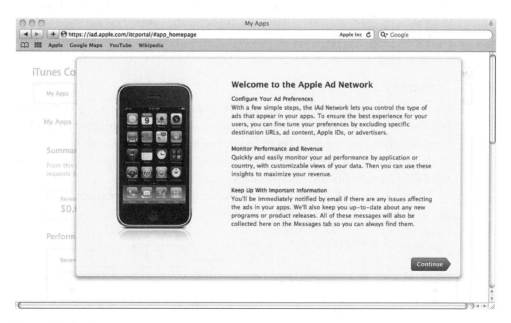

Figure 20.10 iAd Network under iTunes Connect

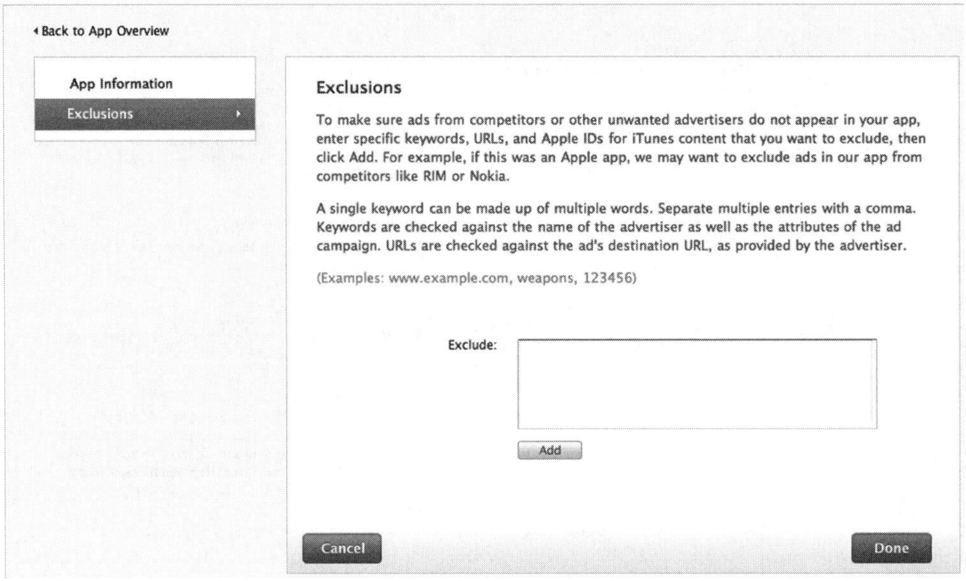

Figure 20.11   Add exclusions to your app.

competitors or certain unwanted advertisers won't show up in your app. Click the app that you would like to add exclusions to, and the Exclusions feature will appear, as shown in figure 20.11.

In this section, we talked about how to get live ads with iTunes Connect on the iOS Developer Program website. With all the tools in hand, you should be able to monetize your app through iAd. When your application is approved and becomes live in the App Store, users will start to download your app; you can come back to the iTunes Connect page and check your revenue through iAd. Have fun!

20.5   *Summary*

You're ready to make money via iAd with your application! Let's recap what you've learned in this chapter. First, you managed to create a portrait mode–only banner view, and then you learned how to handle some real problems, such as screen rotation or advertisement download errors. Now you can get live ads from iAd Network, monitor the ads' performance, and get a revenue report.

Hope you've had a good time with iAd so far. Sit tight, because you're heading to a fun and important part of iOS 4: multitasking.

Introducing multitasking

This chapter covers

- Overview of multitasking on iOS 4
- Fast app switching
- Finishing a task in the background
- Monitoring location change in the background

iOS 4 is muscled up with tons of exciting new features. We've covered the Game Kit framework, local notifications, the Event Kit framework, GCD, and iAd in previous chapters. In this chapter, it's time to introduce multitasking! Multitasking is a feature that has been requested on iOS since its first release. But there's limited screen size and battery life on the iPhone or iPad, so generally only one application is visible and active at a time. In iOS 4 and later, with multitasking introduced, applications can continue running in the background.

What's multitasking? It's one of the important and exciting API features in iOS 4. When the user quits an application, instead of terminating, the application will enter the background state; you can use this feature to support fast app switching and running tasks in the background.

In this chapter, we'll first cover the multitasking basics, the application's lifecycle on iOS 4, followed by the background state and best practices based on an app's lifecycle transitions. Then we'll talk about how to adopt fast app switching on the iPhone and iPad and how to update the application interface with the correct user data when the application gets restarted from the background state. Finally, we'll use a demo app to explain how to finish a task in the background with an expiration handler. First, let's explore some basics on multitasking.

21.1   *Overview of multitasking*

Multitasking is the ability to let the device run more than one application at once. For example, you may want to listen to music using the Pandora application while performing other tasks such as checking your email.

In the past, Apple had a few arguments against multitasking on iOS; the primary ones were that it slows down the device, degrades the battery life, and makes for an overall poor user experience. If you allow the user to run too many applications at once, the device will eventually run out of memory and start killing those applications. Running many applications at the same time quickly drains battery life. Because running an app requires processing power, the constant strain on the processor will soon result in a drained battery.

In iOS 4, Apple has implemented the ability for programs to run in the background. Figure 21.1 shows the multitasking UI on the iPhone and iPad. This isn't true multitasking per se, but it's getting closer and addresses most of users' other gripes.

Figure 21.1   Multitasking UI on the iPad and iPhone

Applications that need to execute operations in the background are restricted to certain tasks, including the following:

- Requesting a set amount of time to finish a task
- Implementing specific services allowed by Apple, including location tracking, audio playback, and voice over IP services

By default, all applications that are compiled for iOS 4 will support multitasking. But after the user taps the Home button, the app will go into the background suspended state unless the background running mode is added.

Because most applications don't require constant usage, the system automatically puts them into a suspended state when the user exits them. When the user resumes the application, it should load into the last state it was in when the user exited it. This is more of a fast application-switching model. A great comparison is that when you're reading a book, you may want to take a break and get a cup of coffee, so you put a bookmark at the page where you stopped. When you return, you can continue from the exact same page where you left off.

Next we'll look at the application lifecycle and how to enable multitasking on iOS 4.

21.1.1 Application lifecycle

With iOS multitasking support, the application lifecycle expands to not running, running in the foreground, and running in the background, as shown in figure 21.2. When the application launches, it will move from the not-running state to the foreground, stay inactive briefly, and become active. That's when the MainWindow.xib file gets loaded into the application. While the application is running in the foreground state, an SMS message or an incoming call could pop out and interrupt the current application, which therefore would become inactive.

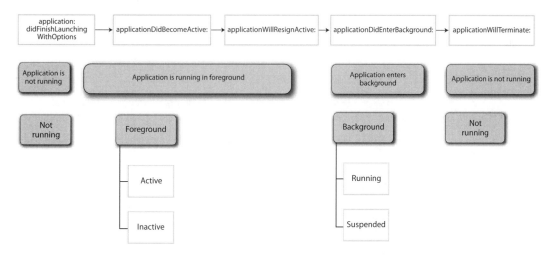

Figure 21.2 Application's lifecycle in iOS 4

When the user taps the Home button, the application will move from the foreground state to the background. The application may continue running if the background mode is supported on the device (iPhone 3G and iPod Touch 2nd Gen don't support the background state at all), such as background audio. When a user is listening to their iPod and taps the Home button, the application still plays music in the background state.

Most applications will stay in the suspended state after moving to background mode and won't execute code in the suspended state. When the user switches back to this application after some time, it will automatically return from the background to the foreground state, where it was left previously.

Sometimes, when the system is running low on memory, applications with heavy memory usage in the background are terminated in order to free up more memory for the foreground application. Another possibility is that the user will manually terminate the application from the multitasking UI stack.

In iOS 4, it's important to understand the application's lifecycle in order to design a responsive and smooth-transitioning application. For example, when you're designing a game application, you should pause the game when there's an incoming call and save important data before the application quits or moves to the background state. How can you monitor the application's lifecycle during runtime?

Two solutions are available on iOS 4. One solution is to respond to each major callback method in the application delegate. Another way is to observe the notifications from the notification center. Table 21.1 has a complete list of application delegate methods and notifications.

Table 21.1   A complete list of application delegate callbacks and notifications

Method	Notification	Description
application: didFinishLaunching- WithOptions:	UIApplication- DidFinishLaunching- Notification	The application launches.
application- DidBecomeActive:	UIApplication- DidBecomeActiveNotification	The application runs actively in the foreground.
application- WillResignActive:	UIApplication- WillResignActiveNotification	During interruption, the application becomes inactive.
application- DidEnterBackground:	UIApplication- DidEnterBackground- Notification	The application enters the background state.
application- WillEnterForeground:	UIApplication- WillEnterForeground- Notification	The application resumes from the background.
application- WillTerminate:	UIApplication- WillTerminateNotification	The application is terminated and not running.

Inside the application's delegate, you can monitor the application's lifecycle state and transitions; at the time of writing, six major callbacks are available in the application delegate:

- `application:didFinishLaunchingWithOptions`—This is the most important method and has been used in the entire book. This method can be used to initialize the application and prepare it for running in the foreground state, such as loading the Main Window nib file.

- `applicationDidEnterBackground`—This is the key callback method to prepare the application for the background state. Use this method to release shared resources, save user data, invalidate timers, and store enough application state information to restore your application to its current state. If the application supports background execution, this method will be called instead of `applicationWillTerminate` when the user taps the Home button.

- `applicationWillEnterForeground`—This method is sent when the application resumes from the background state and will enter the foreground. You can use this method to restore the application and undo the changes before the application enters the background. For example, the application can load the resources and restore the data.

- `applicationDidBecomeActive`—This method can be used to customize application behavior when the application becomes active in the foreground. For example, it will be called when the interruption is gone or when the application continues transition from inactive state to active state after the method `applicationWillEnterForeground` gets called. Use this task to restart the tasks paused previously. For example, you should continue the game, restart the timer, and update the user interface.

- `applicationWillResignActive`—This method gets called when the application is about to move from active to inactive state. This can occur for certain types of temporary interruptions (such as an incoming phone call or SMS message) or when the user quits the application and it's about to start the transition to the background state. You can use this method to pause ongoing tasks, disable timers, and tune down OpenGL ES usage.

- `applicationWillTerminate`—This method is called when the application is about to be terminated. The application will transit back to the not-running state.

You can use the notifications in table 21.1 to monitor the application's transition states with the notification center. For example, you can use the following code snippet to register a notification for `UIApplicationWillResignActiveNotification` inside the view controllers:

```
NSNotificationCenter *notifCenter = [NSNotificationCenter defaultCenter];
[notifCenter addObserver:self selector:@selector(resignActive:)
name:UIApplicationWillResignActiveNotification object:nil];
```

As you can tell, in order to smoothly support multitasking in the application, you need to consider saving the application's data properly before the application moves to the background and reload the necessary data before the application launches from the background mode.

You may have more questions related to the background state at this point, which is important to understand for multitasking in iOS 4. We'll take a closer look at the application's background state in the following section.

21.1.2 *How to enable multitasking*

The applications built under iOS 4 are automatically enabled for multitasking. But in order to support certain constantly running types of multitasking, the background mode must be declared in advance. To do so, include the `UIBackgroundModes` key in the application's Info.plist file. Table 21.2 contains a detailed list for the multitasking mode.

Table 21.2   Multitasking mode list in Info.plist

UIBackgroundModes	Descriptions
Audio	The application plays audible content to the user while in the background, such as the music application Pandora or a turn-by-turn audio navigation application.
Location	The application keeps the user informed about current location updates, even while running in the background. This mode is designed for a turn-by-turn navigation application. Note that a significant location change or region-monitoring location service doesn't have to register for the location mode because the specific location update isn't required.
VoIP	The application provides the ability for the user to make phone calls using an internet connection.

The value for the `UIBackgroundModes` key is an array that may contain one or more strings. For example, the turn-by-turn navigation application will need both location service and audio running in the background mode, so you must add both audio and location to the Info.plist. We'll touch on how to monitor significant location changes in the background in section 21.5 and continue with advanced background audio in the next chapter.

21.2 *Background state*

Background state is important for iOS 4. In this section, we'll look at the definition of the background state under iOS 4 and explore the application lifecycle with the background state.

21.2.1 *Understanding the background state*

When the application is about to enter the background state, a couple of application delegate methods will be called. The process flow chart in figure 21.3 demonstrates the process. When user taps the Home button, the application will move from the foreground to the background. The application delegate method `application-DidEnterBackground:` gets called.

The application delegate method `applicationDidEnterBackground:` has only about 6 seconds to finish the task; then it may enter the suspended state. You want to make sure your application performs some best practices before the application transitions to the background:

- *Save user data*—Save important user data in a few seconds or incrementally, such as saving data at each stage in the middle of the game.
- *Reduce memory usage*—The system will terminate apps in the background when the memory is exhausted in order to free up memory for the foreground application.
- *Stop GPU usage*—OpenGL framework–related objects must be released or the application will be terminated.
- *Finish long-running tasks*—We'll cover this in detail in section 21.4.

After the application continues running in the background for about 6 seconds, the system will move the application to the suspended state. The system takes a snapshot of the application's current image, and the application can't perform any task or execute code after it's suspended.

How does the application resume in the foreground? When the user launches an application that's in the background state, the application delegate sends a message to the `applicationWillEnterForeground:` method in order to restart any services or tasks. Once the application resumes running in the foreground, a second message, `applicationDidBecomeActive:`, will be sent, as shown in figure 21.4.

In the stage when the application moves from the background to the foreground, you should undo the changes made before the application entered the background. For example, OpenGL framework objects need to be re-created. You may also want to respond to screen-rotation events and update the user interface.

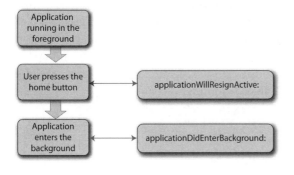

Figure 21.3   Application moves from the foreground to the background.

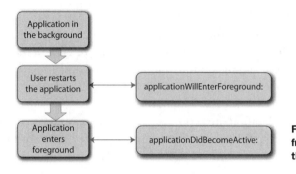

Figure 21.4   **The application restarts from the background and resumes in the foreground.**

21.2.2 *Opting out of the background state*

The background state provides many possibilities for applications on iOS. But if for some reason you wish to turn off the background state, you can add the `UIApplicationExitsOnSuspend` key to your application's Info.plist file and set its value to YES. If your application does opt out of the background state, the application will directly move to the not-running state once the user taps the Home button, which means the `applicationWillTerminate:` method of the application delegate is called instead.

In this section, you learned the basics of multitasking on iOS 4, saw how to monitor the application's state change in the lifecycle, and thoroughly explored the background state. Next, you'll practice writing real code for multitasking.

21.3 *Using fast app switching*

As we mentioned earlier, fast app switching offers a great user experience. When users want to switch between two apps, they double-tap the Home button to enable the multitasking UI, as shown previously in figure 21.1. All applications built on iOS 4 will support fast app switching automatically—no additional setup is required. In this section, you'll build an application that will handle fast app switching smoothly.

21.3.1 *Building a simple application for fast app switching*

Start Xcode, and create a new project with the iOS template Navigation-Based Application. Name the application Quick. In this application, you want to keep track of each time the application launches from the not-running state or resumes from the background state. All the data collected will be listed on the table view.

In order to collect user data every time the application starts, you'll use the application delegates `application:didFinishLaunchingWithOptions:` and `application-WillEnterForeground:` to save the launching time. Single-click the QuickApp-Delegate.m file, and add the changes from the following listing.

Listing 21.1 Implement QuickAppDelegate to collect user data when app launches

```objc
#import "QuickAppDelegate.h"
#import "RootViewController.h"


@implementation QuickAppDelegate

@synthesize window=_window;
@synthesize navigationController=_navigationController;

- (NSString *)getCurrentTime {
    NSDate *lauchtime = [NSDate date];
    NSDateFormatter *formatter = [[NSDateFormatter alloc] init];
    [formatter setDateFormat:@"yyyy/MM/dd HH:mm:ss"];
    NSString *stringFromDate = [formatter stringFromDate:lauchtime];
    [formatter release];
    return stringFromDate;
}
- (void)saveCurrentData {
    NSUserDefaults *defaults = [NSUserDefaults standardUserDefaults];
    NSMutableArray *savedData = [[NSMutableArray alloc] initWithArray:
                                     [defaults objectForKey:@"kQuickData"]];
    [savedData addObject:[self getCurrentTime]];
    [defaults setObject:savedData forKey:@"kQuickData"];
    [savedData release];
}
- (BOOL)application:(UIApplication *)application
      didFinishLaunchingWithOptions: (NSDictionary *)launchOptions {
    [self saveCurrentData];
    [_window addSubview:_navigationController.view];
    [_window makeKeyAndVisible];
    return YES;
}

- (void)applicationWillEnterForeground:(UIApplication *)application {
    [self saveCurrentData];
}

- (void)dealloc {
    [_navigationController release];
    [_window release];
    [super dealloc];
}

@end
```

1 Get launch time

2 Save data

3 App launches

4 App resumes from background

In the application delegate, you want to get the system time when the application starts. You define the method `getCurrentTime` **1** to get the system time using `NSDate` and convert the time to string format including the date and time as "yyyy/MM/dd HH:mm:ss"; then you define another method, `saveCurrentData` **2**, to save the launch time with `NSUserDefaults`, which you learned how to do in chapter 8. There are two callback methods in the application delegate related to the application launch time. First is `application:didFinishLaunchingWithOptions:` **3**. It occurs when the application initially launches from the not-running state, so you want to save the new launch data here. The second method, in applicationWillEnterForeground: ❹, occurs when the application relaunches from the background to continue running in the foreground state, so you need to save this new user data as well.

You've now prepared the application delegate for collecting the launch time data; in the next section you'll make sure the table view can display the user data correctly.

21.3.2 *Updating the user interface in the view controller*

Single-click the RootViewController.h file, and add in the changes from the following code snippet:

```
#import <UIKit/UIKit.h>

@interface RootViewController : UITableViewController {
    NSArray *events;
}
@property (nonatomic, retain) NSArray *events;
@end
```

You'll use the array events as the table view's data source. Move to the RootView-Controller.m file. You want to make sure that each time the application launches, the table view will reload the data that you've saved inside the application delegate, as shown in the following listing.

Listing 21.2   Implementing the RootViewController.m file to update the user interface

```
#import "RootViewController.h"

@implementation RootViewController
@synthesize events;                                    ❶ Update UI in
                                                           table view
- (void)updateUI {
    NSUserDefaults *defaults = [NSUserDefaults standardUserDefaults];
    self.events = [defaults objectForKey:@"kQuickData"];
    [self.tableView reloadData];
}

- (void)viewDidLoad {                                          ❸ Register
    [super viewDidLoad];                                          relaunch
    self.title = @"App Tracking List";        ❷ Load            notification
    [self updateUI];                             init data
    NSNotificationCenter *notifcenter = [NSNotificationCenter
                                            defaultCenter];
    [notifcenter addObserver:self selector:@selector(updateUI)
        name:UIApplicationWillEnterForegroundNotification object:nil];
}

- (NSInteger)numberOfSectionsInTableView:(UITableView *)tableView {
    return 1;
}

- (NSInteger)tableView:(UITableView *)tableView
        numberOfRowsInSection:(NSInteger)section {
    return [events count];
}
```

```
- (UITableViewCell *)tableView:(UITableView *)tableView
      cellForRowAtIndexPath:(NSIndexPath *)indexPath {
  static NSString *CellIdentifier = @"Cell";
  UITableViewCell *cell = [tableView
    dequeueReusableCellWithIdentifier:CellIdentifier];
  if (cell == nil) {
     cell = [[[UITableViewCell alloc]
             initWithStyle: UITableViewCellStyleDefault
             reuseIdentifier:CellIdentifier] autorelease];
  }
   cell.textLabel.text = [events objectAtIndex:indexPath.row];
   return cell;
}
- (void)dealloc {
   [events release];
   [super dealloc];
}

@end
```

In listing 21.2 you use the array events as the table view's data source. Each row will display the launching date you've saved in the application delegate methods. First, you create a new method updateUI ❶ to reload the data from NSUserDefaults and update the table view's data and the table view's user interface. When the table view controller is first created, you need to load the data with the method updateUI ❷. Then you define the notification ❸ to get notified by the system in order to reload the table view's data when the application relaunches from the background. Inside the table view delegate methods, you define the table view's row number and display content. Then, when the view controller is released, you need to release the retained object events in the memory.

With all the new changes included, save the project. Build and launch the application. You should see a UI display similar to the one shown in figure 21.5.
Quit the application, double-tap the Home button when the multitasking UI appears, relaunch the application, and notice that the new time stamp is successfully added to the table view even though the application is launched from the background.

Congrats: you've learned how to save the application's user data inside the application delegate callback methods and how to update the user interface when the application launches from background to foreground by using the notification inside the view controller. You can use this demo application to test out different application state changes. Playing around with different cases will help you understand how to update the user interface and respond to changes correctly.

Next, we'll look at a more in-depth use for the multitasking API: how to finish a task in the background.

Figure 21.5   The Quick application keeps tracking the application's launch time and updating the table view's UI whenever the application starts.

21.4   Task completion in the background

In the previous sections, we went through multitasking basics and fast app switching. Most of the time, it will be good enough for an application to use only fast app switching. But some applications may need extra time to finish the task in the background state before being suspended: for example, uploading a photo to the cloud, tweeting your current status, or downloading the latest RSS feeds. When the user taps the Home button, the application can continue running for about 6 seconds in the background before the application is suspended. In this section, we'll look at the task-completion API and build a demo app for practice.

21.4.1   Task-completion API

With the task completion in the background, the user doesn't have to wait until the task is completed, but you need to tell the application how to start and when to end the task in the background. How can you do that? iOS 4 provides a pair of methods under UIApplication to wrap up a big task in between. You can begin the task assignment by calling beginBackgroundTaskWithExpirationHandler:, and when it's done, you call the method endBackgroundTask: to end the task.

Here are the basics to use the task-completion API:

1 Define the identifier for the background task in the application's delegate `applicationDidEnterBackground:` method.

2 Indicate the start of the task by assigning the expiration handler, calling the method `beginBackgroundTaskWithExpirationHandler:`. The definition of this method is listed here:

```
-(UIBackgroundTaskIdentifier) beginBackgroundTaskWithExpirationHandler:
 (void(^)(void))handler
```

This method will take a block as an argument and return the task's unique identifier.

3 End the task. Call the method `endBackgroundTask:` to end the task by calling the task identified in step 2.

As you can tell, the task-completion API is easy to follow. The remaining time in the background for task completion can be accessed from the `UIApplication`'s property: `backgroundTimeRemaining`. In case a few tasks are waiting to be done, you can use this property to check the remaining time in between tasks.

21.4.2 *Finishing a task in the background*

Back in section 21.1, you learned about the application's lifecycle in iOS 4. When the application moves from the foreground to the background state, its delegate method `applicationDidEnterBackground:` will be called.

Listing 21.3 is an example of a task-completion API, showing how to finish a task in the background before the applications gets suspended. You can create a window-based project from the iOS template project in Xcode, because this part of API will only make changes to the app delegate file. In the app delegate header file, add in the task identifier: `UIBackgroundTaskIdentifier bgTask`. Define `bgTask` as a property of the app delegate, and synthesize it in the .m file.

Next, add the new changes from the following listing to the app delegate file.

Listing 21.3 Task completion in the background

```
- (void)uploadPhoto {                                    ←—❶ Background task
    [[UIApplication sharedApplication] cancelAllLocalNotifications];
    UILocalNotification *localNotification = [[UILocalNotification alloc]
                                              init];
    if (localNotification == nil)
        return;
    localNotification.fireDate = [NSDate dateWithTimeIntervalSinceNow:3];
    localNotification.timeZone = [NSTimeZone defaultTimeZone];
    localNotification.alertBody = [NSString stringWithFormat:
                               @"Your photo is uploaded!"];
    localNotification.alertAction = @"View Details";
    localNotification.soundName = UILocalNotificationDefaultSoundName;
    [[UIApplication sharedApplication]
     scheduleLocalNotification:localNotification];
    [localNotification release];
}
```

```
- (void)applicationDidEnterBackground:
    (UIApplication *)application {
    UIApplication *app = [UIApplication sharedApplication];
    self.bgTask = [app
        beginBackgroundTaskWithExpirationHandler:^{
        [app endBackgroundTask:self.bgTask];
        self.bgTask = UIBackgroundTaskInvalid;
    }];

    dispatch_async(dispatch_get_global_queue
                (DISPATCH_QUEUE_PRIORITY_DEFAULT, 0), ^{
        [self uploadPhoto];
        [app endBackgroundTask:bgTask];
        self.bgTask = UIBackgroundTaskInvalid;
        }
    );
}
```

❷ Begin background task

❸ End task

In this application, you want to finish a task, and after completion, send a local notification out to notify the user that the work is done. This example uses a simple method uploadPhoto ❶ to demonstrate the local notification setup in the background state. If you're interested, you can look up Flickr's photo-uploading API and add real photo uploading code into this method.

Because the main purpose of this listing is to demonstrate the task-completion API, let's take a closer look at how the job is done here. In the method applicationDidEnterBackground: you start the bgTask by calling the method beginBackgroundTaskWithExpirationHandler ❷. The argument for the expiration handler is a block to end the task and release the bgTask. Then, with the help of Grand Central Dispatch (GCD), the task uploadPhoto gets called, and you end the task by calling the method endBackgroundTask: ❸ and release the task identifier by assigning the UIBackgroundTaskInvalid value to bgTask ❸. We covered the GCD back in chapter 16.

Save the changes, and build and run the application. Tap the Home button to let the application enter the background. When the application completes the task in the background, it will send out a local notification, as shown in figure 21.6.

Cool! You just managed to finish a task in the background. Always keep in mind that the permission and time limit are not guaranteed when you use the task-completion API. That's why it's a good practice to end the task gracefully instead of letting it get suspended when it doesn't finish in time.

Next, we'll cover how to monitor location changes in the background on iOS 4.

21.5 *Monitoring location changes in the background*

We covered the Core Location framework in chapter 10 and the Map Kit framework in chapter 18. Because iOS provides an easy-to-use Core Location framework and Map Kit framework, developers have the chance to build creative and amazing applications. For example, Foursquare is one of the most-famous location-based social applications. With iOS 4's location service, you can even check in to places through

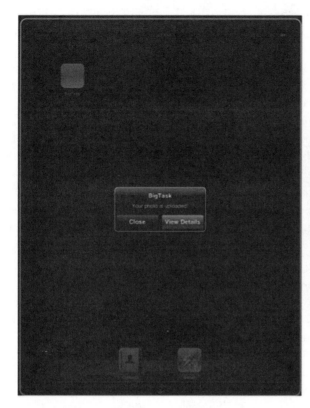

Figure 21.6 The application finishes the task in the background and sends out a local notification on the iPad and iPhone.

Foursquare while the app isn't running. You may ask, "How did they do that? Will the battery drain quickly because the location service consumes a lot of power?"

In iOS 4, an application can monitor location changes even though the application isn't running. The best part is, you don't need to worry about battery usage in this case. In this section, we'll first look at the techniques behind background location monitoring and then explore the new API under iOS 4 for background location monitoring.

21.5.1 An overview of the location service in the background

As mentioned in chapter 10, the location service will use more battery power when the accuracy requirement is higher. Of the three location service providers—cell phone tower, wi-fi, and GPS—cell phone tower uses the least power and provides acceptable accuracy (the 300-meter accuracy is good enough for the majority of cases).

There are several ways to track the user's location in the background, some of which don't require the application running regularly in the background:

- *Significant location changes and region-based location monitoring*—The significant location change service offers a low-power way to receive location data through cell phone towers and is highly recommended when precise location data isn't required. With this service, location updates are generated only when the user's location changes significantly—for instance, when the user moves from one cell tower range to another. If the application is suspended or not running when an updated location occurs, the system will wake it up in the background to handle the event. This service is available in iOS 4 and only on devices that contain a cellular radio, such as the iPhone and iPad with 3G. The region-based location monitoring works exactly the same way as significant location changes.

- *Regular location updates before the application gets suspended*—Before the application gets suspended, you can access the regular location service for a few seconds. The application won't be restarted once it's suspended and a new location update occurs.

- *Accurate and continuous location updates*—An application needs accurate location updates, both in the foreground and background states, for example, a turn-by-turn navigation application. It should add the `UIBackgroundModes` key to its Info.plist file and add the location string to the array value.

If your application doesn't need to provide precise and continuous location information to the user, the significant location change service works out the best. This service provides location updates in the background and can even wake up a suspended or not-running application. Combine this feature with the region monitor in the core location, and you can create an awesome application.

In case the application requires precise and continuous location data, such as a navigation application, you need to declare the location service in the Info.plist. Keep in mind that it increases power consumption because of the GPS usage, but it's available for applications that truly need it. The device should be plugged into the power supply in the real-time case.

We focused on the significant location change service here, mainly because the other options are the same in the background as the regular location updates in the foreground, which we covered in chapter 10.

21.5.2 *Monitoring significant location change*

The significant location change service offers a low-power location service for devices with cellular radios. The location data isn't as accurate as that of the GPS, but it's suitable for most cases. For example, you can use this background location service to trace how far the user has driven their car.

Use the method `significantLocationChangeMonitoringAvailable` to check if the current device supports significant location change monitoring. You can use the following code snippet to verify the availability:

```
BOOL available = [CLLocationManager
significantLocationChangeMonitoringAvailable];
```

When this service is available, you can use two methods in `CLLocationManager` to start and stop receiving the updates:

```
-(void)startMonitoringSignificantLocationChanges;
-(void)stopMonitoringSignificantLocationChanges;
```

Remember to turn off this service when you no longer need to receive the updates. Otherwise, the system will still wake up the application whenever new updates are available. That may annoy the user because it's unnecessary.

When the application isn't running, the new location updates will wake up the application. How can you handle this update in the application? Remember the application delegate method in the application's lifecycle that we discussed in section 21.1? In this case, the `application:didFinishLaunchingWithOptions:` method gets called, and the dictionary `launchOptions` contains the `UIApplicationLaunchOptions-LocationKey` key. You can use this method to restart the `CLLocationManager` if it's not available. You can use the `CLLocationManager` delegate method `location-Manager:didUpdateToLocation:fromLocation:` to get the new location data.

21.5.3 *Monitoring region-based location change*

The region-based location updates service works exactly the same way as the significant location updates. The new location update wakes up the application, even though the application may be suspended or not running at all. You can use two methods available in `CLLocationManager` to start and stop the monitoring for a region:

```
- (void)startMonitoringForRegion:(CLRegion *)
    desiredAccuracy:(CLLocationAccuracy);
- (void)stopMonitoringForRegion:(CLRegion *);
```

Before using the region-based location monitoring service, make sure the application has this service available. For the hardware availability, you can use the `CLLocation-Manager` class method `+ (BOOL)regionMonitoringAvailable;`.

But even if the device can support the region-based location monitoring service, the user can enable or disable the region monitoring service in the settings. Therefore, you also need to check to see if this service is currently enabled. Use the `CLLocationManager` class method `regionMonitoringEnabled` to do so.

The region-based location service will send the new location to the `CLLocation-Manager`'s delegate methods. Table 21.3 lists the important delegate methods for the region-monitoring location service.

Table 21.3   Region-based location-monitoring methods

Description	Methods
User entered the specified region.	`- (void)locationManager:(CLLocationManager *)manager didEnterRegion:(CLRegion *)region;`
User left the specified region.	`- (void)locationManager:(CLLocationManager *)manager didExitRegion:(CLRegion *)region;`
A region monitoring error occurred.	`- (void)locationManager:(CLLocationManager *)manager monitoringDidFailForRegion: (CLRegion *)region withError:(NSError *)error;`

The region-based location service can be helpful and is easy to implement. For example, you can use this service to notify the user that a grocery store is nearby, or in a to-do list application you can remind the user to pick up clothes from the dry cleaner when they are near it.

21.6   *Summary*

Multitasking is useful in many ways. With the application running in the background, you can provide an amazing user experience with the iOS 4 platform. Instead of yanking the user out of the application when the app quits, with a little extra work you can have the application return to the previous state or, even better, perform operations without the application running in the foreground.

Try to adopt fast app switching in your application. It will give the user a chance to resume the application.

In the next chapter, we'll spend more time on continuous location updates in the background and build an application together. We'll also tackle multitasking in depth; we'll show how to enable audio playing in the background and control the background audio through remote-control events.

Multitasking in depth

This chapter covers

- Monitoring the location service in the background
- Building an audio-playing application
- Enabling background audio playing
- Handling remote-control events

In the previous chapter, you learned the multitasking basics in iOS 4 and how to finish a task in the background with blocks and Grand Central Dispatch. When the application needs to (or for better user experience) continue running in the background, remember that these multitasking features are available on iOS 4:

- *Audio*—The application can continue running and play audio to the user while in the background. The user can use the multitasking UI or the lock screen UI to remotely control the audio play, pause, fast-forward, and so on.
- *Location*—The application can receive location updates to support location-related tasks or navigation in the background, such as the significant location change service and turn-by-turn directions.
- *VoIP*—Allows the application to receive voice calls through the internet even though other applications are in the foreground.

These multitasking features are useful and can boost your application to a brand-new level. In this last chapter of the book, first we'll continue the background location-monitoring service from the previous chapter by building a location-tracking application. Next, we'll focus on background audio playing and cover some additional advanced topics, such as handling interruptions and remote-control events.

22.1 *Using the location-monitoring service*

In the last chapter, you learned the features of significant location change updates and region-based location monitoring in the background. Now let's continue exploring the location service by building a location-monitoring application. In this section, we'll build a demo application that tracks location updates in the background.

22.1.1 *Updating the UI when the app relaunches*

The first step is to create the application to display the location data collected. First, open Xcode and create a project using the Navigation-Based Application template in the iOS application projects. Name it Locations. In this application, we'll use a table view to display all the new location updates from the location service running in the background.

The application's view controller needs to update the user interface with location data when the app is restarted from the background state. You learned how to do that in the last chapter's fast app-switching section, section 21.2.

Inside the RootViewController.h file, define an NSArray called `locationData` and use it as the table view's data source, as shown in listing 22.1. Then in the Root-ViewController.m file, display the location data on the table view. Keep in mind that the table view needs to reload the data when the application is restarted from the background.

> **Listing 22.1 RootViewController's header file and implementation file**

```
HEADER
#import <UIKit/UIKit.h>
@interface RootViewController : UITableViewController {
    NSArray *locationData;
}
@property (nonatomic, retain) NSArray *locationData;
@end

IMPLEMENTATION FILE
#import "RootViewController.h"
@implementation RootViewController
@synthesize locationData;

- (void)updateUI {
    NSUserDefaults *defaults = [NSUserDefaults standardUserDefaults];
    self.locationData = [defaults objectForKey:@"kLocationData"];
    [self.tableView reloadData];
}
```

```
- (void)viewDidLoad {
    [super viewDidLoad];
    self.title = @"Locations";
    [self updateUI];
    NSNotificationCenter *notifcenter =
      [NSNotificationCenter defaultCenter];
    [notifcenter addObserver:self selector:@selector(updateUI)
        name:UIApplicationWillEnterForegroundNotification
  object:nil];
}

- (NSInteger)numberOfSectionsInTableView:(UITableView *)tableView {
    return 1;
}

- (NSInteger)tableView:(UITableView *)tableView
    numberOfRowsInSection:(NSInteger)section {
    return [locationData count];
}
- (UITableViewCell *)tableView:(UITableView *)tableView
    cellForRowAtIndexPath:(NSIndexPath *)indexPath {
    static NSString *CellIdentifier = @"Cell";
    UITableViewCell *cell = [tableView
                            dequeueReusableCellWithIdentifier:CellIdentifier];
    if (cell == nil) {
      cell = [[[UITableViewCell alloc]
            initWithStyle:UITableViewCellStyleDefault
            reuseIdentifier:CellIdentifier]
            autorelease];
    }
    cell.textLabel.text = [locationData
                            objectAtIndex:indexPath.row];
    return cell;
}
- (void)dealloc {
    [locationData release];
    [super dealloc];
}
@end
```

When the table view controller gets loaded, the `locationData` array will fetch the data stored with `NSUserDefaults` and then update the table view based on the `location-Data` array. The notification center will observe the event when the application resumes from the background state and reload the table view's data.

Now the table view is ready to display the location data. Next, let's look at how to get the location updates from the Core Location framework with the significant-change location service.

22.1.2 Enabling the significant-change location service

In this section, we'll add the significant-change location service to our Locations application. First, add the Core Location framework to the project and include the core location header (CoreLocation/CoreLocation.h) in the app delegate file.

Then add the Core Location Manager to the app delegate as an instance variable: CLLocationManager *locationManager;. You must also modify the definition of the LocationsAppDelegate @interface to state that CLLocationManagerDelegate is implemented, like this:

```
@interface LocationsAppDelegate : NSObject <UIApplicationDelegate,
    CLLocationManagerDelegate>
```

Now add changes from the following listing into the app delegate implementation file to enable the location-monitoring service when the app launches.

Listing 22.2   Implementing location updates in the background

```
#import "LocationsAppDelegate.h"
#import "RootViewController.h"

@implementation LocationsAppDelegate
@synthesize window = _window;
@synthesize navigationController = _navigationController;

-(void)initLocationManager {                                        ❶ Start location
    if (locationManager == nil) {                                     service
        locationManager = [[CLLocationManager alloc] init];
        locationManager.delegate = self;
        [locationManager startMonitoringSignificantLocationChanges];
    }
}
- (void)saveCurrentData:(NSString *)newData {                       ❷ Store
    NSUserDefaults *defaults = [NSUserDefaults standardUserDefaults];   data
    NSMutableArray *savedData = [[NSMutableArray alloc]
      initWithArray:[defaults
      objectForKey:@"kLocationData"]];
    [savedData addObject:newData];
    [defaults setObject:savedData forKey:@"kLocationData"];
    [savedData release];
}
- (BOOL)application:(UIApplication *) application
    didFinishLaunchingWithOptions:(NSDictionary *)launchOptions
{
    if (![CLLocationManager                                        ❸ Test if location
      significantLocationChangeMonitoringAvailable])                  service is available
    {
        UIAlertView *alert = [[UIAlertView alloc] initWithTitle:@"Sorry"
              message:@"Your device won't support the significant"
                    "location change."
              delegate:self cancelButtonTitle:@"OK"
                otherButtonTitles:nil];
        [alert show];
        [alert release];
        return YES;                                                ❸ Test if location
    }                                                                 service is available
    [self initLocationManager];
    [self.window addSubview:navigationController.view];
    [self.window makeKeyAndVisible];
    return YES;
}
```

```
- (void)locationManager:(CLLocationManager *)manager
    didUpdateToLocation:(CLLocation *)newLocation
    fromLocation:(CLLocation *)oldLocation {
  NSString *locationData = [NSString stringWithFormat:
                            @"%.6f, %.6f", newLocation.coordinate.latitude,
                            newLocation.coordinate.longitude];
  [self saveCurrentData:locationData];
}

- (void)locationManager:(CLLocationManager *)manager
    didFailWithError:(NSError *)error {
  NSString *errorData = [NSString stringWithFormat:@"%@",[error
    localizedDescription]];
  NSLog(@"%@", errorData);
}
- (void)dealloc {
  [[NSNotificationCenter defaultCenter] removeObserver:self];
  [locationManager release];
  [_navigationController release];
  [window release];
  [super dealloc];
}

@end
```

Update ④
location data

Error handling ⑤

Inside the application delegate, you use the Core Location Manager to monitor the significant location change. When the application first launches, you call the method `initLocationManager` ❶ to initialize the Location Manager and start the significant location update service. In order to make sure the location service is actually available on this device, you use the method `significantLocationChangeMonitoring-Available` ❸ to test the availability, and if it's not possible to use the location update service on this device, you give the user an alert.

Once the new location is available, the Location Manager delegate method gets called ❹. You need to store the new location data using `NSDefaults` in the method `saveCurrentData` ❷. That's how the table view can get all the new location updates from the application delegate.

In case an error occurs during location updating, the Location Manager calls the delegate method ❺. You can read the error message inside the console window under Xcode.

You need to test this application on your iPhone or iPad with 3G because the Simulator doesn't support the location change service. Build and run this application on the device. Quit the application to let the location service run in the background.

The location application will continue receiving updates in the background, and once it's relaunched, you can track all the places you've been. Notice that even if the application is suspended in the background or the application isn't running at all, the location service is running. You can tell by the indicator on the status bar of your iPhone or iPad 3G, as shown in figure 22.1.

Figure 22.1   Significant location updates application running in the background

You can combine this significant location updates service and notify the user with local notifications. The region-based location monitoring service works exactly like the significant location updates service. You can define which region to monitor; when the user enters that specific region, the application will receive the location update through Core Location delegate methods. The system will wake up the application even if the application isn't running or suspended. We covered the key methods in the previous chapter.

Next, we'll dive into the background audio techniques and build an advanced application to support background audio together, step by step.

22.2 *Building an audio-playing application with the Audio Toolbox framework*

In order to demonstrate the background audio API, we need to have an application playing audio. Back in chapter 12, you learned how to use the AV Foundation framework to play music inside the application. Let's start by building a MySong application to play music with the AV Foundation framework. We're going to use the AV Foundation framework's audio player that you've already learned and add in the new Audio Toolbox framework to support background audio-playing and remote-control events.

The Audio Toolbox framework sits one level below the AV Foundation framework, so there are more methods available. The new class we're going to use is AVAudio-Session in the Audio Toolbox framework.

First, you may want to spend some time learning new methods in AVAudioSession. AVAudioSession is a singleton object that helps you configure the audio behavior in your application. Call the following class method to get the singleton audio session:

[AVAudioSession sharedInstance];

There are a few reasons for using an audio session:

- To define the audio session category
- To respond to the headset plug-in or unplug it
- To handle interruptions during audio playing

Why do you need to define the audio session category? Table 22.1 show the six categories in iOS that allow you to customize the audio role in your application.

Table 22.1 Audio session category

Audio session category	Definition
AVAudioSessionCategoryAmbient	Audio playing is not the primary purpose but it allows another application's audio to play. Will be muted when the screen is autolocked or the Silent switch is on.
AVAudioSessionCategorySoloAmbient	Default value. Only the current application will play the audio. Will be muted when the screen is autolocked or the Silent switch is on.

Table 22.1 Audio session category *(continued)*

Audio session category	Definition
AVAudioSessionCategoryPlayback	Audio playing is the primary purpose in this application. Won't allow other applications to play along. Won't be muted even if the Silent switch is on. Supports background audio playing.
AVAudioSessionCategoryRecord	Audio recording is the primary purpose. Continues recording when the screen is autolocked.
AVAudioSessionCategoryPlayAndRecord	For audio playing and recording at the same time or not, i.e., voice over IP. This setting will mute the other application's audio.
AVAudioSessionCategoryAudioProcessing	Not playing audio or recording but processing the audio, such as format conversion.

When you set the category to playback, the system knows your application's main purpose is to play music, and it should continue playing even when the application isn't active. By default, this value in the audio session's category is AVAudioSession-CategorySoloAmbient, and the system will stop the audio playing when the application is inactive. Because we're building an audio-playing application that supports continuous audio playing in the background, we need to set the audio session category to playback.

Use this code snippet to define the audio session's category to playback:

```
[[AVAudioSession sharedInstance] setCategory:
    AVAudioSessionCategoryPlayback error: nil];
```

Let's build the audio-playing application with both the Audio Toolbox and AV Foundation frameworks in Xcode. Create a new project, use the View-Based Application template in the iOS application, and name it MySong. Because we're going to use the AV Foundation and Audio Toolbox frameworks in this application, go ahead and add in the needed extra frameworks. Include the header files inside the MySongView-Controller.h file:

```
#import <AVFoundation/AVFoundation.h>
#import <AudioToolbox/AudioToolbox.h>
```

Let's add an audio file called backgroundmusic.m4a into our project. That's the audio file we'll play in the application. You can use any music or audio file available on your own computer; just make sure the name matches the example in this project.

What is M4A format?
Files in M4A format are actually the audio layer of (nonvideo) MPEG 4 movies. M4A is slated to become the new standard for audio file compression.

Next, we'll design the UI inside the MySong view controller. There will be a text label to display the current audio file's name in the center of the screen, and below the label will be three buttons: one button for play/pause events, one for fast-forward, and another one for rewind. When you tap the Play button, the button image will flip to Pause, indicating you can pause the currently playing audio.

In order to have a better user experience, let's add the background images for the three buttons into our project.

Select the MySongViewController.h file, and add in the new changes, as shown in the following listing.

Listing 22.3   Project MySong's view controller header file

```objc
#import <UIKit/UIKit.h>
#import <AVFoundation/AVFoundation.h>
#import <AudioToolbox/AudioToolbox.h>
@interface MySongViewController :
  UIViewController <AVAudioPlayerDelegate> {
    AVAudioPlayer          *myPlayer;
    IBOutlet UILabel       *fileName;
    IBOutlet UIButton      *playButton;
    IBOutlet UIButton      *ffwButton;
    IBOutlet UIButton      *rewButton;
}
@property (nonatomic, assign)    AVAudioPlayer    *myPlayer;
@property (nonatomic, retain)    UILabel          *fileName;
@property (nonatomic, retain)    UIButton         *playButton;
@property (nonatomic, retain)    UIButton         *ffwButton;
@property (nonatomic, retain)    UIButton         *rewButton;

- (IBAction)playButtonPressed:(UIButton*)sender;
- (IBAction)rewButtonPressed:(UIButton*)sender;
- (IBAction)ffwButtonPressed:(UIButton*)sender;
@end
```

In the header file, you add in one label for the filename and three buttons for the audio playing control. Three methods are defined to handle each button's touch event.

Save the changes for the header file. Next, let's add the new objects to the nib file and connect them to the view controller's header file.

Click the MySongViewController.xib file to open it for editing, and then open the object library. First, add a new text label into the view, and then drag three buttons into the view. By default, the button's type is a rounded rectangle. Let's change the button's attributes to a custom type and assign the background image to each button. Once it's complete, you'll see the view controller's UI, similar to the one shown in figure 22.2.

Single-click the file's owner under the MySongViewController's File panel. Go to the connection inspector and make sure all four UI outlets in the file's owner are connected to new subviews. Hook up the three action buttons and save everything.

Now we'll move on to implement the MySongViewController.m file. There are many changes in the next step, considering this is a comprehensive audio playing project.

Figure 22.2 MySong's view controller UI

Select the file and add in the code according to the following listing.

Listing 22.4 MySongViewController.m file

```
#import "MySongViewController.h"

@implementation MySongViewController
@synthesize myPlayer;
@synthesize fileName;
@synthesize playButton;
@synthesize ffwButton;
@synthesize rewButton;

#define SKIP_TIME 3.0
- (void)updateViewForPlayerState:(AVAudioPlayer *)player
{
    UIImage *buttonImg;
    if (player.playing)
      buttonImg = [UIImage imageNamed:@"pause.png"];
    else
      buttonImg = [UIImage imageNamed:@"play.png"];
    [playButton setBackgroundImage:buttonImg forState:UIControlStateNormal];
}

-(void)pausePlaybackForPlayer:(AVAudioPlayer*)player
{
    [player pause];
    [self updateViewForPlayerState:player];
}

-(void)startPlaybackForPlayer:(AVAudioPlayer*)player
{
```

❶ Update Play button bgimage

❷ Pause audio playing

❸ Start audio playing

```
    if ([player play])
      [self updateViewForPlayerState:player];
}

- (void)rewind                                        ◀━━④ Rewind
{
    myPlayer.currentTime -= SKIP_TIME;
}

- (void)fastforward                                   ◀━━⑤ Fast-forward
{
    myPlayer.currentTime += SKIP_TIME;
}
```

⑥ **Play/Pause button pressed**

```
- (IBAction)playButtonPressed:(UIButton *)sender
{
    if (myPlayer.playing == YES)
      [self pausePlaybackForPlayer:myPlayer];
    else
      [self startPlaybackForPlayer:myPlayer];
}
```

⑦ **Rewind button pressed**

```
- (IBAction)rewButtonPressed:(UIButton *)sender
{
    [self rewind];
}
```

⑧ **Fast-forward button pressed**

```
- (IBAction)ffwButtonPressed:(UIButton *)sender
{
    [self fastforward];
}
```

Audio player finishes the audio file ⑨

```
- (void)audioPlayerDidFinishPlaying:(AVAudioPlayer *)player
     successfully:(BOOL)flag {
  [player setCurrentTime:0.];
  [self updateViewForPlayerState:player];
}
```

⑩ **Interuptions start**

```
- (void)audioPlayerBeginInterruption:(AVAudioPlayer *)player
{
    [self updateViewForPlayerState:player];
}

- (void)audioPlayerEndInterruption:(AVAudioPlayer *)player
     withFlags: (BOOL)flags
```

Interuptions end ⑪

```
{
    if (flags & AVAudioSessionInterruptionFlags_ShouldResume)
      [self startPlaybackForPlayer:player];
}
```

⑫ **Create audio player**

```
- (void)viewDidLoad {
  NSURL *fileURL = [[NSURL alloc] initFileURLWithPath:
    [[NSBundle mainBundle]
                   pathForResource:@"backgroundmusic" ofType:@"m4a"]];
  self.myPlayer = [[AVAudioPlayer alloc] initWithContentsOfURL:
    fileURL error:nil];
  if (self.myPlayer)
  {
```

```
        fileName.text = [[myPlayer.url relativePath] lastPathComponent];
        [self updateViewForPlayerState:myPlayer];
        myPlayer.numberOfLoops = 10;
        myPlayer.delegate = self;
    }
    [[AVAudioSession sharedInstance] setDelegate: self];
    NSError *setCategoryError = nil;
    [[AVAudioSession sharedInstance] setCategory:
     AVAudioSessionCategoryPlayback
     error: &setCategoryError];
    if (setCategoryError)
        NSLog(@"Error setting category! %d", setCategoryError);
    [fileURL release];
    [super viewDidLoad];
}

- (void)viewDidUnload {
    self.fileName = nil;
    self.playButton = nil;
    self.ffwButton = nil;
        self.rewButton = nil;
}
- (void)dealloc {
    [fileName release];
    [playButton release];
    [ffwButton release];
    [rewButton release];
    [myPlayer release];
    [super dealloc];
}
```

⑬ **Define audio session**

⑭ **Release retained objects**

```
@end
```

Let's review what you've changed inside this view controller file.

You want to use the Play/Pause button to toggle between play and pause, so you define the method updateViewForPlayerState ❶ to update the Play/Pause button's background image, indicating the audio player's status. The method pausePlayback-ForPlayer ❷ can pause the audio player and update the UI. The method startPlay-backForPlayer ❸ will start playing the audio file if the audio player is not playing.

The method rewind ❹ can control the audio player's timeline to go back 3 seconds, and the method fastforward ❺ will control it to fast-forward 3 seconds.

The action method playButtonPressed ❻ will respond to the Play/Pause button's action event. The action methods rewButtonPressed ❼ and ffwButtonPressed ❽ will respond to the Rewind button's action and the Fast-forward button's action, respectively.

Then you define the audio player's delegate callbacks in audioPlayerDidFinish-Playing ❾, audioPlayerBeginInterruption ❿, and audioPlayerEndInterruption ⓫. In audioPlayerDidFinishPlaying ❾, when the audio playing task is complete, you reset the timeline back to the beginning. When an interuption occurs in the system, the delegate callbacks give you the chance to update the UI. When the interuption is gone, you need to resume playing the music.

Finally, in `viewDidLoad` ⑫, you first define the audio player's music file as back-groundmusic.m4a and then customize the view controller's UI by displaying the file's name in the label `fileName`. In addition, you want to autoplayback this music file 10 times and set the delegate to `self`.

Then inside the audio session ⑬, you define the category as `AVAudioSession-CategoryPlayback` to inform the system that this application will use audio playing as a primary function.

Finally, you release the retained objects inside the `dealloc` ⑭.

That's all! Change the target to a universal application for both iPhone and iPad. Save all the changes, click Build, and run it in Xcode.

If everything runs smoothly, you should see a comprehensive audio-playing application launch on your iPhone or iPad that contains a Play/Pause button, Fast-forward button, and Rewind button. The text label will display the audio file's name, as shown in figure 22.3.

Play with this application a bit, and you will find that our application has the first priority in audio playing. For example, try to play music using the iPod system app in the background, and when this application starts playing audio, the system will mute the iPod music; this application will continue playing even if the screen is autolocked.

When you have an incoming phone call, this application will pause playing the current music as defined in the interruption-handling methods.

Figure 22.3   The audio-playing application when it's launched on the iPhone and iPad

This application uses fast app switching to automatically handle the different application's life transitions. You just built an advanced audio-playing application with the Audio Toolbox and AV Foundation frameworks. Keep in mind that the audio session category is important for audio-playing applications.

Now let's continue with our multitasking project to enable background audio playing and handle remote-control events.

22.3 Enabling audio playing in the background

Under iOS 4, when an application is playing music in the background, such as an iPod application or Pandora, the status bar on the iPhone or iPad has an audio-playing indicator (a Play icon) on the right corner indicating that the music is playing, as shown in figure 22.4.

In the previous section we created a pretty nice audio-playing application, but the music will stop playing if the user taps the Home button. How can we continue playing the music in the application when it's in the background? Even more, how can we control the music playing through the remote-control UI just like in the iPod application, as shown in figure 22.4? We'll explain the details in the next section.

22.3.1 Adding the UIBackgroundModes in Info.plist

The first step to enable the background audio playing is to tell the system that this application will continue playing audio while in the background. How can we do that?

In iOS 4, there's a new key inside the application's Info.plist called `UIBackground-Modes`, and we need to define the value of this key as "App plays audio."

Inside our MySong project, go to the Resources folder and select MySong's Info.plist. Add in a new row, `Required background modes`, and define the item's value as "App plays audio," as shown in figure 22.5.

That's the important step to tell the system that we need to enable the background audio for this application. Let's give it a try right now.

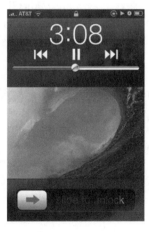

Figure 22.4 Two remote-control UIs on the iPhone when the audio application is playing in the background

Figure 22.5   The info.plist with the background audio key enabled

Save the change, and hit Build and Run under Xcode. When the application launches on your iPhone or iPad, tap the Play button to start playing the music. Then tap the Home button to quit the application. Notice that there is an audio-playing icon on the right corner of the status bar, indicating that you have a background audio application running.

   Are you listening to the music playing in the background? Congrats! You just learned how to enable the background audio in iOS 4.

> **NOTE**   At the time of writing, background audio is not supported on the Simulator, so make sure you're testing your application on a real device, either on an iPhone, iPod Touch, or iPad. That will save you some time trying to figure out what the problem is with the background audio playing.

Now you might want to try the remote-control UI to pause the music, but it won't work. Why? That's because the response is not defined yet, so the system doesn't know what to do when the remote-control events occur. We'll work through the new changes in the next section.

22.3.2   *Handling the remote-control events*

You've already learned how to enable background audio in the MySong application. Now it's time to handle the remote-control events.

   There are two kinds of remote-control user interfaces in iOS 4. One is on the multitasking UI deck, as shown in figure 22.4 on the left side; when you swipe from left to right under the multitasking UI deck, the remote-control UI will present. A few buttons are available: Fast-forward, Play/Pause, and Rewind. The other remote control UI appears when you lock the screen and double-tap the Home button, it's the iPod remote control UI that you've been familiar with since iOS 3, as shown in figure 22.4 on the right side.

   It turns out that you just need to define the remote-control events once, and they'll work for both remote control user interfaces. Let's get started.

   First, you need to tell the application that you want to begin receiving the remote-control events. Call the method `beginReceivingRemoteControlEvents` under `UIApplication` and define the view controller as the first responder when the Remote-control button is tapped. Use the following code snippet:

```
-(void)viewDidAppear:(BOOL)animated {
    [[UIApplication sharedApplication] beginReceivingRemoteControlEvents];
    [self becomeFirstResponder];
}
```

```
- (BOOL)canBecomeFirstResponder {
    return YES;
}
```

Then you can start to define each event's action method in the view controller:

`-(void)remoteControlReceivedWithEvent:(UIEvent *)event`

There are quite a few touch events inside the subtypes, and you want to define the related method inside our application so the system will know how to handle different remote-control events. The `UIEvent`'s subtypes related to the audio remote-control events are listed in table 22.2.

Table 22.2 `UIEvent`'s remote-control subtypes and descriptions

UIEvent subtype	Description
UIEventSubtypeNone	The event has no subtype.
UIEventSubtypeRemoteControlPlay	Playing audio.
UIEventSubtypeRemoteControlPause	Pausing audio.
UIEventSubtypeRemoteControlStop	Stopping audio from playing.
UIEventSubtypeRemoteControlTogglePlayPause	Toggling audio between play and pause.
UIEventSubtypeRemoteControlNextTrack	Fast-forward, skipping to the next audio.
UIEventSubtypeRemoteControlPreviousTrack	Rewind, skipping to the previous audio.
UIEventSubtypeRemoteControlBeginSeekingBackward	Start seeking backward through the audio.
UIEventSubtypeRemoteControlEndSeekingBackward	End seeking backward through the audio.
UIEventSubtypeRemoteControlBeginSeekingForward	Start seeking forward through the audio.
UIEventSubtypeRemoteControlEndSeekingForward	End seeking forward through the audio.

Now with the new remote-control method you learned, we'll start coding with the background audio application and handle the remote-control events in the next section.

22.4   *Building the background audio application*

In our MySong application, three action methods are defined already: when the Play/Pause button is tapped, when the Fast-forward button is tapped, and when the Rewind button is tapped. Therefore, in the method `remoteControlReceivedWithEvent:`, we'll use the three action methods to handle the remote-control events:

- `UIEventSubtypeRemoteControlTogglePlayPause:`—Toggle between Play and Pause
- `UIEventSubtypeRemoteControlNextTrack:`—Next track, fast-forward 3 seconds
- `UIEventSubtypeRemoteControlPreviousTrack:`—Previous track, rewind 3 seconds

With the methods from the last section, define the view controller to be the first responder and begin to receive the remote-control events. Then define the reaction method for each remote-control event in the view controller's method `remote-ControlReceivedWithEvent:`, as shown in the following listing.

Listing 22.5 Enabling remote-control and handling remote-control event reactions

```
-(void)viewDidAppear:(BOOL)animated {
    [[UIApplication sharedApplication] beginReceivingRemoteControlEvents];   ⇠ Begin receiving
    [self becomeFirstResponder];                                               remote-control events
}

- (BOOL)canBecomeFirstResponder {        ⇠ View control is
    return YES;                             first responder
}
-(void)remoteControlReceivedWithEvent:(UIEvent *)event      ⇠ Remote-control
{                                                             events occurred
    switch (event.subtype) {
        case UIEventSubtypeRemoteControlTogglePlayPause:
            [self playButtonPressed:nil];
            break;
        case UIEventSubtypeRemoteControlNextTrack:
            [self ffwButtonPressed:nil];
            break;
        case UIEventSubtypeRemoteControlPreviousTrack:
            [self rewButtonPressed:nil];
            break;
    }
}
```

With new methods added in the MySongViewController.m file, the new audio-playing application MySong can now handle the remote-control events.

Save all the changes, build the application under Xcode, and launch the app on the device. When the application launches, first tap the Play button to start the music playing, and then tap the Home button to quit. The music will continue playing in the background.

Double-tap the home screen to enable the multitasking UI dock, and swipe from left to right to launch the remote-control UI on the multitasking dock, as shown in figure 22.6.

**Figure 22.6
Remote-control UI of My-Song application on the multitasking dock**

Now this application can support the remote-control play/pause feature. When you tap the Fast-forward button, the music timeline will jump 3 seconds forward. Tap the icon, and this app will launch from the background to the foreground.

In addition, when you have an incoming phone call or some other notification from the system, the audio player delegate callback methods will handle the interruption and resume playing music when the interruption is dismissed.

> **Remote-control UI dock is last-in, first-out**
> In the remote-control UI dock, the application queues are last-in, first-out. So, if you have the application running in the background and change to another music-playing application, such as the iPod application, the latter one will be on the remote-control dock.

Now enjoy this audio-playing application! You did a great job of building an awesome application that supports background audio.

22.5 *Summary*

In this last chapter of the book, we dug further into the multitasking topic, built the location-tracking application with background significant location updates, and then focused on the background audio topic. We enhanced the audio-playing application with the audio session from the lower-level Audio Toolbox framework and multitasking API for background audio playing. This application will not only continue running in the background but also react to remote-control events. Even more, it's capable of handling system interruptions. When you combine background audio with internet streaming data, such as Pandora, there's unlimited potential.

iOS 4 provides many enhancements to the user's experience. By default, fast app switching is supported on all applications built on iOS 4. Moreover, multitasking gives developers the power to use local notifications, enable background audio playing, finish a task in the background, and track location updates in the background with lower power consumption. With multitasking knowledge, you can create amazing applications with all the frameworks covered throughout the book.

As always, we encourage you to explore more with the iOS SDK.

So long, my friend! Thanks for staying with us. You started with a basic application and mastered the solid foundation and advanced features of iOS 4. You're ready to build the next best-selling application in the App Store.

We wish you the best of luck on the application development journey!

appendix A
iOS class reference

After reading this book, your main resource for learning more about iOS development should be the references at http://developer.apple.com. To help you find documents that might interest you, this appendix lists the major classes in the UIKit and Foundation hierarchies that you may want to know more about, excluding classes that only appear as a part of another class.

A.1   UIKit framework classes

The UIKit framework contains those classes most tightly connected to the devices, including all the graphical classes you use to make up pages. A partial listing appears as table A.1. It's current as of iOS 4.3 and will probably be mostly correct when you read this, but the UIKit does sometimes change between releases.

Table A.1   The most important user interface classes

Class	Parent	Summary
UIActionSheet	UIView	A pop-up window that includes options; similar to a UIAlertView
UIActivityIndicatorView	UIView	An indeterminate progress display
UIAlertView	UIView	A pop-up window that includes options; similar to a UIActionSheet
UIApplication	UIResponder	The main source for application information and control
UIButton	UIControl	A push button
UIColor	NSObject	A color output class
UIControl	UIView	An abstract class that is parent to many user controls
UIDatePicker	UIControl	A wheeled date-selection device
UIDevice	NSObject	A class that holds info about the device itself
UIEvent	NSObject	A container for touches; part of the event model

Table A.1   The most important user interface classes *(continued)*

Class	Parent	Summary
UIFont	NSObject	A font output class
UIImage	NSObject	A nondisplaying image holder
UIImagePickerController	UINavigationController	A modal controller for image selection
UIImageView	UIView	An image display that holds one or more UIImage objects
UILabel	UIView	A small, non-editable text display
UINavigationController	UIViewController	A hierarchical controller; often linked with a UITableViewController to produce hierarchical menus
UIPageControl	UIControl	A toolbar for navigating among pages using dots
UIPickerView	UIView	A wheel-based selection mechanism
UIProgressView	UIView	A determinate progress display
UIResponder	NSObject	An abstract class that defines all classes that can receive and respond to events
UIScreen	NSObject	A class containing the device's entire screen
UIScrollView	UIView	A parent class for views with multiple pages of content
UISearchBar	UIView	A text-input mechanism specialized for searches
UISegmentedControl	UIControl	A control for making one of several choices
UISlider	UIControl	A control for setting discrete values
UISwitch	UIControl	A control for selecting binary values
UITabBarController	UIViewController	A controller for moving among multiple screens
UITableViewController	UIViewController	A controller for displaying tables of content; often linked with a UINavigationController
UITextField	UIControl	A control for inputting short text
UITextView	UIScrollView	A display for text of any size
UITouch	NSObject	An individual touch on the device's screen
UIView	UIResponder	The abstract class that lies at the core of most UIKit objects
UIViewController	UIResponder	A simple view controller

Table A.1   The most important user interface classes *(continued)*

Class	Parent	Summary
UIWebView	UIView	A Safari-like web browser
UIWindow	UIView	The root for the view hierarchy

A.2   *Foundation framework classes*

Foundation framework classes, whose names begin with *NS*, are almost as important as the UI classes because they represent foundational variable types, like strings and numbers. Table A.2 only lists the major classes that have some relevance to the sort of work you've done in this book; for more, look at Apple's developer site under Core Services Frameworks.

Table A.2   A listing of the most important Foundation classes

Class	Parent	Summary
NSArray	NSObject	An array
NSAutoreleasePool	NSObject	A memory-management class
NSBundle	NSObject	A pointer toward a project's filesystem home
NSCharacterSet	NSObject	Methods for managing characters
NSCountedSet	NSMutableSet	An unordered collection of elements
NSData	NSObject	A wrapper for a byte buffer
NSDictionary	NSObject	An associative array
NSError	NSObject	Encapsulated error information
NSFileHandle	NSObject	A methodology for controlling files
NSFileManager	NSObject	A manager for filesystem work
NSIndexPath	NSObject	A node path
NSLog	NSObject	A very important object for debugging; logs a formatted string to the system log
NSMutableArray	NSArray	An array that can be changed
NSMutableCharacterSet	NSCharacterSet	A character set that can be changed
NSMutableData	NSData	Data that can be changed
NSMutableDictionary	NSDictionary	A dictionary that can be changed
NSMutableSet	NSSet	A set that can be changed
NSMutableString	NSString	A string that can be changed
NSMutableURLRequest	NSURLRequest	A URL request that can be changed

Table A.2 A listing of the most important Foundation classes *(continued)*

Class	Parent	Summary
NSNotificationCenter	NSObject	A notification manager
NSNumber	NSValue	A way to encapsulate many types of numbers
NSObject	N/A	The root class for Cocoa Touch
NSString	NSObject	A class for various sorts of string storage and manipulation
NSURL	NSObject	A simple URL object
NSURLRequest	NSObject	A URL plus a cache policy
NSValue	NSObject	A simple container for data
NSXMLParser	NSObject	An XML parser

A.3 Other classes

The UI and NS classes should contain most of the objects you use when programming.

We've also covered several other frameworks throughout this book, including the Address Book framework (chapter 9), the Address Book UI framework (chapter 9), the Core Location framework (chapter 10), the Core Audio framework (chapter 12), the Media Player framework (chapter 12), the Core Graphics framework (chapter 11), the Quartz Core framework (chapter 13), the OpenGL ES framework (chapter 13), the CFNetwork framework (chapter 14), the Game Kit Framework (chapter 15), the Event Kit framework (chapter 16), the APNS framework (chapter 17), the Map Kit framework (chapter 18), the Store Kit framework (chapter 19), and the iAd framework (chapter 20). Finally, you may wish to pay some attention to the Core Foundation framework, which we've used (as infrequently as possible) throughout the last part of this book.

appendix B
External sources
and references

What follows are web resources that we suggest for continuing your exploration of iPhone and iPad development.

General resources

Site	URL	Summary
iCodeBlog	http://icodeblog.com	Brandon Trebitowski's iPhone and iPad development blog. Updated weekly with great tutorials related to iPhone OS development.
iPhone Atlas	www.iphoneatlas.com	iPhone news blog.
iPhone Dev Forums	www.iphonedevforums.com	Forums for SDK or web discussion.
Stack Overflow	www.stackoverflow.com	Great community of developers where you can ask and answer programming questions for any language.
iPhone in Action	http://iphoneinaction.manning.com/	Christopher and Shannon's blog for this book. Keeps you up to date with new links of interest and occasionally covers some of the topics that aren't covered in this book.
The Apple Blog	http://theappleblog.com	General Apple blog, including some iOS discussion.

SDK resources

Site	URL	Summary
Apple Developer Site	http://developer.apple.com/devcenter/ios/	Official Apple site for developer resources; requires ADC login
Apps Amuck	www.appsamuck.com/	Thirty-one programs with source code in 31 days
Cocoa Dev Central	http://cocoadevcentral.com/	A hub of Objective-C and Cocoa information
Cocoa Is My Girlfriend	www.cimgf.com/	News and tutorial blog
Cocoa Samurai	http://cocoasamurai.blogspot.com/	Cocoa and iPhone discussion
Furbo.org	http://furbo.org/	General blog that's mostly iPhone discussion
iPhone Dev SDK	www.iphonedevsdk.com/	Forums
iPhone Development	http://iphonedevelopment.blogspot.com/	Blog with extensive original content
Mobile Orchard	www.mobileorchard.com/	News blog
Safe from the Losing Fight	www.losingfight.com/blog/	Blog about Macs with some emphasis on iPhones

Other technologies

Site	URL	Summary
JavaScript.com	www.javascript.com/	A comprehensive JavaScript site
Mozilla.org	https://developer.mozilla.org/en/JavaScript	A comprehensive Javascript reference and tutorial site
SQLite	www.sqlite.org/	The official SQLite site
W3C XML	www.w3.org/XML/	The official XML site

appendix C
Publishing your application

All of your programming will be for naught if you don't sign up for the iOS Developer Program with Apple. This is a multistep process that can take quite some time, so make sure to get it all in hand well before you want to upload your program to the App Store.

C.1 Signing up with Apple

To get started, you must register as a developer at http://developer.apple.com/devcenter/ios/. When you register, you're asked for some basic information about what you'll be developing, and you need to sign Apple's Terms & Conditions for working with the iOS. You've probably already done this step, because it's required in order to get access to the SDK and the online documentation.

Sometime afterward—maybe in a few hours, maybe in a few weeks—you'll get a call from Apple confirming your signup information and giving you the OK for the program. Apple will then send you an email that allows you to finish your registration. At this point, expect to pay a fee, currently $99/year (standard) or $299/year (enterprise), to become a full-fledged developer. The standard program allows for distribution via the App Store, and the enterprise program allows distribution of in-house applications to over 500 employees.

C.2 Compiling to the device

The first advantage of being a registered iOS developer is that you can compile programs directly to your device. This is fairly critical for certain types of testing. As you've seen in this book, features like altitude detection, volume control, and the accelerometer don't work correctly when tested in the Simulator.

To compile to a device, you must create a provisioning profile, which is a multistep process. You need to use some new tools that appear under a Program Portal link at the top of http://developer.apple.com after you finish your signup and pay your fee. Apple has a complete "iTunes Connect Developer Guide" that explains how to use everything here, but we'll outline the main steps:

1 *Add team members (admin)*—If you registered as a company, you can add additional team members under the Team tab. The initial creator of a team is the Team Agent, who has the highest-level powers in the Developer Program; other users are Team Administrators or Team Members. From here, individual members can set themselves up to compile to their devices, with some steps requiring interventions from Team Admins.

2 *Create a certificate signing request (member)*—This is the first step required to generate the certificate you need to sign (and thus run) applications on your device. You create a certificate signing request (CSR) inside Keychain Access on your Mac and then upload it from the Certificates > Development tab; a Team Admin must then approve it.

3 *Download a certificate (member)*—After your Admin (who may be you) has approved your CSR, you can download a certificate. From Certificates > Development, download the WWDR Intermediate Certificate, and double-click to install it. Afterward, download your developer certificate, and double-click to install it.

WARNING Your certificate will be permanently installed in your keychain; if you rebuild your machine or move to a new machine, you'll lose it. To avoid this, be sure you export the private key associated with your developer certificate. You can then import it on a different machine, and redownload the two certificates from Apple. If you fail to do this, a Team Admin may need to revoke your certificate so that you can create a new one.

4 *Add devices (admin)*—Add any devices (iPhones, iPods, or iPads) that you want to build on using the Devices tab.

5 *Create an app ID (admin)*—Each application needs an app ID, which controls its access to devices. For the purposes of testing, you'll probably use one general wildcard ID that you create by appending a wildcard (.*) to your app ID bundle identifier.

6 *Create a provisioning profile (admin)*—A provisioning profile is a unique combination of multiple developer certificates, multiple device IDs, and a single app ID. It's what ties your device to your overall development profile and what allows you to run programs. You create a provisioning profile from the Provisioning > Development tab, at which point you're asked to enter the three elements that make it up.

7 *Download a provisioning profile (member)*—Download the profile from Devices, and drag it your Xcode dock icon or the organizer window of Xcode.

Although the setup can be a bit extensive for an Admin, after the initial work is done, a member can create a CSR, download a certificate, and download a provisioning profile. From that point, the member can choose to compile onto a device rather than to the iOS Simulator by changing the pop-up window at upper left in Xcode.

C.3   *Preparing for distribution via the App Store*

Preparing your program for distribution via the App Store follows much the same process as preparing your programs for testing on iPhones on iPads, except that the steps can only be undertaken by the Team Agent:

1   *Create a certificate (agent)*—As before, you must upload a CSR, but here you should create a certificate from the Certificates > Distribution tab, rather than Certificates > Development.

2   *Create a provisioning profile (agent)*—Create a provisioning profile in the Provisioning > Distribution tab. It's usually an App Store profile. As before, drag your new profile to Xcode.

3   *Prepare to compile (anyone)*—Create a new Distribution configuration that uses the distribution provisioning profile. Update other info in the configuration, update your Info.plist as appropriate, and then build.

4   *Prepare media (anyone)*—Prepare a set of 57 x 57 (required), 72x72(required), 114x114(recommended), 29x29(recommended), 50x50(recommended) and 58x58(recommended). PNG icons, a 512 x 512 JPG/TIFF large application icon, and full-screen portrait and landscape screenshots, as well as other information required by the App Store.

5   *Upload (agent)*—Go to the Distribution tab, and create the new app under iTunes Connect. Upload the binary file with Application loader.

6   *Wait (everyone)*—It will take some time for your application to be approved and go on sale.

These procedures may change over time; but for now, this is what you need to do to get your program from your desktop to the App Store.

There are also two alternative ways to distribute your software: enterprise distribution lets you distribute an in-house application to employees within your company, and ad hoc distributions let you distribute to up to 100 other users by email or a website. Both are explained further in Apple's documentation.

appendix D
Updating current applications for the iPad

Developing for the iPad is nearly identical as developing for the iPhone, so you should almost always release a version of your application for both. iPad users can always run your iPhone application in 2x mode (which stretches your iPhone application to fit the dimensions of the iPad screen), but this makes for an overall poor experience.

In a development document[1] called "Introducing Universal Application for iPhone OS", Apple provides a clear and concise document for creating your application for both the iPhone and the iPad. Rather than restating that document, we felt it would be more beneficial to walk you through how to update an iPhone app to support the iPad in converting an actual application.

You'll follow a few standard steps to convert iPhone applications into iPad applications:

1 Configure Xcode. Add iPad to the build target.
2 Update the Info.plist, which is needed to support multiple interface orientations.
3 Add iPad-specific interface components.
4 Update the views. Because the device is larger, you need to update the frames of all your views.
5 Add multiple-orientation support.

In this appendix, you'll convert the collage application that you created in chapter 11 to an iPad application.

D.1 Configuring Xcode

The process for updating your build target to include iPad support is simple. This is because the latest version of Xcode includes a tool that performs the migration for you. Apple strongly recommends against manually updating your files to support the iPad.

---

[1] http://devimages.apple.com/iphone/resources/introductiontouniversalapps.pdf

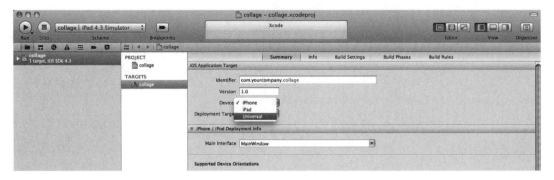

Figure D.1   Upgrading your build target for the iPad

Follow these steps:

1   Open the collage project in Xcode. This is a project we created in chapter 11, section 11.4.

2   Select collage project in the navigation view. The editor view will display the project summary. Select your collage target, and choose Universal for Devices option (see figure D.1).

3   Xcode will present a dialog to confirm that you would like to transit to universal target. Select Yes.

As soon as you perform the upgrade, you'll notice that an iPad folder is added to your project. It contains a new Main-Window-iPad.xib file for the main window of your application. Now run the application in the iPad Simulator. Because you have multiple targets, you must specify which target to run. Make sure the target is iPad 4.3 Simulator. (see figure D.2).

Your application should now run in the iPad Simulator (see figure D.3)

Figure D.2   Collage application running on the iPad

Notice that most of the interface is resized for you. This is because you have a simple interface composed of native UI elements. More complicated interfaces would require more updates.

D.2   *Updating Info.plist to support multiple orientations*

In all iOS applications you can define the support interface orientations. In order to do this, you must add the `UISupportedInterfaceOrientations` key to your project's Info.plist. The steps to do this manually are as follows.

1   Open the Info.plist file, right-click in the plist window, and select Add Row.
2   In the Key column, type `UISupportedInterfaceOrientations~ipad`. The `~ipad` after the field denotes that this field applies to the iPad only. You can just as easily add `~iphone` or `~ipod` to apply the field to the other devices.
3   Right-click the field and set the value type to Array.
4   Right-click again, add a row, and add each of the three interface types. Figure D.4 shows what the plist should look like when you're finished.

Alternatively, you can simply update Info.plist to support multiple orientations by several mouse clicks. Select collage Targets and under Summary tab, drag down to iPad

Key	Type	Value
CFBundleDevelopmentRegion	String	en
CFBundleDisplayName	String	${PRODUCT_NAME}
CFBundleExecutable	String	${EXECUTABLE_NAME}
CFBundleIconFile	String	
CFBundleIdentifier	String	com.yourcompany.${PRODUCT_NAME:identifier}
CFBundleInfoDictionaryVersion	String	6.0
CFBundleName	String	${PRODUCT_NAME}
CFBundlePackageType	String	APPL
CFBundleSignature	String	????
CFBundleVersion	String	1.0
LSRequiresIPhoneOS	Boolean	YES
NSMainNibFile	String	MainWindow
NSMainNibFile~ipad	String	MainWindow–iPad
▼ UISupportedInterfaceOrientations~ipad	Array	(3 items)
Item 0	String	UIInterfaceOrientationPortrait
Item 1	String	UIInterfaceOrientationLandscapeLeft
Item 2	String	UIInterfaceOrientationLandscapeRight

Figure D.4   Collage application running on the iPad

Deployment Info. You will find the Supported Device Orientations. Click on Portrait, Landscape Left and Landscape Right options.

If you tap the arrow in the lower-left corner of the screen to add images, the application present the "UIImagePickerController modally instead of via the UIPopover-Controller". You'll now make the necessary change to correctly display the picker.

D.3   *Adding iPad-specific interface components*

With the iPhone, the UIImagePickerController is presented modally. The iPad screen is much bigger, so it's recommended to present a list of options using a UIPopover-Controller instead. As you start experimenting with iPad development, you'll notice little changes like this that vary from project to project. The compiler generally notifies you of these issues by printing a message to the terminal.

You can use a simple method from the SDK to determine the device for which you're building. Based on the build device, you handle the UIImage-PickerController differently. Open the file collageViewController.m, and update the choosePic method to look like the following listing.

Listing D.1   Adding compiler directives in collageViewController.m

```
-(IBAction)choosePic:(id)sender {

    UIImagePickerController *myImagePicker =
        [[UIImagePickerController alloc] init];
    myImagePicker.delegate = self;
    myImagePicker.allowsEditing = YES;                          ❶ Building
                                                                   for iPad?
    if (UI_USER_INTERFACE_IDIOM() == UIUserInterfaceIdiomPad) {  ⟵
        UIPopoverController *popover = [[UIPopoverController alloc]
            initWithContentViewController:myImagePicker];
        [popover presentPopoverFromBarButtonItem:sender
            permittedArrowDirections:UIPopoverArrowDirectionAny animated:YES];
    } else {
        [self presentModalViewController:myImagePicker animated:YES];
    }

}
```

As of this writing, this is the currently accepted way to determine if you're building for the iPhone or the iPad. Although the condition of the if statement is likely to change in the future, the logic will remain the same.

You first determine if the build target is the iPad ❶. If so, the code displays the UIImagePickerController inside of a UIPopoverController that is oriented around the button that was tapped. The picker's behavior remains the same—it's just presented in a different manner. Finally, the code presents the picker modally if you're building for the iPhone.

The application is now almost fully functional. You can choose photos, add them to the screen, and move and scale them. But one problem remains: if you notice, the area that you have to work with is restricted to 320 x 400 pixels. This is because you need to update the frame of the working area.

D.4 Updating your views for the iPad

When you're updating applications, you'll spend the most time updating your view frames. If you're an iPhone developer, you're probably so used to the 320 x 480 resolution that you have no problem hardcoding those numbers in your applications. Because you now have a 1024 x 768 interface, you must make your view sizes a little more dynamic.

The best approach to resizing views is to make all of their sizes relative to the device size. That way, you can build for all devices without using compiler directives. You can obtain the size of the screen by using the following method call on `UIScreen`:

```
[[UIScreen mainScreen] applicationFrame]
```

This returns a `CGSize` containing your device's height and width. What makes it even more dynamic is the fact that these values are automatically adjusted when the device is rotated. This will aid you in the next section as well.

In the collage application, two major areas break on the iPad. The first is the working area in which you can place images: currently, you're restricted to the 320 x 480 resolution. Second, the `UISlider` has been absolutely placed and appears in the center of the screen. Figure D.5 shows these issues.

Let's start by solving the issue of photos being restricted to the 320 x 480 frame. Open tempImageView.m, and change the `touchesMoved:` method to look like listing D.2.

Figure D.5 Broken interface on the iPad

Listing D.2 Updating the image-view frame in tempImageView.m

```
- (void) touchesMoved:(NSSet *)touches withEvent:(UIEvent *)event {

    UITouch *thisTouch = [touches anyObject];
    CGPoint thisPoint = [thisTouch locationInView:self];

    float newX = thisPoint.x+self.frame.origin.x;
    float newY = thisPoint.y+self.frame.origin.y;

    if (newX < 0) {
        newX = 0;
    }

    if (newY < 0) {
        newY = 0;
    }
    CGRect scRect = [[UIScreen mainScreen] applicationFrame];
    if(newX > scRect.size.width) {
        newX = scRect.size.width;
    }
    if(newY > scRect.size.height) {
        newY = scRect.size.height;
    }

    if (thisTouch) {
        self.center = CGPointMake(newX,newY);
    }
}
```

❶ Gets screen size

Restricts photo's x position to ❷ screen area

Restricts ❸ y position

You get the current dimensions of the device's screen ❶ and then restrict the x position of the user's photo to the screen bounds ❷. You do the same thing for the y coordinate ❸.

If you run the application at this point, you can drag the photos all around the screen. But there is still a problem with the UISlider: it's obviously in the wrong area.

In the original application, the UISlider was positioned to appear on top of the toolbar. You did this by placing it on top of the UIToolbar at the bottom. This wasn't the best approach for building on multiple devices. The solution is to add the UISlider as a subview of the UIToolbar. That way, as the UIToolbar scales and rotates, so does the UISlider. Open CollageViewController.m, locate imagePicker-Controller:didFinishPickingImage:, and update the lines

```
mySlider = [[UISlider alloc] initWithFrame:CGRectMake(90,415,210,44)];
[self.view addSubview:mySlider];
```

to the following:

```
mySlider = [[UISlider alloc] initWithFrame:CGRectMake(90,0,210,44)];
  [myTools addSubview:mySlider];
```

Now that the UISlider is a subview of the toolbar at the bottom, you won't have to worry about its positioning. It will always appear in the toolbar next to the Done button. Figure D.6 shows the updated interface with these improvements.

Figure D.6　Updated iPad interface

The application is starting to look much more complete. But one problem remains: when the user rotates the device, the interface stays in portrait mode. You need to tell the interface to rotate as well as update the frames of the main views.

D.5　*Adding multiple-orientation support*

As we mentioned earlier, adding support for all orientations is necessary for iPad applications. To do this, you must implement the `shouldAuto-rotateToInterfaceOrientation` method on all your views. This method should respond to the interface changes and return YES. To update the application, open col-lageViewController.m and add the following code:

```
- (BOOL)shouldAutorotateToInterfaceOrientation:
    (UIInterfaceOrientation)interfaceOrientation {
if (UI_USER_INTERFACE_IDIOM() == UIUserInterfaceIdiomPad) {
    return YES;
} else {
    return (interfaceOrientation == UIInterfaceOrientationPortrait);
}
}
```

Because you've been careful when updating your view frames in the previous chapters, no real work is needed here. The code returns YES if you're building for the iPad device and returns YES for the iPhone if in portrait mode.

Figure D.7   The collage application in landscape mode

All built-in interface components should rotate and resize automatically. Problems generally occur when you create custom views with hardcoded sizes. Making sure you develop according to the device's screen size will drastically reduce the amount of work you have to do in this method. Figure D.7 shows what the final interface looks like in landscape mode.

For the most part, converting applications won't be as simple as this, because the collage is such a basic application. But the conversion patterns are the same. For more information about how to support universal applications please read the Apple's developer article titled "Introducing Universal Application for iPhone OS" as listed in the beginning of this appendix.

index